Law and Governance in Postnational Europe

This book argues that Europeanization and globalization have led to ever more intensive legalization at transnational level. What accounts for compliance beyond the nation-state? The authors tackle this question by comparing compliance with regulations that have been formulated in a very similar way at different levels of governance. They test compliance with rules at the national level, at the regional level (EU), and at a global level (WTO), finding that in fact the EU has higher levels of compliance than both international and national rules. The authors argue that this is because the EU has a higher level of legalization, combined with effective monitoring mechanisms and sanctions. In this respect it seems that the European Union has indeed achieved a high level of legalization and compliance, though the authors add that this achievement does not settle the related queries with the legitimacy of transnational governance and law.

MICHAEL ZÜRN is Director at the Science Center, Berlin and Founding Rector of the Hertie School of Governance, Berlin. He is author of *Frieden und Krieg* (co-authored with Bernhard Zangl; 2003), *Regieren jenseits des Nationalstaates* (1998), *Gerechte internationale Regime* (1987) and *Interessen und Institutionen* (1992).

CHRISTIAN JOERGES is Professor of European Economic and Private Law and Private International Law at the Law Department of the European University Institute, Florence. Recent publications include *Transnational Governance and Constitutionalism* (co-edited with Inger-J. Sand and Gunther Teubner), *Darker Legacies of Law in Europe: The Shadow of National Socialism and Fascism over Europe and its Legal Traditions* (co-edited with Navraj S. Ghaleigh), and *Good Governance in Europe's Integrated Market* (co-edited with Renaud Dehousse).

T0370554

Themes in European Governance

The evolving European systems of governance, in particular the European Union, challenge and transform the state, the most important locus of governance and political identity and loyalty over the past two hundred years. The series *Themes in European Governance* aims to publish the best theoretical and analytical scholarship on the impact of European governance on the core institutions, policies and identities of nation-states. It focuses upon the implications for issues such as citizenship, welfare, political decision-making, and economic, monetary, and fiscal policies. An initiative of Cambridge University Press and the Programme on Advanced Research on the Europeanization of the Nation-State (ARENA), Norway, the series includes contributions in the social sciences, humanities and law. The series aims to provide theoretically informed studies analyzing key issues at the European level and within European states. Volumes in the series will be of interest to scholars and students of Europe both within Europe and worldwide. They will be of particular relevance to those interested in the development of sovereignty and governance of European states and in the issues raised by multilevel governance and multinational integration throughout the world.

Other books in the series:

Law and Governance in Postnational Europe

Compliance beyond the Nation-State

Edited by

Michael Zürn and Christian Joerges

CAMBRIDGE
UNIVERSITY PRESS

CAMBRIDGE UNIVERSITY PRESS
Cambridge, New York, Melbourne, Madrid, Cape Town,
Singapore, São Paulo, Delhi, Tokyo, Mexico City

Cambridge University Press
The Edinburgh Building, Cambridge CB2 8RU, UK

Published in the United States of America by Cambridge University Press, New York

www.cambridge.org
Information on this title: www.cambridge.org/9780521176361

© Cambridge University Press 2005

First published 2005
First paperback edition 2011

A catalogue record for this publication is available from the British Library

ISBN 978-0-521-84135-1 Hardback
ISBN 978-0-521-17636-1 Paperback

Contents

Tables

Notes on contributors

CHRISTIAN JOERGES has been a full-time Professor at the European University Institute since 1998, and was formerly Professor at Bremen University and Co-director of the Center for European Law and Policy. His present teaching and research projects deal with risk regulation at European and international level, the Europeanization of private law and anti-liberal traditions of legal thought in Europe.

JÜRGEN NEYER is Heisenberg Fellow of the *Deutsche Forschungsgemeinschaft* at the Department of Political and Social Sciences of the Freie Universität Berlin. He has served as a Professor of International Political Economy at the Geschwister Scholl Institut of the Ludwig-Maximilians-University, Munich, and as a Research Fellow and Lecturer at the University of Frankfurt, the Center for European Law and Policy at the University of Bremen and the Robert Schuman Center for Advanced Studies of the European University Institute in Florence, Italy. His research interests include European integration and international political economy.

DIETER WOLF is executive manager of the Research Center on "Transformations of the State," University of Bremen, and was formerly Research Fellow and Lecturer in the Department of Political Science, Technische Universität München. His teaching and current research deal with theories of European integration and multilevel governance, foreign policy analysis and international as well as comparative political economy (monetary, tax, and competition policies).

MICHAEL ZÜRN, formerly Professor of International Politics and Transnational Relations at the Institute of Political Science, University of Bremen and Director of the Special Collaborative Research Center on "Transformations of the State" at the University of Bremen, is now Director at the Science Center, Berlin and Founding Rector of the Hertie School of Governance, Berlin.

Preface

It is difficult to find a book on compliance that would not refer to Louis Henkin's *How Nations Behave*, citing his classic observation: "Almost all nations observe almost all principles of international law and almost all of their obligations almost all of the time." A second disciplinary observation by Henkin is a bit less well known: "The student of law and the student of politics . . . purport to be looking at the same world from the vantage point of important disciplines. It seems unfortunate, indeed destructive, that they should not, at the least, hear each other." Together, these two quotes point directly to the core of this book. *Law and Governance in Postnational Europe: Compliance beyond the Nation-State* discusses the sources of compliance and non-compliance with legal rules. It originated from an interdisciplinary project that involved both vantage points: law and politics.

And it took its time. Back in 1997, Christian Joerges, a lawyer focusing in his research on European and international economic law, asked Michael Zürn, a political scientist focusing on international relations, to join the Center for European Law and Policy (ZERP) at the University of Bremen. Since then we have been continuously engaged in comparing and discussing the perception of law by legal and political science. That co-operation led to a project submitted to the *Deutsche Forschungsgemeinschaft* (DFG) as part of the program on *Regieren in Europa* (Governance in Europe). The funds we received were used to bring Jürgen Neyer and Dieter Wolf on board this project. This enabled Christian Joerges, Jürgen Neyer, Dieter Wolf and Michael Zürn to act for some time as team-mates in this project in Bremen. Our co-operation became more complicated when Christian Joerges moved to the European University Institute in Florence, Jürgen Neyer joined him there for some months as a Jean Monnet Fellow, but then moved further to Berlin, while Dieter Wolf accepted a position in Munich.

Complex structures need not be unproductive, however. The European University Institute hosted two workshops on which we could discuss our work extensively and systematically with colleagues from both disciplines. In addition we have presented individual chapters at various occasions at changing places: at the ECPR workshop "Why do social actors comply?" in Mannheim in March 1999; at the Max Planck Institute for the Study of Societies, Cologne, in June 2000; at a workshop at the Humboldt University, Berlin, funded by the DFG programme on "Governance in Europe" in July 2000, and a panel at the annual conference of the International Studies Association in August 2000 in Los Angeles, at the University of Osnabrück in November 2000, and at the University of Toronto in 2001. Last but not least: with the start of the DFG-funded Research Center (*Sonderforschungsbereich*) on "Transformations of the State" the majority of the group could be brought together again in Bremen and finally finish and polish the manuscript.

It took a time-consuming effort to arrive at *Law and Governance in Postnational Europe: Compliance beyond the Nation-State*. The many changes in affiliations and the interdisciplinary approach came at a price; but that price was to some degree unavoidable – and hopefully as rewarding as envisaged by Robert J. Beck in 1996: "Students of both International Relations and International Law have begun in earnest to address variations of this 'compliance' question, and it would appear to constitute an area where significant gains can be jointly achieved."

We are at any rate indebted to many institutions and individuals, to the *Deutsche Forschungsgemeinschaft* for funding the project, to the Center for European Law and Policy (ZERP) at the University of Bremen for hosting it initially, the European University Institute in Florence and the *Sonderforschungsbereich* on "Transformations of the State" in Bremen for their support. It is hardly possible to list all the scholars who have helped us with useful comments. Special thanks go to Beate Kohler-Koch, the co-ordinator of the *Schwerpunktprogramm* on Governance in Europe, who has given us much advice, and to Karen Alter, Tanja Boerzel, Klaus Eder, Josef Falke, Thomas Gehring, Oliver Gerstenberg, Peter Katzenstein, Martti Koskenniemi, Alexandra Lindenthal, Markus Jachtenfuchs, Thilo Marauhn, Renate Mayntz, Ronald B. Mitchell, Andrew Moravcsik, Claus Offe, Louis Pauly, Ernst-Ulrich Petersmann, Thomas Risse, Fritz W. Scharpf, Christoph Schmid, Beth Simmons, Anne-Marie Slaughter, David Victor, and Bernhard Zangl. We would also like to thank Joseph Corkin who corrected our continental English and Monika Sniegs for her editing of the whole book.

1 Introduction: Law and compliance at different levels

Michael Zürn

Is law – understood as a normatively meaningful form of social regulation – conceivable or indeed possible beyond the nation-state? This is the guiding question that informs our inquiries in *Law and Governance in Postnational Europe: Compliance beyond the Nation-State*. It is based on the conviction that governance beyond the nation-state must contain elements of law if it is to be considered legitimate. The focus therefore is on compliance as an element of social order, not only as a means of effective problem-solving. We will demonstrate that a record of good compliance in multilevel systems does not depend on an agent that is generally able to enforce rules on the basis of a superior availability of material resources. Our case studies show that with respect to some regulations the EU displays better compliance records than comparable regulations in the Federal Republic of Germany. Even compliance with WTO regulations can be compared favorably with compliance with German regulations. A high degree of legalization, combined with well-functioning verification and sanctioning systems, seems to be more important. However, smart institutional designs can cause their own problems. If the intrusions into the constituent units of a multilevel system are too strong and compliance works too well, then compliance crises may result, which involve an open, normatively-driven rejection of the regulation. This is especially true if social integration lags behind and a common public discourse is absent.

Our project on law and governance in postnational Europe can be distinguished from two international, multi-disciplinary research programs which in many ways have inspired and shaped our work. One important strand of research on international environmental politics looks into the conditions necessary to ensure effective environmental policies, i.e. policies that succeed in doing what they were intended to do. "Effective regimes cause changes in the behavior of actors, in the interests of actors, or in the policies and performance of institutions in ways that contribute to positive management of the targeted problem" (Young and

Levy 1999: 5).[1] This strand of research also focuses on the implementation of international commitments as well as on those actors whose behavior the relevant accord ultimately aims to change (Victor, Raustiala and Skolnikoff 1998: 4). It includes studies in which rule compliance is seen as one aspect, or even a fundamental criterion, for the effectiveness of a rule.[2] The other strand of research investigates the problem-solving capacity of the EU.[3] Our approach differs from these research strands in the following two ways:

- Apart from the simple "effectiveness" or "problem-solving capacity" of international regulations, our focus is also on the process – or to be more precise, the normative integrity – of regulatory creation (as an independent variable) and regulatory application (as a dependent variable).
- Our interest is not so much in the problem-solving capacity of a specific international regulation, but rather in the *potential* of constitutional political orders in general. The aim is to identify the central elements of a democratically legitimate and effective multi-level form of governance beyond the nation-state and we do this by raising the question that is crucial to all political systems – why do the addressees of regulations comply with them?

In this introductory chapter, we develop in section 1.1 two principal answers to our guiding question – is law possible beyond the nation-state. One states an unconditional 'No', the other a conditional 'Yes'. These two principal hypotheses have a foundation in both the theory of law and the theory of international relations. In section 1.2 we discuss the selection of cases across levels and why the study and comparison of those cases is appropriate to help answer the questions that drive this project. Section 1.3 differentiates the second hypothesis by introducing four theoretical perspectives on the sources of non-compliance and the conditions for good compliance records beyond the nation-state. The four theoretical perspectives are labeled "rational institutionalism," "management," "legalization," and "legitimacy." In this way, section 1.3 identifies the major variables that have to be taken into account when studying compliance issues. Finally, in section 1.4, the substance of the ensuing chapters

---

[1] See especially the edited volume by Young (1999b) and the recent work of Miles et al. (2002) for major contributions to this field of study. See Levy, Young and Zürn (1995) for a survey on concepts and research strategies.

[2] See especially the major volume by Weiss and Jacobson (1998). Early and seminal contributions are Chayes and Chayes (1993, 1995), contributions to Cameron, Werksman and Roderick (1996), and Mitchell (1994).

[3] See among others Grande and Jachtenfuchs (2000), Héritier et al. (1996), Scharpf (1999), Leibfried and Pierson (1995).

will be outlined, thereby carefully unbundling the empirical and normative aspects of the project.

1.1   The principal contest

Although there are different notions of what sets legal norms apart from
non-legalized social norms, all concepts of law adhere to the principle of
legal equality, according to which like cases are treated alike. The very
notion of the *rule of law* is based on norms that are public, relatively
stable, consistent, and prospective, thus guaranteeing legal equality and
legal certainty.[4] The rule of law requires that the authors of law are bound
by the law as well as ordinary people. It protects people from the arbitrary
(ab)use of power and is thus a core principle of any notion of constitutionalism within and beyond the nation-state (see Petersmann 2002).
In that sense, the rule of law demands less than democracy, which in
addition requires that the objects of law are also the authors of that law.
Although the rule of law does not require democracy, it does presuppose legal equality. Law thus requires that like cases are treated in a like
manner. This, in turn, requires a high compliance rate with any given
regulation. Without an adequate compliance rate, it is hardly possible to
speak of law. Although sufficient compliance is not enough on its own to
turn social norms into legal norms, it is certainly a necessary component
of law.[5]

This leads directly to the most fundamental objection to the notion
of law beyond the nation-state: legal equality and high compliance rates
require an agent that can generally enforce rules on the basis of a superior
availability of material resources and can cast a shadow of hierarchy. In
this view, law is distinct from moral and ethical norms by the method of
sanctioning by which compliance is fostered. The formulation of Hans
Kelsen (1966: 4) is famous: "The antagonism of freedom and coercion
fundamental to social life supplies the decisive criterion. It is the criterion of law, for law is a coercive order. It provides for socially organized
sanctions and thus can be clearly distinguished from religious and moral
order." Whereas Kelsen and Max Weber (1980: 18), who subscribe to

---

[4] See Böckenförde (1969) and Peters (1991: Chapter 4) on the use and development of
this concept.
[5] To consider sufficient compliance as an integral part of law runs counter to the view of
many international lawyers who, understandably, often argue that compliance is external
to law and that the occurrence of non-compliance does not devalue international law.
Nevertheless, the lack of compliance has led to doubts about the lawfulness of international law from Hobbes through Spinoza to Hegel. Arend (1996), for instance, is
one of those international lawyers who also argue that compliance is a prerequisite for
law.

coercion theories of law, see the potential for a law-like use of sanctions in the international sphere and thus do not completely deny the notion of international law, many others see a monopoly of legitimate force as a necessary condition for law (see Koskenniemi 2002: Chapter 6). To cite, for instance, one introductory textbook, written by a continental lawyer: governing in the form of law is the "embodiment of the state-guaranteed general norms to regulate human interactions and to resolve interpersonal conflicts through decision" (Horn 1996: 3). This 'decision-ist' point of view is also reflected in "Realism" as a theory of international relations (Morgenthau 1949, Waltz 1979, Mearsheimer 2002). Realism regards international politics as structured by an anarchic environment that is defined by the absence of a superior agent with the authority to enforce agreement, thus necessitating self-help strategies on the part of the units of the system – in other words, the states. Realism views legal constraints beyond the nation-state as non-existent or at best very weak. In so far as international rules appear to be legal, they emanate from dominant powers and represent their interests. While those norms may be normatively justifiable, they are "in themselves" not founded on the principle of legal equality (see e.g. Krasner 1999 on human rights). The constitutional reflection of the dichotomy between domestic and interna-tional contexts is the notion of final decision. In national political systems an ultimate decision-making authority stands above all the other actors at the central level – either a parliament or a supreme court (Mayer 2000). In the international system the final decision-makers are decentralized and territorially fragmented.

It is not only Decisionists and Realists who are very skeptical about law beyond the nation-state. Those authors who point out that questions of law and justice can only meaningfully be dealt with in communities whose members share common values and ideas (Goodin 1988; Miller 1995) are equally doubtful about the feasibility of law beyond the nation-state. The existence of such communities is, however, closely bound up with nations with shared memories and traditions (Kielmansegg 1994: 27). Such national identities are required before individuals are prepared to subordinate their interests to collectivities and regularly comply with inconvenient commitments. The compliance-pull of rules beyond the nation-state thus becomes unlikely, since they cannot build on state-like polities that are consolidated internally as communities.

Against this background it is easy to understand why many writers doubt whether law is possible beyond the nation-state. Law requires that like cases are treated in a like manner. This, in turn, requires a high com-pliance rate for any given regulation. A high compliance rate, however, is believed to depend on two conditions that are scarcely available outside the institutionalized framework of the developed nation-state: an established monopoly of legitimate force, and a national identity that determines the consent of those who are the targets of a regulation, even if they consider the rule inconvenient. In this sense, it seems fair to describe the question of compliance as the Achilles' heel of international regulations (see Werksmann 1996: xvi; Young 1999a: Chapter 4).

Those who challenge the skeptical view of law beyond the nation-state start with the observation that at least some international norms and rules are complied with to an astonishingly high degree. "Almost all nations observe almost all principles of international law and all of their obligations almost all of the time" is the frequently cited conclusion that is drawn by Louis Henkin (1979: 47). This observation – which against the background of the previously mentioned arguments of the skeptics is not necessarily inexplicable, even if it is to some extent puzzling[6] – has been revived by those scholars who endeavor to understand how international regulations in the environmental field work.[7] According to their findings, it is not so much powerful coercion, but rather good legal management that leads to a satisfactory level of compliance. In the words of Abram Chayes and Antonia Handler Chayes (1993: 205): "Enforcement through these interacting measures of assistance and persuasion is less costly and intrusive and is certainly less dramatic than coercive sanctions, the easy and usual policy elixir for non-compliance." It is the power of the legitimacy of legal norms, the way legal norms work once they are established, and the smart management of cases of alleged non-compliance, which in this view lead to compliance.

In general terms, one may thus distinguish between two competing principal hypotheses. The first one holds that law requires centralized coercion administered by an agent with superior resources and can take place only within an established national community, otherwise compliance with inconvenient commitments becomes a question of opportunism – a notion that is alien to any concept of law. Following this hypothesis, high compliance rates with regulations beyond the nation-state are *per se* impossible, at least as long as they require powerful signatories to a treaty to do things that they would otherwise prefer not to do. High compliance rates with international environmental regulations are

---

[6] Keohane (1997: 487) puts it eloquently: "Governments make a very large number of legal agreements, and, on the whole, their compliance with these agreements seems quite high. Yet what this level of compliance implies about the causal impact of commitments remains a mystery."

[7] See especially the work of Bothe (1996); Chayes and Chayes (1993, 1995); Haas (1998); Mitchell (1994); Underdal (1998); Victor et al. (1998); Weiss and Jacobson (1998); Young (1999a: Chapter 4). See also Young (1979).

put down to shallow treaties, which involve little "depth of co-operation" (Downs et al. 1996). Accordingly, the first principal hypothesis is as follows: *Any given regulation, and especially those with significant incentives to defect (deep co-operation), enjoys better compliance within a national political system, with a material hierarchy and an established national community, than it does within a system beyond the nation-state.*

The counter-hypothesis points to the possibility that the institutionalization of law enforcement among territorially defined political units, that is in a horizontal context, may develop in parallel to the horizontalization of law making. The notion of the *institutionalization of horizontal law enforcement*[8] encapsulates two separate processes. First, the role of coercive sanctions of external origin, with the role of communality becoming relatively less important than other forms of compliance-generation such as incentives, capacity-building, dispute settlement, legitimacy-building, shaming, the internalization of law etc. This focus on the softer means of inducing compliance, that are based on rational consent rather than on a sense of community, is typical of the so-called managerial school and those who focus on the link between legitimacy and compliance. Secondly, to the extent that coercive sanctions are used as a legitimate means of compliance-generation, they need not only be applied in a national context but, in order to be effective, may also be used in an institutionalized horizontal setting.[9] This aspect of horizontal enforcement is typical of the institutionalist approach within the rationalist tradition that seeks to explain co-operation and legalization. The principal hypothesis that emerges from this combination is: *Compliance with regulations varies with, among other things, the legitimacy, the legalization, the reflexivity and the availability of institutionalized horizontal coercion, and is not dependent on the existence of a national context.* A process of horizontalization of law enforcement takes place to the extent that we move from cell one to cell four in table 1.1.[10]

The first principal hypothesis expects sufficient compliance rates only within the nation-state. The second principal hypothesis points to a

---

[8] According to *Black's Law Dictionary* "enforcement" is defined as "the compelling of obedience to law." In our study the use of the term "enforcement" is more generic, and is closer to its use in the citation of Chayes and Chayes. Enforcement is thus the process by which addressees of a regulation are induced to act in compliance with it. It is the process of compliance-generation, independent of the means chosen. The use of negative sanctions to generate compliance – the compelling of obedience – is termed "coercion" (see also Hurd 1999: 383).

[9] This is different from the traditional notion of counter-measures, according to which "the injured state enforced its own rights through self-help" (O'Connell 1995: 2).

[10] The juxtaposition of these two principal hypotheses is not identical with Keohane's (1997) two optics of international law. The second principal hypothesis contains elements of the instrumentalist as well as the normative conceptualization of law.

Table 1.1 *Enforcement mechanisms in a vertical and horizontal setting*[11]

	Means	
Setting	Hard	Soft
Vertical within a community	*Principal hypothesis 1: shadow of hierarchy within a national community*	Managerial school[12]
Horizontal between communities	Co-operation under anarchy	Shaming, reputation and ideas

number of mechanisms that can also be found beyond the nation-state, which might substitute for the compliance-generating mechanisms of the shadow of hierarchy and communality that are only available to the nation-state.

1.2   Comparing compliance across levels

The juxtaposition of the two principal hypotheses leads to two more concrete questions that guide our study in empirical and analytical terms.

- Who is right? Is it true that compliance is generally lower beyond the nation-state than it is within nation-states?
- If material hierarchy and communality are not the only determinants of compliance, what else motivates norm-compliance and the regulated treatment of cases of non-compliance?

In order to answer these questions, it is best to conduct a systematic comparative survey of different sets of regulations that exist in very similar ways both within and beyond nation-state boundaries. In this way, the case selection is based on variations in the independent variable and thus approaches the notion of a quasi-experiment (King et al. 1994). In order to conduct such a study, it is necessary both to find regulations that are effective at different levels, but which are nevertheless similar in

---

[11] One could add "privatization" as a third dimension, that is, the increased importance of private actors in law making and law enforcement, as can be observed in the so-called public-private partnerships. See e.g. Reinicke (1998) from an international relations point of view, and contributions in Applebaum, Felstiner and Gessner (2001) from the point of view of the sociology of law. As to the general theory of law, the debate on private governance regimes and the role of private law is most interesting (cf. Gerstenberg 2000; Teubner 2000).

[12] The managerial school argues mainly in the context of a horizontal setting. However, it focuses primarily on *means* and much less on the other dimension, and is thus compatible with new approaches of governance in the national context, which also emphasize soft and participatory forms of steering societal relations.

content and depth, as well as to develop an appropriate measurement of
the dependent variable, that is compliance.

1.2.1 Compliance

Compliance needs to be distinguished from other areas of study that are
related to the effects of regulations, especially their implementation and
effectiveness. Of course, there are many points of contact, overlaps and
links between these different areas. The focus of implementation research
is, however, the analysis of the difference between legislative enactments
and how they are actually put into practice (see Victor, Raustiala and
Skolnikoff 1998: 4). In contrast, the focus of effectiveness research is the
capacity of political regulation to solve commonly perceived problems
(Young 1999b).

Compliance research is distinct from both these approaches in that it
examines the extent to which rules are complied with by their addressees.
"Compliance can be said to occur when the actual behavior of a given
subject conforms to prescribed behavior, and non-compliance or violation occurs when actual behavior departs significantly from prescribed
behavior" (Young 1979: 3; Mitchell 1994: 430). Hence, "compliance is
a noun that denotes a particular type of *behavior, action or policy* within a
specific regulatory or situational context" (Simmons 2000b: 1). It does
not refer to the *willingness* of the actors to comply. The main object of our
empirical study is therefore the directly ascertainable actions of actors
rather than their attitudes or motives. The intrinsic ambiguity of law
always necessitates application and interpretation and thus makes it hard
to assess objectively whether or not compliance is taking place. As a "living
being," law is not constant over time, but is subject to changing interpretations of its meaning and to new case law, which interprets and changes
the meaning of statutory law (Dworkin 1986). Nevertheless, it seems
possible to assess compliance from an external perspective by systematically using indicators of internal estimates of compliance: "the point is
to compile objective evidence of subjective socially-based interpretations
of behavior" (Simmons 2000b: 24).

Compliance cannot, however, be reduced to a one-dimensional concept, assessed simply by calculating the disparity between obligations and
actual behavior. It is necessary to bring in a second dimension of compliance without setting apart the focus on behavior. In line with Jacobson
and Weiss (1998a: 4), who distinguish the procedural from the substantial
dimension of compliance, we look at the treatment of accusations of non-
compliance in the second dimension. Compliance and non-compliance
are, at least at the margins, perpetually contested concepts, the meaning

of which develops over time once a rule is put into practice. Charges of non-compliance can, for instance, arise out of the ambiguity of a rule, without any desire of either side to cheat or to challenge the validity of the rule. In such cases, it is to be expected that compliance is no longer problematic once any differences about the correct interpretation of the rule have been settled. These complexities in the concept of compliance cannot be disregarded. Compliance, therefore, comprises, in addition to the (perceived) differences between obligation and actual behavior, the way those differences are dealt with once they are on the table. Compliance is thus assessed by dealing with two related questions: (1) What are the demands made on the behavior of the addressees and to what extent do the addressees comply with these demands (the first dimension of compliance)? (2) How are accusations of non-compliance handled (the second dimension of compliance)?

In combining these two dimensions of compliance, we use four values for (non-)compliance: every single rule-related action by the addressee of a rule may be categorized in decreasing order of compliance as:

- "good compliance" if the difference between the prescriptions and proscriptions of a norm is non-existent or negligible and its addressees do not publicly voice their discontent with a rule;
- "recalcitrant compliance" if the difference between the prescriptions and proscriptions of a norm is non-existent or negligible but nevertheless its addressees publicly voice their discontent with it;
- "initial non-compliance" if we observe both a significant difference between the prescriptions and proscriptions of a norm and a change in the behavior of its addressees due to allegations of non-compliance and the activities following the allegation;
- "compliance crisis" if we observe both a significant difference between the prescriptions and proscriptions of a norm and no change in the behavior of its addressees although the practice has been detected, alleged and/or outlawed by a decision of an authorized dispute settlement body or court.

In each case study we also use two different lenses to look at compliance. On the one hand, the overall rate of compliance is assessed with the help of this categorization and, on the other hand, specific cases of alleged non-compliance are analyzed. The aggregate record of compliance is then assessed on the sum of this information.

1.2.2   Similar regulations at different levels

Studies that suggest good compliance with international agreements and interpret such findings as evidence of a compliance-pull by international agreements are often challenged on methodological grounds. The most significant objection to the finding of a remarkable compliance with, for instance, international environmental agreements in horizontal settings has been those arguments concerning the type and depth of the regulation in question. On the one hand, some regime analysts have argued that some malign problems are more difficult to solve at the international level than benign problems (see Underdal 2002). This observation has led to a so-called problem-structural approach, which contends that the properties of issues (or conflicts) predetermine the ways in which they are dealt with (see e.g. Rittberger and Zürn 1991: 26). To the extent that problem structure accounts for the variation in co-operation and compliance, it is necessary to hold the effect of problem structure constant when inquiring into the role of other factors. In the words of Arild Underdal (2002: 23), the problem-solving capacity of different settings "can be determined precisely only with reference to a particular category of problems and tasks." On the other hand, George Downs and colleagues (1996) challenge what they call the managerial school by pointing to an endogeneity problem. According to them, the managerial school focuses on co-operative agreements with little depth, that is measured in terms of "the extent to which it requires states to depart from what they would have done in its absence" (*ibid.*, 383) and it is only for this reason that they discover a correlation between a managerial approach to co-operation and a low degree of defection from the agreement. Raustiala and Victor (1998: 662) support this theoretical observation with a large empirical project: "Whereas many analysts have seen high compliance as a sign that commitments are influential, our cases suggest that compliance often simply reflects that countries negotiate and join agreements which they know they can comply with."[13]

The obvious solution to these problems is to be selective about the kind of agreements we spend time researching. A major challenge in designing this project has therefore been to identify comparable cases in three different issue areas, across three levels of politics. In order to control for the issue area, the type of problem, and the policy type, we employed, in a first step, the distinction between policies termed by Lowi (1972) as constitutive (market-making), regulative (market-correcting) and (re-) distributive (market-breaking).[14] For each policy type we looked, as a second step, at specific policies that are implemented at different levels. In this way, we controlled for problem type as well as the underlying interest

---

[13] See also Raustiala and Slaughter (2002) for a good discussion on this issue.
[14] See Streeck (1995) and Zürn (1998: Chapter 7) for more recent attempts to use and modify this typology.

structure in each of the comparisons *and* we ended up with an analysis of a set of policies which may be considered sufficiently representative for all policies. Moreover, all the policies that we compared across levels are, in general, very similar in depth. For instance, the percentage of GDP transferred in German interstate financial adjustments (*Länderfinanzausgleich*) is remarkably similar to that transferred by the European Regional Development Fund (ERDF) Structural and Cohesion Funds. The major net recipient of EU redistribution via the ERDF Structural and Cohesion Funds is Portugal with a net gain of 2.93 percent of GDP per year; the major recipient in the German *Länderfinanzausgleich* – Berlin – receives almost exactly the same proportion, that is 2.89 percent of GDP per year (see chapter 5 by Jürgen Neyer). Though less quantifiable, it is agreed that European subsidy regulations are at least as "deep" as the agreement within Germany, and the depth of intervention on the issue of beef hormones at the international level is similar to that concerning BSE at the European level.

We ended up with three sets of comparisons.

- Our analysis of *market-making policies* focuses on *subsidy controls* and covers all three levels. At the national level, compliance with the regulation preventing subsidized competition between federal states in Germany is studied. This control is based chiefly on two so-called subsidization codes that are issued by the economic ministers of the German states (*Länder*). The corresponding regulation at the European level is laid down in Articles 87–89 of the Consolidated Version of the Treaty Establishing the European Community (formerly Articles 92–94) and the agreements regarding secondary law making based on these Articles. Finally, for international subsidy control, the study includes Article XVI of the General Agreement on Tariffs and Trades (GATT) complete with the agreement on the interpretation and the application of Article XVI, known as the "Subsidization Code" (GATT/26S/56). The international regulation was strengthened in 1994 by a separate agreement on subsidies (see chapter 3 by Dieter Wolf).
- The two cases chosen for analyzing compliance with *regulative policies* focus on trade in foodstuffs. Both the EU and the WTO have developed exemption rules from the principle of non-discrimination and free trade, which allow import restrictions provided that they are imposed to protect human health and life and cannot be considered arbitrary discrimination or a disguised restriction of trade among member states. Both of these regulations have come under severe pressure on various occasions. Regarding foodstuffs, the European Commission's decision in 1999 to end the embargo on British beef and the decision by the appellate body of the WTO in 1998 to declare the EC ban on five

Table 1.2 *The cases*

	Policy type		
Level	Market-making	Regulative	Redistributive
Germany	Subsidy controls	–	*Länderfinanzausgleich*
EU	Subsidy controls	Trade in foodstuffs	ERDF Structural Funds/Cohesion Fund
WTO	Subsidy controls	Trade in foodstuffs	–

growth hormones incompatible with WTO law are especially telling. In both cases, a highly elaborate institutional design and a decision that was widely perceived as meeting the criteria of valid law met with open non-compliance on the part of its addressees over a considerable period of time (see in more detail chapter 4 by Jürgen Neyer).

• The *redistribution* of financial resources between territorially defined political units is the object of our last comparison. Both the inter-governmental system of the German *Bundesländer* and that of the EU have developed parallel market-making and redistributive market-correcting mechanisms. In both systems, redistribution is considered of constitutional importance and is explicitly codified as an essential element in the political order. Its realization, however, is in both cases the product of intergovernmental bargaining, and is therefore heavily influenced by a variety of political concerns. The legal principles, the political practice, as well as the degree of redistribution are all quite similar at both levels. Both mechanisms redistribute a similar amount of resources among a similar number of states.

Table 1.2 indicates that the study is only partially successful in identifying comparable policies for each policy type at each level. Nevertheless, we came up with three meaningful sets of comparisons and at least two policies for each level. The specific set of cases under question indicates a special focus on the EU, which should allow for additional insights into the characteristics of this multilevel governance system.[15]

In all the three sets of comparisons, the addressees of the regulation are territorially defined political units, which claim some element of

---

[15] It should be added that all three policies that are compared across levels are strongly politicized. Each case attracted attention from the media and public opinion. While, strictly speaking, this feature of our selected cases restricts the generalizability of our results to similarly politized policies, it helps to highlight the issue of legitimacy.

statehood.[16] Although this feature of our design undeniably increases comparability, it requires elaboration on at least three counts. First, this design does not aim to compare the difference in compliance on the part of addressees of a regulation. For this reason, the currently quite popular "goodness of fit" explanation of compliance (see e.g. Cowles et al. 2001) is of secondary interest to our study. By comparing regulations on different levels that are similar in depth, we can assume that the "average" goodness of fit remains more or less constant for each level. The respective differences among addressees has little relevance to the question we pose. We focus on those addressees that display little goodness of fit and therefore may present real compliance problems.

Secondly, the focus on regulations which address themselves to territorially defined units does not imply an exclusion of societal actors from the study in general. On the contrary, we systematically differentiate between the immediate addressees of a regulation and those who are affected by it in other ways. While the former are those actors that are primarily required by the regulation to undertake or refrain from certain activities (and to whom the question of compliance or non-compliance applies), the number of those who are ultimately affected by the regulation can be far greater than the number of its direct addressees. They include, in some instances, the ultimate targets of a regulation – those whose behavior needs to be changed to solve the problem (e.g. producers in many environmental treaties) as well as those who just feel the effects of a given regulation (e.g. workers and consumers in many free-trade treaties). In our study, we therefore include and distinguish between regulatory addressees, regulatory targets, and affected actors. However, only territorial political units – as regulatory addressees – appear as dependent variables. Regulatory targets and affected actors are included on the side of the independent variable.

The focus on territorially defined political units that claim some degree of statehood as addressees of a regulation and thus as those actors who can or cannot comply with regulations raises a third issue. On the one hand, the relations between the Federal German Government and the *Länder* in the issue areas examined are not especially hierarchical when measured in legal or institutional rules. In the case of Germany, this general characteristic of federalism is emphasized additionally by the fact that the ultimate jurisdiction on the interpretation of the constitution lies

---

[16] This is also true of the German *Länder*. In a discussion paper on the future of federalism in Germany in the light of European integration, the Governors of North-Rhine Westphalia (Wolfgang Clement) and of Saxony (Kurt Biedenkopf) start from the position that "a statehood of its own for the *Länder* is the essential substance of the principle of a federal state" (*Frankfurter Allgemeine Zeitung*, 13 December 1999, 2).

with the Constitutional Court and not with the Parliament or the Federal President. No central agent is in charge of coercing the *Länder* into complying with the regulations in question. In the EU, on the other hand, the institutional role of central agents in implementing the agreements seems more pronounced. According to Article 211 of the Consolidated Version of the Treaty Establishing the European Community (following the Treaty of Amsterdam) it is the Commission that shall "ensure that the provisions . . . are applied," and according to Article 220 (formerly Article 164) the European Court "shall ensure that in the interpretation and application of this Treaty the law is observed." The imposition of sanctions to punish non-compliance has only been possible since the Maastricht Treaty came into effect (i.e. since 1993). Now the Commission can demand penalty payments from member states after a judgment to that effect has been passed by the Court (Article 228, formerly Article 171 (2)). A similar though far more common practice leading to the sanctioning of member states is the procedure that allows other member states to initiate this process (Article 227, formerly Article 170). In addition, the principle of direct effect holds open the possibility of states being required to pay compensation to societal actors if non-implementation results in damages.[17] Even the WTO agreements under question make more legal provisions for sanctions than the German constitution, through compensation and the suspension of concessions, in cases of non-compliance (Article 22 of the Understanding on Rules and Procedures Governing the Settlement of Disputes). However, these provisions are less pronounced than in the case of the EU. Most importantly, there is no centralized procedure, as there is in the EU, to investigate potential transgressions. Moreover, compensatory penalties serve more as restitution for the affected victim than as a coercive means to change the behavior of the violator. Sanctions, which can be defined as secondary collective goods,[18] are not imposed by a third party but must

[17] Direct effect has been established by a number of court decisions. This doctrine declares that, as long as they are sufficiently precise, the rules of the EEC Treaty are binding not only on the Community and the member states but are also valid "directly" and create subjective rights: anyone may claim the subjective rights contained in the Treaty, and domestic courts must guarantee their protection as if national law were at stake. The most important court decision was the direct effect decision in Case 26/62 *Van Gend en Loos* [1963] ECR 1. In 1964 (Case 6/64, *Costa* v. *ENEL* [1964] ECR 585) the Court sought to distance the early Community legal order from the conventional structure of international law by identifying the importance of the relationship between Community law and individual citizens of the member states, and by asserting the superiority of Community law over the laws of the member states. The Court argued that there had been a transfer of sovereign powers by the member states to the Community. Moreover, in Joined Cases C-6/90 and 9/90, *Francovich* v. *Italy* [1991] ECR I-5357, the Court has established the right for individuals to receive compensation if non-implementation results in damages.
[18] Theoretically the provision for sanctions is a secondary co-operative problem, which

be executed by the inflicted party. Although the influence of the Dispute Settlement Body is significantly enhanced by the fact that its decisions cannot be simply repudiated by the apparent losers of a dispute, but only "by consensus not to adopt" (Article 17(14)), the "execution" of these judgments still remains decentralized and legitimate sanctions are limited to compensatory penalties.[19]

Does this mean that the relationship between *Länder* and the federal level in Germany is less an expression of the national context than is the relationship between states and either the EU or the WTO? Does this undermine the thrust of this study? No, it rather points to an important distinction: one between a generally *vertical national setting* on the one hand and a *legal or institutional hierarchy* with respect to certain issues on the other. The issue specific institutionalization of independent agents, and even the introduction of an institutional hierarchy, is independent of the national context and can take place in the absence of a material or coercive hierarchy.[20] One can certainly have independent agents and institutional hierarchy beyond the nation-state – indeed it is only this that makes law beyond the nation-state attainable. These institutional features will be discussed under the label of legalization. They need more detailed analysis in relation to each of the case studies, given that they vary from one issue area to the next.

In contrast, Realists and Communalists point to other features of the national context which distinguish it from the international setting. These features are properties of the national context as such and do not vary from one issue area to the next. The first of those features is the *communality* aspect, according to which questions of law and justice can only be dealt with meaningfully within communities that share common values and ideas. This variable is easy to assess. According to the Communalists, such communities are closely bound to nations with shared memories and shared traditions. In the international context, such communities have hardly developed at all. The exception is the EU, which may show some signs of a regional community, but which is – at least from the point of

can hamper co-operation, because the actual provision of sanctionary measures can be a collective good. See Ostrom (1990) and Zangl (1999). In the WTO, the institutional solution to this secondary problem has been performed so skillfully that the problem is now hardly perceptible. The high costs involved in imposing penalties on large competitors are generally not perceived as costly.

[19] See Victor (2000) for an excellent study of compliance conflicts in the WTO, relating specifically to the Agreement on the Application of Sanitary and Phytosanitary Measures (SPS). See also Godt (1998).

[20] Legal hierarchy comes close to what can be labeled "authority," as discussed by Caporaso (2000: 8–9). This concept refers to the right to rule without resting necessarily on power or common reason. It is "the hierarchy itself, whose rightness and legitimacy" are recognized by both those who command and those who obey (see Arendt 1961). However, since the concept of "authority" is so contested, we do not use this term.

view of the Communalists – still underdeveloped when compared with national communities. The second feature refers to the shadow of *material hierarchy*. Material hierarchy is created by an independent agent that is able to enforce rules generally on the basis of a superior availability of material resources. In the national context, the same agent generally also establishes legal or institutional hierarchy. Yet material hierarchy is different from institutional hierarchy. The EU, for example, has some institutional and legal hierarchy characteristics but does not work under the shadow of a material hierarchy. In fact, there are no provisions to coerce member states further in the case of non-payment of penalties or compensation. Although Article 7 (formerly Article F.1) of the Consolidated Version of the Treaty on European Union does contain procedures for restricting membership rights, it applies only with reference to Article 6 of the same treaty, that is, violations of the principles on which the Union is founded such as "liberty, democracy, respect for human rights and fundamental freedoms, and the rule of law" and it is unlikely that member states would treat non-payment of penalties or compensation as a violation of the rule of law. Thus, although there is a legal hierarchy within the EU institutions, it is not backed by a historically established material superiority of any central power. The same applies to the WTO. In contrast, in Germany the federal states do work under a shadow of material hierarchy. As Weiler (2000) points out, unlike federal states such as Germany, the WTO and the EU, in spite of their sanctioning instruments, do not have the capability to coerce addressees into compliance.

To be sure, the legal requirements that need to be fulfilled before material hierarchy can be employed in Germany are quite demanding. Although – according to Article 37(1) of the Basic Law – the Federal Government may "with the consent of the Federal Council, take the necessary coercive Federal measures to urge a *Land* to fulfill its obligations" and then has "authority over all the *Länder* and their administrative offices" (Article 37(2)), before it can subject a non-compliant *Land* to constitutionally valid coercive (but non-military) measures it must have its position validated by the Federal Constitutional Court, take into account the principle of proportionality and win the support of the majority of the *Länder*. Yet the concept of the shadow of hierarchy, as used here, refers mainly to material backing. According to the Realists, at least, it is the Federal Executive which controls the armed forces. It is the federal level that is seen as the supreme authority. Whereas relationships between the states in a federal system are not in all respects legally hierarchical, they take place under the shadow of a material hierarchy, as is indicated by a historically established superiority of material forces on the part of the central state – this is seen most clearly in the US. This point of view

Table 1.3 *Hierarchy vs. anarchy disaggregated*

	Institutional/legal hierarchy in the issue areas in question	Communality	Shadow of material hierarchy
Germany	*Low*	High	High
EU	*High*	Modest	Low
WTO	*Modest*	Low	Low

is shared by Realists and Decisionists who are, after all, the principal opponents of the notion of valid law beyond the nation-state, and who emphasize a structural difference between federal states and international anarchy so as to demonstrate the weakness of international institutions: "To the extent that a federal organization has developed a quality as an actor of its own, the power and security dilemma between the states is resolved, yet it persists in the relationship of the federation with other states, especially great powers" (Link 1998: 107; see also Mearsheimer 1994).[21]

In sum, the test of the two principal hypotheses, that is whether compliance is systematically higher in the national context than it is beyond the nation-state, refers to the variables "communality" and "material hierarchy." The presence of both communality and material hierarchy necessarily locates this within a political system which possesses the authority to settle ultra vires conflicts, be it the Parliament of Great Britain or the supreme courts of federal states. Although communality and material hierarchy can vary along a continuum and are not just dichotomous, Germany – even regarding the relationship between the different territorial units – represents a national case, whereas the EU and the WTO clearly do not. By comparing compliance with regulations which share a similar content and depth, across different political settings (with varying degrees of material hierarchy and communality), we can directly test the two principal hypotheses. To the extent that compliance is not perfectly explained by the national context hypothesis, further explanatory questions arise. Keeping the policy type constant and varying the institutional context seems a promising way of probing the explanatory power of institutional compliance mechanisms outside the national setting, for example the legal hierarchy that is referred to in table 1.3.

---

[21] Policy analysts come to the same conclusion on the difference between the EU and federal states: "The EC has no institutional authority with which to threaten, coerce, or otherwise influence recalcitrant members . . . By contrast, the US government has considerably more enforcement capacity" (Vogel and Kessler 1998: 26).

Table 1.4 *Sources of non-compliance*[22]

	Rule is not challenged	Rule is challenged
Voluntary non-compliance	Cheating	Norm is considered wrong
Involuntary non-compliance	Ambiguity / impreciseness of a norm	Lack of capacity to implement / inadvertent non-compliance

1.3   The causes of and cures for non-compliance beyond the nation-state: Four theoretical perspectives

If the second principal hypothesis holds, compliance with regulations varies, among other things, with the legitimacy, the legalization, the reflexivity and the availability of horizontal coercion, and is not dependent on the existence of a national context. Clearly, we want to know more about the additional determinants of compliance, other than national context. We categorize these determinants by focusing on the different *sources of non-compliance*. Presumably, these are important factors in the way in which cases of non-compliance are dealt with. We may distinguish four sources of non-compliance (see table 1.4), by examining first whether non-compliance is voluntary or involuntary, and secondly whether the non-compliance amounts to a substantial challenge to the rule in question in terms of its rightness, or whether it is essentially an expression of a "technical" problem.

Cheating takes place when actors with a perfect understanding of the rule secretly violate it to their own advantage. The advantage gained is opportunistic, that is it depends on the persistence of the obligation as such. For instance, the use of hidden subsidies in order to place domestic industry in an advantageous position would be a case of cheating. Non-compliance due to the *ambiguity of a rule* is different in that it does not necessarily require secret activities and does not even necessarily benefit the party that is charged with non-compliance. For instance, expenditures that are motivated by the desire to strengthen regional research and

[22] The fourth source of non-compliance – lack of capacity to implement – needs further elaboration. The underlying "challenge" to the rule in this case is somewhat different from an outright questioning of its validity. It is not its normative validity but its practicability that is challenged. Hence, the immediate response to these cases of non-compliance is more often a discourse about the possibility of changing its details, so that the rule can become effective, than giving it up entirely. In this sense, the rule is challenged less than in the case of cell 3 (ambiguity/impreciseness of a norm).

development – be they efficient or not – might be interpreted as rule-breaking subsidies. When a *norm or rule is considered wrong*, parties may openly and voluntarily disregard it, in spite of the precise formulation of the rule. In these cases, transgressors point to the wrongness of the rule as their reason for non-compliance. In the BSE case, for instance, some governments openly declared the obligation to readmit British beef to be wrong. Civil disobedience is the most clear-cut example of this type of non-compliance. An open, but involuntary violation occurs when an actor discovers that it *does not have the capacity to fulfil obligations*. In these cases, the non-compliance is open; there is neither any debate on the correct interpretation nor on the validity of the norm in principle, but reference is made to practical limitations in fulfilling it. Less developed states often run into such difficulties when they sign ambitious international environmental treaties.

Each of the four sources of non-compliance relates to a certain theoretical perspective on compliance.[23] We label the four theoretical perspectives on compliance "rational institutionalism," "legalization," "legitimacy," and "management" respectively. These four perspectives are not so much clear-cut theories of compliance, but rather point to a set of perspectives, as well as a set of processes and variables, that help us to understand compliance issues. These four theoretical perspectives overlap significantly. For instance, none of the perspectives denies the importance of the adequate monitoring of a regulation; however, they put different weight on the relative importance of different variables. While these perspectives do not flow directly from different theories of international relations, in the same way as the first principal hypothesis flows from Realism, they are nevertheless clearly related. While the term "rational institutionalism" is directly used as a label for a theory of international relations, both "liberalism" and "social constructivism" – other theories of international relations – contribute to the legalization as well as the legitimacy perspectives. The management perspective draws on various theories of international relations. At the same time, the four perspectives have affinities to different theories of law. In sum, each of the four theoretical perspectives on compliance are problem-driven attempts at theorizing, with a grounding in compliance issues and they draw upon and combine processes and factors that are emphasized by different theories and disciplines.

---

[23] For other categorizations of approaches explaining compliance see, among others, Haas (1998); Hathaway (2002); Hurd (1999); Jacobson and Weiss (1998a); Underdal (1998); and Vogel and Kessler (1998).

1.3.1   Cheating and rational institutionalism

This theoretical perspective on compliance with intergovernmental agreements regards cheating as the major problem and positive and negative incentives (coercion) as the only solution. The primary focus is clearly on the first dimension of compliance, that is, the difference between obligations and actual behavior. It is based on the assumption of rational, unitary actors who are only willing to co-operate on the basis of a common agreement if the cost-benefit calculations predict positive results. Costs and benefits must not only be seen from the narrow economic perspective, but can also include, for example, power or prestige. This has two implications for rule compliance: on the one hand there is a high incentive for each of the participating actors to enjoy the benefits of co-operation without meeting the costs themselves (free-riding or cheating). On the other hand, there is the perpetual concern that cheating by some actors changes the cost-benefit calculus for all participants, resulting in a breakdown of co-operation with negative repercussions for all participants.

This perspective on compliance is somewhat related to a view of law which lays emphasis on the role of sanctioning by an independent central agent, which can be distinguished by its superior force (e.g. Kelsen 1966). It also strongly emphasizes the use of threats and sanctions against non-compliant actors as a means of reducing cheating. Thus, a "punishment strategy is sufficient to enforce a treaty when each side knows that if the other cheats it will suffer enough from the punishment that the net benefit will not be positive" (Downs et al. 1996: 385). Hence, this perspective is related to one component of the first principal hypothesis, according to which agreements and regulations are not really law-like unless they are backed by a coercive force and are accompanied by "enormous resources devoted to enforcement and surveillance" (Hurd 1999: 384). However, it does not necessarily restrict law to the national setting, since it is open to the notion of horizontal coercion and acknowledges that some agreements manage to work in the absence of coercion.

Rational institutionalism considers a high rate of compliance with regulations beyond the nation-state to be possible. It points out that in most cases the participants' interests and motives for co-operation are mixed. Besides an interest in the short-term maximization of individual gains, future considerations might also make actors act cautiously in a way that does not endanger co-operative outcomes. In this sense, compliance can work on the basis of the actors' belief that this promotes their self-interest (Hurd 1999: 385). Consequently, the process of rule implementation is itself due to compliance bargaining (Jönsson and Tallberg 1998). Two important differences to Realist thinking should thus be emphasized. First, coercion in the form of threats and sanctions is not necessary for all types of co-operation. In some successful institutions there is no significant requirement for threats and sanctions, whereas others indeed require coercion to work. In order to understand this discrepancy, attention should be paid to situations in which actors seek to form institutions. Accordingly, threats and sanctions are only required if some actors have an incentive to defect.[24] Secondly, although all regulations with an incentive to defect must be underpinned by threats and sanctions in order to guarantee their durability and reliability, it seems possible to achieve this even in the context of a symmetrical power relationship. In these situations, tit for tat allows the evolution of co-operation under anarchy (Axelrod 1984; Keohane 1984). In other words, horizontal coercion can function as an equivalent to material hierarchy.

A sustainable regulation depends, however, on a number of additional conditions that make horizontal coercion effective in the first place. It is in this regard that international institutions, once established, gain an independent role and are of the utmost importance in international politics. These conditions can be derived from secondary co-operation problems, that is the costs involved in constructing and maintaining a regulation (Axelrod and Keohane 1985; Keohane 1984; Martin 1993; Ostrom 1990; Zangl 1999; and Zürn 1992). First of all, verification procedures for parties' (non-)compliance need to be reliable and not too costly. For instance, the verification of tariff levels in international trade is much easier than the verification of subsidies. Besides the type of regulation, the extent of verification problems can, among other factors, also be influenced by an intelligent institutional design (see Mitchell 1994; Wettestad 1999). Secondly, the sanctioning of a non-compliant party should not be too costly for the sanctioning party. Sanctioning by military means, for instance, is by necessity extremely costly, while sanctioning in the form of penalty tariffs is considered beneficial. Again, a skillful combination of the underlying problem structure and the institutional design determines the costs of sanctioning. In sum, rational institutionalism points to an institutional setting and a problem structure that

---

[24] For discussions about the underlying situation structure and appropriate institutional design, see Martin (1993), Mitchell and Keilbach (2001), Scharpf (1997), Stein (1983), and Zürn (1992). In any case, the most important determinant of co-operation and compliance is, in the view of rational institutionalism, the so-called situation structure, that is, the interest structure that constitutes the collective action problem (see Oye 1986, Zürn 1992, and Martin 1993; and see Hasenclever et al. 1997 for an overview). In our study we aim to keep the situation structure constant by comparing similar regulations across levels.

facilitates the verification of rule-compliance, and does not involve high costs for the party that seeks to impose sanctions.

This general perspective on compliance with intergovernmental agreements has been used in an array of studies. O'Connell (1992) and Baker (1992) provide evidence that international environmental agreements only work if threats and sanctions are applied. These could, for instance, be export and import limitations for goods to and from countries that do not comply with, or even enter, such agreements. In addition, Morgan and Schwebach (1997) suggest that, in order to take effect, the cost of sanctions to a potential rule-breaker must considerably outweigh the advantages to be gained by their non-compliance. In line with rational institutionalism it has been argued that institutions increase compliance by taking on the role of an independent and credible third party to ensure the fair distribution of co-operation costs and benefits (Mills and Rockoff 1987; Gibson 1989). They encourage the reliability of all participants by administering the monitoring procedures (Raustiala and Victor 1998; Subak 1997; Széll 1995; Macrory 1992; and Wettestad 1999), and finally, by sanctioning infringements of the rules without giving rise to a direct confrontation between participating actors (Väyrynen 1996; Weitsman and Schneider 1996; and Boyle 1991).

1.3.2   Ambiguity and legalization

This perspective sees ambiguities, their strategic abuse, as well as inconsistencies in rule development and application, as the major sources of non-compliance. The solution is a process of legalization, which allows the regulation in question to become incorporated as deeply as possible into pre-existing rule of law systems. Moreover, this perspective stresses the "preciseness" of norms and the need for so-called secondary rules that help to settle disputes over the content and the application of the norms themselves.[25] It therefore focuses quite evenly on both dimensions of compliance, trying to bring in the integrity of law as an explanatory variable for compliance. It is, in a sense, the attempt to "take law seriously" in theories of political science (cf. Joerges 1996b: 86–92).

The most fundamental assumption in this reasoning is probably that a legal system is usually more legitimate than a specific law, which suggests that a specific, law-like rule may be complied with because the legal system as a whole is deemed legitimate. This line of argument applies

---

[25] The major work on this view is H. L. A. Hart's *Concept of Law* (1972). The classic formulation of Oliver Holmes's (1897) legal realism, "Law is what courts do", should also be noted.

not only to national legal systems (Dworkin 1991), but also to international law (Hurrell 1993). International law may be observed, even in the context of contrary self-interests, not least because it is perceived as being part of an all-encompassing normative superstructure. The blatant, unjustified transgression of international legal regulations is thus deemed to be akin to a general repudiation of the normative fundaments of international co-operation. In this sense, legal rules possess a compliance pull of their own (Franck 1990). It follows that the more a rule is considered to be part of a legal system or, to put it differently, the more an international institution is legalized, the more likely compliance with the rule becomes.

The question then arises as to what makes decision-makers perceive a rule as law. We consider two sets of features as fundamental to the process of legalization; one may be called juridification, the other internalization. *Juridification* refers to the process by which it is ensured that regulations fulfill certain criteria, such as clarity, pertinence, stringency, adaptability and a high degree of consistency, both within themselves and in relation to other laws. Abbott et al. (2000: 401) identify three elements in this process:[26] "Obligation," meaning that states or other actors are bound by a rule or commitment; "precision," meaning that the rules accurately and unambiguously define the conduct that they require, authorize or proscribe; and "delegation," meaning that authority has been granted to third parties to implement the rules, including their interpretation, application, dispute settlement, and further rule making. Whereas, for our purposes, the element of obligation is a little too close to our *explanandum* (compliance), the other two elements point directly to the problem of ambiguity. The major mechanism for dealing with ambiguity is to establish procedures that interpret rules and their application on the basis of legal reasoning, that is "an effort to gain assent to . . . judgments on reasoned rather than idiosyncratic grounds" (Kratochwil 1989: 119). Governance beyond the nation-state cannot be justified in legal theory on the basis of "bargaining" alone; it also calls for "arguing" against the background of commonly accepted legal norms.[27] The major instrument for establishing these argumentative procedures is the delegation of "authority to designated third parties – including courts, arbitrators and administrative organizations – to implement agreements" (Abbott et al. 2000: 415). The delegation of authority includes such different tasks as

---

[26] See also Goldstein et al. (2000). Legalization, following our terminology, describes a double process of juridification and internalization. What Abbott et al. (2000) define as legalization is in that sense very close to our concept of juridification.

[27] Cf. Elster (1992, 1998b) and Gehring (1996) on this pair of terms. See Risse (2000) for a treatment of communicative action in world politics.

fact finding, dispute settlement, and rule development in the process of
rule application, each task being restricted by the principles and terms of
the agreement. The greater the autonomy of these designated authorities
with respect to each of the three tasks, the greater the extent of juridification.

In many respects, a very high level of juridification resembles the
concept of supranationalism as applied in recent studies, according to
which supranational institutions develop rules that are considered superior to national law and involve agents who have some autonomy from
national governments – the European Commission and the European
Court of Justice are the best-known examples.[28] Reference to the notion
of supremacy to national law, however, implies that supranational rules
have to a certain extent already been internalized within national legal
systems. In our view, *internalization* constitutes the second component
of legalization besides juridification.[29] We build here on the theory of
the internalization of law, according to which norms above and beyond
national societies only attain full legal status when they are legally, socially
and politically internalized by those to whom they are addressed (Koh
1997: 2645–58; Raustiala 1995). Reformulating this definition slightly,
we draw a distinction between legal and civil internalization. Legally internalized refers here to the fact that norms of conduct, developed beyond
the nation-state, directly affect their addressees; civilly internalized means
that those who are affected by the regulations have actionable civil rights
(Zürn and Wolf 1999). This leads to a situation in which "enforcement
through domestic courts" is the principal means by which compliance
with international regulations is attained (O'Connell 1995: 5–7; Alter
2001).

- In its strongest form, legal internalization is based, above all, on two
  foundations that are best illustrated by the EU: on the one hand the
  supremacy of European law over national law, and on the other hand,

---

[28] See Bogdandy (1999) and Neyer (1999) for a constructive use of the term "supranational governance." Moravcsik (1998: 67) distinguishes between "pooled sovereignty,"
when governments agree to decide future matters by non-unanimous voting procedures,
and "delegated sovereignty," when supranational actors are permitted to take certain
autonomous decisions without an intervening interstate or unilateral veto. On the basis
of this distinction between two subtypes of supranationality even some intergovernmental
institutions can be said to contain supranational components.

[29] Keohane et al. (2000) discuss delegation – the major component of our notion of juridification – in such a way as to include what we conceptualize as internalization. Besides
independence, defined as "the extent to which formal legal arrangements ensure that
adjudication can be rendered impartially," they also consider "access" ("ease with which
parties other than states can influence the tribunal's agenda") and "embeddedness"
(which "denotes the extent to which dispute resolution decisions can be implemented
without governments having to take actions to do so") as part of "delegation."

the direct enforcing effect of ECJ case law, via the preliminary reference procedure that is contained in Article 234 (formerly Article 177).
These features guarantee that European law possesses an unquestionable validity throughout all the member states, such that Community
provisions must be seen as an inseparable part of the body of laws that
are valid for EU citizens (Weiler 1993).[30]

- Civil internalization requires a definitive allocation of individual, subjective rights. These subjective rights must, first and foremost, be *individually* actionable, that is, they must not be attributed to collectivities
or communities, but must be actionable as individual rights, so ensuring
that all those affected by a regulation have the same rights, thus realizing the principle of equality and guaranteeing reciprocity. Second, these
rights must be *directly* actionable. Only where rights infringements can
be brought directly before the relevant judicial body by those who are
affected can the individually allocated rights be said to take effect.

The more extensive the legal and civil internalization of international
regulations, the more likely it is that individual states and actors will
comply with them.

In sum, legalization consists of a double process of juridification and
internalization. These two components of legalization are closely related
to each other and develop their dynamics only in interaction (see Stone
and Caporaso 1998). Legalization beyond the nation-state is most developed if (i) there has been a significant delegation of the power to implement rules to agents with some degree of autonomy, (ii) the supremacy of
the international or transnational law is accepted and is ideally backed up
by direct effect, and (iii) the rules are individually and directly actionable.

Empirical studies that utilize such a conceptual framework are rare.
Besides the seminal work of Franck (1990), some studies in the recent
special issue of *International Organization* on legalization illustrate the
theoretical argument. In particular, Keohane et al. (2000) have explored
some assumptions relating to legalized dispute resolution. With respect
to the EU, the work of Mattli and Slaughter (1998) and Alter (2001)
is the most influential. In addition, Kiss (1996) argues, in his study of
international and European environmental legislation, that the coherent
and consistent integration of international and supranational regulations

---

[30] While the principle of direct effect is unique to the EU, some domestic legal systems
allow the direct enforcement of international law, without prior implementation by the
national legislature. O'Connell (1995: 5) cites *Paquette Habana* as the most famous case
in the United States. "In *Paquette Habana* U.S. Navy ships arrested Cuban fishing vessels
during the Spanish-American War. The Navy wanted to sell the vessels as prizes of war.
The United States Supreme Court held that under international law, fishing vessels
cannot be captured as prizes of war."

into national or regional legal systems results in a decisive improvement in the compliance they enjoy. In addition, some empirical studies that belong to the social constructivist tradition of international relations have contributed to our understanding of the process of internalization and socialization of norms (see Checkel 1998, 2001; Schimmelfennig 2000).

1.3.3   Non-acceptance of rules and legitimacy

This perspective regards reservations about the normative validity of a rule as the most significant source of non-compliance, and therefore the generation of legitimacy as the solution to compliance problems. Its primary focus is on the first dimension of compliance, that is the discrepancy between the obligations that are created by the norm and actual behavior of its addressees. This perspective operates on the assumption that when making and applying a law, general precepts of justice and fairness must play a recognizable part in order for it to be legitimate. Accordingly, the *manner in which* norms are generated and applied distinguishes law from other social norms. In this sense, regulations count as law when they are produced in the context of a legitimate norm-forming process *and* their application is marked by a rational linkage to the objectives they are associated with as well as certain general principles. In finding and applying a law, then, general precepts of justice and fairness must directly play a recognizable part (see Dworkin 1986; Habermas 1994a). In this perspective, the insistence on a link between legitimacy and compliance is even more accentuated than in the legalization perspective.

In so far as law constitutes a genuinely argumentative social practice, the required precepts of justice and fairness can best be determined procedurally. In this sense, both the discourses that are used to justify a law and those who apply it must approximate to the principles of rational discourse and, at the same time, include all the addressees of the regulations. In this sense, the legitimacy of a rule is determined by the extent to which rule-related decision making is considered to be fair. A procedure is likely to be considered fair by the addressees of a regulation provided that they have an opportunity to participate in the rule-related decision making and it does not systematically favor certain interests over others. Participation and impartiality are not only the major ingredients of a normative theory of procedural justice but also enjoy a broad popular support (see Tyler 1990). At a minimum level, participation and fairness must apply to all governments which are the immediate addressees of a regulation. In addition, one might require the direct or indirect participation of the final targets of a regulation (those societal actors who have to change their behavior), most often represented by associations.

A conception of law that is based on the integrity of decision making and its application points in addition to a role for law that previously did not seem to be required of international institutions. Law may be seen as constituted by carrying out a pivotal function between the normative framework of the social and political system on the one hand, and the perceptions of good and bad by the regulatory addressees and other affected parties on the other. In the words of Jürgen Habermas (1994a: 78): "The law acts, as it were, as a transformer, ensuring in the first place that the network of socially integrative pan-societal communication does not break down. It is only in the language of law that normatively meaningful messages can circulate throughout society." Law hereby develops a socially integrative function of its own by, on the one hand, facilitating a codification of normative claims on the real world, while on the other hand remaining equally responsive to problem pressures from that real world. This social integration comes about through a common language, and presupposes a direct linkage between the law and the individuals concerned. This view of law leads directly to what one may call the societal internalization of legal norms (Koh 1997; Zürn and Wolf 1999). This means that not only all the potential regulatory addressees and targets, but also *all others who are affected* must have a chance to take part in these discourses. Publicity, or public discourse, is consequently crucial if the instrumentalization of law, for the purposes of gaining power, is to be avoided. Publicity, and public discourse, averts the danger of social power becoming transformed into administrative power.

In sum, the legitimacy perspective emphasizes two determinants of compliance: (i) the degree to which rule-related decision making is considered as procedurally just, through its incorporation of all regulatory addressees as well as all the associated targets of the regulation and (ii) the extent to which all those affected by the rule know and recognize the rule as being the result of a public discourse.

The legitimacy perspective is reflected in the literature in three connected strands of theory. First, Gaubatz (1996) challenges the argument, well-known in older studies, that democracies are unreliable at the international level, since they only adhere to agreements as long as the domestic balance of power permits. Gaubatz argues that it is precisely because of their pluralistic participatory structures that democracies are reliable partners. This result is reflected by the studies into the effect of participation in international environmental treaties (Victor, Raustiala and Skolnikoff 1998: Part II; Wettestad 1999: 176–178).[31] Secondly, there

---

[31] See, however, Simmons (2000a), who disaggregates democracy into a participatory and a rule of law component, and argues that participatory structures negatively affect compliance rates, while the rule of law has a positive effect.

are several studies that emphasize the fundamental significance of procedural justice in generating rule compliance (Tyler 1990, 1997; Lind 1995) and which repudiate recourse to sanctions as a means of enforcement, because this simply leads to deadlock. It is more important to involve the participants in the formulation and realization of a legal "co-production" (Curtis et al. 1991). Thirdly, in several studies, Gibson points out the distinction between "diffuse" and "specific" support (Gibson and Caldeira 1993, 1998; Caldeira and Gibson 1995), emphasizing that in order to attain a high degree of compliance the relevant regulations must be bolstered by broad "diffuse" support for the decision-making system itself.

The legitimacy perspective also sheds light on the tension that is inherent in the relationship between the external restrictions and the internal demands on the decision-making process, as emphasized in the liberal theory of international relations. While some claim that international agreements are a proven means of disciplining domestic political and social interests and of strengthening the position of governmental actors (Wolf 2000; Moravcsik 1997b; Rieger 1995), others argue that they put executives in a permanent state of conflict with important interest groups regarding their scope of action, thus making them highly dependent on dominant domestic interests and normative convictions (Moravcsik 1998; Müller and Risse-Kappen 1990; Slaughter 1993, 1995; Zangl 1999). Studies on compliance can be categorized according to these views. Goldstein (1996) and Haas (1998), for instance, argue that governments are able to hold national interest groups at bay by complying with international agreements, which they, after all, concluded and which presumably therefore reflect their own interests. Sometimes, for example in the field of trade and commerce, governments even use international agreements as a pretext to enforce domestic deregulatory measures that they had in mind anyway. In contrast, Underdal (1998), Mendrinou (1996), Raustiala (1997), and Lukas (1995) emphasize the predominance of societal interest groups and private actors in the implementation of regulations. If these domestic actors cannot be persuaded to co-operate, then many agreements might collapse anyway due to national resistance to their government's policies.

1.3.4   Resources and management

This theoretical perspective regards the continuing presence of implementation problems as a major challenge to compliance, and proposes a reflexive solution, which would manifest itself in regulatory deliberation by experts.[32] This approach perceives law as a process of permanent interactive adjudication based on reasoning (Joerges 2000; Selznick 1985). The focus of this perspective is thus primarily on the second dimension of compliance, that is, the way in which charges of non-compliance are dealt with after they have been put forward. This involves a challenge to the coercion perspective because it points to two empirical anomalies. In international treaties, "sanctioning authority is rarely granted by treaty, rarely used when granted, and likely to be ineffective when used" (Chayes and Chayes 1995: 32). Nevertheless, overall, compliance with international obligations is remarkably high (Young 1999a: Chapter 4). It is concluded that mechanisms other than coercion are more important. Moreover, this perspective even challenges the view that cases of non-compliance can easily be identified from the perspective of an outsider. Regulations, compliance and non-compliance should rather be regarded as elements in a continuous process in which, by means of a form of "managed compliance," rules are applied and modified, with the object being to ensure that the criteria for effective regulation are continually fulfilled. The production and implementation of rules is thus an iterative process, and it is hard to distinguish one from the other at any given point in time.[33] In this connection, the authors assume that "foreign policy practitioners operate on the assumption of a general propensity of states to comply with international obligations" (Chayes and Chayes 1995: 3). Hence, they draw particular attention to the fact that non-compliance is often unintentional. Unintentional non-compliance may occur for a number of reasons. Ambiguity and the indeterminacy of rules certainly amount to one reason, but a state's inability to fulfill its obligations, as well as the failure of a treaty to adapt to changing conditions, count as equally important, if not more important reasons for non-compliance (Chayes and Chayes 1995: 9–17).

Those who hold this perspective are able to draw upon studies that emphasize two aspects of good compliance, each of which are compatible with the managerial approach to compliance. Compliance management is thus successful if sufficient resources for implementation are available to all parties, and if the compliance management system displays a high level of reflexivity and flexibility by heavily utilizing expertise, so as to be responsive to new problems.

---

[32] From this perspective, deliberation is mainly a reference to a dyadic setting, in the sense of communicative action, and has little to do with legal reasoning in a triadic setting, which is bound up with the legalization perspective.

[33] This emphasis on the legal *process* demonstrates the significant similarities that exist between this perspective on compliance and the so-called New Haven School (see McDougal, Lasswell and Reisman 1968).

Studies in this tradition demonstrate that it is of the utmost importance that the necessary financial and technological resources are available to all the addressees of a regulation. Unintentional non-compliance is often due to a lack of administrative, technological and financial resources. Therefore the availability of mechanisms to ensure that resources are transferred to those addressees who lack resources improves compliance as well as effectiveness. In particular, studies on compliance with international environmental agreements have shown the significant role played by resources, especially when addressees are obliged to undertake action, rather than merely refrain from certain activities (Haas, Keohane and Levy 1993; Chayes and Chayes 1995; Ponce-Nava 1995; Zürn 1998: Chapter 6).[34]

Moreover, a high degree of regulatory reflexivity seems to require a constant and reliable flow of information concerning solutions to both problems and efficient compliance. Again, studies on international environmental agreements have emphasized this aspect. Haas (1998) underlines the role of epistemic communities in drawing up standards so as to identify acute problems and in finding adequate solutions. Underdal (1998) points out the importance of ideas and learning processes to reach a high degree of compliance in politically amicable contexts. So-called comitology procedures in the European Union seem to provide a prime example of this. The implementation of EU regulations is to a large extent managed by committees, which work on the basis of expert arguments, and can consequently be interpreted as operating a form of deliberative supranationalism (Joerges and Neyer 1997a, 1997b).

The review of these four perspectives on the causes of and cures for non-compliance generates a set of variables that will be taken into account in our study, which seeks to explain compliance and non-compliance beyond the nation-state (and see table 1.5). This set of hypotheses enables us to move beyond the dichotomy that is presented by the two principal hypotheses discussed in section 1.1. Ideally, they provide an explanation for the variations in compliance that one can observe in different cases across different levels.

1.4   Empirical and normative results

This project is a product of co-operation between lawyers and political scientists. Political science is mainly concerned with *descriptive* questions such as the degree to which rules are obeyed and why some rules are better

---

[34] See, e.g., the contributions to Cowles, Caporaso and Risse (2001) and Knill and Lenschow (1999) which point to similar effects in relation to EU policies.

Table 1.5 *Perspectives and variables*

Rational institutionalism	• easy verification of rule-compliance • sanctioning does not involve high costs for the sanctioning party
Legalization	• autonomous third party supervision of rules (juridification) • supremacy and direct effect (legal internalization) • rules are individually and directly actionable (civil internalization)
Legitimacy	• participation of all executive addressees and all associative targets of the regulation • involvement of the broad public in rule-formulation and application
Management	• sufficient capacities for implementation are available to all parties[35] • flexibility through reflexivity

complied with than others. "Law, by contrast," as international relations theorist Martha Finnemore (1996: 142) eloquently writes, "is largely *prescriptive*, concerned with codifying and reconciling rules of behavior for states. Questions about why these rules and not others exist or why states comply or do not comply with them are peripheral to the realm of law." The question that millions of lawyers around the world are regularly paid to answer is not *why* there is, or is not, compliance, but *what* does the law command? Therefore, an interdisciplinary project on compliance necessarily combines factual and normative approaches. Indeed, the comprehensive treatment of any complex, real-world problem necessarily involves both factual and normative statements. Nevertheless, as a single proposition, the distinction between the descriptive and the prescriptive sphere remains valid. It is therefore our aim logically to link descriptive and prescriptive statements, thereby avoiding an impenetrable intermingling of normative and empirical questions. Our understanding of interdisciplinary research is thus one that takes the identity of the disciplines as the starting point of a discourse, but in no way advocates the dissolution of the boundaries between the disciplines.

1.4.1   The principal contest – who is right?

Central to our study is the *empirical* question: what constitutes the social and political requirements for rule-compliance? Is a satisfactory rate of compliance – to the extent that one can justifiably speak of legal equality – only possible within the framework of the nation-state, or is it also obtainable within a structure that extends beyond the nation-state? Our

---

[35] In none of our empirical cases is there a practically restrictive lack of resources so that implementation becomes impossible. This variable will therefore not be dealt with in the ensuing chapters.

study rejects the hypothesis that any given regulation is better complied with within a national political system than within a system beyond the nation-state. In none of our sets of comparisons is compliance systematically better in the national context than in settings beyond the nation-state. The case of subsidies (ch. 3) is especially telling. Subsidy controls, as agreed upon by the *Länder* in Germany, are more often disregarded than similar European and international regulations. They display a low compliance rate and are accompanied by perpetual compliance crises. Moreover, the pressures on the redistributive programs within Germany seem to be at least as heavy as on the redistributive programs in the EU (ch. 5).

This finding in no way negates the importance of institutional hierarchy and institutionalized coercion as a means for generating compliance. It does show, however, that a legal hierarchy, as well as institutionalized monitoring and sanctioning, can develop effectively within a horizontal context. In fact, all three sets of comparisons in our study demonstrate the relative success of the EU in generating compliance. In all three issue areas under question, the EU achieves the best rate of compliance. In these issue areas it is the EU that has a legal hierarchy and that works most extensively with institutionalized mechanisms for monitoring compliance and sanctioning non-compliance. Compared with the EU, a legal hierarchy and institutionalized monitoring and sanctioning are much less developed in the relations between the *Länder* in Germany. While the WTO contains some weak elements of legalization and institutionalized monitoring and sanctioning, it is much less developed in these areas (see section 1.2). We conclude that a legal hierarchy and institutionalized monitoring and sanctioning seem to be more important determinants of compliance than the shadow of material hierarchy and strong communal bonds.

1.4.2   *What accounts for compliance beyond the nation-state?*

Although institutionalized enforcement in relationships between states can be as successful as a shadow of hierarchy and communal bonds in achieving compliance, it is dependent on a number of interacting conditions. Against the background of our four perspectives on compliance in horizontal contexts, the ensuing chapters will develop the following points.
- To the extent that horizontal sanctioning is built into the enforcement process, it is also necessary that the verification of rule-related behavior works, and that sanctioning measures do not impose high costs on the sanctioning party. The WTO Treaty, which provides a prime example

of a horizontal coercion mechanism, is a case in point (ch. 3). The comparative analysis of foodstuffs points in the same direction (ch. 4). Hence, the relevance of the variables emphasized by *rational institutionalism* plays an important role in the generation of compliance beyond the nation-state.

- Institutional designs that are based on the theory of rational institutionalism remain highly vulnerable to external shocks, especially when instances of deep intrusion are involved, such as BSE and subsidy controls. Compliance management through *legalization* in the form of juridification and legal as well as civil internalization can stabilize compliance and partially replace horizontal enforcement. In particular, initial non-compliance is easily handled when a regulation is heavily legalized. Legalization is accomplished when juridification, that is the delegation of rule supervision to a third party that acts on the basis of legal reasoning, is complemented by a process of internalization, that is the incorporation of regulations which originated in a realm beyond the nation-state into the national legal system. Probably the most likely reason for the success of the EU in generating compliance is that the legalization of its compliance systems is the most developed. It seems fair to say that legalization is more developed within the political system of the EU than in relations between the *Länder* in Germany. The guidelines of rational institutionalism, coupled with high levels of legalization, seems to create a more superior enforcement mechanism than does hierarchical coercion, not least because in a highly legalized context sanctioning becomes legitimate (Schoppa 1999). Hence, our studies uniformly demonstrate the positive effects of legalization on compliance.

- Legalization, combined with the guidelines of rational institutionalism, seems to work very well in most situations and can explain a high rate of compliance with a given regulation. This mechanism may come under severe stress, however, if an issue reaches the *agenda* of a broader public *and* in particular when the different national public discourses are both *fragmented*, in the sense that they do not relate to each other, and *polarized*, in the sense that they lead to completely different outcomes. Both the issues of BSE and growth hormones are cases in point. In spite of good overall compliance rates, the respective regulations experienced compliance crises. On these issues, national politicians, who were in principle willing to comply with the rules, came under pressure from national interests, backed by a more or less homogenous public opinion (see in more detail ch. 4). By contrast, as long as structurally similar issues are not the concern of public discourse, as in the case of subsidy controls (ch. 3), compliance is no problem and, at worst, in some initial cases non-compliance might occur. Even if an issue, characterized by strongly opposing interests, becomes public, compliance can be maintained and severe compliance crises avoided (recalcitrant compliance) if the issue is the subject of an integrated as opposed to a fragmented public discourse, such as is the case with the *Länderfinanzausgleich* (inter-regional financial equalization) in Germany. In short, even the best institutional design for attaining high levels of compliance with intergovernmental agreements will break down and lead to compliance crises when it is not backed by a public discourse among the people who are affected by the rules. The link between *legitimacy* and compliance seems to be most important when heavily legalized regulations come under stress. Then it becomes obvious that international courts cannot draw from a cache of legitimacy.

- Compliance management seems to be only partially relevant to our set of cases. While we cannot deny the general importance of resources for the implementation of regulations, this factor obviously cannot explain the variance in our cases. The countries that we studied do not face resource problems with respect to the implementation of those regulations that we studied. The second aspect of the management approach – that is the degree to which the application of rules is conducted by means of reflexive interaction – seems to be much more important, however. Both in the foodstuffs as well as in the redistributive cases, one of the most important reasons for compliance difficulties, which resulted in mere recalcitrant compliance (without the presence, however, of either routine non-compliance or compliance crises), was the addressees' perception that they had insufficient opportunities to feed their concerns back into the adaptation of rules so as to represent their changing wants and needs.

In sum, while sufficient compliance can be achieved with regulations beyond the nation-state, this is highly conditional on the interplay of a number of different compliance determinants.

1.4.3   Is law beyond the nation-state a valid normative project?

These descriptive findings are by no means relevant only for political scientists. Both the point of view that "laws need coercion from above" and the statement that "most nations comply with international law without the need for coercion" are taken directly from current debates on legal theory. Our empirical findings are therefore relevant for lawyers in that they contribute to debates on the theory of law. The findings demonstrate that the once fundamental difference between national and international law has become fuzzy, and has even partially withered away. Institutional hierarchy, communal bonds and the shadow of material hierarchy no longer need necessarily to accompany each other. Moreover, the study of the causes of and the cures for compliance is also normatively driven and is thus familiar to the thinking of lawyers. One of the concerns of all the participating authors is the investigation of the potential for normatively substantial international and supranational forms of regulation, i.e. the development of modules for a project on complex world governance. In the light of globalization and denationalization, it seems to us that a paramount concern of the study of politics ought to be a reflection on constitutional forms of governance beyond the nation-state that are both democratically legitimate *and* effective in solving problems.[36] For this reason it does not suffice merely to qualify the role of a material hierarchy in inducing compliance. Rather, put in more positive terms, the question is whether and to what extent the legitimacy and the legal content of a regulation has any influence on compliance with it. We hold that the notion of law beyond the nation-state depends on a strong empirical link between legitimacy and compliance. The establishment and concretization of this link is therefore of particular interest to those who believe in the need for governance beyond the nation-state. It is in this area in particular that the interdisciplinary quality of our project proves to be so fruitful. Juridical concepts can be useful in expanding on rational co-operation theory and are also helpful in specifying constructivist co-operation theory in more detail.

In this respect our study is in line with other recent studies on the "legalization" of the EU, and now also of international institutions, and especially those that appeared in a special issue of *International Organization*.[37] These studies have observed a general shift towards an increased legalization of international and transnational relations. Against this background, a better understanding of "the use and consequences of international law" is needed. Our argument differs from these studies in two respects.

- Our understanding of legalization involves more than the more or less formal aspects of "obligation," "preciseness," and "delegation."[38] Although we are also interested in the clarification of the role of law in

---

[36] See Joerges (1996b) and Joerges and Neyer (1997a, 1997b) with regard to the EU, and Zürn (1998) on the notion of complex governance beyond the nation-state.

[37] See also the work of Weiler (e.g. 1998), Burley and Mattli (1993), Mattli and Slaughter (1998), Stone Sweet and Caporaso (1998) and Alter (1998) on the EU and Chayes and Chayes (1993, 1995), Romano (1999), and Stone (1994) on international relations.

[38] See Finnemore and Toope (2001) for a critique of the conception that is developed by Abbott et al. (2000). The study of Keohane et al. 2000, however, expands the notion of delegation to include elements of what we call internalization.

international politics, our understanding of law also includes aspects such as the legal incorporation and the legitimacy of rules.

- Legalization in our research is an explanatory variable to account for variance in compliance. In this sense, we aim to identify the effects of legalization on the basis of a research design that makes allowance for causal inferences (taking all due care to avoid typical pitfalls). On the basis of our case selection, we move beyond a purely explorative discussion of the possible causes and consequences of legalization.

In general, elaborating on the link between legitimacy and compliance, as well as on the importance of this link to other theories, places our research project together with other studies that consider a denationalized political order in which law making and law enforcement is horizontalized. Establishing a link between legitimacy and compliance could have significant implications for reflections both on law and on international politics. On the one hand, it could significantly weaken the notion that law is restricted to the framework of a democratic nation-state, and would thereby impact on debates on the theory of law. On the other hand, the presence, or even the possibility of legitimate institutions beyond the nation-state could indicate the presence of authority and question the notion of anarchy in the international realm (see also Hurd 1999: 399).

1.4.4   How to promote law beyond the nation-state?

The normative background to our straightforward empirical inquiry requires us to elaborate further on the *normative implications* of the whole study. With our project we would also like to make an original contribution to a theory of good governance in supranational and transnational contexts by determining the characteristics which a just political order should have in the age of denationalization. Each of the two disciplinary perspectives has its own typical way of examining this question.

Political scientists usually base their recommendations on relatively fixed principles and concepts of democracy, and concentrate on the question of how these principles can best be institutionalized under the given socio-cultural and socio-economic circumstances. This approach is therefore particularly concerned with formulating proposals for institutional reform. Our empirical findings can therefore be used in the development of international institutions that are designed to induce compliance. This development uses building blocks to develop regulations which enjoy sufficient compliance and integrity to be considered law. In this regard, as a first step, it seems important to design international institutions so that they allow for institutionalized coercion in a horizontal context.

Compliance is further enhanced if institutionalized horizontal coercion is complemented by compliance management mechanisms as well as with juridification. More advanced compliance tools include processes of law internalization. Finally, intensive co-operation necessarily raises the issues of public opinion and public discourses. It is not the absence of hierarchy in the international sphere, but rather the lack of acceptance of governance beyond the nation-state, which seems to be the real Achilles heel of international co-operation. Thus, governance beyond the nation-state requires a qualitative step away from the *executive multilateralism* of the post-World War II period to a form of *socially consented multilateralism* in the age of globalization (see ch. 6). This Achilles heel also hampers the development of a "globalization of law."[39]

Lawyers, by contrast, tend to develop a constitutional perspective of law production out of a precise understanding of emerging legal practices. A constitution in this view is "a body of metanorms governing how low-order norms are produced, applied and interpreted" (Stone 1994: 443). One critical empirical test for a constitutionalist perspective on European and international political processes is whether there are procedures which ensure the coherence of "facts and norms." Only against this empirical background does it make sense to consider the practical possibilities of a "democratically legitimate" polity within that context and then to classify law systematically. In chapter 7, therefore, Christian Joerges builds on our findings about the link between legitimacy and compliance. He puts forward a constitutional notion of deliberative supranationalism that is conducive to compliance and could provide the basis for law beyond the nation-state. Deliberation becomes the normative leitmotiv that inspires the organization of transnational problem-solving and assessment. A supranational charter is, thereby, neither required to represent a territorial state nor does it presuppose the dissolution of national political systems. What it does require, however, is that the interests and concerns of non-nationals should be considered and legalized through juridification at levels beyond the nation-state and through the internalization of international regulations. This deliberative supranationalism must guarantee (i) that in the deliberations surrounding the enactment of a particular regulation the grounds brought forward for and against it are acceptable to all the parties involved, (ii) that it requires "arguing" about the relevant problems, and (iii) that the general public is given the chance to articulate its opinions on matters that would otherwise only be dealt with in specialist media (see Habermas 1994a; Weiler, Haltern and Mayer 1995; and Koh 1997).

---

[39] On the globalization of law see Gessner and Budak (1998) and Voigt (1999).

1.4.5   What is special about the EU?

Finally, this study on law and governance in postnational Europe obviously also has a specific European component. A European regulation appears prominently in each of our three comparative studies and thus, with all three policies examined, we compare the methods and the relative success with which compliance is achieved with obligations created by the EU, national political systems and international institutions. An extraordinary feature of the EU seems to be its high level of legalization, which, in turn, seems to account to a large extent for the high rate of compliance it achieves. These findings have implications for Europeanists.

First, the more skeptical analyses of compliance in the EU, which emphasize the high number of infringement proceedings (e.g. Knill and Lenschow 1999), must be put in perspective. They point to the growing number of infringement proceedings, now numbering over 1,000 a year, and conclude that the swift and diligent implementation of ECJ decisions has been anything but the rule (Tallberg 2002). Although these studies are essential to understanding compliance in the EU, to some extent they merely reproduce the perspective of the European Commission, which complains about non-compliance partly in order to increase compliance. The fact that the "Commission itself recognises that infringement proceedings and fines are not an effective means for enforcing environmental policies" (Börzel 1999: 10, citing the Commission) may not only be good evidence of self-critical evaluation, but may also be strategically motivated. In relative terms, the EU seems to be a success story in terms of compliance. We will discuss these questions further in the concluding chapter.

Moreover, our analysis addresses the debate over "neofunctionalist" versus "intergovernmentalist" interpretations of European integration.[40] It shows that the role of legalization is of central importance in eliciting compliance with European regulations. To some extent, the relationship between the constitutive political units within the EU is more legalized – in terms of both juridification and internalization – than it is within a federal state like Germany.[41] Moreover, the member states gradually become socialized within a network of transnational legal reasoning. In this sense, legalization contributes to the dynamics of European integration independently of the member state governments' preferences. Thus, our findings show an affinity to the notion of integration by law (see Burley and

---

[40] Although neofunctionalism is established as a term, we consider it to be problematic. Neofunctionalism, as a statement about the driving forces behind European integration, has little to do with functionalist reasoning.

[41] See Garrett, Kelemen and Schulz (1998) for a somewhat more skeptical view.

Mattli 1993; Alter 1998; Stone Sweet and Caporaso 1998; Shapiro and
Stone Sweet 2002). Our results therefore underline the insight of Walter
Hallstein, President of the Commission between 1958 and 1967, according to whom the EU is merely a legal community, but is not a coercive
community.[42] Indeed, it turns out that the focus on law, instead of com-
pelled obedience, seems to be the strength of the Community. At the
same time, it becomes obvious that the EU has the same Achilles heel
as other international institutions. The fragmentation of national public
discourses can undermine the most intelligently designed and legalized
regulation. In this respect, the EU is still far from being a political community, which is something we usually associate with nation-states. The
problem for the EU, then, is that it is not a community with an integrated
public discourse. There is no discursive community at the societal level.

[42] See also Bogdandy (1999: Chapter B 8).

2 The analysis of compliance with international rules: Definitions, variables, and methodology

Jürgen Neyer and Dieter Wolf

2.1 Introduction: Cross-level comparison

The aim of this chapter is to prepare the dependent (section 2.2) and independent (section 2.3) variables – as identified in the introduction – for the empirical analysis conducted in the case studies of chapters 3 to 5. Our approach to the analysis of compliance differs from other research in the field. Unlike the bulk of pre-existing studies, we aim to explain compliance by comparing similar rules at different levels. The main reason for our comparative approach is that it allows us to select cases based on variations in the independent variable and thus to approach our topic in a quasi-experimental fashion. Although the comparative method promises to provide new insights by systematically focusing on the distinction between politics in the nation-state and politics above the nation-state, we are well aware that the literature advances a number of reservations to such an approach. Some argue that the EU is a too specialized polity and therefore cannot be compared to either a nation-state or an international regime. Caporaso (1997: 1) has summarized this view: "Processes of integration in Europe are specialized, and qualitatively different from processes elsewhere. The historical thrust of the EC is so novel that it truly represents a Hegelian moment, a novelty that, however prescient in terms of future developments, has no current analogies." Although rarely made explicit, this argument is especially prevalent in a number of legal approaches which categorize the EU as an economic community (Mestmäcker 1994), as a special purpose association (*Zweckverband funktionaler Integration*) (Ipsen 1972) or, more abstractly, as a type of governance which must be understood in its own terms. The basic argument in all of these approaches is that the EU shows a number of attributes and normative underpinnings which make it a polity *sui generis* (Schneider 1969; Mancini 1991). As such, it is assumed to constitute a third category between the nation-state and international organizations, which neither can nor should be compared with any of them. This, however, would leave us with the simple, but nevertheless unsatisfactory argument that European law is the way it is because it is European in character and its record of compliance is due to the fact that European law is European in kind. There has to be something more to this.[1]

In order to find out what this might be, this project treats the EU, federal politics in Germany and international regimes as governance systems which share important similarities. Federal politics, the EU and international regimes are similar to the extent that all three represent forms of governance which:

- establish binding rules that are intended to promote the collective well-being of their addressees;
- are occasionally faced with the situation that governmental addressees are unwilling to comply with the rules; and, therefore,
- must find means to promote compliance.

By emphasizing these three shared elements, we can, in a first step, abstract from the uniqueness of the three levels of politics and approach them as comparable governance systems which face similar problems and must look for the means to cope with them. This does not mean that we ignore the differences between them. The purpose of this exercise is to find a point of reference (all three are governance systems with the three elements described above) from which we can discern observable differences (institutional variation) as variations in an underlying dimension (the ability to promote compliance). The results expected are far from obvious. Although some would probably argue that different degrees of hierarchy can be used to explain both the results, in terms of the observed degree of compliance and the tools used to promote this end, others point to factors such as management capacities, juridification, epistemic communities and so forth. Our comparative approach is therefore not motivated by the desire to demonstrate that the EU is similar to either a nation-state or an international regime. We do not side *a priori* with any of the descriptions in the literature, but instead conduct an empirical investigation to find out to what extent the EU, a nation-state and the WTO differ in their ability to promote compliance as well as in the instruments they use for that purpose.

2.2   Conceptualizing compliance – the dependent variable

Compliance needs to be distinguished from the concepts of implementation and effectiveness. Unlike these two concepts, compliance focuses neither on the effort to administer authoritatively public policy directives and the changes they undergo during this administrative process

---

[1] Cf. for a more detailed discussion, Moravcsik (1997a) and Marks (1997).

(implementation)[2] nor on the efficacy of a given regulation to solve the political problem that preceded its formulation (effectiveness).[3] Compliance research is primarily concerned with the degree to which the addressees of a rule "adhere to the provision of the accord and to the implementing measures that they have instituted" (Jacobson and Weiss 1998a: 4).[4] Assessing compliance is restricted to the description of the discrepancy between the (legal) text of the regulation and the actions and behaviors of its addressees. Perfect compliance, imperfect implementation and zero effectiveness therefore are not necessarily mutually exclusive. They may coexist, for example, if a rule is limited to prescribing a change in applied technology without listing quantitative performance parameters. In that case perfect compliance (a change in technology) may coexist with both complete ineffectiveness and an impressive record of implementation, if the new technology proves to be inadequate for solving the problem for which it was chosen. Because compliance with commitments is a necessary precondition for effective governance, however, compliance and effectiveness are nevertheless closely related. This is especially the case if the rules require inconvenient behavioral changes of the addressees. In such cases, explaining the conditions under which inconvenient rules enjoy a high likelihood of compliance can be understood as an important step towards understanding if and how effective governance beyond the nation-state can be realized. In assessing compliance we distinguish between two dimensions: non-compliance as the difference between facts and norms and non-compliance as a process.

2.2.1 Non-compliance as the difference between facts and norms

Before any assessment of compliance can be undertaken, a point of reference (a rule) must be identified. Without a rule detailing clear prescriptions or proscriptions, (non-)compliance is difficult to assess. In identifying such rules, the project abstains from analyzing implicit or tacit norms, which are not clearly codified and/or lack a more than marginal consent as to their substantial content. Such rules include, for example, "reciprocity" (Keohane 1986), "fairness" (Franck 1995), or "justice" (Gibson 1989). Although these norms are by no means unimportant in achieving collective well-being, they have too little intersubjective clarity to represent a point of reference for the assessment of compliance. Likewise, the project does not analyze compliance with a whole set of

---

[2] Cf. the research by Victor, Raustiala and Skolnikoff (1998); Mayntz (1980); Pressman and Wildavsky (1984); and Siedentopf and Ziller (1988).
[3] Cf. Haas, Keohane and Levy (1993); Miles et al. (2002); and Young (1999b).
[4] Further research in this tradition can be found in Cameron, Werksman and Roderick (1996) and Chayes and Chayes (1995).

rules (for example the EC Treaties or WTO law in general), but only inquires into compliance with specific rules.

Even if rules are specific and clearly formulated, however, assessing the discrepancy between text and action is no easy undertaking. The intrinsic ambiguity of law always necessitates acts of interpretation. To establish the criteria which have to be fulfilled in order to determine whether there has been "non-compliance" is therefore far from trivial. One intuitively plausible way of conceptualizing non-compliance is to say that it exists only when an authoritative dispute settlement body (or, even better, a court) has decided that a rule has been broken. Unfortunately, such an approach is rather problematic for several reasons. First, everyone is aware of many cases of obvious non-compliance with specific rules in daily life, which do not reach any court or dispute settlement body because the cases are settled beforehand. Consider, for example, incidences of shop-lifting or traffic violations, which in most cases do not reach the desk of any judge, but which everyone instinctively considers to be classic cases of non-compliance with specific rules. Or regarding statutory limitations to legal redress consider, for example, the case of the International Court of Justice in The Hague, which excludes the right of individuals or private parties to bring cases and limits this right to the governments of sovereign states. There are also many situations imaginable in which no court or dispute settlement body is available. In the field of international relations such judicial institutions are a fairly recent development. To restrict the definition of non-compliance to judicially-decided cases would bind the notion of compliance to the existence of a traditional division-of-power system with a developed judicial branch.

Secondly, there are also difficulties in defining a court or an author-itative dispute settlement body. Consider, for example, the old GATT system, which required the consent of all parties involved in order to vest the rulings of the arbitration body with the necessary validity. Thus, if the loser refused to accept the decision no authoritative settlement could be obtained from such a procedure. Intuitively, however, everyone would agree that some kind of non-compliance had taken place. Hence, relying on legalistic formalism is of little use when assessing compliance. Any good assessment of compliance needs to broaden the analytical scope in order to take into account subjective valuations on the part of other addressees, statistical data as provided by international organizations, and expert opinions of scholars who work in the field. In all the cases col-lected in this volume we utilize all three kinds of sources. In the analysis of compliance with state aids regulation and foodstuffs we started by col-lecting statistical data, as provided by the EU, the WTO and the relevant German authorities, which we interpreted by reference to expert opinions and the concerns voiced by other addressees of the relevant rules. Unlike the last two comparisons, such statistical data on compliance issues in the redistributive cases is of rather limited use, since no complaints of outright non-compliance were voiced by anyone. We, therefore, put more emphasis on the discourse among the addressees and their subjective perceptions of the degree of compliance other actors have shown.

In all three comparisons we inquired into whether a specific rule was being systematically violated, violated only in individual cases, or was always complied with. Whilst perfect compliance refers to the absence of any clear evidence of defection, individual instances of non-compliance and systemic non-compliance are not easy to distinguish. How many violations of a rule, by how many actors, are necessary before it constitutes systemic non-compliance? One option is to categorize non-compliance as transcending the category of single case non-compliance (and becoming systemic) if it has an observable effect on the compliance level of other actors. If, for example, an addressee practices non-compliance as a matter of routine, such that it becomes the standard rather than the exception, it is most probable that other actors will also feel less obliged to comply with the rule. To be sure, any such assessment is always difficult. In some cases it might happen that a single incident of open non-compliance is already enough to reduce significantly the sense of obligation felt by other addressees. For example, a party to a bilateral treaty that openly and comprehensively disregards its obligations may have an impact that is sufficiently strong to torpedo the whole treaty. If the defecting party, however, is only one of a hundred parties, and is not among the most important (for example a small African country in the WTO), the impact will be rather limited.

Furthermore, the significance of non-compliance varies with the degree to which a rule is violated: a slight deviation from a rule will generally have a different impact on the sense of obligation felt by third parties than would an open rejection of the rule. Any assessment must therefore be carefully argued and formulated with all the necessary reservations. Assessing the level of compliance at a certain point in time is, however, one of the most important issues. If the most basic requirement for a legal norm is the condition that like cases are treated alike, the aggregate level of compliance with a rule should be taken seriously. A further distinction employed by this project is that between "compliance" and "recalcitrant compliance". Whilst the former denotes a type of rule-related action which not only accords with the prescriptions and proscriptions of a rule but also avoids openly criticizing the rule, the latter is defined as a type of rule-related action which combines adherence to the rule with the voicing of an intention to change it. The act of voicing opposition to a norm reflects, in this understanding, an incomplete acceptance of the rule on the part of the addressee together with the announcement of the reluctance to obey it. Thus, compliance is only perfect if the addressee not only behaves according to the rule but also accepts its legitimacy and refrains from trying to challenge or change it.

Although these distinctions might look clear-cut from an analytical point of view, it is often rather difficult to apply them empirically. First of all, it is sometimes somewhat difficult to assess whether an allegation of non-compliance is well founded. We may either lack the necessary facts for a thorough assessment, or there may be difficulties in putting the facts in a meaningful order to assess their relevance. And, secondly, even if we thought we had all the necessary information, as well as the knowledge to interpret its meaning, we might still be wrong by reason of simple subjective misjudgment. Any satisfactory assessment of non-compliance therefore should also analyze compliance as a process and inquire into the extent to which actors are prepared to accept the authority of shared dispute settlement bodies.

2.2.2   Compliance as a process

One way to assess this readiness is to ask for the procedural significance of non-compliance. Procedural significance refers to what happens after a complaint of non-compliance has been voiced. From this procedural perspective, a vital distinction is that between initial non-compliance and more serious compliance crises. Initial non-compliance refers to non-compliance which does not last beyond the point of its identification by authorized bodies such as a court, a monitoring agency, or another party to the relevant regulation. Such behavior is most likely if non-compliance happens by accident and is against the explicit intention of an addressee (benevolent initial non-compliance) or the addressee is attempting to take a free ride, but still prefers compliance over a breakdown of co-operation (malevolent initial non-compliance). The former is the case, for example, if a government does not have access to the necessary technological know-how and thus unintentionally violates the rules. Many international environmental agreements are, for example, plagued with this problem, because developing countries sign them in good faith, but become unintentional violators due to a lack of resources to comply with the rules (Chayes and Chayes 1995). The latter may occur if the monitoring capacities of an international institution are rather weak and an addressee tries to cheat by reaping the benefit of a rule, while avoiding the cost of complying itself. Initial non-compliance is also the case if an addressee claims to act in accordance with the treaty obligations, using legal arguments to defend its action, but agrees to change that practice in reaction to a decision taken by an authorized dispute settlement body.

The process of establishing the Single European Market provides ample examples of such behavior. In a lot of cases of non-tariff trade barriers, such as technical standards or national consumer and environmental laws, the European Commission called on the European Court of Justice to force member states' governments to open their national markets to goods and services from other member states (Stone Sweet and Caporaso 1998; Tallberg 1999). Accordingly, a reason for initial non-compliance might be an interest in overcoming legal ambiguities so as to clarify the meaning of a certain rule by referring the matter to a court. It may, however, also reflect the desire on the part of one addressee to use asymmetrical bargaining power to force other addressees to agree to a reinterpretation of a rule. Initial non-compliance therefore can have many motives. In any case, initial non-compliance leads to a process, at the end of which either the non-compliant party has to change its behavior or the complaining party withdraws its complaint.

Analytically speaking, "compliance crisis" can be clearly distinguished from cases of initial non-compliance. We define it as non-compliance persisting even after the decision of an authoritative body to declare the disputed measure or action inconsistent with the obligations created by the regulation. Empirically speaking, however, it is frequently difficult to assess whether this disregard for the decision of an authoritative body is present. Addressees will rarely say simply "I do not want to follow the Court's ruling" and will instead usually produce legal arguments to justify their non-compliant behavior or will substitute one illegal measure for another equally illegal one. A prominent example of such behavior is the European Union's response to several rulings by GATT and WTO panels on the question of its banana quota system for the imports of so-called "dollar bananas" from countries that are not associates to the Lomé conventions. For years, Brussels either ignored the rulings, accepted countervailing duties, or played for time by substituting the obviously illegal quota system with an equally illegal one, thereby forcing the complainant states to take recurrent legal actions to reaffirm the illegality of the European Union's actions (Stevens 1996; Thagesen and Matthews 1997). In such cases, the formalistic argument that non-compliance only exists after it has been authoritatively assessed is obviously highly problematic and must be replaced by a subjective assessment of the validity of the claims produced. In any case, it is of the utmost importance that one does not simply assess who is right and who is wrong, but rather offers an overview of both sides of the argument as presented by the relevant actors.

In combining these analytical distinctions, the studies in this book use four categories to distinguish the different degrees of compliance (see table 2.1). The compliance of addressees will be categorized as:

Table 2.1 *Categories of compliance*

Facts and norms	Process	
	Compliance	Non-compliance
Compliance	(1) Good compliance (2) Recalcitrant compliance	–
Non-compliance	(3) Initial non-compliance	(4) Compliance crisis

(1) "good compliance" if the rule-related actions of an addressee show little or no difference from the prescriptions and proscriptions of a norm *and* the addressee does not publicly voice its discomfiture with the rule;

(2) "recalcitrant compliance" if the rule-related actions of an addressee show little or no difference from the prescriptions and proscriptions of a norm but the addressee publicly voices its discomfiture with the rule;

(3) "initial non-compliance" if we observe a significant difference between the prescriptions and proscriptions of a norm and the rule-related actions of an addressee, as well as a change in the behavior of the addressee in response to allegations and/or a withdrawal of the complaint;

(4) a "compliance crisis" if we observe a significant difference between the prescriptions and proscriptions of a norm and the rule-related actions of an addressee, but no change in the behavior of the addressee despite the practice having been detected, challenged and/or out-lawed by the decision of an authorized dispute settlement body or court.

In order to assure reliable information on the degree of compliance in each case we attempt to observe it in two dimensions. First, we try to provide data (statistics, opinions of experts and actors in the field) on a general level. Secondly, we support this overall picture with specific case studies on each political level in order to offer a detailed analysis of at least one characteristic case.

2.3   Conceptualizing the independent variables

As outlined in the introductory chapter, the choices made by the addressees of a rule that is considered by them to be inconvenient are not only contingent upon the extent of that inconvenience but also on a great number of other factors. Whilst some emphasize the importance of sanctions, others point to the relevance of discursive processes, the responsiveness of a rule to changing preferences, or the degree to which a rule is legalized. It is at this point that the search for additional variables becomes important. Therefore, in order to explain the rule-related behavior of the addressees, we need to explore to what extent other variables, apart from the inconvenience of a rule, change the decisions they make. The degree to which addressees comply with inconvenient rules is therefore conceptualized as a function of the degree to which an institutional setting or the requisites of a rule provide incentives that are strong enough to motivate actors to adapt to the requirements of the rule. The introductory chapter has already identified a number of important variables which should be considered in explaining compliance. In the sections below we briefly review each of the variables and prepare them for the empirical investigations that are detailed in chapters 3 to 5.

2.3.1   Rational institutionalism

Rational institutionalism basically emphasizes two causal mechanisms, namely monitoring and sanctions.

2.3.1.1 Sanctions   Different sanction mechanisms can be distinguished according to their relative costs, i.e. whether they imply costs which less than offset, offset, or more than offset the expected benefit to be reaped by an addressee from non-compliance. It is not always easy, however, to categorize specific sanctioning mechanisms along this range. A comparatively inexpensive sanctioning mechanism, such as publicly blaming an addressee for its violation of a rule (Weaver 1986), can sometimes prove to be highly effective. If states are publicly blamed for systematically violating human rights, this can easily result in a significant drop in income from tourism and therefore prove very costly to the non-compliant state. The distinction, however, is very helpful in highlighting the difference between the practice of the WTO, which authorizes counter-measures in cases of non-compliance, and the practice of the EU, which imposes fines or lump sum penalties on non-compliant member states. The former regime does not aim to punish a violator but only to offset the damage that has been inflicted on another contracting party. Because the intensity of the counter-measures authorized by the WTO may not be more than the damage (as assessed by the dispute settlement body), counter-measures offer a non-compliant state the option to continue with its non-compliant practice.

In contrast, administrative fines or lump sum penalties imposed by the European Court of Justice are intended to be set at a prohibitive level (Vervaele et al. 1999). They leave the violator no real choice between paying and complying but are supposed to force it to do the latter. Finally, an even more intense form of punishing non-compliance can be found in provisions that accord the legal competence to interfere in the sovereign competences of an addressee so as to compel compliant behavior. Article 37 of the German Basic Law, for example, provides that the federal government may use "the necessary measures" to motivate a *Land* (state) to comply with its legal obligations and shall give orders which the government of the *Land* is obliged to follow. Any such measures, however, are of a legal nature only, must be approved by the federal council (*Bundesrat*), are subject to judicial review, and may not be enforced by coercive (military) means (Article 87a).

A second important distinction for categorizing sanctioning mechanisms is the distinction between horizontal and vertical enforcement. Sanctions can be imposed and enforced in basically one of two different ways. First, the traditional self-help strategy, in which actors that are negatively affected by the non-compliance of another hold them accountable for their behavior and seek to punish them directly by adopting the appropriate measures. This horizontal enforcement was, for example, common practice in pre-state societies, in which clans or families were responsible for avenging violations of the rules and traditions. Also, before international or supranational institutions took over such tasks by transforming them into vertical enforcement, it was usual for states to retaliate when treaties or agreements were violated. However, these means of horizontal enforcement are not equally available to all actors or addressees. A small state must think carefully before imposing counter-measures such as duties on the imports of a state on which it is heavily dependent in terms of development aid or military support (Downs et al. 1996). The use of sanctions therefore becomes far more efficient if counter-measures are both authorized and enforced by an independent common institution (vertical third party enforcement).

Secondly, vertical enforcement, which presupposes an independent common institution, which on the one hand is able to determine whether an actor has violated the rules and on the other hand possesses the power to enforce sanctions against the violator (irrespective of the content of these sanctions – whether compensatory or penal). The importance of an independent common institution rests on two elements. It must possess a considerable degree of independence when deciding on cases of non-compliance and the imposition of sanctions. Only its independence can assure the universal acceptance of its rulings by the addressees.

Furthermore, the common institution must command the power to impose sanctions and enforce compliance. One can think of hierarchical structures like the monopoly of power enjoyed by the classical nation-state over its own societal actors. However, hierarchy is not always a necessary prerequisite for vertical enforcement. The dispute settlement system of the WTO comprises a common independent institution, the Dispute Settlement Body, with the power to deal with cases of non-compliance and enforce the treaty provisions, but to sanction non-compliant behavior the dispute settlement body relies on the power of the complainant state to impose countervailing duties.

While in many respects vertical enforcement is much better than horizontal enforcement, it is not without its problems. International politics is still strongly influenced by the heritage of diplomacy and its implications for co-operative interaction. To challenge legally the practice of other states (especially if they are close partners in other affairs) or to impose sanctions against them – even if authorized by an international institution – is still widely perceived as an act that is incompatible with the practice of friendly co-operation and mutual respect. Judicial action in this context might only lead to the hardening of the contradictory positions and the complete breakdown of co-operative behavior, possibly extending into areas that were previously unaffected by the dispute or the non-compliance.

2.3.1.2 Monitoring   The most threatening sanctions lose credibility if they are not backed by mechanisms to detect incidents of non-compliance. There is once again a wide spectrum of different ways to monitor compliance (Kent 1995; Széll 1995). One way of classifying these methods is to focus on the actors who perform the task. Adopting this approach, we distinguish between decentralized monitoring, centralized monitoring and societal monitoring.

- The traditional way of monitoring compliance with international obligations is decentralized; awarding the task of monitoring to the sole authority of a contracting party. The basic handicap of the pure form of decentralized monitoring is obviously that it either presupposes an interest on the part of the addressee to deal faithfully with its obligations or it requires a high degree of transparency to allow other parties to detect incidences of non-compliance. In most issues relating to international politics, however, neither of these can be taken for granted. More elaborate forms of decentralized monitoring exist where international or supranational institutions formulate mechanisms and procedures which define how addressees report their compliance. Such a system of indirect control exists if contracting parties are under a duty to report regularly upon the implementation of rules. In the international human rights regime, for example, every two years contracting parties have to present a report listing in detail all measures taken by them to implement the rules of the regime (Klein 1998). Likewise, in the WTO and the EU, member states are required to give notice of any national legislation which might have an impact on the realization of free trade (Laird 1999). Another interesting case is that of the monitoring of the implementation of the EU's regional funds: while the formal task of monitoring the compliance of the recipients of European funds remains with the member states, the EU establishes standards and guidelines defining how the member states must carry out this task. Such decentralized mechanisms have the important benefit of using the EU's scarce administrative resources to co-opt member state administrative resources to monitor the behavior of domestic actors. In practice, however, the whole system works on the (sometimes problematic) assumption that the member states do not merely establish monitoring systems on paper, but also put them into practice.[5]

- Against this background, it is clear that centralized monitoring by the author of a rule might have important advantages over decentralized monitoring by the addressees themselves. Centralized monitoring, however, presupposes that the institution in charge of the task is not only equipped with the right to collect information, but also commands the resources that enable it to conduct on-the-spot inspections. This independent form of monitoring certainly holds out the promise of more objectivity, but it often requires an enormous amount of resources to be effective. As students of European or international politics are aware, this precondition is rarely met. On the contrary, even the EU, as the most sophisticated international organization, has neither the legal competences nor the necessary manpower to conduct anything more than sporadic on-the-spot checks.

- The most effective form of monitoring would therefore seem to be monitoring by societal actors. Societal monitoring refers to a form of monitoring in which not only states and the competent authorities of international organizations but also affected non-governmental parties have the capacity to monitor governmental compliance and report non-compliance to the authors of the rule (cf. Klein 1998). For example, in the EU any affected legal person can either complain to the Commission directly if it believes that a company has been awarded illegal subsidies, or it can ask a national court to declare a national

[5] See Court of Auditors: *Annual Report concerning the Financial Year 1998* (OJ C 349/01): Chapter 3.

law or practice to be contrary to European law. Similarly, in the case
of human rights violations, affected individuals who are of the opinion that their national governments have violated their rights under
the European Convention of Human Rights can ask the European
Court of Human Rights (ECHR) to declare the practice or law illegal.
One of the major strengths of societal monitoring is that the process
of monitoring and establishing cases of non-compliance moves out of
the international realm with its emphasis on political considerations.
The importance of depoliticizing the monitoring process becomes very
clear if one compares the number of reported cases of alleged non-
compliance by individuals and by states. In the entire history of the
EU, there have only been two complaints by member states about the
non-compliance of another member state, whereas the ECJ received
a total of 264 demands for preliminary rulings for individuals in 1998
alone.[6] Even more remarkable are the relative numbers in the European
human rights regime: whilst the ECHR dealt with more than 10,000
individual complaints in 1999, the number of complaints by states
was zero.[7] Against the background of these figures, it is evident that
decentralized governmental monitoring, relying on member states to
control one another, is rather problematic. Although one might argue
that the relative numbers in the EU and the ECHR might be different
if no mechanism of societal monitoring existed, it is difficult to dispute that issues such as reciprocity, tit for tat strategies and political
pressure distort the operation of decentralized monitoring (cf. Sevilla
1997).

2.3.2   Legalization

In our understanding, legalization consists of three different variables,
namely juridification, legal internalization and civil internalization. Juridification refers to the degree of autonomy delegated by the parties of a
treaty or rule to a body charged with resolving disputes concerning the
application of that treaty or rule. Legal internalization refers to the degree
to which a given rule is part of an addressee's domestic law and civil internalization inquires into the extent to which a rule confers rights, rather
than just obligations, on individuals.[8]

---

[6] See Commission of the European Communities: *Sixteenth Annual Report on the Monitoring of the Application of Community Law* (1998), COM(99) 301 final of July 7, 1999.
[7] Cf. *Yearbook of the European Convention on Human Rights* and statement of the president of the ECHR on 21 June 1999, in *Europäische Grundrechtezeitschrift* 1999: 361.
[8] For a similar conceptualization of legalization cf. Keohane, Moravcsik and Slaughter (2000).

2.3.2.1 Juridification   A rich body of legal theory emphasizes that all legal rules are intrinsically ambiguous, have no objective meaning and are in need of permanent interpretation. Judicial or dispute settlement procedures are prominent instruments for coping with this ambiguity. Their function is both to identify authoritatively addressees' non-compliance as well as to adapt rules to changing understandings and steering requirements (Charney 1997; Stone Sweet 1997; Chayes and Chayes 1990). Following Kratochwil (1989), two basic types of dispute settlement procedures can be distinguished: the dyadic and the triadic variant. The former relies on the ability of the contracting parties not only to formulate their individual interpretations and preferences but also to reach mutually acceptable solutions. The process of applying general norms to specific circumstances is purely a matter of negotiation between the actors ("interactoral") and very often subject to a unanimity requirement. Factually, it is rather difficult to distinguish such procedures from legislative interactoral action, and it could even be argued that they do not deserve the label of dispute settlement at all.

Triadic dispute settlement procedures are different in that they delegate the authority to (re)interpret rules to a third party, which may be an individual or a collective of lawyers, diplomats, or even scientists. An important distinction exists between "weak" and "strong" triadic procedures. The old GATT serves as a perfect example of a weak triadic procedure. It was triadic in so far as it allowed for authoritative opinions by a third party (a panel). But it was weak because the adoption of the panel's reports and therefore its legal status was dependent on the precondition that all affected parties agreed to its ruling. Unsurprisingly, such weak triadic procedures are not seen as particularly effective means of eliciting compliance. As the history of the GATT has shown, in the case of reports that were inconvenient to at least one affected party, the use of the veto was the rule rather than the exception (Stone Sweet 1997). Unlike the old GATT, the dispute settlement system of the WTO places far more emphasis on the efficacy of its rulings and greatly reduces the potential impact of the veto. Since its adoption, any report by a panel becomes legally binding unless all affected parties disagree with its ruling (Petersmann 1997c). Likewise, the European Court of Justice can only be overruled if the number of member states so minded would have been enough to change the relevant legal act which was the point of departure for the ruling in the first place.

Furthermore, the degree of juridification is also strengthened by the degree of (political or judicial) autonomy of the dispute settlement system. This refers especially to the procedure with which the mediators or judges are selected and to the question of how long they are in office and whether it is possible to recall them in case of disagreement. The degree of political autonomy usually depends on the influence of addressees or affected parties on the selection process. Hence, there is always the danger of jeopardizing the independence of dispute settlement bodies by appointing "political" candidates. The attempt of successive Republican US Presidents to alter the liberal Supreme Court majority by naming conservative candidates for the bench is just one example. The political pressure on the selection process can be eased in two ways. One is to define professional standards for possible candidates. Thus, in the case of the judges for the German Federal Constitutional Court the candidates are not only required to be members of the bar but also to be specialists in a particular legal field (i.e. civil, public or labor law) or to be chosen from the bench of the federal court system – for example Federal Administrative Court (*Bundesverwaltungsgericht*), Federal Court of Justice (*Bundesgerichtshof*), or Federal Labor Court (*Bundesarbeitsgericht*). This considerably limits the chance for politicizing the selection process. The other option is to entrust the selection of the judges to an independent body.

Additionally, the independence of the dispute settlement institution can be strengthened by appointing its members indefinitely or at least for a long fixed term of several years and without the possibility to recall them. The US Supreme Court judges for example serve a life term with the option to decide themselves on their retirement. German Federal Constitutional Court judges usually serve a twelve-year term without the possibility of renewal in order to exclude any political deal.

Judicial autonomy depends on the supremacy of rulings or judgments over decisions of other judicial or dispute settlement bodies. For years the authority of the European Court of Justice was endangered by the opinion of the German Federal Constitutional Court to reserve the final authority in cases in which European law threatened fundamental human rights of German citizens. If used, this authority would have called into question the universal application of European law in all member states, tantamount to the dependence of the European Court of Justice on the consent of a national court. Generally, the higher the degree of independence of the dispute settlement system, the higher the degree of juridification of the dispute settlement process.

2.3.2.2 Legal internalization   Rules differ not only in their compliance enforcement mechanisms but also in their legal character. Some rules are of a merely declaratory status, some are legally binding on the signatories and others are even domestically enforceable. International resolutions and declarations, for example, frequently carry no legal obligation but are merely non-binding statements of intent. By consenting to a declaration or resolution, the parties express their intention to use those measures and instruments that are laid down in the text to realize the goals to which they had consented. If they do not succeed in mobilizing the necessary resources to apply the measures and instruments, or they fail to realize the goals, this does not entail any legal consequences. Declarations and resolutions are therefore a rather weak means of binding a rule to a legal system. Legally binding rules extend significantly beyond that point. The use of legal instruments means that non-compliance carries with it the threat of legal consequences and proceedings. Any member state that fails to comply with EC rules, for example, risks having that failure challenged by another member state or the Commission and being subject to judicial proceedings. Likewise, WTO rules are legally binding to the degree that they carry with them legal obligations which must be met by the contracting parties.

An important difference between EU and WTO rules, however, exists in relation to their domestic effect. Although WTO law has, for example, in Germany or the United States the status of statutory law, it enjoys no direct effect and cannot be invoked by their national courts. It is only relatively recently that the European Court of Justice confirmed that WTO law and the decisions of its dispute settlement body are not valid criteria for assessing the legality of measures adopted by European institutions.[9] Because the decisions of the Dispute Settlement Body require contracting parties to look for mutually acceptable solutions by means of intergovernmental bargaining, the ECJ argued that there can be no legal supremacy for the decisions of the dispute settlement body over European law. Otherwise, the EU would be handicapped in its relative bargaining power as compared with that of other states. European law goes significantly beyond this point in asserting its supremacy over the law of its member states. According to Article 234, national courts are obliged to ask the European Court of Justice for a preliminary ruling in all matters that concern the application of European law. This mechanism has contributed significantly towards conferring "direct effect" on European law, thereby making it domestically enforceable.

2.3.2.3 Civil internalization   Rules not only differ in the obligations they impose but also in the rights they confer on affected parties. Traditionally, international rules have restricted themselves to giving states the right to be treated according to the prescriptions and proscriptions of a given treaty and have taken little notice of affected domestic

---

[9] Case 149/90, *Portugal* v. *Council* [1999] ECR I–8395.

parties. Any individual rights that did flow from the international rules arose strictly as a result of domestic legislation and were in the discretion of the nation-state. Since the landmark decision of the European Court of Justice in *Van Gend en Loos* in 1963,[10] European rules have gone far beyond that point. The ECJ proclaimed in that decision that the European Community constituted a new legal order which comprised not only the member states but also their nationals. Independent of a member state's legislation, European law not only imposes obligations on individuals but also confers rights upon them: it becomes "the law of the land." Where European rules impose "direct effect," national courts must apply their prescriptions and proscriptions (for details see Weiler 1994; Burley and Mattli 1993). Whilst initially, individuals could only invoke Treaty provisions, the ECJ has subsequently developed its case law to extend this right to areas of secondary European law such as Council directives and decisions. In *Francovich*,[11] the European Court of Justice further enhanced the impact of European law by holding states liable for economic damage incurred by citizens because of the failure of member states to implement European law (for details see Harlow 1996).

2.3.3   Legitimacy

To conceptualize the variable of legitimacy we follow the distinction made by Scharpf between input-legitimacy and output-legitimacy (Scharpf 1999). The former inquires into the degree to which the procedures used to decide upon a rule were in accordance with the basic principles of democratic governance. There is no consensus in the literature, however, about the substantial content of these principles (for a good overview see Held 1995). Whilst the legitimacy of national democratic procedures is broadly acknowledged to depend upon both majority voting and the rule of law based on constitutional principles, the question of what conditions must be fulfilled in order to have (input-)legitimate governance beyond the nation-state is heavily contested. Some argue that international governance must live up to the same requirements as governance in the democratic nation-state (Greven 2000; Kielmansegg 2003) while others emphasize that politics beyond the nation-state is restricted in scope and therefore needs to satisfy rather more limited normative criteria (Majone 1998; Scharpf 1999). Most authors, however, would agree that the participation of addressees and affected parties is crucial to securing legitimacy both inside and beyond the nation-state (Zürn 2000). Only if those who

---

[10] Case 26/62, *Van Gend en Loos* v. *Nederlandse Administratie der Belastingen* [1963] ECR 3.
[11] Case 6, 9/90, *Frankovich & Bonifaci* v. *Italy* [1991] ECR I-5357.

are expected to comply with a rule have a say in its making, can a rule be accepted as democratically legitimate.

Unlike the basically procedural concept of input-legitimacy, output-legitimacy focuses on the response of the addressees and other affected parties to the prescriptions and/or proscriptions of a rule. Output-legitimacy therefore asks whether a rule is accepted by its addressees as adequate, just or fair, independently of the procedures that were used in its enactment. Although input-legitimacy and output-legitimacy may run in parallel in a great number of situations, they are not necessarily always identical. One and the same democratic procedure, for example majority voting, may lead to very different results in terms of social acceptance, depending on the relative size of the winners and losers in a vote or on the subject matter at hand. So as to take both understandings of legitimacy into account, we will in the following sections distinguish between input-legitimacy, conceptualized as participation, and output-legitimacy, conceptualized as social acceptance.

2.3.3.1 Participation   A basic dimension of participation refers to the relationship between the author of a rule and the rule's addressees. Only if the addressees had a chance to participate in the making of a rule can they be expected to feel bound by the rule. Traditionally, international politics had no problems with this. Binding rules were negotiated among the states and were unanimously agreed upon before entering into force. And the addressees of the rules were only the states themselves. Today, especially in the EU, however, it is increasingly the case that decisions are referred to a third party (the European Commission, the WTO's Dispute Settlement Body, the European Central Bank) for it to decide according to its own criteria. Although the criteria are formulated by the addressees (the member states), sometimes they review them only once every couple of years and can then only change them by unanimous decision. Article 202 of the EC Treaty, which confers powers on the European Commission to implement directives, is a case in point (Pollack 1997). Article 202 gives the Commission broad discretionary powers specifically to allow it to deal effectively with a great number of issues. Although member states may in general want the Commission to have these powers, from time to time they are confronted by Commission decisions which require them to make painful domestic policy-changes and which are difficult to sell to the addressees and affected third parties, i.e. their citizens.

It is not only the participation of the governmental addressees but also the participation of societal actors (affected parties) which may be an important factor in securing compliance. Issues such as health and safety regulations demand a great degree of societal know-how as to how to define and solve problems. Governments alone neither command the necessary expertise to assess the different potential solutions for a given problem nor do they always have the resources to implement their chosen solution if it contrasts with experts' opinions or the public's concerns. Because they must justify their policies to a critical public and an institutionalized opposition, they are well advised to build broad coalitions, which take on board as many societal actors as possible. In international politics the very same logic applies. Reacting to the criticism of their remoteness from domestic democratic discourses, both the EU and the WTO increasingly rely on advisory bodies and/or informal meetings with non-governmental organizations (NGOs) so as to gather societal know-how, learn about societal concerns and try to take the demands formulated seriously. In the EU this process has led to the setting up of hundreds of advisory bodies, which are in regular contact with the Commission, whereas the WTO has only recently started to react to this challenge. Since the disaster of Seattle in 1998, the WTO has also begun to conduct (informal) consultations with NGOs on a regular basis and has even started to institutionalize regular contacts with the European Parliament.

      2.3.3.2 Social acceptance   Because rules have to take into account a great diversity of problem definitions and problem-solving philosophies, their acceptance may vary from the domestic context of one addressee to the next. Even a high degree of participation, therefore, is no guarantee that a rule will meet acceptance in all constituencies. Whilst autocratic regimes may deal with such opposition by using repressive instruments such as the control of the media or the prohibition of protest, democratic regimes lack that possibility. Because they must meet the voter every couple of years at the ballot, they are highly dependent on a benevolent media and only to a limited extent able to withstand concerted public opposition when it comes to implementing an inconvenient rule. Not only are interest groups able to threaten to withhold co-operation in the process of implementing agreements, and can thereby impose serious technical difficulties on the implementation of commitments (Reinicke 1998), but they can also use the media to mobilize domestic opposition and thereby significantly increase the political costs of compliance (Cameron 1996). Although a high degree of social acceptance makes compliance more likely (and is more politically wise) than does a low degree of social acceptance, this cannot be easily equated with compliance. In most cases it is ultimately the addressee's decision whether to shoulder the burden of additional domestic political cost by complying with the rule or whether to succumb to domestic pressure and to pay with public reputation for non-compliance.

To conceptualize the different degrees of domestic opposition to and social acceptance of a rule, we assume that social acceptance can be adequately measured by reviewing the leading articles in the major national news magazines and newspapers. Although we are well aware that public opinion and published opinion are not always identical, we have chosen that method to take into account the fact that public opinion most often communicates itself to decision-makers indirectly through the media. If, for example, Germany is the addressee of an international rule, social acceptance will be measured by assessing the extent to which the leading commentators in journals such as *Die Zeit, Der Spiegel* and the *Frankfurter Allgemeine Zeitung* criticize or approve of the German government's compliance with the rule. In assessing social acceptance we distinguish between high acceptance, medium acceptance and low acceptance. High acceptance applies if the public opinion by and large accepts a rule as worthy of being implemented. If public opinion is split into two camps of roughly equal size, social acceptance is medium. Low acceptance applies if public opinion by and large rejects a rule.

2.3.4   Management

The management perspective on compliance distinguishes between two dimensions: the reflexivity of a rule, that is its responsiveness to changing circumstances and societal perceptions of its purpose; and the question of resources or capacities of the addressees (and affected parties) to fulfill the obligations conferred upon them by the regulations.

2.3.4.1 *Reflexivity/responsiveness*   Rules not only need to be established, monitored and equipped with effective means to sanction non-compliance, but the degree to which addressees are willing to comply with them also depends on the responsiveness of the rule to changing perceptions of what should be regulated and which instruments should be used for that purpose (Snyder 1993; Selznick 1992). It is important to emphasize that every rule can only reflect a certain understanding of how to define and cope with a problem. Any such understanding is time-contingent and needs to be permanently updated so as not to lose its pertinence. The importance of flexible mechanisms allowing rules to be adapted to changing circumstances is underlined by empirical studies which point out that divergences in interests, in the perceptions of what is a problem and how it is to be solved, need to be permanently reconciled

with one another (Héritier 1996). However, operationalizing the extent to which administrative practices are capable of realizing such a continual adaptation is difficult. Different topics need different intensities of reflection and therefore different institutional provisions. For example, rules in human rights affairs, such as the prohibition of torture, require less permanent adaptation than do health standards in foodstuffs. The example also underlines how the responsiveness of a rule can become dysfunctional if there are no provisions to limit its openness and exclude those preferences which are incompatible with its basic intentions (for example the promotion of human rights). It is important therefore to distinguish not only between flexible and inflexible rules but also to take account of whether and to what extent provisions are foreseen which safeguard against the misuse of flexibility.

One way of taking both dimensions into account is to distinguish between responsiveness and opportunistic adaptation. In the words of Selznick (1992: 463), a responsive institution is "an institution which maintains its integrity while acknowledging the legitimacy of an appropriate range of claims and interests." Such institutions must be guided by a spirit of consultation, while the institution's basic commitments, and its capacity to function, must be preserved and protected. Opportunistic adaptation, on the other hand, refers to an institution which is open to all demands from the outside without possessing the capacity to protect its integrity (Selznick 1992: 336). A basic requirement of responsiveness is the deliberative character of an institution, which implies that all arguments put forward must be backed by reasons that explain how they promote the basic commitments of the institution. Responsiveness therefore corresponds with openness and deliberation and must be distinguished from strategic bargaining, which is the effort to change a rule by means of threats or promises (Elster 1998a). Such forms of bargaining are not only problematic in terms of their capacity to deal effectively with an identified problem, but – by implication – they cannot be expected to realize any significant compliance-pull (Chayes and Chayes 1995).

Deliberative forms of interaction increase the chances that a rule's addressees will be convinced that the rule is appropriate in terms of the policy goals it promotes and that it is in their own interest to comply with the rule. Within the comitology system of the EU, for example, highly controversial issues are frequently dealt with first in scientific committees or working groups before a regulatory committee gets to take its final vote (Falke 1996). In this way, deliberation among scientific experts or other professionals reduces the potential for conflict on specific policy issues and thereby increases the chances of voluntary compliance.

2.3.4.2 Resources and capacity   Sometimes, however, addressees are involuntarily in breach of commitments they negotiated in good faith and wholeheartedly support. But during implementation of the provisions they realize that they are short of resources or capacities necessary to reach the intended goals successfully. Thus, there are sometimes compliance problems due not to bad intentions of the addressees but to the lack of the necessary means to comply with the rules. Necessary resources for compliance usually comprise two important elements: technology and scientific know-how to deal with the problems at hand and/or financial means to implement the necessary measures. A prime example of a situation in which the lack of important resources prevented states from complying with an international agreement is the international regime against the depletion of the ozone layer and the situation of developing countries. The Third World countries basically agreed with the general intention of the Montreal Protocol but pointed to the fact that they neither possessed the necessary technology to replace the ozone-depleting chemicals nor the financial resources to modernize the existing production facilities to accommodate the chemical replacements. Hence, although the developing countries basically acknowledged the detrimental effect of CFCs on the ozone layer and agreed to phase out their production, they realized that they did not command the necessary technological and financial resources to comply with the provisions of the already established international agreements (Chayes and Chayes 1995). In the following rounds of negotiations this situation led not only to opening clauses for certain patents on chemicals for developing countries but also to the introduction of an assistance fund in order to provide financial support for the necessary restructuring and modernization of chemical production facilities in Third World countries; important steps to increase the degree of compliance of developing countries.

The lack of capacities usually refers to missing institutional, especially administrative, structures to deal with the problems. Sometimes addressees are readily prepared to comply with the rules, but are overwhelmed by the task of implementing and enforcing all the provisions. A prime example of this form of compliance problem are the EU accession countries in Central and Eastern Europe which are still in the process of creating the necessary institutional and administrative capacities effectively to implement and enforce EU policies in a broad spectrum from various market regulations of the Common Agricultural Policy to the border control regime at the external borders of the EU. One important aim of EU support is to foster the creation of the necessary institutional capacities, to train and expand these capacities, and to introduce them to the EU's modes of operation. Without these measures it would be impossible for these countries to take over the *acquis communautaire* successfully.

It is obvious that in this perspective the degree of compliance depends on the amount of financial and technical resources as well as institutional capacities available for the implementation and enforcement of rules. Lack of either resources or capacities or both results in deteriorating and eventual poor degrees of compliance by both addressees and affected parties.

2.4   Perspectives, variables, hypotheses, and values

The preceding sections distinguish different theoretical perspectives and identify specific variables, hypotheses, and values belonging to each perspective (cf. the overview in table 2.2). The rationale behind this endeavor was to separate discrete analytical perspectives, which can be assessed empirically, and to question to what extent they are capable of explaining observable differences in compliance. Although this methodology may suggest that we treat the different perspectives as competing explanations for compliance, we are well aware that a number of interactive effects among the different variables exist. To begin with, monitoring and sanctioning (rational institutionalism) may be closely connected with juridification and legal and civil legalization (legalization). Legalization, of course, only makes sense if it is supported by close monitoring, and it may be far more effective in changing state behavior if it is backed up by serious sanctions. Furthermore, there can be little doubt that a rule that is viewed as legitimate requires less enforcement and legalization than a rule viewed by all addressees as despotic in origin. The same argument is valid with regard to the management perspective: rules that are subject to permanent deliberation and adaptation to the steering requirements of their addressees have a better chance of being perceived as deserving a high degree of compliance than do inflexible rules. Thus, they require less monitoring, sanctioning, and legalization to realize the same results. In sum, although we treat the four perspectives as discrete, we are well aware that any sound understanding of the workings of most compliance mechanisms necessitates taking all four perspectives into account. The basic challenge therefore is not simply to dismiss one or two of the perspectives discussed above but to arrive at a balanced picture that highlights the interactive effects among the different variables.

Table 2.2 *Overview of the independent variables*

Perspective	Variable	Hypothesis		Values
Rational institutionalism	Sanctions	Actors will comply if they are threatened by credible sanctions that offset the expected benefits of non-compliance	Content	• less than offsetting • offsetting • more than offsetting
			Competence	• horizontal coercion • vertical coercion
	Monitoring	Actors will comply if non-compliance is likely to be detected		• decentralized monitoring • centralized monitoring • societal monitoring
Legalization	Dispute settlement	The less that arbitration reflects political concerns the higher will be the precision of, and thus the compliance with, the rules		• dyadic dispute settlement • weak triadic dispute settlement • strong triadic dispute settlement
	Legal internalization	The more international rules are part of domestic law the less likely is non-compliance		• no legal effect • legal effect on signatories • legal effect in domestic law
	Civil internalization	If individuals can enforce rules against their governments, non-compliance becomes less likely		• only obligations • enforceable rights

(*cont.*)

Table 2.2 (*cont.*)

Perspective	Variable	Hypothesis	Values
Legitimacy	Participation	The broader the participation in the making of a rule the greater the readiness of addressees to accept a rule	• neither addressees nor affected parties • only the addressees • addressees plus affected parties
	Social acceptance	Governments are highly dependent on public support and will only comply if public opinion does not demand otherwise	• public opinion supports compliance • public opinion is split into two camps • public opinion rejects compliance
Management	Reflexivity/ Responsiveness	The more administrative procedures are conducted by means of deliberation, the greater the compliance with the rules	• no procedures foreseen at all • only procedures on the basis of bargaining • procedures on the basis of deliberation
	Resources/ Capacity	The more financial and technical resources and the more institutional capacities the greater the compliance with the rules	• no resources, no capacities • either resources or capacities available • both resources and capacities available

3 State aid control at the national, European, and international level

Dieter Wolf

Any integrating or already integrated market that encompasses several jurisdictions or states is usually confronted in one way or another by the problem of state aids or subsidies, which are handed out by governments or governmental agencies to businesses that settle or have already settled in their jurisdiction. Economic theory posits that such measures distort the markets for investment and employment because they influence the decision making of enterprises, luring them into allocating resources according to political rather than economic, market-driven reasons (Färber 1989; Zippel 1993). Other strands of economic theory, however, disagree with this assessment of the impact of political interference on market forces. Whereas Keynesian demand-side approaches favor such interventions in order to correct for market failures, as well as smooth out and stabilize the steady growth of the economy (Hall 1989; Ikenberry 1993; Franz 1992), neoclassic supply-side economics considers such financial support to be part of the problem. Significant financial support requires big government, high taxes and equally high budget deficits. These usually lead to higher inflation and unnecessarily high interest rates, which – taken together with the high taxes – reduce investment in the real economy and, hence, lead to unemployment (Siebert 1990, 1995, 2000).

As far as empirically oriented economic literature goes, it is difficult to settle this debate once and for all because the decision of an enterprise about where to locate its investment seems to be based on a very complex set of reasons, including market access, transaction costs (infrastructure, suppliers), taxes, labor costs, and the amount of state aid available (Liemt 1992; Heise et al. 1998). However, it is safe to assume that in one way or another subsidies are one of the major reasons for choosing where to allocate investment and that state governments consider them their most effective instrument for influencing the decision making of private investors (Thomas 2000; Krüger 1998). Hence, independently of the answers to those questions that are posed by economic theory, state aids constitute an important element in competition or industrial policy in all jurisdictions (Brösse 1999). In an integrating or already integrated market with different jurisdictions, this necessarily leads to the question of how to co-ordinate these presumably different policies.

State aid policy is usually a form of a distributive or redistributive political measure. Interjurisdictional state aid control, however, is clearly regulative in character. Governments agree to abstain from supporting their businesses or agree to some code of conduct that limits the amount of financial support they can provide or specifies those cases eligible for such aid. In the absence of a hierarchical or hegemonic power distribution, such political decision-making and implementation resembles the game-theoretic concept of a mixed-motive game in the form of a prisoners' dilemma (Scharpf 1997; Zürn 1992; Zangl 1999). Each government would certainly welcome the co-operation and compliance of its partners, with an agreement to limit state aid, but at the same time it prefers a free-rider position for itself. Thus, even after an agreement is reached there remain incentives to free-ride and the rules are not self-fulfilling or self-enforcing. Furthermore, the governments do not need any particularly important societal co-operation so as to be able to comply with the regulation. While societal demands might be a major reason for distributing subsidies, compliance with state aid control measures only requires governments to retain rather than distribute their funds. It does not – as for example with respect to environmental politics – require the active co-operation of societal actors to reach the intended goals.

The analysis ventures to compare three empirical cases of state aid control on different political levels. First, the intergovernmental co-operation between the German *Länder* in the context of German federalism; secondly, the state aid control concerning the member states of the European Union; and, thirdly, the state aid control concerning the member states of the World Trade Organization and the General Agreement on Tariffs and Trade. In each case, the analysis focuses on the regulations that limit the amount of state aids to be given to industry and business, deliberately excluding agriculture and fisheries, since these sectors are governed by special regulations usually excluded from state aid control agreements (even though the WTO is attempting to regulate these sectors as well).

Before turning to the task of assessing the degrees of compliance with these provisions and then comparing the findings, it is first necessary to deal with the question of whether these regulations are comparable in the first place. Traditional accounts (from both political scientists and legal scholars) often point to the alleged qualitative difference between national and international policies or laws. While national law is backed by the state's monopoly of force – the Leviathan – international law is still commonly regarded as "soft law" – some kind of official declaration of intent and sometimes not even that. It is not something to be strictly implemented, let alone enforced. If this premise were correct, such a comparison would be either impossible or tautological. Different regulations are comparable if they exhibit similar characteristics with respect to the following aspects: the type of addressees, the way the regulations address them, the kind of problem the regulations seek to tackle, and the depth of the regulatory interference with the problem. Only if the regulations seek to regulate the same kind of problem, address the same type of addressees and interfere in a similar manner and to a similar depth with the behavior of those addressees, is it possible to compare them directly and to do so without hesitation, despite the fact that they belong to different political levels.

The three cases of state aid control regulations at the national, European and international levels are perfect candidates for such an interlevel comparison. All three are regulatory instruments which address governments or governmental agencies and all establish guidelines concerning their financial support of enterprises. All regulations contain specific rules and provisions governing the appropriate behavior of the addressees and they are essentially all aimed at reducing the amount of state aids, standardizing the cases in which subsidies are allowed and, thus, preventing the addressees from engaging in a financially detrimental subsidies race with each other. They focus on industrial goods (although WTO regulations potentially extend to agricultural subsidies) and address state governments or state agencies. In all three cases perfect compliance would be reached if all state aid programs were terminated, that is, absolute restraint in distributing public money to businesses. Hence, there is no reason to believe that these regulations are of different quality or character and, hence, that they are not comparable with each other.

The three empirical cases are presented in four steps. First, it is necessary to describe the contents of the regulations and to offer – for each separate case – an empirical example of how the respective political institutions at the different political levels handle complaints concerning, or even outright instances of, non-compliance. This offers the opportunity to detail both the actual status of compliance or non-compliance (the rate of compliance) and the procedural dimension of dealing with disputed cases and handling compliance crises. Secondly, the degree of compliance, both in general and in procedural terms, is assessed for each regulation and a comparison made between the three regulations analyzed. Thus it is possible to establish some kind of ranking according to the degree of compliance achieved by each of these regulations. Thirdly, this comparative result is used to test the hypotheses that are derived from the four theoretical perspectives for explaining compliance, which are described in the previous two chapters. The aim is, again, to establish some form of ranking according to the capacity of these four theoretical perspectives to explain the empirical results. Finally, this provides an opportunity to discuss the strengths and weaknesses of the different theoretical explanations for compliance or non-compliance, with respect to the regulatory policies at the different political levels.

The analysis of the state aid control regulations on three different political levels shows that – contrary to the wisdom of conventional political science – the EU regulation achieves the best rate of compliance, followed by the WTO rules and, finally and surprisingly, the inter-*Länder* regulation in Germany. In the German case, from the very outset the rules were never complied with. The GATT basically had the same problem but improved its grip with the strengthening of its institutional capacities at the Uruguay Round and the creation of the WTO in 1995. The EU not only has the strictest state aid control regime but, since the introduction of the common market in 1993, has been able to achieve a considerable degree of correspondence between member state practice and the actual law in the books.

Furthermore, this analysis shows that, as far as the theoretical perspectives are concerned, this comparative empirical result is best explained by the legalization approach and rational institutionalism. The legal quality and character of the rules are the most important indicators in explaining the degree of compliance, or non-compliance, with the state aid control regulations at the three different political levels. Rational institutionalism is similarly successful, except in the case of the EU before 1990. The existence of strong, independent multilateral institutions, including an effective judicial body that is able to monitor and ultimately sanction the behavior of non-compliant addressees, also makes for a good indicator in the state aid control cases.

3.1   State aid control regulations and the cases of dispute settlement

This chapter offers a descriptive summary of the regulations governing state aid control at the three different political levels. It also presents a characteristic example of dispute settlement, in order to exemplify the procedural dimension of the compliance problem and give some insight into the way in which the different institutional settings deal with alleged or proven cases of non-compliance.

3.1.1 State aid control at the national level: The co-operation between the German Länder

Regarding the German economy, it is possible to distinguish four major sources of state aids to enterprises, namely the financial support of the European funds, especially those directed at the East German *Länder*; the state aids from the federal government; the subsidies that are distributed through *Länder* budgets; and, finally, the aid from municipal and local budgets. If one considers the amount of money distributed, by far the largest sources are federal and *Länder* governments, followed by the European Union and local sources. Thus, the federal German government increased its financial support from 7.7 billion Euros in 1970 to roughly 27.9 billion Euros in 2001, while the *Länder* governments distributed some 6.9 billion Euros in 1970, 23.9 billion in 1997 and 21.9 billion in 2001. These funds allocate money to (or refrain from taxing) an average of 4,500 cases of private investment every year in Germany (Becker 1977: 34). The 16 *Länder* governments, however, focus their attention especially on some 250 cases a year in Germany where businesses are seeking new locations for their investment and are not simply expanding their existing plants (Schmid 1989: 93). The central aim of all regional jurisdictions is to increase their own share of these new investments, to create new employment opportunities for their constituencies and to strengthen the tax base for further taxation. In this competition, all governments use tax cuts and financial support to improve their attractiveness to potential investors. At the same time, all governments consider the emerging "subsidies race" as economically and fiscally harmful and some of them suspect that big multinational corporations in particular are playing one state government off against another in order to gain the best financial support for their investment (Staudt 1987).

Especially since the 1970s, when both rising unemployment and increasing budget deficits marked the end of the classic Keynesian demand-side approach to economic policy, the regional governments, as well as the federal government, came to the conclusion that it was necessary to control the distribution of state aids and to contain locational competition between the regional jurisdictions. However, Article 74 of the federal German constitution – the *Grundgesetz* – allows for the federal regulation of this locational competition between the *Länder* only with the support of the majority of the Upper House of the German Parliament (*Bundesrat*), which represents the *Länder* governments in the federal decision-making process. When the bureaucracy of the Federal Ministry of Economic Affairs attempted to introduce the proposal for such a federal law in the 1960s, the federal minister himself surprisingly vetoed further considerations in this direction because the *Länder* governments perceived it as a move towards more centralized economic policy-making in Germany (Bleckmann 1984: D57).

The proposal for a federal law establishing guidelines for the financial support of enterprises, put forward by the state government of North Rhine-Westphalia, met a similar fate in the 1970s. Several comments criticized the proposed law because it gave enterprises the right to receive comprehensive financial support rather than limit their access to subsidies (Harzem 1988: 176) and the proposal never reached the floor of any chamber of Parliament. Finally, in 1984, the government of Lower Saxony prepared a proposal for a federal law on the principles of subsidizing businesses. The central elements of this proposal were guidelines laying down those cases eligible for financial support and a requirement placed upon federal, *Länder*, and local governments to report in detail the financial benefits given to enterprises, as well as the creation of an independent expert commission to scrutinize the subsidies given at the federal, regional, and local levels. Again, this proposal failed to reach even the floor of the Upper House, because most *Länder* governments feared that this law would restrict their competences in the areas of budget and economic policies (Bleckmann 1984).

After failing to reach a hierarchical solution via federal law, in the 1980s, the *Länder* governments attempted to solve the problem using inter-governmental co-ordination of their competition policies. As a result, in 1982 and 1983, the ministers for economic affairs signed two so-called "Codices on State Aids." These two codices form the core of a common effort to limit the subsidies race between the German *Länder*. Additionally, one option for the centralized, hierarchical control of state aids has been in existence since 1969. The federal law on the "Joint Task to Improve the Regional Economic Structure" gives the federal government the right to reclaim misspent money from state governments and, thus, to enforce state aid regulations. Although this federal law exists independently of the two codices on state aid, it nevertheless offers an important monitoring and sanctioning mechanism for the federal government to enforce the compliance of the *Länder* governments with any kind of guidelines laid down for state aid control. Thus the following three provisions must be mentioned in the context of limiting subsidies in Germany:

(1) The "Codex on State Aid" assented to by the *Länder* on July 7, 1982;
(2) The "Codex on State Aid with Respect to Single Enterprises" assented to by the *Länder* on May 30, 1983;[1] and

---

[1] The two codices are published as Annex 10 and Annex 11 of the *Ninth Report of the Federal German Government on State Aids*, Deutscher Bundestag, Drucksache 10/352, 310–312.

(3) Article 11, para. 2, of the federal law on the "Joint Task to Improve
   the Regional Economic Structure."[2]

The 1982 "Codex on State Aid" stipulates in eight paragraphs the
central principles for the distribution of state aids to enterprises. In paragraph I the *Länder* governments underline their opinion that coping with
structural changes in the economy is primarily the task of private enterprises, not the political system. The political system must offer attractive
background conditions that give private enterprises the opportunities to
achieve economic success but it must not support them on a continuous
basis to maintain their competitiveness. Thus, paragraph II allows state
aids only if structural change would otherwise lead to unbearable economic or social conditions and other responses have proven unsuccessful.
Governments are barred from distributing subsidies that are not in the
public interest. Paragraph III lays down that state aids should not interfere with or impede market forces, they should be as small as possible and
definitely smaller than the amount allocated by the benefiting enterprise
itself towards the overall restructuring costs. Furthermore, they should
be limited in time, regressive in their amount and if possible should be
based on the principle that after a successful restructure the beneficiary
pays back at least part of the state aid it received. Paragraph IV requires
that state aids have clear, quantifiable and controllable aims. Paragraph V
stipulates that *Länder* governments should refrain from distributing direct
financial support and should rather use indirect measures, such as tax
expenditures or infrastructure improvements. Subsidies intended simply
to preserve certain enterprises are not allowed except to secure the unim-
peded supply of strategic resources like oil. Financial support for the
restructuring of companies is only allowed if the whole economic sector
is in danger.

   Paragraph VI calls for a clear division of competencies between the
federal, regional and local levels. State aids should only be paid from
one source; a mixture of subsidies from different political levels should
be avoided. Paragraph VII authorizes periodical evaluations of the success of programs of financial support, possibly leading to their eventual
termination. Finally, paragraph VIII requires the *Länder* governments to
revise their already existing state aid programs and to adjust them to the
principles of the new codex.

   The 1983 "Codex on State Aid with Respect to Single Enterprises"
underlines these central principles and rejects the idea that the rescue of
private enterprises is the task of the state, since this would disadvantage
the competitors of potential beneficiaries, set precedents for further financial support and lead to a dangerous subsidies race between the *Länder*

---

[2] See *Bundesgesetzblatt* I, 1969, 1861–3.

governments. Hence, the codex stipulates that state aids should only be given to enterprises if: these aids are limited in time so as to encourage self-help; the owners of the company have already exhausted their capabilities of financing the restructuring; major regional or social reasons necessitate the state intervention (the simple rescue of jobs being insufficient); the state aids do not endanger the competitors of the beneficiary; the benefiting enterprise discloses its books and proposes a restructuring plan; there is enough time to check the books and the new business plan; and the EU regulations on the notification of aid schemes are not violated. Furthermore, the codex prohibits in all cases the transfer of ownership from private to public hands in order to support the rescue of the enterprise.

Although the two codices are horizontal intergovernmental agreements, there exists a traditional hierarchical federal element, which is older than the two horizontal codices. The federal law on the "Joint Task to Improve the Regional Economic Structure" was adopted in 1969 with the aim of supporting less developed areas in certain regions with federal funds. The central idea was to share the costs of improving the competitive position of these areas equally between the federal and the responsible regional government. Some observers originally feared that this would lead to the centralization of regional structural policy but the federal government essentially was limited to co-financing *Länder* projects (Scharpf et al. 1976). With respect to limiting the subsidies race, however, Article 11, para. 2 of the federal law stipulates that the federal government has the right to demand the repayment of any funds spent by a regional government in violation of the subsidies program. With this law the federal government possesses de jure both the carrot of financial support for regional measures as well as a limited stick with which to enforce the statutory regulations, which can be used to combat the subsidies race. Although the federal law is independent of the codices and fifteen years older, its regulations focus on the very same subject, the co-ordination of state aid (especially of the *Länder* governments) and the prevention of unfair locational competition in the distribution of subsidies to business. A strict state aid control policy in the federal system of Germany could have used this provision to back up the horizontally agreed upon codices with considerable vertical monitoring and sanctioning power.

As far as the procedural dimension of compliance is concerned, no official charge of non-compliance is on record. And while there are hints of a lot of unofficial complaints,[3] no effort has ever been made to enforce these

---

[3] The anonymous answers to a questionnaire sent to all the administrators responsible for state aid in the sixteen German *Länder* reveal a high degree of mutual distrust and

codices, or use Article 11, para. 2 of the federal law on the "Joint Task." There is no case on record in which the federal government attempted to reclaim misspent funds from any state government on the grounds of Article 11, para. 2. And while state aid administrators of the *Länder* governments hint at unofficial discussions with non-compliant state administrations (Eick 1981), at the same time they complain about larger, multinational enterprises exploiting the competition between the *Länder* to extract considerable amounts of financial support.[4] Yet, no further measures have been taken since the 1980s.

3.1.2 State aid control at the European level: The EC Treaty provisions on subsidies control

The rules governing the distribution of state aids to businesses by the governments of the member states are among some of the oldest and least changed elements of the treaties establishing the European Union. The Treaty on the European Coal and Steel Community of 1952 already included Articles which dealt with state aids. Also, the central elements of the still valid primary law of the EU concerning this topic are included in the 1958 Treaty on the European Economic Community. These rules are considered to be one of the major aspects of European competition policy (together with the matters of anti-competitive behavior, merger control and measures against partitioning of the common market). The drafters of the treaty intended it this way in 1958; not only did they include a special form of access to the European Court of Justice in state aid cases but also some special provisions to allow for the enactment of European secondary legislation in this policy field.

While the latter option was rarely exercised and only most recently used to clarify and expand upon the provisions contained in the original treaty, the former option became the virtually exclusive means of interpreting, exemplifying and expanding the meaning of the treaty provisions on state aid control in the European Community (Winter 1993; Hancher 1994). Hence, the application of these Articles has been guided by a multitude of Commission decisions, official and unofficial guidelines and some 250 rulings of the European Court of Justice since 1964. Only in 1999 did Council Regulation 659/99, OJ 1999 No. L83/1 summarize the essential

---

many allegations concerning state aids. However, it seems equally important to solve such questions in the context of inter-*Länder* committees or through bilateral discussions.

[4] Several anonymous respondents to the questionnaire were of the belief that the *Länder* state aid administrations are played out, one against the other, by large enterprises. At the same time they saw no necessity for further legislative activity in the field. Rather they call for increasing interadministrative co-ordination.

procedural requirements and material provisions, which had been established through the case law over the previous 35 years of the Community's state aid control. This regulation was enacted as the first major piece of secondary legislation in this policy area. Today, the Commission receives some 800 official notifications a year from member state governments informing it of their intention, or that of their agents, to distribute some form of state aid. In addition it receives word of some 150 cases of national aid schemes that were not notified, for example through media reports or complaints from the competitors of a beneficiary.

The core provisions regulating member states' subsidies are Articles 87, 88 and 89 of the EC Treaty as well as Council Regulation 659/99 which lays down detailed rules for the application of Article 88. Additionally, reference must be made to several other Articles in the EC and the ECSC treaties, for example Articles 36 and 73 of the EC Treaty, or Articles 4 and 54 of the ECSC Treaty, as well as to the decisions and guidelines of the Commission and the rulings of the European Court of Justice.

Article 87 of the EC Treaty is unambiguous in its general prohibition of market-distorting state aids awarded by member state governments. Basically, any form of market-distorting state aid is incompatible with the European common market. The only general exceptions are:

- subsidies to agriculture (Article 36 of the EC treaty);
- subsidies to the transport sector (Article 73 of the EC treaty);
- subsidies to some forms of public enterprises (Article 86 of the EC treaty);
- subsidies to coal and steel companies (Articles 4, 54 and 95 of the ECSC treaty);
- aid schemes intended to achieve social purposes for consumers, provided such subsidies do not discriminate against the origin of products (Article 87, para. 2a of the EC treaty);
- aid intended to support reconstruction after natural disasters or similarly unexpected occurrences (Article 87, para. 2b of the EC treaty); and
- aid granted to businesses in certain areas of Germany to compensate for the disadvantages caused by the division of Germany (Article 87, para. 2c of the EC treaty).

Furthermore, Article 87, para. 3 of the EC Treaty gives the Commission and Council the option of legalizing certain types of national subsidies provided they:

- promote the economic development of areas with an extremely low standard of living or a very high rate of unemployment;
- support an important project of common European interest or remedy serious economic disturbances in a member state;

- facilitate the development of certain economic activities or areas, where such aid does not adversely affect trading conditions to such an extent that it is contrary to the common interest;
- promote culture and the conservation of local, regional or national heritage and they do not adversely affect the common market;
- are specified by a decision of the Council, acting with a qualified majority on a proposal from the Commission.

Article 88 of the EC Treaty invests the Commission with the power to monitor the state aid policies of member state governments, decide on the compatibility of these policies with the treaties, and call directly on the European Court of Justice if a member state fails to comply with its decision. Furthermore, the article requires the member state governments to notify the Commission of all their major state aid programs and not to implement them until they have received the consent of the Commission.

And finally, Article 89 of the EC Treaty offers the opportunity to enact secondary legislation in the realm of state aid control so as to specify, clarify or amend the provisions of the treaty. The appropriate decision-making procedure is the co-decision procedure (Article 251 of the EC treaty). This option, however, has only been used once – in the case of Council Regulation 659/99, which effectively legally codified the pre-existing procedural practices of the state aid control regime in the European Union: the requirement on the member states to notify the Commission of their state aid schemes; the standstill clause; the preliminary and formal examination by the Commission; and, finally, the ultimate decision of the Commission. Furthermore, if the Commission believes that a member state has granted unlawful aid, the regulation details additional steps: a call for more information; an injunction; direct access to the court in case of member state non-compliance; and the decision on the basis of the available information, if a member state refuses to submit evidence. The overall aim is to recover from the enterprise the unlawful state aid and the accumulated interest. The Council Regulation also establishes a ten-year limitation period, opens the procedures up to interested third parties, requires member states to submit annual reports about their state aid programs, permits on-site monitoring by Commission officials, and invests the Commission with the right to seek lump sum penalties according to Article 228 of the EC Treaty if it considers that a member state is disregarding the ruling of the European Court of Justice. Finally, the regulation establishes an Advisory Committee on State Aid, which must be consulted by the Commission before the adoption of further implementing provisions concerning the primary and secondary legislation on state aids in the Community.

Probably the best example illustrating the procedural dimension of state aid control at the European level is the so-called "Alcan" case.[5] The German subsidiary of the Canadian aluminum producer Alcan operated an aluminum smelting plant in Ludwigshafen in the German state of Rhineland Palatina from 1979 to 1987. Because of a large-scale increase in electricity prices in 1982 Alcan Germany planned to close its Ludwigshafen plant and lay off some 330 employees. In order to dissuade Alcan from so doing, the state government of Rhineland Palatina offered 8 million DM (some 4.1 million Euros) to offset the increase in energy costs, but it failed to notify the European Commission of its intention. Nevertheless, Brussels became aware of this projected scheme and in a telex, dated March 7, 1983, it asked the federal German government to provide the information. In the meantime on June 9, 1983, the state government paid Alcan the first half of the aid package – 4 million DM. On July 25, 1983 the federal government responded to the Commission's inquiry by simply acknowledging that the state government of Rhineland Palatina intended to subsidize Alcan. On being pressed by the Commission for more details, Bonn responded on August 3, 1983 with some general declarations.

On October 11, 1983 the Commission opened a preliminary investigation and on November 25, 1983 it informed the federal government that it would follow this up with a formal investigation under Article 88, para. 2 of the EC Treaty. This decision was communicated to the state government on November 28, 1983. Unimpressed by this development, the government of Rhineland Palatina paid the second slice of the promised aid package to Alcan on November 30, 1983 – another 4 million DM. Only on December 13, 1983 was Alcan informed by the German administration that the aid had not been notified to the European Commission.

After concluding its formal procedures, Brussels decided on December 14, 1985 that the aid package to Alcan had been in violation of Article 87 of the EC Treaty and, hence, was unlawful and had to be reclaimed by the German authorities. On January 15, 1986 Alcan was informed of this decision. Neither it nor the German authorities appealed this decision. But on April 21, 1986 the German federal government informed the Commission of important political and legal difficulties, which effectively barred Bonn from reclaiming the subsidy. The Commission, however, pointed to the fact that its decision had not been appealed and on February 2, 1989 it gained a ruling from the European Court of Justice, which stated that the German federal government had violated its

---

[5] ECJ Case 24/95, *Land Rheinland-Pfalz* v. *Alcan Deutschland* [1997] ECR I-1591. See also Classen 1997, Scholz 1998, and Winkler 1999.

obligations under the EC treaty by its failure to comply with the Commission's decision.

This led the state government of Rhineland Palatina, on September 26, 1989, to cancel its state aid decisions of June and November 1983 and to reclaim the subsidies. Alcan petitioned the local administrative court to annul this new decision. Both the local and the regional administrative courts of appeal decided in favor of Alcan and the state government appealed these decisions before the Federal German Administrative Court, which itself referred the case to the European Court of Justice for a preliminary ruling. Alcan essentially claimed that Article 48 of the Federal German Administrative Procedures Act (*Verwaltungsverfahrensgesetz*) provides for a limitation period of one year that applies to all administrative decisions which distribute financial benefits, even if unlawful. After one year, the beneficiary, according to the federal German law applicable in the state of Rhineland Palatina, is entitled to retain its financial aid, especially if it has already spent the allotted money. Given that, according to the EC Treaty, it is national (German) law which governs the recovery of unlawful state aids, Alcan argued that Article 48 of the German Administrative Procedures Act protected it from having to repay the illegally received state aid; an argument that had been upheld by two consecutive rulings of lower German administrative courts.

In its judgment of March 20, 1997, the European Court of Justice, however, pointed to three important aspects. First, neither Alcan nor the German government had appealed the Commission's initial decision, effectively allowing it to become legally binding. Secondly, Alcan could not claim to have received the subsidies in the belief that the German authorities had complied with the notification requirement without it first having made sure that this was really the case. And thirdly, the stipulation in the EC treaty that, in the absence of common regulations, national law governs the recovery of illegally awarded state aids, cannot be interpreted in such a way that in effect denies the Community the opportunity of effectively applying and enforcing its treaty provisions. Hence, Alcan had forfeited its rights, both under the EC Treaty and under German law, and it was obliged to repay the state aid it had received plus interest. On April 23, 1998 the Federal German Administrative Court ruled according to the answer it received to its preliminary reference from the European Court of Justice, provoking a fierce debate among legal scholars on the question of subsidiarity, legitimacy and legal empowerment (Classen 1997; Scholz 1998; Winkler 1999). Alcan, finally, brought the case before the Federal German Constitutional Court and claimed that its rights under Articles 14 and 20 of the German constitution (*Grundgesetz*) had been violated. Alcan argued that the ruling of the Federal German

Administrative Court (and by implication the previous ruling of the European Court of Justice) denied it due process and ignored the principle of democratic decision-making in Germany. In its ruling of February 17, 2000 the Federal Constitutional Court, however, found there had been no violation of Alcan's constitutional rights and refused to hear the case.[6] Alcan had to repay the aid.

3.1.3   State aid control at the international level: The WTO/GATT provisions on subsidies

The central aim of the negotiations after the Second World War, which led to the conclusion of the General Agreement on Tariffs and Trade (GATT) in 1947, was the liberalization of trade, with the special focus on industrial goods and resources rather than services and agricultural goods. One of the major causes of the economic problems of the 1920s and 1930s was widely acknowledged to have been states' increasingly protectionist reactions, which had in fact aggravated the problems more than they had contributed to their solution. So, the postwar economic order needed to be based on the idea of reducing barriers to trade – that is reducing tariffs and eventually non-tariff barriers. The original treaty did not focus a great deal on state aids, but Article XVI of the GATT contained the requirement to reduce or avoid export subsidies, to notify such aid schemes and consult in case of injuries to other partner states. Article XVI became closely linked with Article VI of the GATT, which dealt with countervailing measures, which one country was allowed to invoke if it believed itself to have been injured by the unfair trade practices of another member state.

This aspect of the GATT did not receive much interest until the late 1960s and early 1970s when the United States increasingly considered itself to be the victim of other countries' unfair state aid programs and the European Community reproached the US by steadily increasing its use of countervailing measures. The following Tokyo Round of the GATT negotiations reacted to this perception with the inclusion in the treaty of a Subsidies Codex, which attempted to specify some of the disputed questions and, most importantly, to define two possible procedural remedies to settle disputes over subsidies. The so-called Track I procedure called on the injured party to prove the seriousness of the injury and then allowed the use of countervailing measures (mostly tariffs) to protect its home market. The Track II procedure sought to get the conflicting

---

[6] German Federal Constitutional Court Decisions: BVerfG, 1 BvR 489/99 of February 17, 2000.

parties to accept a multilateral dispute resolution with the aim of reconciling the interests of the protagonists and avoiding recourse to countervailing measures (Senti 1986; Adamantopoulos 1988).

Because of a widespread dissatisfaction with the effect of this Subsidies Codex, the Uruguay Round of the GATT negotiations once
again strengthened the treaty provisions governing unfair state aids by
introducing the so-called "Agreement on Subsidies and Countervailing
Measures" as an integral part of the new GATT of 1994. The new agreement not only contained a definition of subsidies but also distinguished
between three categories of state aids: prohibited, non-actionable and
actionable subsidies. Strictly prohibited are all subsidies (except those in
the agricultural sector) which support the export of domestic goods or
discriminate against the import of non-domestic goods. So called non-
actionable subsidies, which the agreement does allow, are non-specific
subsidies: non-discriminatory financial support, research and development programs, regional and structural policies and environmental aid.
Actionable subsidies, which other governments are allowed to challenge, are all specific subsidies with a serious negative impact on other
countries.

The agreement offers a three-step process to settle disputes between
GATT members over subsidy questions. The first step is to initiate consultations between the conflicting parties to exchange the different views,
which are even permitted in cases of non-actionable subsidies. If these
consultations do not lead to the resolution of the conflict, the second
step (now only in cases of prohibited or actionable subsidies) calls for
the appointment of an expert panel by the so-called Dispute Settlement
Body to study the disputed questions and propose a remedy on the basis
of the GATT. It is against this panel decision that the conflicting parties –
as the third step – have the right to appeal to the Appellate Body. The
ruling of this Appellate Body is automatically legally binding as long as
the Dispute Settlement Body does not veto it by a unanimous decision
of its members.

Furthermore, the Dispute Settlement Body has the opportunity to
sanction non-compliant behavior. If a party does not comply with the
ruling of the Dispute Settlement Body it has the right to allow the complainant to take countervailing measures, which usually consist of puni-
tive tariffs on specific trade goods exported by the non-compliant state
and which are intended to hurt the offender in sensitive trade areas,
thereby forcing it to comply. Finally, the new agreement reaffirms the
obligation on all the GATT member countries to give notification of all
existing state aid schemes and it created the Committee on Subsidies and
Countervailing Measures to receive and monitor these notifications.

The still ongoing dispute between Canada and Brazil over alleged unlawful export subsidies for producers of small civil aircraft is very instructive on the procedural dimension of compliance with international state aid control provisions.[7] Both countries are home to important manufacturers of such aircraft: Canada has Bombardier and de Havilland and their various subcontractors and Brazil has Embraer and some of its suppliers. Not surprisingly, these enterprises are fierce direct competitors on the world market for regional civil aircraft and are, thus, very sensitive to any kind of perceived or real market distortion which benefits their competitors. This resulted in a series of nine cases and rulings from various WTO panels, the Appellate Body and the Arbitrators. A final solution is still not at hand.

Officially, the dispute started on June 18, 1996 with a Canadian request for consultations with Brazil on the alleged export subsidies which were being granted by the Brazilian government to foreign purchasers of civil aircraft produced by Brazil's Embraer aircraft manufacturer. Canada was especially critical of one element of the so-called PROEX program, set up in 1991, under which the Brazilian government undertook to support its export industry. Under the special PROEX clause, Brazil offered so-called "interest rate equalization" to foreign banks that financed the sale of Brazilian aircraft. In such cases the Brazilian central bank covered up to 3.8 percent of the interest rate payable by the foreign bank to refinance its loan for the aircraft sale. Canada alleged that this constituted an illegal export subsidy under the GATT and especially its Subsidies and Countervailing Measures Agreement, since it enabled banks to offer cheaper loans to foreign airlines that chose to buy Brazilian instead of, for example, Canadian aircraft.

Several bilateral consultations between 1996 and 1998 failed to achieve any mutually satisfactory solution. So Canada, on July 10, 1998, finally asked for the establishment of a WTO panel, which the Dispute Settlement Body set up in the fall of 1998. The panel met with the parties in November 1998, submitted its interim report to them on February 17, 1999 and presented its final report on March 12, 1999. It concluded that the interest rate equalization under Brazil's PROEX program was indeed an illegal export subsidy, according to the Subsidies and Countervailing Measures Agreement of GATT. The panel called on the Brazilian government to terminate this program within 90 days.

In May 1999, Brazil appealed the panel report, prompting Canada to file a conditional appeal in the event that the Brazilian motion should

---

[7] See the various WTO panel and Appellate Body reports on the dispute settlement cases WT/DS46 and WT/DS70.

prove successful. In June 1999, the Appellate Body heard the case and it reaffirmed the Panel's ruling on August 2, 1999, especially the demand on Brazil to end its PROEX interest rate equalization program in support of the export of Brazilian civil aircraft.

This was not, however, the only dispute between Brazil and Canada relating to alleged subsidies for aircraft exports. On March 10, 1997 the Brazilian government had requested consultations with Canada, essentially complaining about four Canadian measures:

- the financing and loan guarantees, including equity infusion, to companies established for the purpose of exporting civil aircraft;
- direct and indirect governmental financial support to the civil aircraft industry;
- the sale of government-owned shares in one aircraft manufacturer to another aircraft manufacturer at less than the market value; and
- the benefits awarded to aircraft manufacturers under various Canada–Québec development agreements and programs.

Since the consultations on April 30, 1997 failed to produce a satisfactory solution, on June 10, 1998, Brazil asked the Dispute Settlement Body to set up a WTO panel, which it did on July 23, 1998. This panel met with the parties and submitted its final report on March 12, 1999. It rejected two of Brazil's allegations, but found that two instances of Canada's financial assistance did constitute illegal export subsidies, contrary to Articles 3.1(a) and 3.2 of the Subsidies and Countervailing Measures Agreement of the GATT. It recommended the termination of these practices within 90 days. Parallel to conducting the first dispute, both Canada and Brazil, in May 1999, also filed their appeals in this case and the Appellate Body issued its ruling alongside the ruling in the first case on August 2, 1999, once again rejecting all arguments of the appellants and upholding the panel recommendations.

Although the Dispute Settlement Body adopted both reports of the Appellate Body, this only led to a subsequent round of allegations. Both Brazil and Canada complained that the measures taken by their adversary to implement the reports were inadequate and, hence, the other government was not complying with the GATT rules. Consultations once again failed, as both governments stuck to their points of view. In November 1999, both governments called on the Dispute Settlement Body to establish two separate panels to review these disputes relating to the inadequate implementation of the two reports. Both panels submitted their reports on April 28, 2000. The panel looking at Brazil's implementation of the Appellate Body's ruling in the case of its PROEX program concluded that no implementation whatsoever had taken place and that Brazil had totally failed to honor the ruling. The panel looking at Canada's implementation of the Appellate Body's ruling on its financial support measures acknowledged that Canada had changed one of the two measures sufficiently to comply with the ruling, but that it had not changed the second one. Consequently, the panel again recommended that Canada change the second financial support instrument for aircraft sales.

Unsurprisingly, in May 2000, both governments appealed the respective panel rulings, which led, on July 21, 2000, to two rulings of the Appellate Body, which rejected both of their appeals and upheld the panel decisions. At the same time Canada requested an authorization from the Dispute Settlement Body to take appropriate countervailing measures against Brazil to the sum of 700 million Canadian Dollars a year. Brazil asked that this amount be referred to arbitration. On August 28, 2000 the arbitrators concluded that Canada had erred in its account of the damages that resulted from Brazil's PROEX program and that the sum of 344.2 million Canadian Dollars in countervailing measures against Brazilian trade was sufficient to offset the damage to the Canadian aircraft industry. Interestingly, to date the Canadian government has refrained from applying these countervailing duties against Brazilian exports.[8] The next move is still to come.

3.2   The degrees of compliance with the state aid control regulations

There is an important difficulty regarding the quantitative measurement of subsidies. The literature cannot agree on a single definition (Boss and Rosenschon 1998; Slotboom 2002). Rather, it is possible to find several competing definitions, from those with a narrow perspective to those with a very broad perspective. The narrow definition considers state aids to be governmental financial support for businesses intended to achieve some economic goal, which could not be achieved by the market (Zimmermann 1979). The loopholes in this definition are obvious: it includes neither tax expenditures nor financial support by governmentally instructed market actors, such as development agencies and investment banks. The broad definition takes into account these shortcomings and defines subsidies as any financial advantage (whether the allocation of money, tax expenditure, or the transfer of valuable resources) given by a state authority (or in the name of a state authority) to an enterprise, which does not entitle the state authority to an equivalent amount of marketable goods or rights (for example shares or ownership) in return for this financial support (Ross 2000). The problem with this broad definition is the lack of empirical data to quantify the degree to which a government subsidizes

---

[8] See *Neue Zürcher Zeitung*, November 3/4, 2001.

its economy. Since tax expenditures form a major part of these financial advantages to enterprises it is not sufficient to look at the state's official budget alone. To some extent it is necessary instead to estimate the amount of money the government could have extracted if it had employed an unbiased tax structure instead of subsidizing certain sectors of the economy or certain locations in the jurisdiction using tax breaks (Howard 1995, 1997).

This, however, is a rather difficult and complicated task, which has only rarely been done in the empirical literature. It entails not only the creation of a "model tax structure" for the country analyzed such that one can locate those instances of tax expenditures (Datta and Grasso 1998), but it is also necessary to look into the accounting rules that govern the preparation of the balance sheets for important corporate taxpayers. Different book-keeping rules result in different tax bases and, thus, different opportunities for governments to extract money from the same kind of business (Break 1985; Cummins et al. 1995). Any attempt to take into account such considerations fails, not only due to insurmountable problems of data collection and computing, but also because of the increasingly abstract and theoretical nature of the resulting figures. The iterative use of *ceteris paribus* assumptions would finally result in a formal tax system, in which no real-world taxpayer would behave the way predicted by the theoretical model.

Although this analysis uses the broad definition of subsidies, it is impossible to support this perspective with satisfactory quantitative data. Nevertheless, most of the statutory regulations dealing with subsidies control explicitly or implicitly employ such a broad definition. Hence, using the narrow definition would only increase the difficulties of an interlevel comparison between national, European and international regulations. The analysis relies on useful indirect empirical data, especially the opinions of politicians involved in the formulation and administration of these subsidies control policies and of scientific experts on the efficacy of these policies – principally economists and legal scholars. Taken together, these opinions allow for quite a reliable assessment of the degree to which state aid control regulations are complied with at the different political levels.

3.2.1 Compliance with the inter-Länder codices in Germany

Since 1967, the German federal government has been required by law to present regularly to the German Parliament a report on the development of state aids. Since the 1980s, the *Länder* governments have agreed to provide overall figures relating to their distribution of financial support to businesses (see table 3.1).

Table 3.1 *Annual total amount of state aids in Germany in billion Euros*[a]

	1970	1975	1980	1985	1988	1989	1990	1991	1992
Fed.	7.7	10.8	13.9	15.6	16.7	17.1	18.0	24.6	24.8
Län.	6.6	10.2	13.9	16.1	16.7	17.2	17.5	22.3	21.2

	1993	1994	1995	1996	1997	1998	1999	2000	2001
Fed.	23.7	23.5	24.4	27.1	27.9	27.8	28.6	28.9	27.9
Län.	23.3	23.6	23.6	24.1	24.8	24.1	22.7	23.2	21.7

[a] Annual amount of state aids in Germany in billion Euros; see Deutscher Bundestag, Drucksachen 14/6748, 13/8420, 13/2230, 12/5580, 12/1525, 14/1500; Bundesrat, Drucksache 430/99.

These figures are heavily criticized by economists who argue that they do not represent the real picture of state aids but rather underestimate the amount of resources that are spent to support German enterprises (Zimmermann 1979; Rosenschon 1991; Boss and Rosenschon 1998). There is good reason to acknowledge the validity of this critique. However, even the official figures show the same obvious trend as the much larger figures given in the analyses of economists. Since 1970, and until the late 1990s, the German *Länder* regularly and year-on-year increased their subsidies to enterprises, regardless of whether the economy was booming or in recession (Boss and Rosenschon 2000, 2002; Deutsche Bundesbank 2000).

A similar conclusion can be drawn from the reactions of politicians, both at the federal and at the regional levels, to the question of the effectiveness of the codices on state aids. Criticism of the state aid programs of the *Länder* governments started before the introduction of the codices and continued until at least the second half of the 1990s, when it was increasingly overshadowed by the debate on the EU state aid control policy. On the federal level, the then Chancellor, Helmut Schmidt, criticized "extreme federalism" in Germany, which, in his opinion, blocked any attempt to co-ordinate state aid policies in the context of the federal law on the "Joint Task" (Schmidt 1977). His Secretary of State in the Federal Ministry of Finance, Manfred Lahnstein, supported this view and argued that the federal level was unable to co-ordinate economic policies in Germany because the regional governments did everything to render such federal efforts useless (Lahnstein 1978). In 1979, Hans-Ulrich Klose, a parliamentary representative in the German *Bundestag*, criticized the divergent aims and the lack of co-ordination of the state aid policies produced by the *Länder* governments.[9] His colleague, Heide Simonis, offered her own view on the basic principle of subsidies control, as between the *Länder* governments: "If you do not touch my program I will not touch yours!" (Simonis 1979; Nägele 1996). In 1982–1983, Birgit Breuel, the Minister for Economic Affairs in Lower Saxony, acknowledged that most of her fellow *Länder* ministers had signed the two codices on the understanding that these regulations would only become obligatory if the ministers with other important cabinet portfolios could agree on similar restrictions in their policy areas (Breuel 1988).

Unsurprisingly, academics unanimously rejected these codices as ineffective and charged the *Länder* governments with gross non-compliance. Both the research groups of Fritz Scharpf in 1976 and Carl Böhret in 1980 came to the conclusion that the federal law on the "Joint Task" was failing to prevent the German regions from engaging in a bitterly fought subsidies race (Scharpf et al. 1976; Böhret et al. 1980). Equally devastating was the academic opinion relating to the effectiveness of the codices. No parties to the agreement ever honored the regulations and the level of compliance was practically zero (Bleckmann 1984; Nieder-Eichholz 1995).

Although this state of affairs was no secret, nothing was done to rectify it, either horizontally or vertically. The federal government never invoked Article 11, para. 2 of the law on the "Joint Task" to ask the *Länder* to repay obviously misused funds and no regional government ever challenged the behavior of another regional government in court. However, there are a vast number of cases in which *Länder* governments have sought the repayment of illegally used state aids from enterprises, based on Article 11, para. 3 of the law on the "Joint Task". Obviously, the federal law was basically in force and the parties involved were aware of its contents, but only in relation to the regulations for societal actors, not in disputes between the federal and *Länder* governments. This is surprising given that the input side of the budget, especially the inter-regional support mechanism, surfaced several times on the agenda of the Federal Constitutional Court. The output side, especially the detrimental subsidies race, however, never did. Hence, not only was overall compliance zero, the procedural dimension was completely missing.

Today, the state aid administrators of the *Länder* governments hint that, although the codices lack any official enforcement mechanisms, they constitute an important unofficial and informal yardstick for decisions in state aid cases. Without the codices, so the argument goes, the subsidies race

---

[9] See Klose's article in *Frankfurter Rundschau*, September 13, 1979.

would have been even stronger and, hence, even more detrimental to the state budgets in Germany (Eick 1981; Hübl and Legler 1983). While it is impossible to deny some plausibility in this line of reasoning, the overall disciplining effect of the codices must have been quite marginal, given that the real turnaround only came subsequent to the increased pressures from Brussels in the early 1990s. On the other hand, it is certainly not true that these codices were simply engineered with a view to public opinion, but they were never intended to be invested with any form of binding power. Several facts refute such a conclusion. First, the codices were negotiated within a special panel of representatives from the state ministries of economic affairs and it took more than a year of intense negotiations to finalize the provisions (Eick 1981). Secondly, the codices contain footnotes with several provisos, included by various state governments, against some of the clauses and wording, which would have been an unnecessary caution if it had been clear that these codices were not intended to be complied with. Thirdly, even after 20 years of non-compliance, the responsible state administrators still regard it as necessary to keep these codices on the books if only to have a common yardstick for decisions in state aid cases. Thus, it is wrong simply to infer from the reduced legal quality and character of the codices that there was an intention by the *Länder* governments to ignore their provisions from the outset.

3.2.2   Compliance with the European Regulation

Regarding the overall status of compliance, it is, once again, difficult to measure directly the extent of compliance with these rules. However, on the basis of the indirect evidence – the official figures on state aids, the opinions of politicians and the opinions of economists, legal scholars, and political scientists – the European Union's regulatory controls on state aid must be considered to be one of its more or less silent success stories. Since 1988 the European Commission has regularly published a so-called "Survey on State Aid" in the European Union. The figures given in these reports provide a very clear picture (see table 3.2).

Until the creation of the Single European Market in 1993 the total amount of subsidies distributed by member state governments increased over the years, both in real terms as well as in proportion to GDP, with some exceptions, for example in 1989 and 1992. Since 1993, however, the figures have shown a strong downward tendency. Even though this trend is supported by independent analysis (Bilal and Polmans 1999), it is still possible to argue that these statistics do not represent the whole picture because governments have taken evasive actions to conceal the

Table 3.2 *Annual total of state aids granted across the EU in billion Euros*[a]

	1988	1989	1990	1991	1992	1993	1994
EU12	43.9	33.6	44.2	39.8	39.1	44.1	41.2
percent GDP	4.1	3.2	4.0	3.6	3.2	3.8	3.4

	1995	1996	1997	1998	1999	2000	2001
EU12	37.4	35.4	34.4	28.4	24.6	24.4	21.3
percent GDP	2.9	2.7	2.6	2.0	1.7	1.6	1.4

[a] Annual amount of state aids of EU member governments in billion Euros, excluding agriculture; see: COM(2003) 225 final, COM(2002) 242 final, COM(2000) 205 final; COM(98) 417 final; COM(97) 170 final; COM(95) 365 final; COM(99) 148 final.

aid they award to enterprises. Nevertheless, from the perspective of compliance research, such a change in the behavior of the addressees must be explained, especially so when one considers their very different behavior in the late 1980s.

Furthermore, this clear trend is confirmed by a multitude of highly critical comments from politicians in the member states on the topic of the European Commission's state aid control. While Commission officials deplore the lukewarm to practically non-existing political support from member state governments (Van Miert 2000), politicians, especially at the regional level, for example in Germany and Austria, have heavily criticized Brussels for effectively depriving them of any independent powers to subsidize enterprises (Nägele 1997). Since the early 1990s the Commission outlawed nearly all direct aid schemes instituted by the West German *Länder* and it is also now on the way to bringing to an end the most important indirect aid schemes, for example the German *Landesbanken*, which are publicly owned banks that are used by the *Länder* to promote industrial policies. The Commission considers the public ownership and the state guarantees given against bankruptcy to constitute unlawful state aid (Doering 2003). At the same time *Länder* politicians deplore the loss of valuable instruments which have been used to regulate investment and employment as well as to support less developed areas. They have thus called for the stricter application of the principle of subsidiarity in the EU in order to defend their political room for maneuver. The examples can be extended to basically all member states and together add up to give the impression that the Community's state aid control has not only found a lot of targets but has also hurt enough of them politically to force national and regional politicians to make the Commission a scapegoat for its efforts in preventing them from distributing money according to their usual schemes (Nägele 1996, 1997; Zimmermann 1990).

Finally, this perspective is supported by the opinion of the overwhelming majority of academics who deal with the question of state aid control in the EU. While most academic commentators criticize the EU for not going far enough to prohibit state aids, for being "political" when some cases are decided, for overlooking major aid schemes, or for being too bureaucratic when making decisions, they are generally in agreement that since the early 1990s the EU system has been the most powerful instrument for reducing the amount of subsidies paid by member states and that the Commission has managed to elicit an unusually high degree of compliance with the provisions of its system (Nägele 1997; Bilal and Polmans 1999; and Lavdas and Mendrinou 1999). During the 1970s and 1980s, most analyses of the EU's state aid control policy tended to discuss the question of why this policy did not work and what requirements were necessary before one might see some improvement (Bleckmann 1977; Seidel 1985). Since the 1990s, the foremost topic in the books and articles has changed. Today, academic debate centers on the reasons why this policy has been so successful, explores ways for the further development of some of its rules and tries to find solutions to the enormous workload placed on the Commission by this area of competition policy (McGowan 2000; Nicolaides 2002). Hence, academics criticize the Commission sufficiently to demand changes which they deem necessary for the reform of the system but, in doing so, most acknowledge that this has been a successful area of EU activity.

This qualification of the overall status of compliance is also confirmed by the procedural dimension. The Commission receives some 500 to 800 notifications of national state aid measures every year. About 400 or 500 of these meet with no objection from the Commission after a preliminary examination. Some forty to sixty cases a year will result in the Commission opening a formal investigation into the details because it suspects they will produce negative effects on the markets. Of these formal inquires, some fifteen to twenty cases end up being accepted, some twenty to thirty cases are found to be non-compliant and a few cases are conditionally accepted. Either the member state government, the potential beneficiary of the state aid, or an affected third party challenges the Commission decision before the European Court of Justice in around ten to fifteen cases a year. Since the 1980s there has been no open refusal by any party to accept the ECJ's decision. Article 228 of the EC Treaty, giving the Commission the power to seek penalties against any party ignoring a court order, has never been used in the realm of state aid control.

Although the judicial process provided one of the most important – if not *the* most important – means of interpreting, expanding and reformulating the EU's primary law on state aid, fundamental challenges to the regulations did occur in the 1960s and 1970s. In this period recalcitrant compliance, or initial non-compliance, with the Community's state aid rules was the common practice of many member state governments (Zuleeg 1978). This has now changed and nearly all recent state aid cases brought before the European Court of Justice have dealt with new forms of state aid, where the ECJ is being asked to subsume them under the relevant provisions. The Alcan case was no exception. Neither Alcan nor the German government challenged the initial decision of the Commission in court, thus accepting both the law on the books and also the power of the Commission. The new question was only whether national rules implementing European regulations could neutralize the intended effect of the European rules. Here, the European Court of Justice extended its previously well-established case law of the supremacy of European law over national law to the effect that national implementation rules, denying the efficacy of Community law, are not compatible with the EC treaty. And even the attempt to invoke the spirit of the so-called Maastricht ruling of the Federal German Constitutional Court did not help Alcan. The state government canceled its illegal decisions and reclaimed the aid, and both the Federal German Administrative Court and the Federal German Constitutional Court decided in favor of the European Commission.

The procedural stability of these state aid control provisions at the European level is also underlined by the fact that for years the Commission refused to initiate secondary legislation on state aid control matters based on Article 89 of the EC Treaty. It feared that the Council would seize the chance to roll back much of what had been achieved by state aid control in the Community and that the new rules would effectively curb the power of the Commission. However, in 1998 the Commission felt sufficiently confident to summarize the existing case law by codifying it in a Council Regulation. The Commission's proposal navigated the decision-making process with only a few minor changes; a clear sign that no member state openly doubted the legal basis of the European state aid control system. Furthermore, the Commission has recently begun to introduce measures that aim to reduce its workload by essentially loosening its tight grip on national state aid schemes, in particular by handling *de minimis* cases more leniently[10] and relieving certain groups of small and medium-sized enterprises from the notification requirement entirely[11] (Sinnaeve 2001). These are obvious signs that the state aid control regulation at the European level enjoys a good rate of compliance.

3.2.3   Compliance with the WTO/GATT Regulations

On the overall status of compliance, there is, unfortunately, no systematic reporting on state aids in the context of the GATT, neither for the "old" GATT, before 1994, nor the "new" GATT/WTO, since 1995. The WTO has only published regular annual reports since 1996. These do include elaborate trade statistics but only a few figures on state aids. Until 1994, some 90 percent of the consultation and dispute settlement cases involved either the USA or the European Community or both. Some 40 percent of the cases brought against the USA concerned countervailing measures, while some 40 percent of the cases brought against the European Community were about targeted subsidies, mostly in the realm of agriculture (Hudec 1993; Petersmann and Jaenicke 1992). Hence, state aid questions became important and gave rise to heavily disputed issues in the context of the GATT. Nevertheless, both governments and academic observers were disappointed about the results of the system, which depended on an injured government taking action, since private third parties possessed no standing (Jackson 1978; Bliss 1987; and Plank 1987). Furthermore, until 1994, panel reports had to be accepted unanimously by all members, including the losing party, which was not often the case. Finally, even if all parties accepted the decision, it was far from self-evident that the measures proposed by the panel report would be implemented. In many cases countervailing measures were taken and the distribution of subsidies continued, both to the detriment of free trade (Hilf 1991; Petersmann 1991).

In summer 2003, the WTO published the reports and rulings made in 294 cases, going back to 1995, which have involved the panels, the Appellate Body or arbitration. Of these, only fifteen dealt with allegedly illegal subsidies under the Subsidies and Countervailing Measures Agreement of the GATT. The bulk of disputes obviously involve anti-dumping measures, questions of risk regulation (foodstuffs), patent questions (pharmaceuticals), non-tariff barriers (shirts, bananas) and environmental protection (dolphins, asbestos). Of the recent cases involving subsidies,

[10] See Commission Regulation 69/2001, OJ 2001 No. L10/30 on the application of Arts. 87 and 88 of the EC Treaty to *de minimis* aid.
[11] See Commission Regulation 70/2001, OJ 2001 No. L 10/33 on the application of Arts. 87 and 88 of the EC Treaty to state aid to small and medium-sized enterprises.

six were part of the ongoing dispute between Canada and Brazil over export subsidies for small civil aircraft. Furthermore, the 2002 annual report of the WTO lists only thirty[12] member countries, out of a total of 146, as being compliant with the requirement in the Subsidies and Countervailing Measures Agreement to notify the WTO of existing and newly introduced state aid schemes. Various questions raised by representatives of several member governments in the Subsidies and Countervailing Measures Committee about the notifications made by other member countries suggest that even these thirty notifications are incomplete or disputed. Both aspects point to certain improvements since 1995, but also to remaining shortcomings, especially relating to the issues of notification and monitoring.

3.2.4   *Comparing the degrees of compliance with state aid rules at the different political levels*

The three empirical examples of state aid control regulations at the different political levels offer an interesting pattern of compliance. The inter-*Länder* codices in Germany were never complied with and, surprisingly, no one ever had recourse to the existing legal means of enforcing compliance. During the 1980s and early 1990s, there was a clear and ongoing compliance crisis. Since the second half of the 1990s the picture of compliance with state aid control in Germany has become overshadowed by the effect of the European state aid control provisions, which have forced the German *Länder* to reduce their financial support for private enterprises, and which have essentially prevented the West German states from undertaking any independently run state aid programs (Färber 1995, 1996).

In assessing the compliance record with the EU regulations, two time periods must be distinguished. Until the 1980s both the overall status and the procedures for handling disputed cases provide overwhelming evidence of a number of compliance crises. It took the Commission years to establish and enforce the simple rule of notification for state aid schemes. And for years the member states were singularly reluctant to honor the Commission's decisions or the ECJ's rulings in such cases (Slot 1990; Lasok 1990). This changed with the gradual introduction of the common market from the late 1980s onwards. Since the early 1990s the overall status has improved to achieve a high degree of compliance and, from a procedural perspective, there have only been a few cases of

---

[12] The EU is counted as a single member. Thus, the figure actually amounts to 44 out of 146 member states.

recalcitrant compliance with references to the European Court of Justice. Since the 1990s no member state has simply ignored a ruling of the European Court of Justice in the area of state aid control. The only observable forms of resistance have been some cases of minimal implementation, which have often simply led to the next court ruling (Rosenstock 1995).

The compliance record with WTO/GATT state aid control regulations exhibits a similar pattern. Until 1994, under the "old" GATT, the overall status of compliance as well as its procedural dimension must be judged as an almost continual compliance crisis (Müller 1984; Scheffler 1993). Most disputes over state aids were to do with agricultural export subsidies, but even in the cases that dealt with industrial subsidies, the GATT's success in changing the behavior of its member governments was extremely limited (Hudec 1993). The new WTO/GATT, in place since 1995, has changed the picture, even though it is still too early to make completely reliable judgments. One-fifth of the member states have complied with the notification requirement and compliance with those cases that have been disputed shows some signs of improvement. Compliance crises still exist, but it is initial non-compliance or even recalcitrant compliance that is increasingly observed (Hudec 1999).

Taken together and measured according to the compliance they secure with their state aid control regimes, the German, European and international levels achieve the following ranking:

German inter-*Länder* codices < WTO regulations < EU regulations.

The lowest degree of compliance can be found in the case of the German inter-*Länder* codices, the WTO regulations elicit a somewhat higher degree of compliance and the EU regulations are by far the most complied with state aid control regulations.

3.3 The independent variables: Explaining the comparative empirical result

The somewhat surprising empirical result that emerges from the comparative assessment of the degree of compliance achieved by the various state aid control regulations at the different political levels immediately begs the question, "Why?" The introductory chapters presented four theoretical perspectives that seek to explain compliance or non-compliance as well as offering a set of independent variables for each. The comparative empirical result enables the testing of these theoretically-derived hypotheses and a comparative assessment of their explanatory power with respect to state aid control regulations at the different political levels. Hence, in the sections below, each set of independent variables is applied to the comparative empirical findings so as to assess the ability of each theoretical hypothesis to explain the empirical picture.

3.3.1   Rational institutionalism

Rational institutionalism focuses its explanation of compliance on two central variables: sanctions and monitoring. In the case of monitoring, the means of its application is important, whereas, in the case of sanctions, two aspects are central: the content and the competence.

3.3.1.1   Monitoring   In order to monitor the compliance or non-compliance of the *Länder* governments in the case of the state aids codices each signatory had to rely on its own unilateral efforts to gather information on the behavior of the other fifteen partners to the agreements. No central agency was created to support these efforts, nor did the *Länder* governments allow the federal government to carry out this task. Rather, the German states generally refused to give any information to the federal government on their distribution of state aids, which meant that the federal government could not include any figures about the behavior of the *Länder* in its regular report to the federal Parliament. When the *Länder* cabinets changed their minds in the 1980s they only agreed to disclose to the federal authorities the total overall yearly figures for direct financial support and tax expenditures of the eleven (and later sixteen) *Länder* combined (Bleckmann 1984). Under no circumstances was the federal level permitted to identify the details of the state aids handed out by each of the regional governments. Since they did not trust the federal level the *Länder* governments even took the precaution of installing a common statistical office for the *Länder* to conduct the simple task of collecting the necessary data and transferring it to the federal government. This statistical office never received any authority to monitor or even control the *Länder* and it has no authority to publish any data, reports or summaries (Neuhaus 1987).

The option of societal monitoring (and possible enforcement) is theoretically open to affected third parties, especially to the competitors of the potential state aid beneficiaries. However, there are only a handful of cases, because the Federal Administrative Court introduced an extremely high burden of proof to achieve a successful court ruling (Zuleeg 1974; Bleckmann 1984). The plaintiff must present evidence to convince the court that the state aid awarded to its competitor will lead to its own bankruptcy. No plaintiff has ever managed to offer such compelling evidence and, hence, the court has blocked all requests by interested societal actors for it to review state aid cases in Germany.

In the case of European state aid control regulations, the treaties established a common central agent – the European Commission – and invested it with the task of monitoring member states' state aid activities, and regularly reporting the results of these monitoring efforts. The Commission, with the support of the European Court of Justice, has developed a very broad definition of state aids and, thus, is able to monitor and seek information on a wide variety of schemes to support business (Smith 1996, 1998).

The task of the Commission to monitor member states' state aid schemes is supported by five additional provisions, which essentially strengthen the position of the common agent:

- member state governments are required to report any form of state aid to the Commission;
- the Commission has the right to carry out on-site monitoring of enterprises or offices that are suspected of concealing evidence relating to state aid;
- the Commission is allowed to use and act upon information obtained from private third parties and has even developed a special reporting form for such cases;
- if the member state government or the suspected beneficiary of state subsidies refuses to provide the necessary information to the Commission, it is empowered to decide on the basis of the evidence available, essentially giving it the power to decide according to reasonably acceptable schemes;
- state aid that is not notified is always illegal even if the Commission would have approved the program had it been notified.

These wide-ranging competencies for multilateral monitoring by the European Commission are, furthermore, supported by far-reaching options for societal monitoring by interested third parties. Under the European state aid control regulations interested third parties – such as the competitors of potential beneficiaries – do not only have the right to inform the Commission and participate in the formal investigation of state aid cases but are also able to challenge Commission decisions in court and can, hence, seek judicial review of any decision affecting their market position (Polley 1996; Schneider 1996).

Although the new WTO/GATT's "Agreement on Subsidies and Countervailing Measures" requires all member states to report their use of subsidies regulated by the GATT and that agreement, there is no common institution or autonomous system to monitor the international subsidies regime that was so created. Rather, the treaty relies on the willingness of its members to report their own state aid schemes and to carry out unilateral monitoring of other members whose subsidies might affect their own interests (O'Brien 1997; Stehn 1996). The new agreement created a Committee on Subsidies and Countervailing Measures, which receives the notifications and monitors the notification process. However, it has no independent status and does not meet frequently enough to control the national administrations. Furthermore, it has no right to carry out on-site monitoring. Hence, the monitoring efforts of the Committee are limited to controlling the formal notification requirements. Finally, all information on state aids intended for the WTO must pass through the hand of a government. There is no provision for direct access to the WTO by societal actors in relation to the international state aid control regime. Thus, the WTO/GATT is left with a monitoring process that is based on bilateral supervision by the member governments (Hoekman/Mavroidis 1996).

3.3.1.2 Sanctions   In the case of the inter-*Länder* codices, Article 11, para. 3 of the federal law on the "Joint Task" stipulates that the *Länder* governments are entitled to demand the repayment of any subsidies given to a private enterprise which were not used according to the regulations governing the grant. This rule has been widely employed to sanction enterprises for wrongly diverting subsidies and there exists a large body of case law, from German administrative courts at all levels (local, regional and federal), interpreting the precise meaning of the law (Götz 1984). Quite to the contrary, Article 11, para. 2, which empowers the federal level to demand the repayment of funds misused by *Länder* governments, has never been utilized and no German court has ever had to deal with a single case. Especially during the 1970s, some notorious disputes erupted between the federal government and the regional governments of Bavaria and North Rhine-Westphalia. In most cases the federal ministry of economic affairs did not concur with the aims pursued by regional governments in their distribution of subsidies. But the federal government in Bonn never attempted to use any form of sanction to force the regional level to accept its view on the proper targeting of state aids.

Similarly, there is no known case in which a regional government threatened to use or used some form of sanction against another signatory of the codices in order to force it to comply with the regulations. Over the years *Länder* governments have made many accusations against each other which have surfaced in public and each has, at one time or another, no doubt considered itself to be a victim of a subsidies race that has been provoked by others. But none of them is prepared to call for stricter regulations, an improvement in the monitoring system, or the use of the federal level as an independent third party, nor have they sought to challenge the behavior of other signatories in court.

Thus, even though both vertical and horizontal means for the judicial enforcement of the codices existed, none of these instruments has ever been used for this purpose. An alternative would have been to offset the benefits received by reclaiming the misspent money. But this option was never exercised either.

The Commission is empowered to enforce the European state aid controls by sanctioning any illegal distribution of state aid to private enterprises. The enforcement process offers the chance of participation to third party interests. The central element is again the decision of the Commission, which tests the compatibility of a member state's subsidy with European law (Rosenstock 1995). The member state government, the potential beneficiary and potentially affected third parties all have the right to seek a court ruling. If, however, the money is spent without a proper legal basis, the Commission is empowered to issue a second decision that calls on the member state government to recover the illegally awarded aid plus interest on usual market terms. The duty to recover interest prevents a member state from illegally giving money to enterprises, delaying legal action by every available means and then only recovering the original sum when forced to do so by the court, as this would essentially amount to a subsidy via cheap credits. Against this second type of Commission decision, direct legal action is once again possible. If the member state government, after having being called upon by the court to recover the subsidy plus interest, continues to refrain from taking the appropriate actions, the Commission has the option to use Article 228 of the EC Treaty in order to seek a court ruling imposing lump sum penalties until the member state government complies with the original court decision (Lasok 1990; Sinnaeve 1999; and Schütterle 1995).

Hence, this vertical enforcement only attempts to offset the benefit provided by the illegal aid scheme. It does offer, however, the opportunity for harsh penalties beyond the recovery of the illegal benefits, if the member state government does not comply with the initial Commission decision and a subsequent ruling by the European Court of Justice.

There is, however, one inconsistency. Although the basic treaty provisions have existed since the introduction of the Treaty on the European Economic Community in 1958, the Commission encountered enormous problems in enforcing these rules until the 1980s. The first major problem was to get the member states to notify it of their aid schemes. It took years and the help of the court to establish a general reporting pattern, so that the Commission usually accepted the validity of all notified aid schemes and concentrated its fight on non-notified member state programs. Hence, the Commission reports in this period show a slowly increasing number of notified programs as well as approved aid schemes

(Seidel 1984, 1985). Only in the 1980s, with the renewed effort to complete the Single Market, did the Commission take a more rigorous stand in scrutinizing notified schemes. Since then, the figures for notified and approved programs have differed significantly over the years. The full array of instruments used by the Commission to fight national subsidies and the willingness of (and probably the possibility for) the Commissioners to use these measures was not in place until the early 1990s and the start of the Single European Market (Seidel 1992).

Since then, however, the Commission has not only become more and more critical of national subsidies and decided against member states in an increasing number of notified cases but, more importantly, it has lashed out against illegal payments that have not been notified and which were often reported to Brussels by the competitors of state aid beneficiaries. Although figures on the amount recovered are unavailable, the Commission has stepped up its measures to ensure the execution of such decisions and the European Court of Justice has not hesitated in lending its support to these efforts (Rosenstock 1995).

In the case of the WTO/GATT there are only limited possibilities for sanctioning the non-compliant behavior of its members. First of all, any attempt to pressure a member to reduce the amount of state aid awarded – even in cases of prohibited subsidies – has to start with a formal complaint by another member state. The treaty provides for neither the possibility of societal, private parties challenging such aid schemes nor a common agent with the autonomous right to open a formal investigation. This certainly reduces the caseload of the state aid control regime and allows it to focus only on important cases. However, it also limits the kind of interests which are incorporated.

After a formal complaint has reached the WTO, the conflicting parties are given time to consult and bilaterally resolve the question. If this does not lead to a resolution of the problem, the conflicting governments are required to call for a dispute settlement procedure. Since 1994 this has been a formalized multi-step process in which an independent panel and if necessary the Appellate Body deal with the accusations and attempt to come up with a solution based on the GATT law (Jackson 2000). In these examinations the complainant must prove it has suffered serious injury to its economy which is the result of the state aid scheme carried out by the defendant. Until 1994 such a proposal from the panel only came into force if all parties, including the losing party, agreed to it. Since 1994 the rulings of the panel, and eventually that of the Appellate Body, automatically come into force if the Dispute Settlement Body does not unanimously reject them. Such rulings may require the defendant to reduce or even abolish its subsidies. If the defendant is not willing to comply with these measures, the Dispute Settlement Body has the power to permit the complainant to introduce unilateral counter-vailing measures, which are usually some form of tariff or quota (Senti 2000). Beyond this, neither the GATT nor the WTO provide for any form of sanctions (except the "nuclear" option of excluding a member country).

The central aim of this dispute settlement procedure, however, is the reconciliation of diverging national interests and the resolution of disputes between member governments which might in the long run endanger the level of free trade achieved thus far (McLarty 1994). However, this aim is not necessarily identical with the systematic and comprehensive reduc-tion of state aids across the world market, since it targets only state aids which are brought to the attention of the WTO/GATT by other mem-ber governments and allows for side-payments, trade-offs and even the continuous unchallenged application of WTO-approved countervailing measures (Jackson 2000). Under such circumstances, formally illegal aid schemes can be maintained provided that the disputing parties agree to such a solution or the defendant state prefers simply to accept the impo-sition of countervailing measures.

Hence, WTO/GATT-approved sanctions have to be enforced horizon-tally by the complainant and are only allowed to offset the benefit that it is assessed accrues to the defendant as a result of the illegal state aid, which is measured in terms of the costs it creates for the complainant (and not for the world trade in general).

Taken together, the rational institutionalist perspective predicts the comparative empirical findings since the 1980s, but has problems explain-ing the finding from the years before then. Central as well as societal monitoring, vertical enforcement and offsetting as well as other types of sanctions well explain the comparatively better record of the EU while the WTO's decentralized monitoring, combined with its horizontal enforce-ment and the offsetting sanctions, obviously explain the WTO's better position against the German *Länder* situation with its decentralized mon-itoring, the refusal to use horizontal or vertical enforcement options and the absence of sanctions. Before the 1980s the EU case creates a prob-lem. Its compliance record improved only during the late 1980s and early 1990s, while the explaining factors of the rational institutionalist per-spective had been in place since the late 1950s and early 1960s. Rational institutionalism would predict a rising degree of compliance following a short transition period of, say, five years in which the common insti-tutions had the time to set up their business and develop their working routines. But in fact it took more than twenty years to establish them, far longer than the institutionalist perspective can explain.

3.3.2   The legalization approach

The legalization approach focuses essentially on three aspects to explain the differing degrees of compliance: the kind of dispute settlement, the degree of legal internalization and the degree of civil internalization of the regulations.

3.3.2.1 Dispute settlement   With respect to dispute settlement, the national inter-*Länder* codices and the "Joint Task" law theoretically offered the option of strong triadic judicial review. A state government could have called upon the Federal Constitutional Court to decide on the alleged non-compliant behavior of another state government with respect to the two codices and both the federal and the state governments (and interested third parties) could have used the administrative courts to challenge any illegal state aid decisions by state governments. These options were never used.

On the European level, triadic judicial review became the central venue for clarifying, expanding and developing the primary European law on state aid control (Winter 1993, 1999). In the 1950s and 1960s, most of the treaty provisions on European state aid control were considered law on the books but did not really find their way into European legal practice. This changed only slowly during the 1970s when the Commission started to press member states to notify it of their national state aid schemes. However it took years to bring the member states to do this regularly and systematically. The situation further improved after the European Court of Justice established the basic legal principles guiding *inter alia* the application of the state aid control provisions, including the supremacy of European law over national regulations, the direct effect of treaty provisions and directives in national legal systems, and the access of private third parties to the decision-making process and the courts (Alter and Meunier-Aitsahalia 1994). With this, the ECJ fulfilled three essential functions. First, it supported the bulk of the Commission's decisions, guarding them from political pressure by member state governments. Secondly, with several major landmark cases, the ECJ opened the way for European law to have an impact beyond the control of the member state governments. Without these major decisions European law might have witnessed the same fate as most statutes of international law, which only address themselves to their signatory governments and, hence, are only applicable if these governments agree to the use to which they are put. Only in the larger context of directly effective European law could the common system of state aid control develop and strengthen (Maduro 1998; Stone Sweet and Caporaso 1998). Thirdly, it was the court which established several principles to structure the process of European state aid control. One example was the general illegality of non-notified aid, even if the aid scheme would have been approved had notification been received. Another was the requirement on the Commission to give reasons for and publish its decisions, instead of simply informing the addressees of the conclusion it had reached; a requirement which in turn opened up the Commission's own decision-making process to judicial review (Tallberg 1999).

At the international level, the old GATT offered the option of using either dyadic or triadic dispute resolution. The new WTO/GATT basically uses triadic judicial review, but requires bilateral consultations before a WTO panel is established by the Dispute Settlement Body to step in to resolve the dispute. Also, the new GATT only offers triadic judicial review but calls on the complainant to enforce the rulings; thus, the implementation of the court decisions still resembles a dyadic practice (Jackson 2000; Senti 2000; and Kelemen 2001).

3.3.2.2 Legal internalization   On the legal internalization of the different state aid control regulations, Germany's inter-*Länder* codices possess the character of a mere declaration (Breuel 1988). In order to avoid any centralizing tendencies the state governments took refuge behind the weak legal instrument of codices. But Article 11 of the "Joint Task" law was and still is legally binding on all state governments and has always been enforceable if the federal government had chosen to use it.

European regulations are legally binding – a quality which took the European Commission and the European Court of Justice some years to establish beyond doubt – as well as internally enforceable with direct effect. Several landmark decisions of the European Court of Justice have ensured that over the years European law has established precedence over national law and the state aid control regulations are directly applicable without the need for national implementation measures. National courts are obliged to apply European state aid control regulations directly and – if clarification is needed – to refer the case to the European Court of Justice for a preliminary ruling according to Article 234 of the EC Treaty (Sinnaeve 1999). The best example here is the Alcan case in which the Commission and the European Court of Justice overruled national state aid decisions and the ECJ also blocked any recourse to national statutes of limitation to avoid repaying the illegally distributed subsidies. The German Federal Constitutional Court accepted this decision as legally binding and denied that there had been any infringement of the constitutional rights of the appellant.

At the international level, the regulations are legally binding but their internal enforcement is heavily disputed. For example, in several recent rulings relating to the status of the WTO/GATT in European law, the European Court of Justice (Griller 2000; Zonnekeyn 2000), as well as the US Supreme Court, denied the direct effect of GATT provisions, essentially arguing that WTO provisions are not specific enough to contain clear instructions regulating conduct, but simply call upon member governments to resolve disputes by negotiation (Lee and Kennedy 1996; Backes 1995; Sack 1997). Although this argument is criticized by several law scholars it remains to be seen whether WTO/GATT law will be directly applied by national courts at any time soon (Petersmann 1997a).

3.3.2.3 Civil internalization   The German inter-*Länder* regulations theoretically offered rights to individuals and societal actors to participate in the application of the state aid control regulations. Theoretically, the competitors of potential beneficiaries have the right to seek judicial review of state aid decisions made by *Länder* governments (Zuleeg 1974; Bleckmann 1984). The local and regional administrative courts as well as the Federal German Administrative Court are responsible for these cases. However, there are few cases on record in which competitors have attempted to use court proceedings to stop subsidies being awarded to their competitors. All of these cases have failed because the Federal German Administrative Court has established a particularly high hurdle for the plaintiff to jump in order to achieve success. Essentially, the plaintiff has to prove that the particular subsidy paid to its competitor will certainly lead to its own bankruptcy. No enterprise has ever been able to discharge this burden of proof and, not surprisingly, few have attempted to do so. This judicial practice offers broad room for maneuver to state and federal governments that wish to distribute subsidies according to their political preferences.

At the European level, the picture is completely different. Both the European Commission and the European Court of Justice have opened up state aid cases to individuals and interested third parties (Slot 1999; Polley 1996). Hence, the Commission is not only receptive to information from third parties regarding state aid schemes, programs, or individual state aid cases which are in need of its consent, but it also publishes its intention to instigate a formal investigation of a specific program or case and invites interested third parties to submit their reasoned opinions. The European Court of Justice has also opened up the judicial review of state aid programs to interested third parties. In effect, this allows the competitors of state aid beneficiaries to challenge in court the Commission's decision to permit a given state aid program (Schneider 1996; Schütterle 1994).

At the international level, no such right of individual participation exists. In the context of the debate on the question of the direct applicability of WTO/GATT law, some argue that GATT regulations should not only be directly applicable but confer individual rights directly on individuals (Petersmann 1997a). This, however, is even more disputed than the question of direct effect. Hence, WTO/GATT regulations still only address their signatories' governments and do not offer the chance of participation to individuals or societal actors (Senti 2000; Trachtman and Moremen 2003).

In sum, the legalization approach predicts very well the comparative empirical findings over the whole timeframe and is able to provide a very useful dynamic explanation for the case of the EU. The EU's strong triadic dispute settlement, its legal effect in domestic national law and its societally enforceable rights clearly predict a higher rate of compliance than the WTO's weak triadic dispute settlement system, its legal effects at least on the signatories of the WTO treaty and the continuing absence of societally enforceable rights. The strong but unused triadic dispute settlement of the German inter-*Länder* case with no legal effect for the codices and no individually enforceable rights offers an obvious explanation for the lowest position in the comparative assessment of the degrees of compliance.

Furthermore, the legalization approach is also able to explain the slow development of the European state aid control regime. Although both the institutions and the primary law were in existence from the late 1950s, it took the Community more than thirty years to establish a clear legal precedence for European law over national law and to allow this precedence to become a simple matter of fact in the day-to-day issues relating to European state aid control (Slot 1990). Hence, the low degree of legal and civil internalization in the early years led to a comparatively low rate of compliance, which gradually improved as the legal and civil internalization of the European state aid control regulations increased.

3.3.3   The legitimacy approach

The legitimacy approach focuses on two important aspects in an attempt to explain the degree of compliance with a regulation: the participation of the addressees in the formulation of the regulation and the social acceptance of the regulation.

3.3.3.1 Participation of the addressees   With respect to the inter-*Länder* codices on state aids, all addressees fully participated in the decision making. All state governments in Germany were fully included in the formulation of the policy. Since the decision making was based on unanimity, each and every state government was in the position to veto any provision included in the codices (Bleckmann 1984; Breuel 1988). The codices were formulated in an ad hoc working group that consisted of representatives from the regional and federal ministries of economic affairs. They met regularly to discuss several proposals and to reach a compromise on the final draft (Eick 1981). This was not totally successful because the codices contain two footnotes in which two *Länder* governments express their dissatisfaction with the final text and suggest an alternative formulation. Nevertheless, the two codices were unanimously accepted by the *Länder* ministers for economic affairs. Hence, every addressee had a fair chance to influence the final agreement, to force the others to consider its position seriously and – if deemed necessary – to veto the draft, avoiding provisions which they considered it impossible to comply with.

In drawing up the federal law on the "Joint Task," the addressees were also included in the decision-making process, albeit with a somewhat reduced influence. The federal law is based on two Articles of the German constitution, which are themselves amendments to the *Grundgesetz* of 1969 to establish a sound legal basis for joint tasks. The amendment required a two-thirds majority in both houses of the German legislature. Thus, *Länder* governments commanding at least two-thirds of the votes had to agree to the new provisions in the constitution. Furthermore, the federal law itself necessitated the consent of a majority of state governments in the Upper House (*Bundesrat*), since it was one of those policies that constitutionally require the endorsement of the second chamber, whose veto cannot be overruled by a majority of the Lower House (*Bundestag*). The same rule applies to the decisions made with respect to the detailed subsidies programs, which were agreed upon in the context of the federal law. Here again, the consent of the federal government and the majority of the *Länder* governments is required. These provisions usually guarantee the fair and comprehensive inclusion of all addressees in the decision-making process (Nägele 1996). Not surprisingly, both the amendments to the constitution and to the federal law were passed unanimously by the Upper House of the German legislature.

Affected third parties, in particular the subsidized enterprises themselves, were only part of the decision-making process in so far as they were able to lobby the *Länder* governments. Furthermore, the intergovernmental decision-making process relating to the codices, which were mostly negotiated by expert groups behind closed doors, effectively limited societal influences, because credit-claiming and scapegoating opportunities encouraged the *Länder* governments to shield their decision making from unwelcome societal pressure (Moravcsik 1997b). Thus, while the addressees were fully included in the decision making, the wider circle of affected third parties was forced to rely on indirect strategies.

At the European level, the picture of fair and equal participation is mixed and complex. Formally, all addressees – the member state governments – had a very strong position in the formulation of policy. The six founding member states, in particular, were in the position to veto any undesirable provision and could thus participate fairly and fully in the decision-making process. The governments of later entrants to the Community were in a more difficult position because they had to accept the *acquis communautaire* if they wished to join. However, none requested any fundamental changes in this area of competition policy, only a few limited exemptions or transition periods. Hence, from a formal point of view, the existence of fair and equal participation for all the addressees is fully confirmed.

However, this result represents only part of the real empirical picture. As described above, most of the details of the European state aid control regime emanated from the judicial activism of the European Court of Justice, in which the member state governments played only one – albeit important – role. The vivid debate surrounding the negotiations leading up to the Maastricht and Amsterdam Treaties, with proposals to circumscribe or even revoke some of the competencies enjoyed by the European Court of Justice or explicitly exclude the home and justice affairs from judicial oversight by the European courts, sheds ample light on the widely shared governmental impression that the court had overstepped its powers too often, using them like a constitutional court to develop European law in ways that had not been envisaged by the founders of the treaties.

Although state aid control policy was certainly not at the center stage of this debate (even though the German *Länder*, for example, considered it to be a real constitutional issue, which endangered their ability to regulate their economies successfully), questions arise as to the validity of the formal role played by the member state governments in the process of developing this policy. At least some governments, some of the time, saw themselves as victims of an integration dynamic, which they considered to run against their interests and to be impossible to control (Burley and Mattli 1993).

So, while there are question marks related to the participation of all addressees of the EU state aid regulations, the question as to the participation of all affected third parties is also complicated. Formally, it seems that societal actors (enterprises benefiting from subsidies or their competitors) were excluded by the scapegoating and credit-claiming practices of national governments in intergovernmental bargaining situations (Rieger 1995). Since most of the state aid control rules were established via case law, the actual picture is more diverse. In a lot of state aid cases, affected third parties were able to have their interests recognized through the consultation processes followed by the Commission or via judicial review by the European Court of Justice. Not only the addressees, but also some affected parties, were able to influence the EU decision-making process on state aid control regulations.

For the international WTO/GATT level the question of input legitimacy, the fair and equal participation of all addressees in the formulation of the rules, is easy to answer. Not only did all governments fully participate in the formulation of the rule but until 1994 they even had the power to veto any panel rulings which did not suit their interests (Senti 1986).

The old GATT, as well as the new WTO, certainly exhibits unequal power distributions among its members. For years the USA occupied the position of the hegemonic leader of the world trade system. This has somewhat changed over the years as both Japan and the European Union have increased their influence over trade policy matters. Still these three powers dominate the GATT/WTO system. Nevertheless, since 1947 no state has ever been forced to enter the GATT, the WTO or its multiple revisions. Thus, the unequal power distribution does not change the basic impression of the full participation of all addressees in the formulation of the rules (Grieco 1990).

With the strengthening of the judicial character and the absence of traditional diplomatic bargaining in resolving WTO disputes, one might expect a gradual reduction in the strong participation of the addressees in the development of the rules. But it is still too early to detect any major steps in this direction in the realm of GATT state aid control.

3.3.3.2 Social acceptance   The question of the social acceptance of regulations refers to the wider audience and to public opinion. In this respect, the public debate in Germany over subsidies seems to present an extremely fragmented and arbitrary picture. Hence, it is very difficult even just to enumerate the different arenas and perspectives, not to mention summarizing the debate in any systematic way. Economic experts and political advisers present a reasonably clear picture. Up until the early 1970s state aids were seen as an aspect of Keynesian market regulation, whereas, from the late 1980s onwards, the neoclassic supply-side and monetarist perspectives came to dominate and they tended to see state aids as part of the problem. According to this perspective, state aids impede market forces and lead to larger government budgets, higher taxes, higher inflation, and higher interest rates and, hence, to less economic growth. Not surprisingly, since the 1980s practically all major economic experts in Germany have called for a massive reduction in state aids and this perspective has became quasi-hegemonic in the German economic discourse (Krieger-Boden and Lammers 1996; Werner 1995).

Regarding interest groups, the picture is different. When the budget committee of the German *Bundestag*, the Lower House of the legislature, organized a comprehensive hearing on state aids in 1981 and invited more than sixty non-governmental organizations and interest groups to present written statements and defend their positions in an open discussion, to the great surprise of the Parliament only around thirty groups bothered to submit written statements and only twenty sent a representative to the hearing itself. Furthermore, all responses – whether from the agricultural, coal and steel, textiles, or other sectors – acknowledged that subsidies are generally detrimental to the economy. However, in every case the interest groups forcefully argued why their situation was exceptional and not only why the already existing subsidies were so necessary but also why they should be increased. No interest group was prepared to name a policy area where the government should start with a reduction in financial support (Deutscher Bundestag 1982).

Furthermore, the broader public debate only rarely concerns state aids. There are very many cases or instances in which subsidies have become the focus of the German media. Regular occasions are the yearly report of the German Court of Auditors and the yearly report of the German Association of Taxpayers. Both, however, tend to focus more on cases of corruption and misspent funds than on subsidies. This leaves us with the few exceptional cases which managed to enter the headlines: the financial support given by Baden-Württemberg for the new Daimler plant in Rastatt (Kiemmer 1986); the subsidies given by Saxony for the Volkswagen plant in Mosel; the rescue of the construction company Holzmann by Chancellor Gerhard Schröder; and the acquisition of the Salzgitter steel company by the regional government of Lower Saxony (headed by the then governor, Gerhard Schröder). But once again, the resulting debate was rather confusing and incoherent. While the first example (Daimler) received negative headlines (except in the city of Rastatt), the second case (Volkswagen) involved a protracted dispute between the European Commission, the federal government, West German newspapers and the regional East German media (Nicolaysen 1996; Hrbek 1996; Falkenkötter 1996). While the Commission, the West German newspapers and the federal government considered the money to be misspent, the East German media were anxious to keep Volkswagen committed to East German employment. The last two examples (Holzmann, Salzgitter) are the result of Chancellor Schröder's crusade to protect endangered employment opportunities in Germany, despite bitter criticism from economic experts. While the support for Daimler was heavily criticized for giving money to an already rich company which could afford to pay for the cost of the new plant itself, Schröder's two rescue actions received widespread public support, percieved as courageous state interventions to prevent the big banks and shareholder-value ideologists from destroying thousands of employment opportunities in the German construction and steel industries.

Unsurprisingly, the codices never appeared in any mainstream public debate on economic questions and the federal law on the "Joint Task" is unknown beyond the circles of experts on financial and regional policies. Symptomatic of this, the major newspaper archive on economic matters in Germany, the Hamburg-based HWWA, does not collect newspaper articles under the special keyword of state aids or subsidies. Rather, these articles are included in files on regional and structural policy, specific companies, budget matters or R & D policy. In Germany, state aids can obviously be considered a form of clientele politics, with a strong influence coming from small, well-organized interest groups, which stand to benefit from these subsidies, but with a weak public opinion, displaying oscillating reactions to different headline cases of state aids, largely ignoring the matter altogether. Hence, a paradox results in which, for example, major German newspapers readily support cutbacks in state aids but this does not lend any power to the bid to implement the codices.

In the European context, the question of social acceptance offers about as fragmented and incoherent a picture as the German case. Until the 1970s, the sectoral epistemic discourse of economists tended to follow a coherent Keynesian pattern of demand-side regulation for the economies of the member states. The European level was seen as a useful instrument for harmonizing these national policies and preventing any form of free-rider or beggar-my-neighbor strategies. Basically, state aid was seen as a valuable tool to correct politically intolerable market results, especially in the realm of structural and regional policies. This, however, has changed drastically since the 1980s. While many North European economists, as well as some of their very influential Italian colleagues, have changed their minds and now consider state aids to be a major cause of economic problems in Europe, most of their Spanish, Portuguese and Greek colleagues have not followed the new neoclassic, supply-side oriented, monetarist paradigm. Rather, they still consider subsidies to be necessary instruments in a government's toolbox for improving the underdeveloped regions in their country. Hence, the sectoral discourse did not project a clear picture of how to deal with the question of state aids and state aid control.

At the level of the interest groups, a two-tier strategy has developed over the years. On the one hand, major interest groups created European associations as well as installing their own representatives in Brussels to lobby the Commission directly. On the other hand, other major interest groups attempted to pressure their national governments into not giving in to the European control measures and to continue their traditional patterns of distribution to private enterprises. This double strategy exploited the opportunity presented by the missing European transnational discourse on such economic problems (Kohler-Koch 1992, 1994; Eising and Kohler-Koch 1994). The media is mostly still nationally oriented and tends to think of the EU as an aspect of foreign policy, where national interests have to be defended. Due to this fragmentation, special interest groups are able to avoid being caught politically for lobbying at the European as well as the national level, employing different arguments, sometimes with conflicting aims.

While this fragmentation might increase the chances of a member state government cheating or free-riding, it can also lead to classic scapegoating strategies by member states and furthermore, it shields the European Commission from much of the media pressure usually directed at national governments. Hence, with respect to the European state aid control regime, the effects of such a fragmented sectoral and general public discourse are not easily discernible. Some aspects support the perspective that such fragmented public opinion offers the opportunity to national governments to evade European measures aimed at curbing their use of subsidies. At the same time, the very same elements can be seen as ample evidence for the increased room for maneuver enjoyed both by the national governments and by the European Commission in their task of reducing the influence of strong national interest groups (Moravcsik 1997b; Rieger 1995).

The question of social acceptance in the case of WTO disputes over state aids leads to a more straightforward answer than in the other two cases. Once again the sectoral epistemic discourse and broader public opinion are very much fragmented. The economists are divided between those from the North, with their more or less hegemonic position based on neoclassic supply-side arguments, and those from the South, who provide very articulate arguments in favor of developing economies that favor the opening up of Northern markets (especially to agricultural products from the South) but also the use of subsidies to improve developing economies. In this epistemic discourse it is practically impossible to draw clear boundaries between the different schools and academic factions. Even proponents of neoclassic ideas sometimes use Keynesian arguments and, during the 1990s development economics, reconsidered many of the typically neoclassic doctrines. Hence, no clear picture arises out of the epistemic debates over state aids.

The wider public debate is rather heavily fragmented along national boundaries. It is still very easy for governments or interest groups to appeal to the widespread protectionist sentiments of the public by pointing to unfair protectionist practices that are allegedly exercised by other countries. This is used to justify taking action by, for example, subsidizing the allegedly negatively affected domestic industry. There are many examples for such cases: shipbuilding with European and Asian competitors; car manufacturing with US and Asian competitors; the aviation industry with European and US competitors; steel production with competition between the USA and newly industrialized countries. In these cases the extremely fragmented and nationally oriented public opinion provided governments with a double opportunity: on the one hand to create a scapegoat given that the public is not well informed about GATT questions and the situation in other countries; and, on the other hand, to cheat and free-ride, since fragmented and nationally oriented media and public opinion sometimes press for protectionism and at the very least do not sanction it.

Altogether the legitimacy approach only poorly predicts the comparative empirical result. The case of the German *Länder* showed full addressee participation, some indirect, if weak, participation for affected third parties and a fragmented public opinion on the issue of cutting back subsidies. The case of the WTO subsidies control regulations looks similar: the full participation of the addressees; some limited indirect form of inclusion for affected third parties; and a fragmented public opinion on the question of compliance with WTO/GATT subsidies control rules. The EU case follows the same pattern: full participation of the addressees; some incorporation of affected third parties, via consultation and case law; and an equally fragmented public opinion on the issue of EU subsidies control. On the basis of these empirical findings, the legitimacy approach would predict a ranking placing the German inter-*Länder* case and the WTO case in the same position, with the EU being in a somewhat better position due to the stronger influence of affected third parties. This prediction, however, only poorly matches the empirical results, which clearly show a major difference in the rate of compliance that is enjoyed by the German regime as opposed to the WTO regime as well as a similar difference between the WTO and the EU regimes.

3.3.4   *The management approach*

This theoretical approach focuses, on the one hand, on the question of responsiveness and deliberation in relation to the process of implementing state aid control regulations and on the ability of a particular political level to use this deliberation to feed back into any reform of regulation. On the other hand the question of capacities and resources to empower the addressees to comply with the rules is of central importance.

3.3.4.1 Reflexivity and responsiveness   At the German inter-*Länder* level, some form of administrative feedback mechanism exists which could function as the institutional basis for fostering deliberation between those administrators responsible for the implementation of the subsidies control codices. The most important institutional forums are the committees which bring together the administrators of the *Länder*'s economics ministries, which meet regularly to discuss common problems of competition policy, as well as the conference of the *Länder*'s finance ministers, which could be called upon to decide politically difficult questions. In both cases, opportunities for arguing and deliberation exist, but in the case of subsidies control, strategic bargaining seems to be the rule. While some experts hint at the possibility of using these forums to discuss compliance crises, whether bilaterally or multilaterally, the reality of continuing compliance problems reveals that these discussions do not strengthen compliance with these codices. Members of the committee of experts on competition policy are especially critical of the subsidies race taking place between the *Länder*.[13] However, no attempt has ever been made to reform the codices or strengthen their enforcement. Rather, the central argument for keeping these codices was that without them the administrators would have no yardstick with which to distinguish "good" industrial policy from "bad" subsidization. But in certain instances, every administrator is quite prepared to ignore the codices if it is to his advantage to do so.

At the EU level even more formal and informal instruments for deliberation and feedback exist especially – but not only – through recourse to legal procedures. Most importantly, the Commission opens up its informal as well as its formal investigations to all interested parties, which provides multiple opportunities to discuss problems and introduce different

---

[13] In the anonymous questionnaire several *Länder* administrators hinted that in cases of grave non-compliance they were prepared to use the committee meetings to confront the non-compliant *Länder* representative. But, at the same time, they also acknowledged that there was not much they could do if this representative stuck to his guns. So, while arguing and deliberation seems to be an option, the result resembles the outcome of strategic bargaining.

opinions. Furthermore, the European state aid control regime provides for multiple opportunities of access to the courts and, since it basically develops through case law, it includes various feedback opportunities. However, it is difficult to support this prima facie institutional perspective with empirical evidence. There is no question that the creation and development of rules, especially through the process of judicial interpretation and the introduction of principles by establishing precedents, has to be seen as an inherently discursive and reflexive process, in which primary rules guide the process of producing applicable and at the same time generalizable solutions for deciding about real life state aid cases. As such, the years up until the 1980s can be seen as a time of common learning and the discursive development of European state aid control law (Volcansek 1997; Armstrong 1998; Easson 1994). However, since the 1990s the decisions on real life cases – whether notified or not – involving the basically well-established system of state aid control regulations in the EU are essentially stripped of any discursive elements, except for maybe a few essential landmark cases. The ratio of landmark cases to simple rule application cases has decreased rapidly over the last ten years because of the now well-established system of state aid control in the EU.

Beyond these special state aid cases involving judicial review, other cases exhibit the unmistakable characteristics of intense strategic bargaining in the shadow of the law. Especially high profile cases, which involve national finance ministers, prime ministers, the Commissioner for Competition Policy or the Commission President, are classic cases of interest-based political bargaining. National cabinet ministers, pressured by special interests or the election promises they have given previously, usually attempt to force the Commission into accepting a bargain, which allows them to continue with their national subsidies program. In this setting of power politics, threats and allegations are commonly used to intimidate the Commission, for example by threatening to use the veto in another policy area. At the same time, the Commission attempts to get the agreement of all other member state governments, if it is not prepared to accept the state aid scheme at issue (Van Miert 2000).

For this reason, it is extremely difficult to judge the influence of such discursive processes on the actual degree of compliance. The most important and – with hindsight – the most successful discourses in this policy area took place during the late 1970s and 1980s. While this ran in parallel with a low degree of compliance with the primary legislation that was already in place, it paved the way for a dramatic improvement in compliance during the 1990s, just when the discursive processes seem to have been marginalized. And, since the establishment of the Advisory Committee on State Aids in 1999, it remains to be seen whether this comitology approach can once again improve the chances for arguing and discursive decision making in the realm of state aid control at the European level (Joerges and Neyer 1997b).

At the international level, empirical evidence of common discourse, understanding and arguing is also very limited. Until 1994, all state aid disputes involving the GATT were strictly dominated by strategic bargaining because the losing party was able to veto the final ruling and, hence, had no incentive to bargain in the shadow of the law or even seek common ground with the complainant. This has certainly changed with the introduction of the new treaty and the WTO in 1994. At least the dispute settlement procedure, with its Panels and Appellate Body, has become more legalized, tending to strengthen the possibility for discourses, arguing and persuading and reducing the effectiveness of simple strategic bargaining to realize one's own interests (McLarty 1994). Unfortunately, the real life disputes over subsidies since 1994 have shown no sign of the parties involved reaching a common understanding on state aids. However, there has been a new common understanding to take the dispute settlement procedures of the WTO seriously (Kelemen 2001; Hilf 2001; and Steinberg 2002).

In this respect, the member governments of the new WTO/GATT are certainly using the reformed dispute settlement procedure as a new instrument for furthering their national interests. And, although major parts of the dispute settlement process itself might contain discursive and deliberative elements – especially those aspects related to the increased judicial review of cases on the basis of the GATT and its annexes – the whole area of dispute settlement continues to be part of a larger process of strategic bargaining. The example mentioned earlier in this chapter of the successive dispute settlement proceedings between Canada and Brazil over the subsidies given by each country to civil aircraft exporters illustrates this strategic use of the dispute settlement procedure very well. Not only did Brazil refuse to honor the Panel's decisions and the rulings of the Appellate Body, but it used every means available to prolong the case. It also established a parallel case against Canada with which to create a bargaining chip for any bilateral resolution of the dispute. Canada still refrains from applying the countervailing duties which the WTO permitted it to use against Brazil. Hence, it remains to be seen whether the WTO is able to follow the European example and develop a coherent body of case law, adjusting the law on the books to the actual problem at hand (Weiler 2001).

3.3.4.2 Capacities and resources   Since all addressees of the regulations on the three different political levels are governments and since the only action required to fulfill the intentions of the rules is to refrain from distributing public money to enterprises in their respective jurisdictions, state aid cases do not entail any compliance problems due to the lack of capacities or resources on the side of the addressees of the regulations. All governments or governmental agencies basically command the necessary instruments and means to live up to their commitments. They do not depend on societal domestic implementation of the rules and even governments in developing countries generally are able to fulfill the requirements without the financial or technical support of the international community.

In sum, the management perspective offers a reasonable explanation for the comparative empirical evidence of compliance with the state aid control regulations at the different political levels. At the German inter-*Länder* level, institutional provisions that allow for formal or informal deliberation between the administrators of the state aid control codices exist and are – at least partially – used. However, reviewing the empirical evidence, it is clear that they do not increase compliance with the codices but rather – to put it harshly – contribute to a common understanding, which is to stick to the codices as some kind of common yardstick but not to bother too much with their details. At the WTO/GATT level, ever more deliberative feedback channels have been created, especially by strengthening the judicial character of the dispute settlement procedure, but actual discussions are nevertheless still characterized by strategic bargaining. At the EU level, institutions and procedures promoting deliberation have existed since the early 1960s and until the 1980s were the basis for the development of secondary law in the realm of state aid control. However, since the 1990s most state aid control cases have exhibited strong signs of strategic bargaining in the shadow of existing (case) law. Furthermore, the addressees on all three political levels are in command of all necessary instruments and means for compliance and, hence, possess the required institutional capacities to adhere to the rules.

Against this empirical background the reflexivity approach would predict the following compliance ranking prior to the 1980s: German inter-*Länder* codices; the WTO/GATT; and finally the EU. Since the 1990s, it would predict that the German inter-*Länder* codices would remain with the worst record on compliance, but that the WTO would manage to achieve the same rank as the EU. The approach faces major difficulties in coming to grips with the strange German situation in which formal and informal channels for arguing exist, but which are not used to strengthen compliance but rather to achieve mutual agreement on the necessity of the codices without investing them with binding force.

3.4   Conclusion: Comparing compliance with state aid control regimes at three political levels

The previous chapters presented the empirical evidence of the rate of compliance with state aid control regulations at three political levels: the national, inter-*Länder* system in Germany; the state aid control provisions of the European Union; and, finally, the rules on control of state subsidies of the GATT/WTO system. Furthermore, they delineated the performance of the four different theoretical approaches in an attempt to explain this comparative empirical result. This leaves two tasks for the conclusion. First, to compare the performance of the different theoretical perspectives and to assess which of these approaches offers the best overall explanation for the comparative empirical result. And, secondly, to determine what insights the results of this comparative analysis of the effects of regulations on the behavior of their addressees has for the special character of European politics. Is it possible to specify the *sui generis* character of the European multilevel polity?

3.4.1   Summary of the performances of the different theoretical perspectives

The empirical evidence of compliance with state aid control regimes at the different political levels offers up a surprising ranking:

German inter-*Länder* codices < WTO/GATT < EU.

The four different theoretical perspectives on compliance reveal different capacities to predict the comparative empirical result. Two theoretical approaches clearly performed better than the rest: first, *rational institutionalism*, albeit only since the 1990s; secondly, the *legalization approach* for the whole timeframe. This allows us to give some tentative answers to the question of what is necessary to secure a high rate of compliance with regulatory rules that are designed to prevent free-riding in a common market. From the results of this theoretically-oriented, comparative analysis of state aid control rules at the three different political levels, two very important insights reveal themselves as potential answers. On the one hand there is the classic answer of the importance of strong monitoring and sanctioning capacities, but on the other hand, and equally important, is the high degree of legal and civil internalization as well as the existence of strong judicial instruments that maintain direct links with societal actors and lower courts.

The classic answer of strong monitoring and sanctioning still makes a big difference. It is not enough to rely on the voluntary participation of a regulation's addressees to ensure a good rate of compliance. Nor is it enough to wait for complaints to come forward and then to blame other addressees for not having complied with the rules. And, finally, it is not enough merely to attempt to reconcile the diverging interests of the parties in dispute – especially in policy areas where the distribution of money is central and, hence, there is the opportunity for quick compromise. Rather, it is necessary to install an independent third party – an independent common agent – and entrust it to monitor the national or regional systems autonomously. This task must be supported by strict rules. For example, any non-notified aid scheme must be considered automatically illegal; any form of state aid has to be approved by the independent agent, even if generally allowed; and the common agent must have the right to obtain the information necessary for its decisions or, if this is impossible, to decide on the basis of the information available. Very useful in this respect is the possibility of using information provided by societal actors – interested third parties – which enable it to avoid the governmental bottleneck.

The same applies to the task of sanctioning non-compliant behavior. It is not enough to rely on the demand to abolish the state aid scheme alone and permit the plaintiffs to introduce countervailing measures if a defendant ignores the decision reached by the common agent or judicial body. Rather, it is necessary to force the government to recover the subsidies with interest, to blame the government publicly so that its non-compliant behavior is there for all to see, and to seek additional penalties if the government refuses to obey the decision handed down by the agent.

However, the institutionalization of a system of strict monitoring and sanctioning is not sufficient on its own. Common agents must not only be created, but must also have the power and will to enforce the rules. In a one-sided political setting, this is sometimes rather difficult to achieve. Strategic bargaining usually comes to dominate the material content of the decision as well as the procedural dimension of the decision-making process. In this respect, politically-based control of governmental spending programs is on its own always in danger of becoming captured by the interests of stronger member governments.

It is here that the second important aspect of securing compliance becomes relevant. There must be some form of judicial control over the decisions that are reached by both the common agent and the member governments (Zangl 2001). Such judicial oversight should include the powers enjoyed by a constitutional court as well as direct links to the societal actors and lower courts. Moreover, the direct effect and supremacy of those rules intended to regulate the markets should be firmly established. The judicialization of rule implementation allows member governments to settle disputes between themselves and the common agent or other member governments. It also creates the opportunity to clarify the rules, expand the task of the common agent to unforeseen cases and, finally, legalize and civilly internalize the whole process into the legal systems of the regulatory addressees. Successful internalization transforms most rule implementation into a routine, ritualized process and, hence, virtually guarantees a continuously high rate of compliance.

While the first aspect – monitoring and sanctioning – attempts to curb the free-riding problem by introducing strict controls or clear threats of harsh sanctions and, ultimately, aims to achieve some degree of trust between the addressees of the rules, the second aspect focuses on depoliticizing and judicializing regulatory implementation. This development initially requires some degree of trust, but holds out the promise of comparatively stable relations between the addressees and the common agent. Stable expectations of individual behavior are the ultimate goal of any form of rules. This is only present when a rule possesses strong legal character and there is equally strong judicial oversight as well as some form of social routine, which incorporates the provisions into the common set of behavioral guidelines.

3.4.2   The compliance perspective: What is so special about European politics?

On the basis of the empirical analysis of compliance with state aid control regimes at the three different political levels, it is certainly a daring move to put forward major conclusions on the special character of European politics. However, the results of the study certainly point to some aspects which might help to identify the special characteristics of the *sui generis*, multilevel governance system of the European Union. The analysis of the regulation of the governmental free-riding problem in common markets suggests at least two important points.

First, successful monitoring and sanctioning is possible beyond the nation-state and can be done without a hegemonic power distribution or constant threats of exclusion or retaliation, by a common agent without centralized power. This sounds unsurprising, especially if the European Union is anyway seen as something special. But it contradicts the expectations of major analyses of international and European politics and, to a certain extent, it liberates the monitoring and sanctioning approach to compliance from the bias of being bound inseparably to the hierarchical structures of the nation-state. But, this power of monitoring and sanctioning beyond the nation-state is only effective and stable if combined with a second element.

This second element is law beyond the nation-state, which is not classic international law oriented towards the preservation of state sovereignty, but rather law beyond the state, which addresses itself directly to both governments and societal or private actors. Such individually oriented law beyond the state provides private parties with autonomous rights that go beyond and can sometimes be used against their governments.

The European Union's law of state aid control is the combination of independent powers beyond the nation-state and individual-oriented law beyond the nation-state. This combination is certainly unique. At the inter-*Länder* level in Germany, the independent power was not created (and the federal level not used) and individual rights were blocked by the Federal Administrative Court by its imposition of an extremely high burden of proof which plaintiffs must surmount to establish their injuries caused by the negative effects of state aids awarded to their competitors. Also at the international level, the GATT and WTO system has not (yet?) created any independent power or any individual rights to participate in the implementation process.

4 Domestic limits of supranational law: Comparing compliance with European and international foodstuffs regulations

Jürgen Neyer

4.1 Risk regulation in the EU and the WTO

The trade in foodstuffs is a particularly interesting candidate for the comparative analysis of compliance with inconvenient market-correcting rules. Analyzing foodstuffs policy underlines the fact that regulatory policy involves a number of difficult regulatory issues, such as the need to integrate expertise, the problem of dealing with conflicting points of view concerning those risks attributable to foodstuffs and/or nutritional habits, the growing importance of new concerns about animal welfare and the environmental dimensions of foodstuff production, as well as the impact of cultural traditions on production and consumption. Furthermore, because of their proximity to the everyday life of consumers, foodstuff issues rank prominently on the public agenda of domestic politics and, as such, can easily become politically sensitive issues.

A comparative analysis of compliance with foodstuffs regulations, however, is difficult to conduct across all three of the levels employed in this project. Due to the increasing relevance of European and international policies to the member states, important regulations are often authored by either international or European authorities (cf. Schlacke 1998; Hilf and Reuß 1997; and Ritter 1997) without reserving many competencies for the federal level. This chapter accordingly avoids conducting a comparison across all three levels and instead concentrates on comparing compliance with the rules of the World Trade Organization (WTO) with the compliance enjoyed by the rules of the European Union (EU). Although it might seem unfair to compare the WTO with an institution that some have already described as possessing some form of statehood (Caporaso 1996; Majone 1994; and Evers 1994), and which builds on nearly fifty years of experience in dealing with cases of non-compliance, such a comparison is useful for a number of reasons: both institutions are supranational, in that they have the competence to settle disputes authoritatively and rely on enforcement mechanisms to make them effective; and in both systems, it is the member states which have the monopoly of force and the competence to implement rules.

By comparing overall compliance with European and international foodstuff rules as well as by looking at two more specific cases of non-compliance, the chapter indicates that neither elaborate enforcement mechanisms nor a high degree of legalization is able to guarantee compliance with inconvenient commitments. Although both are important for the day-to-day conduct of compliance management, they are inadequate in situations where rules enjoy only limited social acceptance. The EU and the WTO are therefore well advised to emphasize the participation of affected parties to avoid any such situation. That argument is advanced in three steps. Section 4.2 will briefly introduce the basic rules that guide the European and international trade in foodstuffs. Section 4.3 presents some aggregate data on the overall level of compliance with WTO and EU rules, and it introduces two cases of open non-compliance. In section 4.4, the four theoretical perspectives which seek to explain compliance and which are outlined in chapters 1 and 2 are employed to explain the values of the dependent variable.

4.2   Basic trade rules in the EU and WTO

The ban on arbitrary trade restrictions is one of the basic rules of international and EU trade policy. In the EU, Articles 28 and 29 prohibit any quantitative restrictions on imports and exports as well as any measures to the same effect. Furthermore, the first paragraph of Article 31 states that "Member States shall adjust any State monopolies of a commercial character so as to ensure that no discrimination regarding the conditions under which goods are procured and marketed exists between nationals of Member States." They must also "refrain from introducing any new measure which is contrary to the principles laid down in paragraph 1 or which restricts the scope of the Articles dealing with the prohibition of customs duties and quantitative restrictions between Member States." Article 28 has become a particularly powerful tool for liberalizing trade in the EC. Interpreting the famous *Cassis de Dijon* decision of the European Court of Justice, the Commission declared in 1979 that it would take it as arguing for a "principle of mutual recognition." In the Commission's view, the ECJ's decision implies that all products legally marketed in one member state must not be restricted in any other member state.[1]

---

[1] Commission communication on the implications of the ECJ Judgment of 20 February 1979 in Case 120/78 ("*Cassis de Dijon*"), OJ 1980 No. C256/2–3.

This liberal bias of the EC's market-making regime, however, is limited by a number of exemptions that are contained in Article 28 (formerly Article 30) of the EC Treaty, which provides that "[t]he provisions of Articles 28 and 29 shall not preclude prohibitions or restrictions on imports, exports or goods in transit justified on grounds of public morality, public policy or public security; the protection of health and life of humans, animals or plants; the protection of national treasures possessing artistic, historic or archaeological value; or the protection of industrial and commercial property." It has never been entirely clear how the tension between the liberal principles and the legitimate exemptions could be resolved. Instead, the EC has relied on a case-by-case approach to decide each dispute as to whether or not an import restriction that has been imposed by a member state is in accordance with Article 28. In foodstuffs policy, this procedural approach was supported by the Commission's Standing Committee for Foodstuffs. Although the Standing Committee is not invested with the formal legal task of deciding whether or not a member state's action is in accordance with the criteria set out in Article 28, in practice it serves as a forum for member states to voice their grievances, justify safeguard measures or demand the withdrawal of unacceptable measures (cf. Joerges and Neyer 1997a). Interestingly, however, both the Standing Committee and the Commission placed particular reliance on a scientific body – the Scientific Committee on Foodstuffs – in their decision making. Supported by the Commission's practice of only accepting health-related and scientifically supported arguments as relevant to the justification of protectionist measures in foodstuffs policy, the Scientific Committee has contributed a great deal to the EC basing its foodstuffs policy on scientific foundations.

Structurally similar to the EU, the GATT is based on a parallel between the principles of non-discrimination, reciprocity and liberalization as well as a multitude of exemptions that define and restrict the normative framework described. To be sure, just as in the EU, the basic purpose of the GATT is to liberalize trade. Its aim is to prevent governments imposing or continuing with any measures that restrain or distort international trade. Such measures include tariffs, quotas, international taxes and regulations which discriminate against imports, as well as subsidy and dumping practices, state trading, customs procedures and a plethora of other "non-tariff measures" which discourage trade. Article I states that government import or export regulations should not discriminate against other countries' products (the so-called "most-favored-nation" clause). Any advantage, favor, privilege, or immunity granted to one contracting party must also be granted immediately and unconditionally to all other contracting parties. In the same vein, Article III sets up a "national treatment" obligation of non-discrimination against imports. Contracting parties are required to impose no internal taxes or regulations that afford protection to domestic production. Imported products must be accorded treatment no less favorable than domestic products. Article II holds that the tariff limits expressed in each contracting party's "schedule of concessions" shall not be exceeded. Interpreting the GATT as being an agreement that is solely oriented towards free trade, however, would be misleading. The GATT also recognizes a number of exemptions, such as those necessary for national security, health and morals, as well as safeguard or escape clauses (which allow for temporary restrictions on imports), free trade agreements and customs unions.

An instructive example for studying how the WTO copes with the tension between free trade and legitimate exceptions is provided by the Agreement on the Application of Sanitary and Phytosanitary Measures (SPS Agreement). The SPS Agreement sets out the basic rules for food safety and animal and plant health standards. It allows countries to set their own standards but requires them to be based on science. They should be applied only to the extent necessary to protect human, animal or plant life or health and should not arbitrarily or unjustifiably discriminate between countries where identical or similar conditions prevail. Member countries are encouraged to use international standards, guidelines and recommendations where they exist. However, members may use measures which result in higher standards if there is a scientific justification. They can also set higher standards which are based on an appropriate assessment of the risks, as long as the approach is consistent and not arbitrary.

As the brief description above has shown, both in European and in international foodstuff politics, the tension between free trade and legitimate protection is largely resolved by reference to scientific expertise.[2] The fact that scientific expertise has been given such a central role is mainly due to the technical innovations taking place in food production and the immediate relevance of issues of public health to the field. Since the 1950s, the foodstuffs industry has increasingly been using additives, coloring agents, preservatives, etc. In European as well as in international foodstuffs politics it is now generally accepted that in the interest of consumer protection these new production technologies require scientific control to guard against possible health risks (Somogyi 1999).

While the necessity of scientific foodstuffs control in general is undisputed, the controversy focuses on the issue whether scientific expertise can be regarded as the only valid criterion for deciding on the legitimacy

---

[2] For EC law see Joerges (1997); for WTO law see Victor (2000).

of trade restrictions that are imposed by individual states. In particular, the so-called precautionary principle, according to which a state is permitted to impose trade restrictions in a case where health risks cannot be completely ruled out,[3] appears to clash with the principle of scientific certainty. Hence, international trading circles regard the precautionary principle with a lot of skepticism. The principle holds that in order to impose trade barriers it is not necessary to establish a scientifically verifiable causal connection (e.g. that a certain concentration of a harmful substance results in a risk to health) – mere suspicion that there might be such a connection is sufficient. This, it is argued, creates an easy invitation to abuse, giving a state the opportunity to legitimize any trade restriction it so chooses. Therefore, the prohibition of arbitrary discrimination and the requirement on states to substantiate their exemptions scientifically are two core principles that are beyond dispute in European as well as international food politics. The acceptance of both these principles reflects the belief that no other standard of assessment is capable of achieving such a high level of public health protection alongside fair trade practices.

4.3   Compliance with European and WTO rules

Despite the ban on arbitrary trade restrictions, non-compliance, i.e. the unilateral hindrance of the free movement of goods by the authorities of a member state without scientific proof of a risk to health, continues. Secondary Community legislation and Commission action based on Article 28 have resulted in the principle of free trade being gradually incorporated into the legal systems and administrative procedures of the member states. However, cases have always existed in which the principle's specific application has led to a certain product being found to be unacceptable in the country of destination.[4] EU data shows that, between 1996 and 1998, 245 violations of the principle of mutual recognition were recorded.[5] Of these, 25 percent were in the foodstuffs sector. Foodstuffs policy is the most affected policy area of the EU. Further statistical support for the omnipresence of compliance issues can be derived from

---

[3] On the precautionary principle in general see Di Fabio (1996). For its relevance to international foodstuffs politics see Eggers (1998); for European foodstuffs politics see Christoforou (2003) and the Commission's Communication on the Application of the Precautionary Principle (COM(2000) 1 final.).

[4] See COM(99) 301 final, 20.

[5] Commission Communication to the European Parliament and the Council: Mutual Recognition in the Context of Successive Measures for the Single Market Action Plan, Orig. Doc. CA15-0136/03/01/00.

Table 4.1 *Infringement procedures in the EU, 1995–1999ᵃ*

	1995	1996	1997	1998	1999
(1) formal notice	1,016	1,142	1,461	1,101	1,075
(2) reasoned opinion	192	435	334	675	460
(3) legal action at the ECJ	72	92	121	123	178
Ratio (3):(1) expressed as percentage	7.1	8.0	8.3	11.2	16.6

ᵃ *Source:* COM(2001) 92 final, 72.

table 4.1, which shows the total number of cases in which the Commission has instituted infringement proceedings against a member state in recent years.

What is most striking about this survey is that inadequate compliance with European law is obviously a significant problem. In each of the years that were monitored, the Commission had to send more than 1,000 letters of formal notice to member states regarding their alleged violations of EC regulations (the first stage of the infringement procedure). Equally striking is the fact that the ratio between the number of formal notices and the instigation of legal action is deteriorating significantly. Whilst only 7.1 percent of all alleged violations in 1995 were dealt with by the ECJ, this ratio has increased over the years and stood at 16.6 percent in 1999. Interpreting this data, however, is not easy. One reason could be an increasing reluctance on the part of the member states to shoulder the domestic cost of adapting to intensified economic interpenetration. Yet the worsening ratio could also signify a certain weariness on the part of the Commission, which is reluctant to conduct time-consuming negotiations with unwilling member states and is increasingly prepared to rely on legal enforcement. This would come as no surprise, considering that, at the end of 1999, the list of cases which had been decided by the ECJ but not yet implemented by the non-compliant member state came to the impressive figure of eighty-two. In three instances member state implementation has been overdue since 1990 (with appellate proceedings or the Article 228 procedure currently in progress). In one instance implementation had been overdue since 1988 (present status: the Commission has applied for the imposition of an administrative fine) (COM(99) 301 final, 247–258). Thus, regulatory compliance in the EU can by no means be taken for granted. Often it is only achieved after lengthy, time-consuming negotiations, with both sides applying legal and political pressure in no-holds-barred negotiations. Although permanent compliance crises are hard to detect, initial non-compliance seems to be a common feature of the EU.

In the WTO, the principle of non-discrimination is equally beyond dispute. But here, even more so than in the EU, a great number of cases of inadequate compliance come onto the political agenda. A direct comparison of WTO and EU data is difficult, because the WTO does not compile a systematic survey of the implementation of WTO law. The data available on the extent of its members' compliance is limited to cases dealt with by the WTO's Dispute Settlement Body (DSB). This points to the second fundamental difficulty of conducting a comparison: apart from the obligation on member states to report their national trade policy measures to the Trade Policy Review Mechanism (TPRM), the WTO does not have the competence to control compliance with WTO law autonomously, let alone to highlight instances of non-compliance and address them by legal means. As a result, only those disputes in which one member complains about the conduct of another and applies to the DSB are known. This renders the entire process of regulatory compliance a highly politicized business in which issues of non-compliance are the more likely to become legal disputes the better organized and the more powerful domestic pressure groups are (see Sevilla 1997).

A WTO survey, conducted in spring 2000, lists a total of 192 complaints since 1992, referring to 150 alleged violations.[6] By 1 April 2000, thirty-two of these had resulted in a final report by the DSB or the Appellate Body (AB). Although an evaluation of the extent of compliance by the losing parties in the DSB's final decisions precludes any systematic analysis of the overall extent of compliance with WTO law, it does emphasize an important difference with compliance in the EU: in the EU, only about 10 percent of all infringement proceedings have ended up before the ECJ and there has not been a single case so far in which a final decision has been explicitly ignored by the defeated party. In the WTO, the ratio of cases of alleged non-compliance to those brought before the DSB is – with thirty-two out of 192 – significantly higher (16.7 percent). Even more importantly, the thirty-two cases (see table 4.2) that have been concluded by the DSB or the AB since 1995 have included four cases of open refusal to comply, three of which belong to the foodstuffs sector (the European banana regime, the European ban on US beef hormones and the Australian obstruction of salmon imports).

These figures reveal that the foodstuffs sector is the policy area with the highest rate of non-compliance in the WTO as well. Furthermore,

[6] Overview of the state of play of WTO disputes of May 15, 2000 (http://www.wto.org/wto/dispute/bulletin.htm).

Table 4.2 *Status of implementation of reports accepted, as at April 18, 2000*[a]

Year of final report	Implementation/ bilateral settlement	Announcement of implementation	Disagreement about extent of implemen- tation	Refusal to implement
1996	2	2		
1997	1			1
1998	6	1		2
1999	1	6	3	
2000		1		1
total	10	10	3	4

[a] *Source:* Overview of the state of play of WTO disputes, as of May 15, 2000 (http://www.wto.org/wto/dispute/bulletin.htm), own compilation. Five of the thirty-two cases listed could not be allocated (WT/DS24; WT/DS222; WT/DS44; WT/DS62, 67, 68; WT/DS60). See also: (1) WT/DS33; WT/DS31; (2) WT/DS2 and WT/DS4; WT/DS8, WT/DS10 and WT/DS11; (3) WT/DS75 and WT/DS84; (4) WT/DS27; (5) WT/DS50; WT/DS56; WT/DS69; WT/DS54, 55, 59 and 64; WT/DS79/1; WT/DS58; (6) WT/DS98/1; (7) WT/DS26 and WT/DS48; WT/DS18; (8) WT/DS76/1; (9) WT/DS90/1; WT/DS103/1; WT/DS34; WT/DS87/1 and WT/DS110/1; WT/DS121/1; WT/DS108/; (10) WT/DS99/1; WT/DS46; WT/DS70; (11) WT/DS132/1; (12) WT/DS126/1.

they also reveal a fundamental difference between European and WTO law: while the EU can (within some limits) rightly be regarded as a community of law in which facts and norms are relatively close together, the WTO's record reveals a number of permanent compliance crises. In fact, it could be argued that the data supports the claim that the violation of international rules is systematic whenever the governmental addressees of a regulation regard the domestic cost of implementation as high.

4.4   Dealing with non-compliance

A closer look at two cases – the decision of the Commission of July 1999 to lift the embargo on British beef[7] and the decision of the WTO Appellate Body of January 1998 to require the EU to lift its embargo on beef hormones[8] – helps to clarify some of the reasons for the weak record of

[7] For a detailed chronology of the BSE affair, see the webpage of the BSE Inquiry (http://www.bse.org.uk) and the Report of the BSE Investigation Committee of the European Parliament (EP 1997). For British government statements see http://www.maff.gov.uk/animalh/bse/index~1.htm. For scientific studies and summaries see Westlake (1997), Wolters (1998), and Neyer (2000b).
[8] For detailed presentations of the case from the US point of view, with numerous relevant documents, see http://www.useu.de/issues/hormonedossier.html. Under the

compliance of both institutional settings. Furthermore, it provides evidence that the WTO is still very much hampered by its diplomatic heritage and that it is in need of structural reform if its performance is to improve significantly.

4.4.1   Initial non-compliance in the BSE case

The case of BSE (bovine spongiform encephalopathy) has a long and unfortunate history of political cover-up and institutional failure. When the European Parliament (EP) published its report on the crisis in 1997, the picture it painted was one of a policy of misinformation that had been pursued by the Commission, of partial and politically instrumentalized science and political blackmail (European Parliament 1997; Neyer 2000b). Although the Scientific Veterinary Committee had had BSE on its agenda from the late 1980s, it was not until 1996 that it managed to overcome British political pressure and introduce more than marginal measures. Only in March 1996 – when new scientific evidence was published by British scientists about the probability of a causal link between BSE and Creutzfeld-Jakob Disease – was the Commission ultimately forced to act. After meetings of the Scientific Foodstuffs Committee and the Standing Veterinary Committee, it declared a comprehensive ban on British beef on March 27, 1999.[9] Three months later, the Florence European Council laid down specific steps that were necessary to lift the ban. After the competent Scientific Committee certified in May 1999 that the protective measures taken by Great Britain were adequate and that there was no danger to consumers, the Commission decided in July to lift the ban on certain beef products from Great Britain, with effect from August 1, 1999, provided that they complied with a special certification requirement.

In reacting to the Commission's decision and in clear contradiction of it, the German Minister of Health, Andrea Fischer, declared that she would not allow the import of British beef without additional guarantees regarding its safety.[10] Only after a couple of months of bargaining between

same address there are also the reports of the DSB and the AB. From the European point of view, the relevant documents can be accessed under http://www.europa.eu.int/comm/trade/miti/dispute/hormones/index_en.htm. For daily compilations of the latest developments see Agence Europe. For scientific analyses see Meng (1990); Engels (1996); Eckert (1995); Godt (1998); Eggers (1998); Hilf and Eggers (1997); and Victor (1999).

[9]   See Commission Decision 239/96/EC on emergency measures to protect against bovine spongiform encephalopathy, OJ 1996 No. L78/47.

[10] Press release by Federal Minister of Health Fischer of October 29, 1999: "It is important for us to secure transparency on the origin of the meat. Everybody must be able to see

the UK, the Commission, and Germany, was a diplomatic compromise found that was acceptable to all parties. Whilst at the beginning of the crisis the Commission reacted to German demands for a special labeling requirement for British beef by stating that this would constitute an illegal discriminatory measure, it started to reassess the legal situation in subsequent months. Succumbing to political pressure from France and Germany, the Commission developed a new position, which was that while a "Made in Britain" label was ruled out by Single Market regulations, it was quite permissible to label British beef "British XEL Beef."[11] Unlike the former label, this informed the consumer that the meat was fit for export and in conformity with European health provisions.[12] Although this solution was, no doubt, a cheap compromise, it formed the basis for the decision by the German Federal Council in March 2000 to lift the ban on British beef. De facto this meant that the Commission had yielded to German pressures by agreeing to a regulation which was in clear violation of the former EU practice of rejecting any discriminatory product labeling rules. Compliance with European law was re-established, but it came at the price of openly showing the vulnerability of the EU to political pressure. The conflict between the Commission and France was even more spectacular. Even though it was fought out in legal forums, it took a very late decision of the ECJ[13] to bring about a solution which seems to have ensured compliance by France.

4.4.2   Permanent compliance crises in the beef hormones case

As with the BSE case, the beef hormones case demonstrates that international trade politics are, after all, not solely about tariffs and quotas, but also complex regulatory tasks. Just like the BSE case, it shows how susceptible institutional structures are to explicitly antagonistic interests, and how difficult it is to resolve these in a non-hierarchical negotiating system. Like the BSE affair, the beef hormones scandal has a history as well. In 1980, the press in nearly all EU member states carried reports about babies in Italy who had grown oversized genitals and breasts because they had been fed beef from hormone-treated cattle. Reacting to the public outcry and a massive decline in beef sales, the European Community restricted the use of growth hormones in 1981 and – after pressure from

---

at the butcher's or in the supermarket where the meat, the sausage or the pizza topping have come from. This transparency, which the consumers need for their independent decision, is indispensable."

[11] "XEL" is the EU's abbreviation for "export eligible."

[12] Agence Europe, November 19, 1999, 11.

[13] Case 1/00, *Commission v. France* [2001] ECR I–9989.

the EP and European consumer associations – totally prohibited the use of six hormones in 1986.[14] This affected not only European producers who had been using growth hormones but, above all, US beef exporters. Less than 10 percent of US beef exports into the EU were hormone-free, which meant that the ban on growth hormones in effect excluded US beef exporters from the European market (cf. Vogel 1997: 159). In the following year the USA (and Canada) initiated a GATT dispute settlement procedure, but EU objections prevented a panel from being set up. During the following years, the dispute between the EU on the one side and the USA and Canada on the other stagnated, with no progress being made on the matter. Following the establishment of the WTO's new dispute settlement modalities, however, the matter attained a new dynamic. After a number of scientific tests had shown that the reasonable use of growth hormones did not create a health risk, the USA and Canada succeeded in persuading the Codex Alimentarius Commission (CAC) to establish upper limits for five of the six disputed hormones. As a consequence, legally binding benchmarks for the application of the SPS Agreement were created. In the future, WTO members would not be allowed to ban the import of hormone-treated beef as long as the permissible upper limits had not been exceeded.

Shortly after the CAC had adopted standards for growth hormones, the USA and Canada demanded that a DSB panel be set up at the WTO. The panels were established in May and October 1996, and reached the same conclusion in August 1997. In almost identical wording they found that the import restrictions imposed by the EU were contrary to SPS regulations because the EU had not sufficiently substantiated its claim as to the carcinogenic nature of growth hormones. This decision was appealed in October 1997, not only by the three disputing countries, but also by three further countries. On January 16, 1998 the WTO Appellate Body confirmed the earlier decision, on the grounds that the European import ban had been based on a scientifically inadequate risk assessment. Accordingly, the Appellate Body asked the EU to lift its import ban by May 13, 1999 or alternatively to supply a more convincing substantiation of its claim by the same date.[15]

Although the EU was unable to produce the required data,[16] it nevertheless upheld its import ban, even extending it, on April 20, 1999, by

[14] For a more detailed account of the case history see Vogel (1997: 154 ff.).
[15] For the decisions in full see the WTO homepage (http://www.wto.org/english/tratop_e/dispu_e/dispu_e.htm#disputes).
[16] On May 3, 1999 the competent Scientific Committee for Veterinary Measures arrived at the unanimous decision that a scientifically substantiated health threat could only be proven for one of the six hormones in question (http://www.europa.eu.int/comm/trade/miti/dispute/hormones/hor0405a.htm).

declaring a total embargo on all US beef products regardless of whether or not the cattle had been treated with growth hormones, to be enforced from June 15, 1999 onwards.[17] At the end of April, the EU Council for General Affairs declared – in clear violation of the SPS Agreement – that consumer protection had to be the first priority and that therefore the import ban on beef containing hormones was justified in spite of the WTO Appellate Body's decision to the contrary. According to European diplomatic circles, the EU was fully aware that it was formally in the wrong, but at the same time was "proud" to represent the interests of European consumers forcefully (Agence Europe, May 13, 1999). Even the Commission – usually in favor of free trade in relation to the internal market – supported this position. In its recent communication on the use of the precautionary principle (COM(2000) 1 final) it maintains that the precautionary principle is a key tenet of international law and that, in cases in which science is as yet unable to give a clear answer, the Community has the right to determine what it considers an appropriate level of protection. Applied to the beef hormones case, the argument implies that the Commission reserves to itself the right to conduct examinations – and thus to delay the lifting of the ban – for as long as it deems appropriate. By giving priority to its own risk assessment over that of the CAC, the Commission not only interpreted the SPS Agreement in a way that was in direct contradiction to the spirit of the Agreement but, moreover, fundamentally called into question the meaning of essential elements of the SPS Agreement. The action of the EU therefore led to a compliance crisis, which may become permanent and shows little prospect of ending in a co-operative settlement in the near future.

4.5   Explaining compliance

How does one explain the vehement opposition of Germany ("initial noncompliance") to the decision of the Commission, and of the EU to the decision of the Appellate Body? And what accounts for the fact that the EU seems to be better at eliciting compliance than the WTO, both in terms of overall data and in the two specific cases? This section uses the four theoretical perspectives outlined in chapters 1 and 2 to explain the degree of compliance in the two case studies and the comparative level of compliance that the law of the two institutions enjoys.

---

[17] According to the Commission, scientific tests conducted in the member states had shown that beef imported from the USA contained traces of illegal hormones, in spite of the exporters' assurances to the contrary. Hormone residues were found in 20 percent of all samples taken (Agence Europe, 21 April 1999).

4.5.1   Rational institutionalism

4.5.1.1 Monitoring   The monitoring of compliance with WTO rules is generally decentralized. The contracting parties must themselves take care that other contracting parties fulfill their legal obligations and – in cases of non-compliance – enter into bilateral negotiations or file a suit with the WTO. With the introduction of the Trade Policy Review Mechanism (TPRM), however, the contracting parties have added a more centralized monitoring instrument. Contracting parties are obliged to submit reports regularly about their trade-relevant national legislation to a Trade Policy Review Body (TPRB), which is entitled to employ its own discussants to comment on the reports and to publish their opinions following their review.[18] Furthermore the contracting parties agreed on a notification procedure that requires them to notify all relevant national legal measures and practices (Laird 1999).

Except for the TPRM and the notification requirement, the WTO has no competence or administrative resources to monitor compliance. Monitoring in the EU is far more centralized. In particular the Commission is empowered to function as the guardian of the treaties, i.e. "to ensure that the provisions of this Treaty and the measures taken by the institutions pursuant thereto are applied" (Article 211). To enable it to fulfill its duty the Commission has been given a wide range of instruments to facilitate implementation of Community law by the member states. One of the Commission's main instruments – frequently used in the veterinary field – is to carry out on-the-spot checks to verify the proper application of EU measures. During these inspections, Commission experts are to be given access to all concerned persons, information and documentation.[19] If the Commission uncovers deficiencies, the member state responsible must thoroughly investigate the general state of affairs in the area concerned and notify the Commission within the time it sets of the results of the investigation and the measures taken to remedy the situation. If the corrective measures are found to be insufficient, the Commission may take all measures it deems necessary. This is, however, subject to the comitology procedure, i.e. it requires a qualified majority of the member state representatives on the committee or, if recourse is had to the Council,

---

[18] WTO Treaty, Annex 3, C, iv–vi. And see http://www.wto.org/wto/reviews/reviews.htm. For an extensive bibliography on the TPRM see http://www.wto.org/wto/reviews/tprmpubs.htm.

[19] Commission Decision 98/139/EC of February 4, 1998, which lays down certain detailed rules concerning on-the-spot checks in the veterinary field in the member states by Commission experts, OJ 1998 No. L38/10–13, Art. 6.

in the event of the Commission being unable to secure that majority, the measures must not be rejected by the Council.[20]

Although the more detailed European monitoring procedures have probably contributed to the better record of compliance with European law, their impact on the rule-related actions of Germany in the BSE case and of the EU in the beef hormones case is far from clear. In both cases the disputed issue was subject to public discourse and all the legal steps taken by Germany were well known to the EU and all those taken by the EU were well known to the US. In refusing to lift their embargoes, neither Germany nor the EU withheld any information as to their motives and the actions they were taking; instead they openly justified their non-compliance by reference to consumer protection.

4.5.1.2 Sanctions   Although in many respects the European Union is far from being a state, its capacity to sanction non-compliance goes far beyond that of any other international organization because it can impose administrative fines to enforce its law. This is permitted, however, only when a dispute has been decided by the ECJ and the non-compliant member state has not implemented the court's decision. In this case the Commission – after giving the non-compliant member state the opportunity to state its case – is entitled to appeal to the court once again and demand the imposition of an administrative fine. Due to their high level, the fines come close to producing a prohibitive (rather than a merely offsetting) effect and a culpable member state is unlikely to withstand this pressure over a longer period of time.

In WTO law, there is no comparable horizontal or vertical enforcement mechanism. Analyzing the enforcement capacities of the WTO, one quickly notices that the supranational character of the WTO is largely limited to applying the law via triadic dispute settlement, but it falls short in terms of its sanctioning of non-compliance. The DSU only stipulates that, once a case has been decided by the DSB, the losing "defendant" is obliged to bring its policy into line with the ruling or recommendations. Although it stresses that "prompt compliance with recommendations or rulings of the DSB is essential in order to ensure effective resolution of disputes to the benefit of all Members," the wording of the Dispute Settlement Understanding (DSU) does not, according to some commentators,

---

[20] In this context, Commission Decision 98/139/EC, Art. 7, para. 4, refers to the procedure laid down in Council Decision 89/395/EC, OJ 1989 No. L186/17, at Art. 17, which is identical with procedure IIIa of the Comitology Decision (Council Decision 87/373/EC, OJ 1987 No. L197/33). For a detailed discussion of comitology, see the contributions in Joerges and Vos 1999.

imply that there is a legal obligation to abide by the rulings of the DSB (see Jackson 1999: 81–89). Furthermore, unlike the EU, the WTO does not have the option of imposing administrative fines on non-compliant members. Therefore, ultimately the enforcement of WTO law depends on the DSB authorizing a party to use its unilateral capacity to re-establish the rule of law. This confines the potential of the WTO to enforce its rules to those instances in which their breach damages the interests of an economically powerful member. But, even in such cases, effective enforcement is limited because the dispute settlement bodies can only authorize, not require, the party that suffered the damage or loss to suspend concessions up to the amount of the damage or loss suffered. Although such measures are supposed to be taken for a limited period only and to lead to the eventual withdrawal of the disputed regulation, once again there are no enforcement mechanisms available.

Thus, the WTO's enforcement mechanisms have neither a deterrent nor a punishing effect but only an offsetting one, such that the non-compliant party is in fact at liberty to choose between compliance with WTO law and the withdrawal of proportionate concessions. Likewise, the credibility of sanctions clearly militates in favor of the EU. Unlike the EU, the WTO lacks the competence to initiate legal proceedings or enforce sanctions. The importance of a third party that is not only able to assess the validity of claims but also has the role of the "Guardian of the Treaties" is highlighted by the European experience. Since 1995 the Commission has initiated more than 4,700 infringement proceedings against alleged cases of non-compliance. In the WTO, over the last eight years, there have been fewer than 200 cases.

The deficiencies of the WTO's sanctioning potential became evident in the hormone dispute. In 1997 Dagmar Roth-Berendt, MEP, declared that, should the Commission's appeal against the DSB panel's verdict fail, the import ban should nevertheless "be pushed through" and that the EU should incur penalty payments instead of endangering consumer protection.[21] This is exactly what the EU did. On July 12, 1999 the DSB decided on the appropriate level of retaliatory measures, determining that the damage suffered by the USA was US$ 116.8 million and that incurred by Canada was US$ 11.3 million. The EU accepted the verdict and conceded that the USA and Canada were entitled to withhold tariff concessions to these amounts. The retaliatory measures would stay in force until an amicable settlement could be reached with the USA and Canada, or until the WTO acknowledged the lawfulness of the European provisions. After the sanctions came into force on July 30, 1999, the EU for a long

---

[21] *Frankfurter Rundschau*, July 8, 1997, 24.

period has seen no reason to reconsider its embargo. In September 2003 the European Parliament and Council adopted a new directive,[22] which upholds the ban on hormones but allows their restricted use for therapeutic purposes. With this the Commission considers that it has now fully implemented the recommendations of the DSB.[23]

Not only the WTO sanctioning mechanism but also the more detailed mechanism of the EU failed to compel compliance in the BSE case. Against the background of the strong coercive potential of the EU, it seems astonishing that Germany was able to avoid its legal obligation and press the EU into agreeing upon the compromise described above. The explanation lies basically in the fact that the infringement procedure in Article 226 is "not necessarily an ideal sanction."[24] It is often too protracted to accomplish immediate improvements.[25] The obligation to demand statements and set deadlines creates long delays in the dispute settlement process. It can easily take eighteen months or more from the time when the Commission inspectors identify a problem until an action is filed at the ECJ.[26] For the Blair government, however, any such delay was politically difficult to accept in the political climate of summer 1999. The British tabloid press had already portrayed the issue as just another instance of the EU revealing itself as an essentially German-French show, at the expense of the other members. This question was all the more important to the British government because Prime Minister Blair had linked the British participation in the third stage of the Economic and Monetary Union (EMU) – of which he is personally in favor – to a positive outcome in a referendum. This referendum, however, could only be won if the idea that EU politics runs counter to British interests could be kept at bay. Therefore Blair was under domestic pressure to achieve an acceptable result as soon as possible and was not too interested in instigating a time-consuming infringement proceeding.

In sum, rational institutionalism adequately explains the better compliance record of the EU in comparison with the WTO. Both monitoring

---

[22] Directive 2003/74/EC of the European Parliament and of the Council of September 23, 2003 amending Council Directive 98/22/EC concerning the prohibition on the use in stockfarming of certain substances having a hormonal or thyrostatic action and of beta-antagonists, OJ 2003 No. L262/17.

[23] European Commission, Press Release IP/03/1393 of October 15, 2003.

[24] Commissioner Franz Fischler at the conference on the lessons to be drawn from the BSE crisis, jointly organised by the EP and the Commission, verbatim (European Parliament/European Commission 1999: 164).

[25] See COM(98) 598 final, 5.

[26] The procedure can be accelerated through an injunction on the part of the ECJ president, but this requires that the disputed measure is causing serious and irreversible damage to the claimant. According to the Commission's Legal Service it was quite difficult to furnish this evidence in the case of BSE. Agence Europe, January 13, 2000, 7.

and sanctioning are more developed and there can be little doubt that both contribute to the EU's better record of compliance. One could also argue that rational institutionalism is able to predict adequately the different level of compliance in the two case studies. At the WTO level compliance with what the DSB had required was achieved only after a long period during which the EU simply accepted the sanctions imposed by WTO law, and even now, after the adoption of the new directive,[27] the assessment of the EU's "compliance" remains controversial. The EU's compliance record looks better. Germany's resistance was overcome. France is unlikely to disrespect the ECJ's judgment.[28] Can we conclude that rational institutionalism with its insistence on monitoring and sanctioning provides a good explanation of compliance? Such a conclusion seems much too simplistic. Monitoring and sanctioning were embedded in both cases in judicial processes.

4.5.2   Legalization

4.5.2.1 Juridification   The EU's most prominently used mechanism for settling disputes on the application of its law by member states is the infringement procedure. According to Article 226 the Commission can react to alleged non-compliance by sending a "letter of formal notice" and demanding a statement from the member state. At the second stage, the Commission submits a "reasoned opinion," and only at the third and final stage does it have recourse to the ECJ. Thus the infringement procedure is not a classic court procedure but aims to facilitate interadministrative co-operation between the Commission and the member state, with the court mechanism providing only a default option (see Snyder 1993; Mendrinou 1996). That the procedure is aimed at achieving political co-operation, rather than legal confrontation, becomes clear from its application in practice: in 1998 the Commission sent 1,101 letters of formal notice, but only in 11 percent of these were legal proceedings instigated. In 1997, the Commission and the member states were able to settle 92 percent of all such issues using extra-judicial administrative procedures: of a total of 1,461 requests for a statement only 121 resulted in court proceedings.[29] The political rather than the judicial nature of the procedure is also emphasized by the fact that it is solely up to the Commission to decide whether or not to instigate proceedings, whether the member state's reactions are sufficient, and whether to bring legal action

---

[27] Directive 2003/74/EC; see footnote 22 above.
[28] Case 1/00, *Commission* v. *France* [2001] ECR I–9989.
[29] Source: COM(99) 301 final, 142; author's own calculations.

before the ECJ. The Commission is also free to decide on the appropriate deadline for taking these steps.

In breaking with the diplomatic tradition of international trade relations, the contracting parties of the WTO have, with the adoption of the Agreement Establishing the World Trade Organization, created a similarly powerful instrument for settling disputes. According to the DSU conflicting parties are required to seek a negotiated settlement. If this fails, the complainant may request a panel at the next meeting of the DSB – a request that is automatically granted. A panel consists of three to five members, all of whom are legal experts, and must complete its report within six months. During that period, the parties to the dispute can submit written statements, present oral arguments and make rebuttals. After the panel has reported its decision, it is automatically adopted by the DSB within sixty days unless unanimously rejected or it is appealed by one of the member states. If an appeal is filed, a Standing Appellate Body (SAB) has ninety days to rule on the legal issues that were decided by the panel. The decision of the SAB is final and enters into force within thirty days.

Compared to the old GATT, the new dispute settlement mechanism is a major step forward. Previously, a defeated party could veto any ruling and even prevent the establishment of a panel. Now the report of a dispute settlement body is valid unless *all* parties oppose it. In terms of overcoming the problem of ambiguity, the DSB appears to be highly efficient. As most lawyers emphasize, its triadic structure, with independent and automatic dispute settlement, makes for high quality reasoning from all parties involved and has proven to be an important element in the settlement of international trade disputes.[30]

4.5.2.2 Legal internalization Whilst the dispute settlement procedure is well elaborated at both the WTO and the EU level, the two legal systems differ significantly in the extent to which their rules are legally internalized, enjoying domestic effect, in the legal systems of their members. WTO law, however, has no direct effect and cannot be invoked by national courts. Likewise, although Article 300, para. 7 of the EU Treaty states that "agreements concluded . . . shall be binding on the institutions of the Community and the member states" the ECJ refuses to honor that obligation. The court has only recently reached a decision holding that WTO law and the decisions of the DSB are not valid criteria for deciding

---

[30] For good discussions of the workings of the DSB see Trachtman (1999); Cameron and Campbell (1998); Hoekman and Mavroidis (2000); Komuro (1995); Petersmann (1997b); Vermulst and Driessen (1995).

whether an act of a European institution is lawful or not.[31] The court argued that because DSU decisions call upon the contracting parties to look for mutually acceptable solutions by means of intergovernmental bargaining, there can be no legal supremacy of these decisions over European law. Otherwise, the EU would be handicapped in its relative bargaining power as compared to other states.

EU law goes significantly beyond that point. While some national constitutional courts, such as the German Constitutional Court, have expressed reservations about the competence of the ECJ to deal with issues of constitutional importance, the supremacy of EU law has been largely unchallenged since the very beginning of the European Communities. According to Article 249, regulations and decisions of the Community are binding in their entirety and are directly applicable either in all member states (regulations) or to those to whom they are addressed (decisions). However, their legal effect in the member states derives not only from Article 249, but also from Article 234, which obliges national courts to ask the ECJ for a preliminary ruling in all matters that concern the application of European law. While national governments can simply ignore an international dispute settlement, this opportunity is denied them by Article 234. Because the national court applies the law, non-compliance on the part of the defendant government would be tantamount to an open breach of the domestic rule of law. This mechanism has brought national courts into the position of domestically enforcing European law, even against the will of the governmental addressee.

The legal implications of the difference in internalization between WTO and EU law are clear in the BSE and beef hormones cases. Legally, both the EU and Germany were obliged to comply with the decisions of the DSB and of the Commission. Only in the latter case, however, did that obligation have domestic legal effect because a national court would have had to apply the decision had it been faced with a corresponding case.

4.5.2.3 Civil internalization   Since the landmark decision of the ECJ in *Van Gend en Loos* in 1963,[32] European rules have not only been directly binding on their addressees but have also conferred rights on individuals. The court proclaimed in that decision that the Community constitutes a new legal order which comprises not only the member states but also their nationals. Independently of the legislation of the member states, EU law therefore not only imposes obligations on individuals

---

[31] Case 149/90, *Portugal* v. *Council* [1999] ECR I–8395.
[32] Case 26/62, *Van Gend en Loos* v. *Administratie der Belastingen* [1963] ECR 3.

but also confers upon them rights which become part of their legal heritage. Following that decision, European rules not only have direct effect (national courts must apply their prescriptions and proscriptions), but individuals can invoke European rules to force their governments to honor the commitments they agreed upon at the European level (Weiler 1994, Burley and Mattli 1993). Following this decision, the ECJ has steadily expanded the scope of individual rights. Whilst at the beginning, individuals were only entitled to invoke treaty provisions, the ECJ included secondary Community legislation in its subsequent case law, including council directives and decisions, and it even granted horizontal effect to Community directives, thus allowing individuals to enforce obligations which had explicitly been created by council directives for member states to impose on other individuals (Stein 1981). Unlike the EU, the WTO does not confer any such rights on individuals. They have neither standing nor a right to be heard (Lukas 1995). WTO law is international law which only binds the contracting parties and does not create duties or confer rights upon individuals.

While the different degree of civil internalization is significant for understanding the structural features of the EU and the WTO, it did not make for too much difference in the achievement of governmental compliance in the two cases. To be sure, the Commission's decision to lift the ban on British beef was formally binding on the member states and could also have been enforced by any German individual. A German beef importer could have filed an action at a German administrative court claiming that the import ban infringed the principle of the free movement of goods. Under the Article 234 preliminary ruling procedure, the German court would have been obliged to send the disputed issue to the ECJ. If – as is most likely – the ECJ had agreed with the plaintiff's argument, the Commission's decision would have been binding on the German government as part of the domestic legal order. However, had a German importer brought legal action, it would have received such bad press in Germany that is it hardly surprising that nobody pursued this option.

In sum, as in relation to rational institutionalism, legalism has explanatory strengths and weaknesses. It is a good theoretical approach if one wishes to explain the overall level of compliance. The EU, being clearly more advanced in its dispute settlement and civil and legal internalization than is the WTO, shows the better overall compliance record. None of these three mechanisms, however, proved to be particularly helpful in overcoming German resistance to a domestically unpopular European rule, or in overcoming European resistance to an equally unpopular international rule. Thus, in seeking to explain the two cases it appears to be necessary to look for additional variables.

4.5.3   Legitimacy

4.5.3.1 Participation   Participation in the process of decision making in the EU differs significantly from decision making at the international level. Today, the EP acts as the co-legislator of the EU and nearly all legal acts which are adopted in the First Pillar of the EU must find its approval. Furthermore, both in legislation and implementation, the Commission is supported by a myriad of committees which provide for administrative and non-governmental policy input, and take care that societal knowledge and concerns are taken seriously. That, however, did not at all apply in the case of deciding whether and when to lift the embargo on British beef. At the Florence summit in 1996, the member states and the Commission agreed on the conditions and timing of the lifting without consulting the EP or any scientific or otherwise composed committee. By means of political bargaining they consented on the criteria which were to be fulfilled by the British government and on a procedure to be followed as a prelude to the eventual lifting of the ban on British beef. The criteria included a bundle of measures which the British government was required to implement to eradicate BSE, as well as an elaborate procedure to monitor the progress and – after full implementation – to lift the ban. This procedure involved on-the-spot checks by the Commission to monitor the progress of implementation, and the eventual use of scientific committees to confirm the safety of British beef.

It is important to note that the deal that was concluded at the Florence summit did not include the basic demand of consumer organizations that British beef only be allowed onto the European market when BSE had been eradicated. The deal was basically a political compromise by the member state heads of government which was an attempt to bring the UK back into a more co-operative line with European politics but without being too soft on tackling the problem of BSE. It is to be understood against the background of the British announcement that "without progress towards lifting the ban," as John Major stated in the House of Commons in May 1996, "we cannot be expected to co-operate normally on other Community business . . . Progress will not be possible in the intergovernmental conference or elsewhere until we have agreement on lifting the ban on beef derivatives and a clear framework in place leading to lifting of the wider ban."[33] Thus, when the European Council in Florence "gave favorable consideration" to a Commission paper based on British proposals, the EU refrained from making a demand of total eradication and declared instead that the measures proposed, as well as

[33] Agence France, May 25, 1996.

the procedure for progress assessment, met with the broad consent of the member states.

When in April 1999 a final inspection by the FVO (Food and Veterinary Office) in Great Britain found that the agreed measures had been implemented,[34] and in May the competent Scientific Committee certified that the protective measures in Great Britain were adequate and that there was no danger to consumers, the Commission came under pressure to act. Although the disease was not yet eradicated, it decided in July to lift the ban on certain beef products from Great Britain, with special certification, with effect from August 1, 1999. Although the Commission might have known that any advance along the lines established in Florence in 1996 would lead to open conflict with some member states, it had no political or legal choice. The Commission was bound by the Florence agreement to decide the matter solely on the basis of scientific criteria and information available as to the implementation of the measures consented to and to lift the ban as soon as the competent bodies had given their go-ahead. Had it not taken these steps, it would have discredited its own scientific bodies, which had repeatedly stated that British beef constituted no danger to public health. Equally importantly, any failure to proceed would have left the Commission in a situation where it would have had to act contrary to its own regulations and practically invite the UK to initiate legal proceedings against it.

France, Austria, and Germany objected to the Commission's decision, but were unable to reverse it. The Commission acknowledged that BSE had not yet been eradicated, but argued that this was not the benchmark for its decision. Instead the decisive criteria were the full implementation by the British government of the measures that had been consented to in Florence and the confirmation of the relevant scientific bodies that beef from Great Britain represented no health risk. France, Austria, and Germany pointed out that contrary to the Florence agreement the Commission had not carried out a final inspection even though the inspection of April 1999 had unearthed some remaining problems. The Commission responded that the last inspection report had not talked of deficiencies, but only of measures that still required implementation, and Britain had confirmed that this would be done by August 1, 1999.

As with the Commission's decision to lift the embargo on British beef, affected parties, such as consumer organizations, had no say in determining the upper limits of the six growth hormones set by the CAC. Whilst consultations among consumer organizations, the European Parliament, and the Commission are at least part of the regular EU

[34] XXIV/1054/99 MR-EN FINAL, DG XXIV, FVO, Unit 2.

procedures for adopting foodstuffs regulations, such consultations are practically non-existent in the WTO. In its "Guidelines for Arrangements on Relations with Non-Governmental Organizations"[35] the WTO General Council stresses the explicitly intergovernmental nature of the WTO and maintains that ad hoc meetings between WTO representatives and non-governmental organizations (NGOs) are not ruled out, but that the appropriate channel for negotiating interests is the national political level.[36] To be sure, of late the WTO secretariat has started to invite NGOs for consultations on specific topics.[37] However, the fact that these consultations have taken place must not be equated with their empirical relevance. Although these consultations are no longer restricted to questions of content, but also concern such issues as public access to documents, the formalization of consultation procedures and the financing of costs accrued, this hardly constitutes anything other than a first attempt at more systematic integration.

International rule-making in foodstuff policy largely takes place without the participation of those affected. This absence of participation is also apparent in the most important body for the elaboration of international foodstuff standards, the Codex Alimentarius Commission (CAC).[38] The CAC is an intergovernmental organization which is open for membership to all members of the WTO. Its basic task is to co-ordinate pre-existing food standards, initiate and guide the preparation of new standards, and publish them in a so-called "Codex Alimentarius." Participation in the plenary meetings is restricted to delegations from the WTO members. They sit under the leadership of a chief negotiator. The composition of each delegation is at the discretion of the member governments and may include representatives from industry, consumer associations, or academic institutions. In principle, the working method of the CAC is directed at promoting the comprehensive participation of all interested parties and at determining international standards on the basis of a common interest in ensuring safe foodstuffs. However, from the beginning the CAC has shown a strong pro-industry bias. In the majority

---

[35] WT/L/162, Decision adopted by the General Council on July 18, 1996.

[36] See the "Report of the WTO Informal Session with Non-Governmental Organizations (NGOs) on Trade and Environment" of November 28, 1996: "As a result of extensive discussions, there is currently a broadly held view that it would not be possible for NGOs to be directly involved in the work of the WTO or its meetings. Closer consultation and co-operation with NGOs can also be met constructively through appropriate processes at the national level where lies primary responsibility for taking into account the different elements of public interest which are brought to bear on trade policy-making" (http://www.wto.org/wto/environ/te016.htm).

[37] E.g. the WTO Symposium on Trade, Environment and Sustainable Development, July 1997.

[38] The CAC is presented in detail at http://www.fao.org/docrep/w9114e/W9114e00.html.

of cases, consumer associations do not possess the required expertise, the administrative capacity or the financial resources to follow the highly technical debates conducted in the CAC working groups and committees (Avery, Drake and Lang 1993). Industrial interests largely determine the process of standardization and in practice leave little room for the concerns of those ultimately affected by such regulation: the consumers (Engels 1996).

4.5.3.2 Social acceptance   Given the high political saliency of both the BSE and beef hormones issues for German and European consumers, the fact that they enjoyed only limited participation in the decision-making process, and that little concern was shown for their risk perceptions, it is unsurprising that both decisions were met by their open protests.

Already in 1996, the press coverage on BSE in Germany had resulted in a dramatic decline in beef sales, of up to 50 percent.[39] A spokesman for the Federal Association of Central Abattoirs in Bonn described the beef market situation as "utterly desolate." Abattoirs had drastically reduced their output, had filed applications to put their workers on a part-time basis and had sent others on holiday. According to the representative association in Thuringia, many of the *Land*'s 1,000 livestock farms faced ruin if the situation prevailed. Similarly, the Federal Association of Food Retailers noted that in the self-service sections with pre-packed beef the market had "collapsed completely." The German weekly, *Der Spiegel*, pointed out that "the island over the Channel is possibly about to experience a worst-case-scenario epidemic of hitherto unknown dimensions." Scientists were quoted forecasting a "galloping spongiform epidemic" with up to 10 million deaths.[40]

When the Commission decided to lift the embargo in 1999, emotions were once again running high. On the continent, and particularly in Germany, angry protests by consumer associations demanded the decision's reversal. A number of *Länder* health ministers called the Commission decision utterly irresponsible and declared that their *Länder* would neither lift the import bans that they had imposed individually in 1996 nor consent in the Federal Council to a nationwide lifting of the ban. In Germany, Hans Kretzschmar, head of the Institute for Neuropathology at the University of Goettingen and a member of the Scientific Steering Committee of the EU, argued in a couple of interviews that the ban

---

[39] *Die Welt*, April 11, 1996.
[40] By the end of 1998 only forty-one cases of new variant Creutzfeld-Jakob Disease had become known in the EU, thirty-nine of those in Great Britain (European Parliament/ European Commission 1999, 109).

should not be lifted under any circumstances before the year 2001, i.e., before the end of the estimated incubation period of five years, as only then would it be possible to establish whether the protective measures that had been in force since 1996 had actually been effective.[41]

Just as the German government was under domestic pressure not to back down until it had won the concessions demanded by the public, the Commission, too, had little room for maneuver in the beef hormones case. During the investigation of the BSE affair by the European Parliament (EP) in the autumn and winter of 1996 it became evident that for years the Commission's competent authorities had pursued a policy of covering up health risks emanating from BSE. The EP was enraged and threatened to suspend the Commission by a motion of censure (a vote of no confidence) before the end of the year, unless it carried out fundamental reforms to its institutional structures and its substantive food policies.

As a result, subsequent to 1996 the Commission found itself in a situation where even the slightest doubt as to the priority it was giving to consumer protection could have had disastrous political consequences. So when, in May 1999, the European Parliament unanimously called on the Commission to keep the ban on hormone-treated beef in place and by a majority rejected the proposal to solve the problem by introducing labeling requirements, the Commission's room for maneuver was non-existent. At the same time the precautionary principle was overwhelmingly endorsed (by a majority of 502 to 2 votes), putting the Commission under even more pressure to cement its position against beef imports from the USA and Canada. In all likelihood, this was the decisive motive for the Commission to publish its communication on the importance of the precautionary principle. All parties, from the Communists to Conservatives, supported the Commission's refusal to lift the import ban and demanded an uncompromising position. Consumer associations and the EU's agricultural associations (European Bureau of Consumer Organizations (BEUC), European Community of Consumer Co-operatives (EUROCCOP), European Group of Farmers' Unions (COPA), and European Group of Farmers' Co-operatives (COGECA)) were also very pleased with the Commission's eventual decision not to lift the ban on American beef.[42] Just like the German government which, for domestic reasons, had had little room to maneuver in the way it handled the import ban on British beef, the Commission, too, was faced with the choice of

[41] Interview in *Süddeutsche Zeitung*, October 30/31, 1999, 7.
[42] The only exception was the federation of business enterprises, CIAA, which warned – largely in vain, however – of the possible economic consequences of an intensifying dispute and demanded the introduction of labeling/identification requirements.

potentially being voted out of office or risking the consequences of dishonoring its legal commitments. While the EU was forced to admit, during negotiations in the CAC, that no objective health risk was ascertainable for the five disputed hormones, it nevertheless insisted on the necessity of continuing with its embargo for reasons of consumer policy.[43]

Unlike the theoretical approaches of rational institutionalism and legalism, legitimacy gives a good indication of both the overall level of compliance with EU and WTO law and of that in the two cases. The comparatively higher level of participation in the EU that is indicated by the participation of the European Parliament in the making of European law, in the myriad of committees, and the comparatively easy access to the Commission and the European Parliament that European lobby groups enjoy, correlates well with its better record of internal compliance, as compared to that achieved by the WTO. In the two cases, however, none of these factors mattered. Due to the intergovernmental decision making that led to the adoption of the compromise at Florence and the following technocratic closure of the process inside the Commission, societal participation in deciding whether to lift the ban on British beef was close to zero. It is little surprise, therefore, that the social acceptance of the measure was very low and can easily be compared to that of the WTO decision on the hormones. Thus, legitimacy can well explain why neither a highly detailed institutional design nor a sophisticated set of legal instruments was capable of eliciting compliance in either of the two cases.

4.5.4   Reflexivity

In the WTO, the most important legal document relating to the trade in foodstuffs is the SPS Agreement. According to its core principle, WTO members are only allowed to implement trade-restrictive measures if they are justified by health concerns and/or the protection of animals and plants. As to whether the trade-restrictive measures of an individual state are arbitrary, the SPS Agreement declares that the members should – if possible – apply the international standards of the CAC. The possibility of continuously reflecting upon the adequacy of the standards adopted by the CAC is, in principle, safeguarded by the right of any member to request the inclusion of specific items on the agenda of the CAC. The main task of the CAC is conducted by so-called "subsidiary bodies"

---

[43] See WT/DS26/R/USA, paras. 2.26–2.33; also Victor (2000: 23). For an assessment of the EU embargo see also Vogel (1997: 158): "The ban . . . represented an important victory for European consumer and environmental organizations; their concerns rather than the judgement of the Commission's own scientific advisory bodies, had carried the day."

which are staffed by persons who "serve in a continuing capacity and shall be specialists active in the fields of the respective subsidiary body."[44] The CAC strongly emphasizes the scientific soundness of its standards and co-operates closely with other relevant bodies in the field, such as the Food and Agriculture Organization of the United Nations or the Scientific Committee for Foodstuffs of the EU. Due to the technical and non-binding character of its standards, the CAC aims to adopt or amend standards by consensus. Only if such efforts fail does it have the right to decide by simple majority voting.

In European foodstuff policy, the basic legal logic is rather similar. The core principle of the SPS Agreement, which is to prohibit protectionist measures that cannot be justified by sound scientific evidence, is mirrored by the principle of mutual recognition and the strict requirements for recourse to the legitimate exemptions to that principle. If a member state objects to the application of the principle in relation to a certain product, it must notify the Commission of its discriminatory measure and provide reasons justifying it. The Commission then requests an opinion from a specialized committee made up of member states' representatives. Two of the most important committees in the area of foodstuffs are the Standing Committee for Foodstuffs and the Standing Veterinary Committee. In both cases the Commission reacts to a member state's notification by informing the Committee that it is minded either to grant permission, or prohibit or delay the member state's proposal. Although any decision of the Commission requires member state approval by a qualified majority, the Commission can call upon a number of scientific advisory bodies to support its proposal. By relying on scientific evidence to assess the validity of the arguments put forward by a member state, the Commission can force the member state to engage in argumentative discourse and apply scientific criteria to assess the validity of arguments.

By relying on administrative expert bodies, both the WTO and the EU can in principle base their legal instruments on science-based expertise and force their members to support their preferences by means of arguments. In both cases, these arguments must be founded on health and safety concerns and must make clear the scientific assessments upon which they are based. Although the discourse among the member states is intended to be deliberative, if no consensus can be achieved final decisions are taken by majority vote both by the CAC and by the Standing Committees of the EU. It is important to note, however, that unlike the WTO, the notification of trade restrictive measures by member states of the EC gives the Commission the option to initiate new legislation that

---

[44] Rule IX of the Rules of Procedure of the CAC.

adapts existing EC regulations to changed scientific evidence regarding a problem. Regarding the international trade of foodstuffs, any such option outside the CAC is missing because the WTO does not itself have the competence to propose new legislation. Thus, whilst disputed issues in the EC can be referred back to the political agenda and rule and political rationality can be mediated, the WTO's emphasis is heavily weighted towards rule rationality.

The difficulty of achieving argumentative interaction over hotly disputed issues became evident in both the BSE and beef hormones cases. After lengthy and controversial discussions between those involved in the decision making in the CAC, Spain demanded, on behalf of the EU member states, that the decision be postponed until the outcome of a further international EU conference had been determined.[45] This motion was rejected by an extremely narrow margin of twenty-nine to twenty-eight votes, with five abstentions. In a subsequent secret ballot, maximum quantities were determined for the five disputed hormones, with thirty-three in favor of the levels set, twenty-nine against and seven abstentions. Thus, the EU was outvoted by the majority and five of the six growth hormones banned by the EU were made integral to the CAC code of standards, becoming legally binding benchmarks for the SPS Agreement.

Equally, in the decision to lift the EU embargo on British beef, argumentative interaction had limited political relevance. After the Commission decided in July 1999 to lift the ban on the export of beef from Great Britain, with effect from August 1, France, Austria, and Germany immediately objected to the Commission's decision. In spite of the Commission's clear decision to the contrary, the French government declared on October 1, 1999 that it would not lift the ban on British beef, justifying its measure with a report by the *Agence Française de Sécurité Sanitaire des Aliments* (AFSSA) which raised serious doubts about the appropriateness of the Commission decision. On September 30, 1999 the AFSSA had published a statement, based on the findings of a government-appointed expert group, setting down a number of reasons why the import embargo on British beef should remain in place.[46] According to the statement, the methods available to identify infected meat had improved dramatically since the time the Commission decided on the criteria to be applied; the number of new BSE cases was declining at a remarkably slow rate, giving rise to new concern; and the findings of the on-the-spot checks by Commission inspectors raised concerns about the proper implementation of the measures that had been consented to in Florence.

---

[45] Regarding the negotiations see Engels (1996: 14) and Eckert (1995: 382–383).
[46] Summarized in http://europa.eu.int/comm/dg24/health/sc/ssc/out62_en.pdf.

On October 29, 1999, after two days of deliberation, the Scientific Steering Committee (SSC) unanimously rejected the French arguments for maintaining the import ban on British beef. According to the SSC, the examination of all relevant data had clearly shown that there was no reason to alter the conclusions outlined in its previous statement which served as the basis for the Council's decision. In particular, the conditions for the lifting of the ban were being complied with and the safety of beef and beef products from Great Britain was comparable to that of food-stuffs produced in the rest of the European Union.[47] Unimpressed by the SSC decision, France refused to lift its import ban.[48] Initially Germany openly refused to comply with the Commission decision as well. The Federal Minister of Health, Fischer, declared that she would not allow the import of British beef and beef products without additional guarantees as to their safety.[49] Only after the Commission initiated the second step of the Treaty violation procedure, did the German government reluctantly give in and lift its embargo.

As with the theoretical focus on legitimacy, a management perspective is helpful in understanding both the overall level of compliance with EU and WTO law and the outcome of compliance crises in the two case studies. It correctly identifies the deficiencies in the WTO's and the CAC's administrative procedures, which are less flexible and are open to constructive compromise when compared with the procedures in the EU. It is also helpful in explaining the diplomatic compromise that was realized by the UK, the Commission, and Germany, and thus sheds light on the limitations of a legalistic understanding of implementation. The management perspective highlights the fact that the enforcement of compliance must be understood as a political process in which arguing, bargaining, and compromise are important elements in the empirical reality.

4.6   Explaining non-compliance

The WTO and the EU clearly differ in terms of their ability to elicit compliance. Whilst compliance is far from automatic in both institutions and often involves intense bargaining and legal proceedings, only

---

[47] Agence Europe, October 30, 1999, 6. The SSC report can be found at http://europa.eu.int/comm/dg24/health/sc/ssc/out62_en.pdf.

[48] For an extremely critical legal assessment of the actions taken by France see the opinion of Advocate General Mischo, delivered on September 20, 2001, Case C–1/00, *Commission of the European Communities* v. *French Republic* (Action for failure to fulfil obligations – Refusal to end the ban on British beef and veal). The ECJ has endorsed the Advocate General's position in its judgment of December 13, 2001, Case 1/00, *Commission* v. *France* [2001] ECR I–9989.

[49] Press release by the Federal Ministry of Health of October 29, 1999.

in the WTO is non-compliance accommodated as a systematic component of the application of rules. The analysis of the four theoretical perspectives demonstrates that the effectiveness of sanctions, the degree of
participation as well as legal and civil internalization, the reflexivity of
the administrative procedures, and the extent to which rule rationality
is mediated by political rationality are all major reasons that go towards
explaining the difference in the overall record of compliance between
the two institutions. Unlike the EU, the WTO still looks very much like a
traditional intergovernmental structure with its scant regard for domestic
politic concerns and the concerns of affected parties. It cannot implement
unconditional compliance but has to live with the option of its addressees
to pay rather than to obey (i.e. to accept symmetrical retaliation). Long-
term non-compliance would be incompatible with the EU's very being as
a legal community, whereas paying is regarded as an accepted alternative
by the WTO.

Against this background, it comes as no surprise that the enforcement
mechanisms of the WTO have had limited effect up until now. The EU's
compliance could not be secured in the beef hormones case for a long time
even though the WTO satisfies all criteria which the institutional literature
considers decisive, including the effective monitoring of the actions of
the regulatory addressees; reduced information uncertainty; competent
institutions with a scientific-technical orientation to fine-tune the general
rules; and, last but not least, a juridification of dispute settlement to solve
differences of interpretation. The beef hormones case has underlined the
fact that the WTO is confronted by serious difficulties when it comes
to enforcing inconvenient rules. Its systematic neglect of the concerns
of consumers provoked open confrontation between its rules on the one
hand and the political rationality of its addressees on the other hand, but
it did not possess the enforcement instruments necessary to overcome
such a division. The BSE case highlighted the limits to the effectiveness
of European law. Although the supranational legal status of the EU's rules
is well accepted and elaborate enforcement mechanisms are in place,
the EU still had to rely on diplomatic bargaining and finally a political
compromise to re-establish the rule of law. Just as in the beef hormones
case, domestic opposition from affected parties and intergovernmental
bargaining trumped supranational law.

Furthermore, both cases underline the fact that public risk perceptions,
diplomatic political processes, open confrontation and asymmetrical
power constellations are acutely relevant, even in highly institutionalized and juridified polities such as the EU and the WTO. The findings
imply that effective political integration beyond the nation-state cannot
be restricted to harmonizing national legal systems and co-ordinating

governmental preferences. If the integrity of supranational law is to avoid head-on confrontation with domestic concerns – and public opposition is not to become the Achilles heel of supranational enforcement – both the WTO and the EU are well advised to put increasing emphasis on the participation of affected parties in the making of rules. Therefore, some skepticism is called for instead of the exaggerated optimism of those institutional approaches that see an intelligent intergovernmental institutional design as the first-best solution for effective governance beyond the state. Both the BSE and the beef hormones cases provide evidence that the effectiveness of trade policy depends crucially on an overlap between consumer preferences, governmental interests and supranational law.

Whether the EU would have been more accommodating if the WTO had had at its disposal enforcement mechanisms similar to those enjoyed by the EU, must remain a hypothetical question. It is true that in both cases the capacity to sanction non-compliance correlates with an observed degree of compliance, but it is inappropriate to deduce from this that the WTO should be given the prerogative to impose penalty payments. Any such strategy would increase the already latent antagonism between domestic politics and supranational law – which in the long run would hardly be conducive to achieving effective international governance. Both cases therefore underline that governance beyond the state is only effective to the extent that it is embedded in and supported by public discourses. Analytically, this finding is restricted to foodstuffs politics. Unlike most other policy areas, the politics of European and international foodstuffs is central to consumer interests and therefore very much an object of public concern. If it is true, however, that members of the WTO and the EU will continue to grow closer and that their interdependence will increase rather than decrease in many areas, then foodstuff politics can serve as a model for identifying future conflict patterns and finding ways and means to address them.

5 Politics of intergovernmental redistribution: Comparing compliance with European and federal redistributive regulations

Jürgen Neyer

5.1 Intergovernmental redistribution

Intergovernmental redistributive arrangements have to date been largely neglected in analyzing international relations and researching questions of international compliance. Game theorists argue that the paucity of intergovernmental redistribution is explained by the fact that redistributive policies are appropriately modeled as zero-sum games in which any gain for one party corresponds to an equivalent loss for the other (Morrow 1994). Since states are taken to be self-referring agents, which "develop their own strategies, chart their own courses, make their own decisions" (Waltz 1979: 96), the emergence of a redistributive regime and compliance with it, on the part of those who have to pay into it, must be regarded as extremely unlikely. Since the enlightened self-interest of the addressees of the regulations cannot be relied upon to ensure payment, an intergovernmental central body is required which is able, in doubtful cases, to enforce compliance even against resistance. It may thus be argued that the fact that there is no significant international redistributive regime is ultimately attributable to the anarchical nature of the international system.

Alongside this state-oriented explanation, one can also find an explanation in the literature that is informed by the communitarian theoretical tradition. Miller (1988) and Goodin (1988) point out that questions of justice can meaningfully be dealt with only in the context of a political community which has a shared understanding of the content of sound policy. Since the existence of a political community is, however, closely bound up with national statehood, the term "political community" must always be understood as a nation-state concept. One important reason for this is that nations are to be understood as communities of memory and experience that are integrated through tradition and in which social actors are perceived as components of a collective subject (Kielmansegg 2003). It is only against this background that one can explain why social actors should be prepared to act in favor of others and identify their well-being with that of others. Thus the concept of "international justice" is considered illusory because it overlooks the precondition of shared normative basic convictions. If communitarians are right, the implications for compliance are straightforward and rather serious. In an international world, without collectively shared normative convictions, in which states unilaterally pursue their own self-interest, eliciting compliance with inconvenient rules would often be a difficult business. Neither the oft-cited "compliance-pull" of legitimacy (Franck 1990) nor the social force of public shaming (Liese 2001) could provide much assistance. In a world inhabited by monological and exclusively self-caring actors, solidarity beyond borders (Smith, Chatfield and Pagnucco 1997) and the readiness to contribute significant resources towards implementing it could be neither expected nor demanded for legitimate reasons (Miller 1995).

In contrast to both the realist and the communitarian analysis of the problem, we show below that the existence of a superior sanctioning power and a shared political identity are not necessary conditions to achieve a high degree of compliance with intergovernmental redistribution schemes. International redistributive policy can also emerge as a result of multilateral bargaining and is characterized, on a basis of individual rational action, by a high degree of willingness to comply. A heavy reliance on the solidarity-creating function of political community may even have counter-productive effects on the willingness of addressees to comply with redistributive provisions if it ignores the basic insight of managerial approaches (Chayes and Chayes 1995) that any regulation needs to be tied into an institutional context open to changes in social preferences.

We shall develop these arguments below in three stages. Section 5.2 describes two intergovernmental redistributive regimes: fiscal compensation between *Länder* in Germany and financial compensation between member states in the EU. Section 5.3 traces the differing degrees of compliance within the two regimes. Section 5.4 employs the four theoretical perspectives that are outlined in chapters 1 and 2 to explain the compliance record of the two regimes. A concluding part, section 5.5, makes the link with the initial question concerning the conditions for governmental willingness to comply with intergovernmental redistributive arrangements.

5.2   Intergovernmental redistribution in the EU and Germany

Two arrangements that suggest themselves for a comparative study of the above hypotheses are the intergovernmental European redistributive regime and the intergovernmental German (federal) redistributive regime. The intergovernmental relations in the EU as well as those in Germany are largely based on a parallelism between market-creating and market-correcting policies. In both cases the accomplishment of a unitary (German or European) internal market was accompanied by the building up of intergovernmental redistributive mechanisms to compensate for territorially defined social and economic inequalities. In Germany the intergovernmental market-correcting mechanism was established with the adoption of the Basic Law in 1949 and the first horizontal fiscal compensation Act in 1951. In the EU the development of redistributive arrangements began with the European Social Fund and European Investment Bank, which were established by the Rome Treaties and were very limited in scope. Both the adoption of the Single European Act and the decision to move to economic and monetary union, as codified in the Maastricht Treaty, were accompanied by significant increases in the resources made available by the richer member states for the poorer ones. Today, both the federal and the European redistributive regimes have constitutional status in their respective political systems. The EU preamble lists among the objectives *inter alia* the reduction of both the gap between individual regions and the lag of the least favored. Article 2 explicitly makes economic and social cohesion and the promotion of solidarity a task of the EU, and Article 3 adds the strengthening of economic and social cohesion to the catalogue of EU competences. The federal redistributive regime is equally central to the German constitutional system, having its basis in Articles 72(2) and 106(3) of the Basic Law, which bestow constitutional status upon the idea of the "creation of equivalent living conditions throughout Federal territory" as well as the promotion of "uniform living conditions."

5.2.1   *Quantitative comparison*

The European and federal intergovernmental redistributive regimes were, until 1 May 2004, thoroughly comparable, both in terms of the range of actors involved and the intensity of redistribution: both redistribute financial resources among a similar number of governmental units (15 member states in the case of the EU, and 16 *Länder* in the case of Germany) and do so with similar intensity. Table 5.1 shows the relative economic importance of the resources redistributed in the context of each regime for the EU and for Germany. In calculating these quantities for the *Länder* the volume of horizontal fiscal compensation includes the redistributive effect of the turnover tax compensation and federal payments are taken as a basis (all vertical payments from the federal government

Table 5.1 *Redistributive volumes absolutely and as a percentage of GDP of the EU and of Germany*

	Federal redistributive regime	European redistributive regime		
		Total 1	Total 2	Total 3
(1) Redistribution per year	12.3 bill. DM	18.2 bill. ECU	25.5 bill. ECU	58.3 bill. ECU
(2) GDP	2942.7 bill. DM	6772.9 bill. ECU	6772.9 bill. ECU	6772.9 bill. ECU
(1):(2) Relative redistributive volume	0.42%	0.27%	0.38%	0.86%

to the *Länder* are excluded). In contrast, for the European redistributive regime three different procedures have been applied. Total 1 calculates the redistributive intensity by taking into account only the allocations realized under Objective 1 (promotion of the least-developed regions) of the European Regional and Development Fund (ERDF) and the Cohesion Fund. Total 2 takes account of all directly redistributive effects of the ERDF Structural Fund and the Cohesion Fund, and Total 3 brings in the redistributive effect of the Common Agricultural Policy (CAP). Table 5.1 shows that the relative economic importance of both redistributive regimes exhibits thoroughly comparable orders of magnitude. Within the framework of the German redistributive regime, in 1996 a total of 12.3 billion DM was redistributed, corresponding to 0.42 percent of German gross domestic product (GDP). The European redistributive regime redistributes amounts ranging from 18.2 to 58.3 billion ECU, which corresponds to between 0.27 and 0.86 percent of European gross domestic product (depending on one's method of calculation) – a highly comparable proportion.

The similarity between the two regimes emerges clearly when one calculates the redistributive effect for all thirty-one EU and German states. Table 5.2 shows, for all member states and *Länder*, the net resource transfer (payments minus receipts) under both regimes. Taking the two narrow definitions of the European redistributive regime, using the Total 1 and Total 2 procedures, *Länder* occupy the first three places as the largest relative net contributors (Hesse, Baden-Württemberg and Bavaria) and the Netherlands, at 0.41 or 0.37 percent of GDP respectively, comes in fourth (Total 1) or fifth (Total 2) place. These rankings change significantly when one adopts the broader Total 3 definition. If one includes the redistributive effect of the Common Agricultural Policy, Hesse, at

Table 5.2 *Redistributive intensity, as a percentage of GDP, of EU and* Länder

Rank	Total 1			Total 2[1]			Total 3[2]		
1	D	HES	−0.94	D	HES	−0.94	D	HES	−0.94
2	D	BW	−0.50	D	BW	−0.50	EU	LUX	−0.68
3	D	BAY	−0.48	D	BAY	−0.48	D	BW	−0.50
4	EU	NL	−0.41	D	NW	−0.40	EU	D	−0.49
5	D	NW	−0.40	EU	NL	−0.37	D	BAY	−0.48
6	D	HH	−0.36	D	HH	−0.36	EU	NL	−0.45
7	EU	BEL	−0.34	EU	BEL	−0.28	EU	BEL	−0.43
8	EU	SWE	−0.30	EU	LUX	−0.27	D	NW	−0.40
9	EU	DK	−0.29	EU	DK	−0.27	D	HH	−0.36
10	EU	LUX	−0.28	EU	A	−0.27	EU	UK	−0.16
11	EU	A	−0.27	EU	F	−0.24	EU	F	−0.03
12	EU	D	−0.21	EU	UK	−0.19	EU	ITA	0.00
13	EU	F	−0.19	EU	D	−0.15	D	S-H	0.01
14	EU	UK	−0.12	EU	ITA	−0.02	D	R-P	0.16
15	EU	FIN	−0.11	D	S-H	0.01	D	NS	0.18
16	D	S-H	0.01	D	R-P	0.16	EU	DK	0.19
17	EU	ITA	0.04	D	NS	0.18	D	SAAR	0.54
18	D	R-P	0.16	D	SAAR	0.54	EU	ESP	1.51
19	D	NS	0.18	EU	ESP	0.97	D	BB	1.52
20	D	SAAR	0.54	D	BB	1.52	D	HB	1.61
21	EU	ESP	1.05	D	HB	1.61	D	SACH	1.69
22	D	BB	1.52	EU	IRL	1.68	D	TH	1.85
23	D	HB	1.61	D	SACH	1.69	D	S-AN	1.88
24	EU	IRL	1.65	D	TH	1.85	D	M-V	1.93
25	D	SACH	1.69	D	S-AN	1.88	D	BER	2.89
26	D	TH	1.85	D	M-V	1.93	EU	POR	3.11
27	D	S-AN	1.88	EU	GR	2.58	EU	IRL	3.72
28	D	M-V	1.93	D	BER	2.89	EU	GR	4.76
29	EU	GR	2.46	EU	POR	3.05			
30	D	BER	2.89						
31	EU	POR	2.93			.			

Notes: [1] No data available for Finland and Sweden.
[2] No data available for Finland, Sweden, and Austria.

0.94 percent of GDP, remains the biggest relative net contributor, but it is followed closely by Luxembourg with 0.68 percent of GDP. Likewise, Germany, with 0.49 percent of GDP, ranks high in fourth place and comes close to Baden-Württemberg, which is in third place with 0.50 percent of GDP.

The economic importance of the European redistributive regime becomes still clearer when one compares the largest relative recipient countries. Using all three methods of calculation, a European member state is the largest relative recipient. Even employing the Total 3 method of calculation, the last three places are occupied by European member states (Portugal, Ireland and Greece). A look at the figures of relative redistribution underlines the similarity: in the two calculations of Total 1 and Total 2, the largest recipient *Land*, Berlin, scores 2.89, which is a very similar level to the largest recipient member state, Portugal, with 2.93 (Total 1) and 3.05 (Total 2) percent of its GDP.

Just like the federal redistributive regime, the European regime can also be described as being largely oriented towards bringing about financial equalization between the above-average and below-average member states, measured in terms of their wealth (cf. Thomas 1994: 473). It does not therefore constitute an empirical marginality but must be seen rather as "implicit fiscal compensation" (Walthes 1996: 69–70) among member states with significant economic importance.

5.2.2   Qualitative comparison

Whilst the two regimes look remarkably similar in terms of redistribution, they differ markedly with regard to the requirements they impose on the recipients in terms of how they spend the resources they are allocated. The federal redistributive regime allocates resources unconditionally and creates no economic incentive to encourage the recipient *Länder* to reduce their reliance on redistributed resources. The reasons for this are attributable historically to the fact that in 1949 the Parliamentary Council (*Parlamentarischer Rat*), which was in charge of preparing a proposal for the German Basic Law, regarded its most pressing task as the promotion of legal and economic unity and the creation of uniform living conditions throughout the whole federal territory. Fiscal compensation was thus subordinated to the desire for a unitary financial system with the objective of "creating uniform living conditions throughout Federal territory" (old version of Article 72(2) Basic Law). The use of allocated funds was not to be tied to particular projects, such as the construction of new industrial structures or investments in infrastructure, but was to be unconditional, i.e. to benefit directly the budgets of the recipient *Länder* and increase their general financial capacity. This hitherto unbroken logic of the federal redistributive regime obliges the financially strong *Länder* to contribute so-called compensatory amounts out of which the financially weak *Länder* receive compensatory allocations to strengthen their general financial power. Compensatory entitlements and obligations are established by setting the financial revenue of each of the *Länder* (financial strength indicator) against a fictitious target revenue (compensation index) which is calculated for each of them on the basis of a federal

average per capita revenue. Comparing these two indices allows a calculation of how each of the *Länder* stands in relation to the federal average.
If it is above average it has to pay, i.e. it has to give out some of its above-
average financial strength to the *Länder* with revenues that are below
average.[1]

Since payments are made unconditionally, they offer no additional
incentive to the *Länder* to aim at high tax revenues and sound financial and economic policies. Should, for instance, the Saarland manage to
raise an additional million DM of tax revenue by successfully attracting
industry, it would be left with a mere 13,000 DM, i.e. only 1.3 percent of
the proceeds of its efforts. The entire remainder, i.e. nearly 99 percent,
would be allotted to the compensation system, with the result that higher
tax revenues scarcely benefit the *Länder*.[2] The opposite effect of a negative incentive structure might even arise, with the result that a rise in tax
revenue could lead to smaller payouts for poor *Länder*, or else higher contributions from rich *Länder*.[3] In connection with the increasingly intense
competition between *Länder* to attract industry, circumstances can arise
under which it is rational for *Länder* to take advantage of the (incorrect)
imposition of tax obligations on firms as a tool to subsidize them indirectly
and thus, contrary to the rules of the system, enhance the attractiveness
of a region. In an empirical survey on the topic, the Bremen Chamber of
Labor in 1998 cited the Bremen Finance Minister to the effect that "firms
ought not to be squeezed harder than by other *Länder*. Being too harsh can
frighten off some firms, and we don't really want that" (Arbeiterkammer
Bremen 1998: 12). That this scarcely concealed call for the instrumentalization of taxation for the achievement of competition policy goals did
not produce open enthusiasm among donor *Länder* is hardly surprising.

Like the federal redistributive regime, the member state regime also
distributes non-repayable financial resources. But, in clear contrast to
the federal arrangement, the funds in the member state system are the
object of both substantive earmarking and central review. Payouts to
entitled member states are made not just on the basis of their needs in
accounting terms, but in all cases require the presentation of multi-year
development programs that formulate detailed development strategies for
whole regions, accompanied by an application to the Commission and

---

[1] On this see the extremely complex provisions of section 10 of the German Act on Inter-
regional Financial Equalization (FAG). However, the rather unclear wording of the Act
does not make it a recommendable read. For a description that is readable, yet detailed,
see Kesper (1998: 110–118) and the ruling of the German Federal Constitutional Court
(*Bundesverfassungsgericht*) of November 11, 1999, 2 BvF 2/98.

[2] Bavarian Finance Minister Faltlhauser in the *Süddeutsche Zeitung*, August 20, 1999.

[3] On this see also Rolf Peffekoven, "Die deutschen Länder am kollektiven Tropf," *Frankfurter Allgemeine Zeitung*, April 18, 1996, 17, and Ebert and Meyer 1999.

156 *Jürgen Neyer*

approved only as the outcome of negotiations between the Commission and member states.[4] In connection with the most important funding instrument, the ERDF, funds applied for are subjected to the objective of the creation of a common market. All funds applied for must be used for productive investment in the industrial sector, infrastructure investments, or investments in education and health. A further requirement on the allocation of funds by the Commission is that structural fund measures must not be substitutes for individual state measures but rather supplement these in their investment potential. Accordingly, in principle, the principle of additionality is to be applied to all investments, so that Community actions must not function as a substitute for structural expenditure by individual states, or member state expenditure of a similar nature, but rather supplement or contribute to corresponding national actions.

The clear subordination of redistributive measures to the higher objective of promoting integration is particularly clear in the case of the cohesion fund. Also here substantive requirements apply to implementation, to the extent that the allocation of funds is limited to a balanced funding of projects in the area of transport infrastructure and environment protection. However, member state beneficiaries are additionally required to submit and comply with so-called convergence programs.[5] In these programs the member states must commit themselves to specific steps to comply with the Maastricht criteria, and agree the precise target figures for the various planning periods with the Commission. The European Council has further laid down in this connection that should the Council establish excessive deficit no new projects can be funded. The conditionality principle in relation to the cohesion fund constitutes a severe limitation on recipient countries' budgetary and financial policy autonomy. It commits them to a long-term restrictive financial policy, which by its comprehensive approach affects all high-expenditure policy areas and compels cuts or at least a stabilization in their volume.

However, the performance-oriented target-setting of the member states' redistribution regime is clear not only from this detailed programming but also from its administrative provisions. To guarantee a high degree of compliance with the legislative requirements, the implementation of structural fund measures is the object of regular review through so-called follow-up committees and by the relevant Commission departments. The follow-up committees have the task of continuously supervising implementation of a measure and making necessary corrections to it.

---

[4] For detailed accounts of the administration of structural funds see Benz and Eberlein (1999); Pollack (1995); and Hooghe (1996).
[5] Article 6 of Directive 1164/94/EC, OJ 1994 No. L 130/1 setting up the cohesion fund.

Additionally, successes or failures are to be reported to the Commission in order that, if necessary, new substantive priorities can be set, which may affect the transfer of funds to another program. Should trouble arise systematically, financial cuts can also be made.[6]

Alongside the substantively oriented follow-up committees, the Commission's financial controllers play a central role in the implementation of the structural fund measures. While the Commission's implementation of the structural funds in the early years depended largely on its own on-the-spot checks, in recent years it has moved increasingly towards a model that depends on self-monitoring by member state controllers. The relevant Regulation[7] requires member states to guarantee, *inter alia*, that the effectiveness of their administrative and control procedures can be demonstrably checked by the Commission; that they co-ordinate their monitoring programs with the Commission at least once a year; and that they annually report progress on improving control and administrative procedures. The Directive further provides that measures can be fully funded only where an independent third party attests in detail that the measure has been implemented in accordance with the provisions.

5.3   Good compliance in the EU and recalcitrant compliance in Germany

While no European member state or German *Land* has ever rejected its obligation to contribute the agreed-upon financial resources, the willingness of the respective net contributors to comply with the two arrangements has been different. The two biggest net contributors in the EU's redistributive regime – Germany (the biggest absolute net contributor) and the Netherlands (the second biggest relative net contributor, topped only by Luxembourg) – have essentially accepted that their payment obligations are appropriate and justified,[8] and have instead confined their political efforts, including those at the 1999 Berlin European Council, to pushing for incremental changes. In contrast, the federal redistributive regime has had to face massive criticism from the net contributing *Länder*, Bavaria, Baden-Württemberg and Hesse, which have used

[6] For a critique of the practical realization of this requirement, however, see the Annual Report by the Court of Auditors (1998: 67) and its Special Report No. 15/98 on the evaluation of structural fund investments in the periods 1989–1993 and 1994–1999, along with the Commission's replies (OJ 1998 No. C347/1), and Lang, Reissert and Schnabel (1998: 62–73).

[7] Regulation (EC) 2064/97 establishing detailed arrangements for the implementation of Council Regulation (EEC) 4253/88 as regards the financial control by member states of operations co-financed by the Structural Funds, OJ 1997 No. L 290/1.

[8] See the Dutch memorandum of November 14, 1994 on "Enlargement of the European Union: Possibilities and Obstacles" and the German White Paper on the 1996 Intergovernmental Conference, vol. II (http://www.europarl.eu.int/dg7/igc).

all available legal and political measures to seek to change the regime. Certainly, the incoming German government, headed by Chancellor Gerhard Schröder, declared in early 1999 – supported by the Netherlands, Austria, and Sweden – that one of its most prominent goals would be to reduce its 60 percent share of redistribution in the EU (Heinemann 1998). During the course of the preparations for the summit in Berlin, however, the four member states quickly came to realize that all politically feasible possibilities for reducing the volume of expenditure would be limited to minor cuts in spending on the Common Agricultural Policy and would therefore be of limited volume. Proposals by the Dutch and German governments relating to expenditure in the area of the structural fund were confined to the demand for further concentration of fund distribution to the least-developed regions, and have thus to be regarded as tending more to harmonize with the interests of the recipient than the contributing countries.

The critique of the three net contributing *Länder*, in the context of the federal redistributive regime, was by contrast principled in nature, alleging incompatibility with the existing system and its democratic and federal principles. To back their arguments, the three *Länder* not only resorted to the Federal Constitutional Court but additionally brought massive political pressure to bear on the recipient *Länder*, in particular by threatening to take up the question of restructuring the *Länder*. *Länder* fiscal compensation could not, according to Baden-Württemberg Minister-President Erwin Teufel (CDU), be any substitute for more effective *Länder* structures, since it only treated the symptoms but did not go to the root of the problem. It would instead be consistent to reduce the number of *Länder*, in particular merging Saxony-Anhalt, Mecklenburg-Prepomerania, the Saarland and Bremen with their respective neighbor *Länder*.[9] Only slightly less extreme was the pronouncement which came from the Bavarian Minister of State, Huber (CSU), who threatened Bavaria's exit from the institutions of the federation and the *Länder* should no progress be made in the matter.[10] Though the three *Länder* at no point stopped meeting their financial obligations, the vehemence of their opposition must nonetheless be seen as the expression of a significantly reduced willingness to comply with the arrangement. It involved not just the exercise of their constitutional right to institute constitutional review proceedings, but also the open threat to call into question

[9] *Weser-Kurier*, January 2, 1999, 2. See also the position taken by Baden-Württemberg Minister-President Erwin Teufel on 22 September, 1999 in connection with the first hearings in Karlsruhe (*Weser-Kurier*, September 23, 1999, 1.)
[10] *Frankfurter Rundschau*, January 8, 1999.

the willingness for federal policy co-operation and the territorial integrity of other *Länder*, should recipient *Länder* not assent to a reduced redistributive effort. In terms of European policy, a similar threat might have involved Germany questioning the territorial integrity of Greece, Portugal or Ireland and announcing a review of co-operation in the European institutions should these member states not accept reduced financial payments from the structural fund.

5.4 Explaining compliance

How is the more vehement opposition by the German *Länder* to be explained? And how can one explain that both the German law and the EU directive are fairly well complied with? Against the background of the communitarian hypothesis we should expect a low willingness by the member states of the EU and a fairly high willingness by the *Länder* to comply. To explain this puzzling finding, this section assesses to what extent the four different theoretical perspectives outlined in chapter 1 and operationalized in chapter 2 can provide sufficient explanations.

5.4.1 Rational institutionalism

The monitoring of compliance is, both at the European and the German level, unproblematic. In the European case, monitoring is primarily conducted by the Commission, which administers the budget of the EU. Any failure on the part of a national government to contribute its financial share would lead directly to a shortfall in the financial resources required to meet the expenditures of the EU and could scarcely go unnoticed. Furthermore, because the financial commitments agreed upon in Edinburgh were ratified by all national Parliaments, non-compliance would presuppose a national Parliament enacting legislation. Any such Act, however, would have little chance of escaping the awareness of the media and would quickly become a hotly disputed public issue. In the German case, the same combination of central and societal monitoring applies. According to § 12 of the FAG, the federal minister of finance, together with the Federal Council (*Bundesrat*), determines in any given year the financial resources which each *Land* has to contribute. However, unlike the European redistributive regime, those resources are not subject to allocations by the respective *Länder* Parliaments but are automatically invoiced by deducting from the share which each *Land* receives from value added tax, which is collected by the *Länder* but distributed by the federal government. Non-compliance with the federal redistributive regime would therefore presuppose a financial secession of a *Land* from the whole federal financial system, which again could barely go unnoticed and would surely be the subject of broad public debate.

It is far more difficult to assess the intensity of sanctions in the two cases. Formally, the competence to enforce the rules in both cases is organized vertically, with the Commission and the federal government in charge of securing compliance. The instruments that these two institutions have to hand, however, differ significantly. In the European case, any failure by a member state to comply with its commitments and withhold the agreed upon contributions, would open the way for the Commission to ask the ECJ to declare such non-compliance illegal. The consequences of such a judgment, however, are far from clear. The ultimate sanction available to the ECJ to compel a member state to comply with European law is for it to impose administrative fines or lump sums. In a situation in which a member state refutes its obligation to contribute financial resources to the EU, it seems a rather inadequate sanction to demand that the state pay an extra fine. The most probable outcome of any refusal by a member state to contribute its share would therefore be a major crisis, which would put into doubt its membership of the EU. Against the background that all member states have a strong interest both in the smooth functioning of the EU and in retaining membership of it, such a sanction (their exclusion from the EU) would surely greatly outweigh any perceived benefit of non-compliance.

In the case of Germany, essentially the same logic applies. Although the federal government does not explicitly have the option to impose fines on *Länder* governments, according to Article 37 of the Basic Law, it has the competence to use "all necessary means" to compel a *Land* to fulfill its legal obligations. This includes the right to issue orders to a *Land* government, or even to hold in trust the constitutional tasks of a *Land*. Holding out against these powers of the federal government would, just as in the case of the EU, ultimately involve rejecting the very foundations of the federal system, which are the rule of law and the principle of loyalty to the federation (*Bundestreue*). Although the resources distributed by the federal redistributive regime are significant, the implications of withdrawing from the federal system would be yet more so.

Against the background of this brief discussion, the explanatory power of the two variables of monitoring and sanctioning, highlighted by rational institutionalism, is mixed. Both variables are strong in that they adequately predict high levels of compliance, both on the part of the *Länder* and the EU's member states. Sanctions and monitoring are well established and leave little room for non-compliance. It is difficult, however, to use the variables to explain why compliance is slightly lower in the case of Germany than it is in the case of the EU. If one were forced to judge whether sanctions and monitoring are more developed in Germany or the EU, one would have to say that monitoring is equal at both levels, whereas there is a slightly higher degree of sanctioning power in the case of Germany. Because compliance is lower in the German case, however, the two variables and therefore the whole theoretical perspective are of only limited value in explaining this difference.

5.4.2   Legalization

As with the two variables of monitoring and sanctioning, the three variables of the legalization perspective "juridification," "legal internalization," and "civil internalization," have very similar values in both cases. Incidents of non-compliance would end up at the ECJ (in the case of the European redistributive regime) or the German Constitutional Court (in the case of the federal redistributive regime). Although some argue that in fact the ECJ very often anticipates the preferences of the dominant member states in its rulings (Garrett 1995), similar arguments also exist with regard to the German Constitutional Court (see Gawron and Rogowski 1996). The vast majority of scholars therefore ascribe to the ECJ a degree of autonomy from its governmental principals which is little different from that of national courts (Alter 2001; Burley and Mattli 1993). In the literature on international governance, the ECJ therefore serves as a prime example of an independent court (see Keohane, Moravcsik and Slaughter 2000).

The degree of legal internalization of the two rules, however, differs slightly. To be sure, both the federal and the European redistributive regimes have indisputable legal status for their signatories. The federal redistributive regime is based on a federal law (the *Finanzausgleichsgesetz*) which is binding on the *Länder* and has clear legal effect because federal law trumps the law of the *Länder*. Likewise, the European redistributive regime has clear legal effect for the member states due to its ratification by the Parliaments of the Netherlands and Germany. The difference, however, lies in the fact that only the European member states had the option of evading their legal obligation by adopting a new law, contradicting the agreed-upon financial obligation. In the German case, no such competence on the part of the *Länder* existed. Because federal law always trumps the law of the *Länder*, the Parliaments of the *Länder* did not have the option of enacting a law with the effect of relieving them of their legal obligation.

In both cases civil internalization is practically zero. Neither within the EU nor Germany is any option foreseen for individuals legally to challenge governmental non-compliance. If the German or Dutch Parliament decided to change national law and discontinue their obligation to contribute to the European budget, neither a Dutch nor a German citizen would have any capacity to challenge that decision in court. Although the courts are required to treat the EU as a source of law in both member states, they most probably would not grant standing to individuals in such a case. In both member states, the right to file a suit against governmental actions is limited to those legal persons who can prove individual damage. In the instance of a legislative Act which has the same consequence for all nationals, that condition would not be met. Likewise, if a German *Land* decided to withstand the federal government by rejecting its competence to enforce federal law, and chose instead to secede from the federal system, any legal claims by individuals against this act would stand little chance of being accepted by the courts of that *Land* for the very same reason.

Whilst the dispute settlement and legal internalization variables adequately predict the high degree of compliance in the two cases, the civil internalization variable would suggest a low degree of compliance and is of only very limited explanatory power. None of the three variables can explain the lower compliance record of the federal redistributive regime. Whilst the juridification and civil internalization variables are in both cases of the same value, the legal internalization variable wrongly suggests that there should be a better compliance record on the part of the federal redistributive regime. Just like rational institutionalism, legalization is therefore helpful in explaining the high overall level of compliance but falls short when it is used to explain the different degrees of compliance in the two cases.

5.4.3   Legitimacy

5.4.3.1 Participation   In both cases the redistributive arrangement was a product of intergovernmental negotiations in which all addressees participated. Nevertheless, in both cases all non-state actors were formally excluded. In the case of Germany, the bargaining surrounding the new financial equalization scheme was conducted amongst governmental delegates from the *Länder* and the federal government only. Neither the German Parliament nor the smaller German parties, such as the FDP, the Greens and the PDS, were involved. A closer look at the practice of participation, however, reveals important differences. While in the case of the EU all member states have the same formal power to exercise their veto and no decision can be taken without the consent of all member states, the German redistributive regime is subject to majority voting and allows for weighted votes. Article 51 of the Basic Law provides

Table 5.3 *Structurally greater weighting of recipient* Länder[a]

Länder	Number of inhabitants in millions	Number of votes
Net contributors		
Hesse	6.0	5
Bavaria	12.0	6
Baden-Württemberg	10.3	6
Hamburg	1.7	3
North Rhine-Westphalia	17.9	6
Total	47.9	26
Net recipients		
Schleswig-Holstein	2.7	4
Lower Saxony	7.8	6
Rhineland-Palatinate	4.0	4
Saarland	1.1	3
Brandenburg	2.5	4
Bremen	0.7	3
Saxony	4.6	4
Saxony-Anhalt	2.7	4
Thuringia	2.5	4
Mecklenburg-Prepomerania	1.8	3
Berlin	3.5	4
Total	33.9	43

[a] *Source: Statistisches Jahrbuch der Bundesrepublik Deutschland* 1997, 32–33.

that each of the *Länder* shall have at least three votes on the Federal Council. *Länder* with over 2 million inhabitants shall have four votes, those with over 6 million inhabitants, five votes, and those with over 7 million inhabitants, six votes. This results in a distribution of votes on the Federal Council which leads to a significant distortion of the relative potential influence of *Länder* populations. Despite their relatively small population of 33.9 million inhabitants, the recipient *Länder* occupy the majority of seats on the Federal Council, with a total of forty-three votes. The donor *Länder*, which account for 47.9 million inhabitants – a majority of the population – are represented by a total of only twenty-six votes on the Federal Council.

Table 5.3 clearly shows the greater structural weight of the recipient *Länder* and also the distortion of the relationship between the population represented and the de facto influence they can exert through their representatives on the Federal Council. Though the donor *Länder* represent almost 60 percent of the population they have less than 40 percent of the votes on the Federal Council. Whereas, until accession by the five new *Länder*, the proportion of votes between the recipient and donor *Länder* was fairly balanced, accession shifted the balance in favor of the small and structurally weak *Länder*. The chances for the majority of the population to give effective expression to their preferences as regards the pattern of the federal redistributive regime have thereby been significantly reduced. This structural defect is clearly expressed by Fritz Scharpf (1994: 52) when he states that "there is little standing in the way of exploitation of the large by the small, and the strong by the weak."

Undoubtedly, if we compare the voting distortion between the two cases, there is little doubt that it is even more pronounced in the case of the EU. Even Luxembourg might veto a deal it dislikes and thereby exert a voting power that goes far beyond its relative size in terms of population. That argument, however, applies to all of the member states. And in practice, it is hardly imaginable that Luxembourg would indeed do so. The political costs it would have to face if it acted against the explicit will of the other fourteen (or twenty-four, since 1 May 2004) member states would probably outweigh anything it stood to gain by so doing. In sum, the argument that this section has raised is that European rule can be assumed to be less controversial than federal rule because all of the member states consented to it, and all had a fair chance to promote their individual interests. In the federal case, no such chance existed. The minority of the net contributors could advance whatever arguments they wanted without having any leverage (apart from through the judicial process) with which to press for a more compromising position on the part of the net recipients.

5.4.3.2 Social acceptance   However, the inflexibility of the federal redistributive regime and its in-built bias towards high levels of redistribution is by no means a problem confined to the Federal Council. It is part of the broader context of the development of federalism in Germany. Through the extensive exercise of its legislative powers the federation, especially in the 1950s and 1960s, took up a whole range of powers, which had originally been solely in the province of the *Länder* (see Abromeit 1992). Subsequently, federal politics largely determined what was to be the object of the public exercise of power by the *Länder*; what standards had to be applied by the *Länder* in improving public infrastructure; and what the cost of this to *Länder* budgets was to be. Whereas this centralizing logic of the federal redistributive regime still enjoyed, in the early postwar period, the consensus of the political elite, which faced the emergency situation of the postwar period and which required especially a concentration on the establishment of effective central state institutions, it stands today in clear contradiction with the far-reaching criticism of centralization in Germany. The complaint against the *Länder* fiscal compensation by the three *Länder* of Bavaria, Hesse and Baden-Württemberg in the late 1990s was thus aimed not just against redistributive intensity and the associated financial burden on the rich *Länder* but was ultimately against the whole traditional system of German federalism. At bottom, the issue was whether the federal system of Germany should tend to a model that was oriented more towards compensation and uniformization or else a competition-oriented and therefore decentralized model.[11] The existing system was said, in a complaint by Baden-Württemberg, for instance, to be based on a basic misunderstanding of the principle of federalism, since it shut out the whole innovation-promoting role of policy competition among the *Länder* and between them in the federation.[12] There were very similar arguments advanced in Bavaria's application for constitutional review, to the effect that the federal state should "guarantee diversity of ideas" and that the best environment for this was "competitive federalism."[13]

The criticisms of Bavaria and Baden-Württemberg met with fairly broad support in the early 1990s. Right through the academic literature one can find the assertion that the federal redistributive regime is marked by large-scale absence of any consideration of economic criteria, and even less systematic considerations.[14] The process of expanding the redistributive intensity and – by implication – enlarging the competences of the federal level of German politics has long been criticized as the establishment of a "disguised unitary state" (Abromeit 1992), in which federalism becomes a purely executive federalism and the *Länder* degenerate into mere political and administrative units of the federation. Alongside the multiplicity of critical voices among scholars, broad support for the complaint can also be found in the media. The daily newspaper, *Die Welt*, pointed out that the existing system meant that "the most stiff-necked *Länder* can turn their vote or silence into cash" and that the Saarland would become richer than Bavaria. The call by the southern *Länder* to reform the FAG is regarded as justified because the current

---

[11] For a summary of the debate see Bull (1999).
[12] Summarized in the ruling of the German Federal Constitutional Court (*Bundesverfassungsgericht*) of November 11, 1999, 2 BvF 2/98.
[13] See Bull (1999).
[14] On the critical literature see e.g. Renzsch (1994), Schuppert (1995), and Peffekoven (1994). The rejection of the 1993 FAG by the ruling of the German Federal Constitutional Court (*Bundesverfassungsgericht*) of November 11, 1999, 2 BvF 2/98, also focuses largely on this lack of justification.

system is hostile to efficiency. Additionally, the real goal is considered to be "restructuring the *Länder* in accordance with economic viewpoints."[15]

Comments in the *Frankfurter Allgemeine Zeitung* and the *Handelsblatt* were fully in line with this position. The *Frankfurter Allgemeine Zeitung* argued that the traditional federal system punished efficiency and rewarded inefficiency, and ought to be adapted to the requirements of a modern competitive economy. The "absurdity" of financial compensation that "made the poor rich and the rich poor" would end up ruining the spirit of solidarity between the *Länder*.[16] The *Handelsblatt* was also convinced that the "high level of redistribution kills the incentives for *Länder* to raise their tax revenues by skilful policy of their own." It suggested instead the merger of *Länder* so as to attack the "high costs of the political apparatus." It concluded that by rearranging the federal redistributive regime one would ultimately strengthen democracy, since at present citizens cannot see whether *Länder* governments are dealing properly with tax funds.[17]

The German media, of course, was not unequivocal in its criticism but instead divided along the political spectrum. Whilst the conservative newspapers sided with the donor *Länder*, the liberal ones were more ambivalent. Liberal newspapers, even in the donor *Länder*, such as the *Nürnberger Nachrichten*, criticized the claims of the donor *Länder* as an "attack on federalism" which was justified only by "absurd accusations."[18] Likewise, the *Ulmer Südwest Presse* from Baden-Württemberg commented on the case under the headline "Rich *Länder* are tired of sharing" and described the reasons given for bringing the case as "daring." Both newspapers, however, also acknowledged the need to reform the system and emphasized stronger economic incentives.[19] The same two-sided assessment can be found in the major German liberal newspaper, the *Süddeutsche Zeitung*, which found that the basic reason for the case was the stinginess of the donor *Länder* and the political motive to highlight the bad economic policy being conducted in the recipient *Länder*.[20] At the same time, however, the *Süddeutsche Zeitung* also opened its pages to voices such as that of the Bavarian finance minister and showed sympathy for reform of the system.[21] In sum, the conservative governments of the donor *Länder* had broad backing for their case from nearly all local and

---

[15] *Die Welt*, July 31, 1998.   [16] *Frankfurter Allgemeine Zeitung*, July 31, 1998.
[17] *Handelsblatt*, July 31, 1998.   [18] *Nürnberger Nachrichten*, September 24, 1999.
[19] *Nürnberger Nachrichten*, June 20, 1998; *Nürnberger Nachrichten*, November 12, 1999 and *Ulmer Südwest Presse*, September 24, 1996.
[20] *Süddeutsche Zeitung*, August 3, 1998.
[21] Bavarian Finance Minister Faltlhauser in *Süddeutsche Zeitung*, August 20, 1999.

federal conservative newspapers, while liberal newspapers – both regional and federal – were rather ambivalent in their assessment.

Whilst public opinion concerning the German case was by and large split into two camps (but with most of the academic literature criticizing the new FAG and pleading for a major reform of the whole system), both the Dutch and German newspapers were largely supportive of the 1993 Edinburgh deal. Likewise, little fundamental criticism of the very structure of the European redistributive regime has appeared in the academic literature. The whole issue of whether the existing mode of organizing intergovernmental redistribution in the EU accords with sound economic or ethical criteria has hardly attracted broad debate among scholars.[22] Even more astonishing, however, is the fact that both Dutch and German newspaper reporting was marked by a uniformly high degree of assent to the outcome of negotiations. Although the two major net contributors did not succeed in their demands to reduce their financial contribution significantly, the simple fact that the agenda had been largely accomplished as well as the fact that slight reductions (590 million Euros for the Netherlands and 700 million Euros for Germany) had been achieved were assessed as great successes. "The Netherlands came back from the Euro summit as the big winners" wrote *De Telegraaf* accordingly.[23] *De Volkskrant* too reported that "there is satisfaction everywhere with the agreement reached in Berlin."[24] In Germany, reports extensively praised the outcome to the negotiations. Though the German Chancellor, Gerhard Schröder, had himself set an extremely ambitious target, with his original calls for a reduction totaling some 3 billion Euros, his defense of the outcome – as "a prudent mixture of budget discipline and social justice between the stronger and the weaker"[25] – met with scarcely any domestic criticism. Media reporting in general concentrated less on the question of the small reduction in Germany's burden and overwhelmingly on the positive implications for enlargement. Even the more pro-opposition *Frankfurter Allgemeine Zeitung* did not adopt the opposition party's criticisms of the small reductions in the German contribution, but only regretted that the reforms to the Common Agricultural Policy had not been incisive enough.[26] The liberal *Süddeutsche Zeitung* even praised the outcome explicitly for bringing about "more justice in the Community" thus expressing acceptance of the federal government's renunciation of harder negotiations.[27] Finally, the *Frankfurter Rundschau* did not even mention Chancellor Schröder's demand of 3 billion Euros and

---

[22] Some exceptions, of course, exist. For review of the debate see Heinemann (1998).
[23] *De Telegraaf*, March 27, 1999.   [24] *De Volkskrant*, March 27, 1999.
[25] *Frankfurter Allgemeine Zeitung*, March 27, 1999, 1.   [26] *Ibid.*
[27] *Süddeutsche Zeitung*, March 27, 1999.

instead criticized on a broad front the selfish conduct of the other member states.[28]

In sum, both the participation and the social acceptance variables provide good explanations for the observable degree of compliance. The structural minority (in terms of number of votes) of the majority (in terms of the size of population) and its exploitation by the minority (in terms of population) is an important reason why the donor *Länder* brought the case. The combination of the two elements in the decision-making procedure resulted in a further entrenchment of a rule which had become the focus of a great number of criticisms. It is little wonder that the donor states felt encouraged to challenge not only the level of redistribution but also the whole logic of the system.

5.4.4   Management

The legislative process which led to the adaptation of the two regimes was in both cases very similar. Neither of the two processes showed more than a marginal degree of arguing. Both were heavily dominated by self-interested bargaining backed by threats and promises. Following directly upon the accession of the five new *Länder*, there was a vigorous debate between the old *Länder* and the federation as to the question of what proportion of the ensuing cost should be loaded on to whom.[29] Whereas the wealthy old *Länder* were not prepared to accept any additional financial burden, the poorer among them fought against retaining the same redistributive amount, which would have meant that the incorporation of the five new *Länder* would ultimately have come at their expense. By contrast the new *Länder* were relatively indifferent as to who should pay, provided they received nothing less than the poor among the old *Länder* had been accustomed to hitherto. The federal government sought to exploit the general quarrelling among the *Länder* by trying to establish a coalition between the financially strong among the old *Länder*, and the new *Länder*. The financially strong old *Länder* were won over by *inter alia* a (long-term) reduction in their burdens under the fiscal compensation scheme and a reduction in the intensity of compensation, whereas the new *Länder* were won over by a promise of extensive special aid. While this solution had the attraction of neither excessively increasing the financial burden on the rich old *Länder* nor denying the new *Länder* additional financial resources, it implied that to achieve this the *Länder* would once again

---

[28] *Frankfurter Rundschau*, March 27, 1999, 3.
[29] For a description of the negotiations in more detail see Renzsch (1994).

have to let themselves be played off, one against the other. Against this background, considered to be rather undesirable, the *Länder* ultimately managed to agree on a common line.[30] At its most basic, the proposal of the *Länder* amounted to leaving everything as it was and raising demands for compensation through the federation only where additional burdens on the *Länder* were to be expected.

The surprising agreement between the *Länder* brought the federal government under pressure. After months of debate the federal government was – in contrast to the *Länder* – under considerable public pressure to reach a speedy agreement. In order to avoid endangering the adoption of the supplementary budget for 1993, a compromise had to be found before the summer break. Since agreement on the reformulation of the federal redistributive regime was in addition directly related to the economic stabilization of the new *Länder*, and the Chancellor had committed himself publicly to his prediction of imminent "flourishing landscapes," any failure would come across as the federal government's inability to act. Against this background, the federal government stood in a very poor negotiating position, with the effect that it had to accept most of the positions taken by the *Länder* if it wanted to strike a deal at all. The very far-reaching adoption of the *Länder's* compromise by the federation was thus less about a reorientation of the federal redistributive regime to the new challenges in regulatory terms and more about the "typical case of a deal at the expense of a third party"[31] whereby the old *Länder* indemnified themselves at the expense of the federation.

Like the 1993 FAG, the Delors II package, agreed to by the member states in 1992, was an outcome of a purely intergovernmental negotiation, in which substantive justifications and argumentative ways of seeking a compromise also played no relevant part. The essential reference point for the redistributive regime between the member states had already been supplied by the Spanish government in the run-up to the summit, with its demand to orient the European Union's financial planning more than it had been before towards a consideration of the relative prosperity of member states, as well as to provide further financial resources in order to reduce regional disparities.[32] While the first significant expansion of redistributive financial resources under the Delors I package had been an important step in the right direction, it was totally unsatisfactory in

[30] See Peffekoven (1994: 282–9) and the reports in *Süddeutsche Zeitung, Die Welt,* and *Frankfurter Rundschau,* March 11, 1993.
[31] Finance Ministry Secretary of State Grunewald in *Focus* 10/1993, 32.
[32] See "Economic and Social Cohesion in Political, Economic and Monetary Union: The Spanish Viewpoint," 5 March 1991, in Laursen and Vanhoonacker (1992: 336–344).

terms of both its volume and its practical implementation. The very fact that economic and monetary union would involve the disappearance of the instrument of flexible exchange rates, while at the same time the Maastricht criteria placed tight budgetary discipline requirements on all member states, made it increasingly hard to keep tax income constant. Spain argued that extensive financial allocations by the EU to the more backward member states were required in order to allow for a realistic prospect of them joining the EMU. In order to achieve this, it was said that the structural funds should be endowed with more resources and a special fund set up for only the least-developed member states with the highest adjustment costs.

Spain's demand for a further significant increase in redistributive intensity met understandably with little favor from either the British presidency or the richer member states. Germany and Britain in particular argued that the process of economic integration would lead to increased prosperity for all member states, so that no compensation payments were needed. In the negotiations, however, Spain was ultimately successful: under Spanish pressure (supported by Portugal, Greece, and Ireland) the member states ended up agreeing to an increase in resources for the four structural funds, which totaled 35 percent in 1999, and which went to benefit the EU's poorer regions in particular. Again, they also yielded to the demand for the establishment of a special fund for the four poorest member states only (the cohesion fund). The success of the Spanish position was attributable essentially to the fact that the financial questions were dealt with together with a whole number of other questions. These included, in particular, the definition of the modalities enabling Denmark to opt out from specific parts of the Maastricht Treaty (no participation in the introduction of a common currency or the West European Union (WEU), or in establishing a common security and defense policy); the British demand to continue with its rebate; and the planned enlargement of the EU to include Austria and the EFTA countries, Finland and Sweden. Since all these questions were resolved as part of a package solution, each individual question had the potential to prevent adoption of the whole package, thus torpedoing both ratification of the Maastricht Treaty in Denmark and Britain and the EU's enlargement negotiations with Austria, Finland, and Sweden.[33]

---

[33] "Without a settlement on future financing, there could be no agreement on the opening of enlargement negotiations, on the way to deal with the Danish requests for opt-outs from the Maastricht Treaty, or on how to deal with the issue of subsidiarity . . . [F]ailure to agree in December 1992 was seen ahead of the summit as . . . threatening its very existence" (Shackleton 1993: 11).

In this intimate mixture of differing interests and interwoven policy objectives, the Spanish government was well-positioned. Since Spain had, by contrast with the richer member states, neither a major interest in the EU's planned enlargement nor an interest in achieving economic and monetary union or allowing Denmark special terms, its government was able credibly to threaten to use its veto in the negotiations on structural measures unless its demand to double, once again, the money earmarked for south European member states was met. Scholars and journalists largely agreed on their assessment of the negotiation process that led to the agreement on the funding volume that was allotted in the Delors II package. While the media labeled the negotiations in terms such as "ruthless interest politics" (*Die Welt*), "hour-long tug-of-war" (*Frankfurter Allgemeine Zeitung*), and "brinkmanship" (*The Times*), the academic literature was only slightly more reticent, for example referring to a "typical outcome of a 'deal' among member states with differing interests" (Franzmeyer 1993: 101).

Whilst both redistributive regimes are similar with regard to their procedures of adoption, they differ significantly in terms of their responsiveness. By ratifying the Basic Law in 1949 the *Länder* accepted *inter alia* the constitutional basis of the *Länder* fiscal compensation. By Article 105(2) the federation was allotted concurrent legislation over the whole tax system provided this served the purpose of "bringing about equal living conditions or upholding legal and economic unity" (Article 72(2)). Since Article 105(3) requires that all federal laws affecting *Länder* taxes must be assented to by the federal council, the rich *Länder* could assume that no excessive extension of redistributive intensity would be imposed on them against their will. But after 1955, with the accession of the Saarland to Germany, the recipient *Länder* gained a majority in the federal council and could thereby increase the amount of *Länder* fiscal compensation without the agreement of the richer donor *Länder*. Consequently, the successive history of the FAG was one of imposing a task-oriented distribution of funds that was largely independent of local tax receipts and regional economic power (see Renzsch 1991; Scharpf 1994: Chapter 2). The intensification of the compensatory effect of the horizontal *Länder* fiscal compensation from the previous 75 percent to the current 95 percent of the average financial strength of all *Länder* is thus also a consequence of the structural majority of the poorer *Länder*. Because the recipient *Länder* benefited from this situation, basic reform considerations such as restructuring the federal territory, changing the expenditure distribution, or introducing limited fiscal autonomy for the *Länder* (see Sachverständigenrat 1992: 212) never had any real chance of entering the political arena.

As opposed to the German redistributive mechanism which is determined by the majority of the poor *Länder* according to the regulatory ideas of the early postwar period, the European redistributive mechanism is far more open to adaptation. Although in the literature the unanimity requirement is by and large viewed as a major obstacle to policy reform (Lewis 1998), the history of the European redistributive regime underlines the fact that this can have important advantages over majority voting in terms of promoting its responsiveness. In 1957 the Treaties of Rome had laid the initial bases for a European regional policy, with redistribution affected through the European Social Fund (ESF) and the European Investment Bank (EIB). Because the European Community was seen from its inception by the original six member states as an arrangement to promote a common market which – against the background of economic growth that was presumed to be long-term – might lead to occasional regional distortions but which would ultimately benefit all (Marks 1992: 193), the redistributive elements were given barely more than symbolic importance.[34] It was not until the early 1970s, with the end of the euphoria over growth and the accession of Ireland and Britain into the European Community, that the question of the distributive implications of European integration began to play a more important role (Wallace 1983). Not entirely without justification, the British government in particular argued that the high financial burden of funding CAP out of the Community budget fell disproportionately on Britain, and that consequently it ought to be compensated. Britain's demand coincided with the demand long advanced by Italy for the setting up of a fund to support less-developed regions. Following prolonged negotiations, the Italo-British compensation demands ultimately led, in late 1974, to the establishment of the European Regional Development Fund (ERDF).[35]

The logic that was applied in setting up the ERDF – that of coupling substantive steps in integration with financial side payments for those states which drew little or no benefit from them – continued to mark the further development of the European redistributive regime. In 1985, as a response to the expected accession of the Iberian countries, Italy, Greece, and France demanded and received compensatory measures under the long-term Integrated Mediterranean Program (IMP), which were to compensate them for the new competitive pressure they could expect. Only a few years later the same game was repeated in the context of negotiations on the Single European Act, with a doubling of the resources

---

[34] On the genesis of European regional policies see Wozniak (1999).
[35] However, at only 1.3 billion accounting units (3.5 billion ECU, or a mere 5 percent of the Community budget), this fund had only very limited means.

that were allotted to the European Structural Fund. The economically weaker member states (Spain, Greece, and Portugal) demanded and received compensation through the doubling of the structural funds so as to offset the economic and political risk that was associated with the completion of the internal market (Anderson 1995: 141; Marks 1992: 202–204). The next big increase in the intensity of the redistributive regime operating between member states was also in the context of a linkage transaction between the richer and poorer member states. The Spanish delegation claimed in its position paper of March 5, 1991[36] that the transition from a mere common market to a political, economic, and monetary union inevitably required efforts by the European Community to compensate for regional imbalances through redistributive financial transfers. This, they claimed, was the only way to set up a mechanism that would enable backward regions to undertake the necessary infrastructural changes to keep pace with intensified competition. The Spanish position was that only the richer states would profit from the currency union, which would also have the effect of imposing additional costs on the poorer member states. Monetary union was accordingly only acceptable to Spain if flanked by additional redistributive measures. Though Germany and Britain in particular cast doubt on the substance of the Spanish argument, the need for Spain's assent to EMU (as well as that of Portugal, Ireland, and Greece) meant that they had to fall in with the demands of the four poorest member states – increasing the ERDF funds yet further and setting up a new cohesion fund.

Though it can scarcely be doubted that the assent of the richer member states to the various intensifications of the European redistributive regime was given reluctantly, both sides were better off after the linked transactions. The richer states secured the systematic inclusion of the costs of the Common Agricultural Policy in the EC budget (benefiting France in particular); the completion of the internal market; several enlargements to the European Community; and finally the move to EMU. Against the background of the high political importance that Germany – the European Community's principal net contributor – attached to these advances in integration, the price, in the form of intensified redistributive financial flows, was entirely in the range of the defensible. Without seeking to overinterpret the empirical finding of hard political negotiations, it therefore seems appropriate to interpret the development of the European redistributive regime as one component in a dynamic linked transaction from which both the net contributors and the net recipients benefited.

---

[36] See "Economic and Social Cohesion in Political, Economic and Monetary Union: The Spanish Viewpoint," 5 March 1991, in Laursen and Vanhoonacker (1992: 336–344).

In positive terms, the expansion of the EU's redistributive regime reflects not only the willingness of the economically more competitive member states to compensate their less competitive partners for the costs of further integration, but also the adaptability of a financial redistribution mechanism in order to accomplish changed social and political preferences.

Although neither of the two regimes shows any significant recourse to deliberative procedures to distinguish between legitimate concerns and pure political pressure, the European regime is nevertheless far more responsive. By forcing member states to renegotiate every couple of years on the basis of unanimity, the regime has an in-built check against the decoupling of its substantive elements from the political steering requirements of the member states. The need for the member states to update their consensus on how to conduct intergovernmental redistribution differs significantly from the federal regime with its in-built mechanism for conserving an outdated consensus. This is probably the single most important factor in explaining the relative level of compliance with the two regimes.

5.5   Compliance with redistributive arrangements

Notwithstanding the differences between the two regimes, the comparison has revealed a number of striking similarities on the side of both the dependent and the independent variables. The two redistributive arrangements are very similar in terms of the range of actors they involve and their redistributive intensity, as well as their similar degrees of monitoring, sanctioning, dispute settlement, legal and civil internalization, and participation. Both enjoy a good record of compliance and differ only slightly in this regard. This fact alone is puzzling if measured against those skeptical approaches to intergovernmental solidarity which restrict the existence of redistributive payments to within a national community. This chapter has shown that intergovernmental redistribution can exist both within and between nation-states and that it follows a very similar pattern in terms of compliance and those factors eliciting compliance. In clear contrast to the communitarian hypothesis, the readiness of the EU's member states to comply with their financial obligations is higher and not lower than is the readiness of the *Länder* to do the same in Germany.

The comparison furthermore provides clear evidence that the degree of compliance is strongly linked to the extent to which the arrangements are tied into an institutional framework, which allows for continual adjustment in the light of changing social preferences. The comparative unwillingness of *Länder* to comply with the federal redistributive regime is attributable decisively to the fact that the form of its institution-alization is associated with an outdated social consensus that has come into contradiction with the prevailing value orientations of German soci-ety. Whereas the regulatory ideal of a community of destiny based on German solidarity may still have achieved some kind of consensus in the early postwar period, today it stands in open contradiction to a clear ten-dency in society to see itself as performance-oriented, with a desire to tie redistributive efforts to economic incentive systems designed to overcome dependency.

Redistributive arrangements concluded for an unlimited or at least a fairly long period (or those seen as a side payment for another arrange-ment that is concluded for an unlimited period) require, like any other arrangement, to be continually rethought. The preferences of actors, the perception of the problems, and philosophies for solving them are also contingent temporally in the area of redistributive policies. One must therefore allow for appropriate possibilities to influence the adjustment and modification of a given arrangement. As to the question of the fac-tors that influence governmental willingness to comply with redistributive arrangements, this connection has a practical importance that should not be underestimated. The 1980s and 1990s saw a broad paradigm shift spanning the various societies. Against the background of the limits to the welfare state, which become increasingly apparent from the late 1970s, social transfer systems in general came under legitimation pres-sure. Increasingly, the conviction took hold that the further expansion of redistributive efforts threatened to overstrain the financial capacities of the modern welfare state, and that existing redistributive systems could be justified only if accompanied by incentives for the recipients to shift their needs away from a dependency on redistribution. Empirically, this social paradigm shift was expressed in the voting out of governments of a social democratic orientation, in the late 1970s and early 1980s, that had favored the maintenance of established social positions. This occurred first in Britain and the US, and shortly thereafter in Germany and France. The voting out of the conservative governments in all four countries in the 1990s by no means reversed this paradigm shift. On the contrary, in the US as well as in Britain and Germany, social democratic govern-ments came to power with social policy programs that had absorbed the lessons of the late 1970s in terms of formulating policies "beyond left and right" (Giddens 1994). Both under Clinton and under Blair and Schröder, social policy in the 1990s counted as "modern" only if it tied redistribution to a demand on the recipients to make a contribution to overcoming their dependency (Seeleib-Kaiser 2001).

The member states' redistributive regime, by contrast with the federal one, encounters a much lower level of criticism because its institutional structures enable it to reflect that paradigm shift. The rise in its redistributive intensity was accompanied by a continuing stress on the conditionality of the transfers. The necessity of continually renegotiating the regime, which is something that is built into the system of intergovernmental financial negotiations, led to linkage transactions, a dynamic over time and to openly changed preferences, that were acceptable to both donor and recipient member states. These negotiations – just like those in connection with the federal redistributive regime – are certainly associated with hard political bargaining but, on the other hand, they are also open to constructive responses to changed social and political preferences.

Thus, the significant political resistance by the three German net contributing *Länder* can be seen as an expression of the tension between a historically outdated – though institutionally cemented – idea of unconditional solidarity and the reality of a plural society, which wishes to link that solidarity to efforts on the part of the recipient *Länder* to overcome their dependency.

5.6   Annex

Table 5.4 *Gains and losses from the EU budget by member states and* Länder, *in percentage of GDP*

			(1) Cohesion fund	(2) ERDF	(3) Objective 1	(4) LFA	(5) EAGGF	(6) Total 1[1]	(7) Total 2[2]	(8) Total 3[3]
1	D	HES	0	0	0	−0.94	0	−0.94	−0.94	−0.94
2	D	BW	0	0	0	−0.50	0	−0.50	−0.50	−0.50
3	D	BAY	0	0	0	−0.48	0	−0.48	−0.48	−0.48
4	D	NW	0	0	0	−0.40	0	−0.40	−0.40	−0.40
5	EU	NL	−0.05	−0.36	−0.32	0	−0.04	−0.41	−0.37	−0.45
6	D	HH	0	0	0	−0.36	0	−0.36	−0.36	−0.36
7	EU	BEL	−0.05	−0.29	−0.23	0	−0.09	−0.34	−0.28	−0.43
8	EU	SWE	−0.04	−0.26	N/A.	0	N/A.	−0.30	N/A.	N/A.
9	EU	LUX	−0.04	−0.24	−0.23	0	−0.40	−0.28	−0.27	−0.68
10	EU	DK	−0.04	−0.25	−0.23	0	0.48	−0.29	−0.27	0.19
11	EU	A	−0.04	−0.23	−0.23	0	N/A.	−0.27	−0.27	N/A.
12	EU	D	−0.04	−0.17	−0.11	0	−0.28	−0.21	−0.15	−0.49
13	EU	F	−0.04	−0.15	−0.20	0	0.16	−0.19	−0.24	−0.03
14	EU	FIN	−0.04	−0.07	N/A.	0	N/A.	−0.11	N/A.	N/A.
15	EU	UK	−0.03	−0.09	−0.16	0	−0.04	−0.12	−0.19	−0.16
16	D	S-H	0	0	0	0.01	0	0.01	0.01	0.01
17	EU	ITA	−0.03	0.07	0.01	0	−0.04	0.04	−0.02	0.00
18	D	R-P	0	0	0	0.16	0	0.16	0.16	0.16
19	D	NS	0	0	0	0.18	0	0.18	0.18	0.18
20	D	SAAR	0	0	0	0.54	0	0.54	0.54	0.54
21	EU	ESP	0.26	0.79	0.71	0	0.46	1.05	0.97	1.51
22	D	BB	0	0	0	1.52	0	1.52	1.52	1.52
23	D	HB	0	0	0	1.61	0	1.61	1.61	1.61
24	EU	IRL	0.34	1.31	1.43	0	2.07	1.65	1.77	3.72
25	D	SACH	0	0	0	1.69	0	1.69	1.69	1.69
26	D	TH	0	0	0	1.85	0	1.85	1.85	1.85
27	D	S-AN	0	0	0	1.88	0	1.88	1.88	1.88
28	D	M-V	0	0	0	1.93	0	1.93	1.93	1.93
29	EU	GR	0.43	2.03	2.15	0	2.30	2.46	2.58	4.76
30	D	BER	0	0	0	2.89	0	2.89	2.89	2.89
31	EU	POR	0.51	2.42	2.54	0	0.18	2.93	3.05	3.11

Notes:
[1] (1)+(2)+(4).
[2] (1)+(3)+(4).
[3] (1)+(2)+(4)+(5).

Table 5.5 *Winners and losers from the cohesion fund 1994–1999*

	(1) GDP in billion ECU	(2) Share in cohesion fund, percent	(3) Share in EU own resources, percent	(4) Gross contribution in billion ECU	(5) Net contribution in billion ECU	(6) Net gain in percent GDP per year
Net contributor countries						
NL	309.4	0	6.4	0.97	0.97	−0.05
B	208.5	0	3.9	0.59	0.59	−0.05
S	199.6	0	3.1	0.47	0.47	−0.04
LUX	13.4	0	0.2	0.03	0.03	−0.04
DK	137.1	0	2.0	0.30	0.30	−0.04
A	180.1	0	2.8	0.42	0.42	−0.04
D	1865.7	0	28.2	4.27	4.27	−0.04
F	1216.2	0	17.5	2.65	2.65	−0.04
FIN	97.5	0	1.4	0.21	0.21	−0.04
UK	894.3	0	11.9	1.80	1.80	−0.03
I	955.4	0	11.5	1.74	1.74	−0.03
Net recipient countries						
E	460.4	52–58 (=55)	7.1	1.08	−7.25	0.26
IRL	55.6	7–10 (=8.5)	0.9	0.14	−1.15	0.34
GR	96.6	16–20 (=18)	1.6	0.24	−2.49	0.43
P	83.1	16–20 (=18)	1.4	0.21	−2.52	0.51
EU 15	6772.9	100	100	15.15	x	x

Table 5.6 *Winners and losers from the structural fund (Objective 1–Objective 5b) for 1994–1999*

	(1) GDP in billion ECU	(2) Allocation of funds in billion ECU	(3) Share in EU own resources, percent	(4) Gross contribution in billion ECU	(5) Net contribution in billion ECU	(6) Net gain in percent GDP per year
Net contributor countries						
NL	309.4	2.194	6.4	8.83	−6.64	−0.36
B	208.5	1.808	3.9	5.38	−3.57	−0.29
S	199.6	1.178	3.1	4.28	−3.10	−0.26
LUX	13.4	0.083	0.2	0.28	−0.19	−0.24
DK	137.1	0.741	2.0	2.76	−2.02	−0.25
A	180.1	1.432	2.8	3.86	−2.43	−0.23
D	1865.7	19.519	28.2	38.92	−19.40	−0.17
F	1216.2	13.334	17.5	24.15	−10.82	−0.15
FIN	97.5	1.503	1.4	1.93	−0.43	−0.07
UK	894.3	11.409	11.9	16.42	−5.01	−0.09
Net recipient countries						
I	955.4	19.752	11.5	15.87	3.88	0.07
E	460.4	31.668	7.1	9.80	21.87	0.79
IRL	55.6	5.620	0.9	1.24	4.38	1.31
GR	96.6	13.980	1.6	2.21	11.77	2.03
P	83.1	13.980	1.4	1.93	12.05	2.42
EU15	6772.9	138.201	100	137.86	0.34	x

Table 5.7 *Winners and losers from the ERDF structural fund for Objective 1 (1994–1999)**

	(1) GDP in billion ECU	(2) Allocation of funds in billion ECU	(3) Share in EU own resources	(4) Gross contribution to Objective 1 in billion ECU	(5) Net contribution to Objective 1 in billion ECU	(6) Net gain in Objective 1 in percent of GDP per year
Net contributor countries						
NL	309.4	0.150	6.4%	6.014	−5.865	−0.32
B	208.5	0.730	3.9%	3.665	−2.936	−0.23
LUX	13.4	0	0.2%	0.188	−0.188	−0.23
DK	137.1	0	2.0%	1.880	−1.880	−0.23
A	180.1	0.162	2.8%	2.631	−2.470	−0.23
F	1216.2	2.190	17.5%	16.445	−14.258	−0.20
UK	894.3	2.360	11.9%	11.183	−8.825	−0.16
D	1865.7	13.640	28.2%	26.500	−12.865	−0.11
Net recipient countries						
I	955.4	14.860	11.5%	10.807	4.051	0.01
E	460.4	26.300	7.1%	6.672	19.627	0.71
IRL	55.6	5.620	0.9%	0.846	4.774	1.43
GR	96.6	13.980	1.6%	1.785	12.476	2.15
P	83.1	13.980	1.4%	1.316	12.664	2.54
EU13	6475.8	93.972	95.4%	93.972	x	x

* Without Sweden and Finland.

Table 5.8 *Winners and losers from the federal equalization scheme* (horizontaler Länderfinanzausgleich) (*LFA*) *for 1996*

	(1) GDP in billion DM	(2) Net funds from LFA in billion DM	(3) Net gain as percent GDP
Net contributors			
Hesse	343.4	−3.245	−0.94
Baden-Württemberg	509.6	−2.525	−0.50
Bavaria	596.0	−2.866	−0.48
North Rhine-Westphalia	787.7	−3.135	−0.40
Hamburg	136.6	−0.485	−0.36
Net recipients			
Schleswig-Holstein	110.9	0.016	0.01
Rhineland-Palatinate	150.1	0.235	0.16
Lower Saxony	315.4	0.553	0.18
Saarland	43.9	0.238	0.54
Brandenburg	67.8	1.030	1.52
Bremen	39.3	0.634	1.61
Saxony	116.5	1.971	1.69
Thuringia	61.0	1.130	1.85
Saxony-Anhalt	66.1	1.244	1.88
Mecklenburg-Prepomerania	44.5	0.859	1.93
Berlin	149.9	4.335	2.89
D 16	2942.7	(12.3)	x

Table 5.9 *Winners and losers from the European Agricultural Guidance and Guarantee Fund (EAGGF) – guarantee section (1994)*

	(1) GDP in billion ECU	(2) Share in own resources in percent	(3) Gross contribution to EAGGF in mill. ECU	(4) Gross payments from EAGGF in mill. ECU	(5) Net payments from CAP	(6) Net from CAP as percent of GDP
B	208.5	4.1	1349.2	1170.4	−178.8	−0.09
DK	137.1	1.9	625.2	1278.4	653.2	0.48
D	1865.7	31.4	10332.5	5179.9	−5152.6	−0.28
GR	96.6	1.5	493.6	2718.9	2225.3	2.30
E	460.4	7.0	2303.4	4408.3	2104.9	0.46
F	1216.2	18.5	6087.6	8001.2	1913.6	0.16
IRL	55.6	1	329.1	1480.0	1150.9	2.07
I	955.4	11.7	3850.0	3460.6	−389.4	−0.04
L	13.4	0.2	65.8	12.1	−53.7	−0.40
NL	309.4	6.2	2040.2	1916.0	−124.2	−0.04
P	83.1	1.7	559.4	708.4	149.0	0.18
UK	894.3	10	3290.6	2939.0	−351.6	−0.04
EU12	6295.7	95.2	31326.6	33273.2	1946.6	x

6 Conclusions – the conditions of compliance

Michael Zürn and Jürgen Neyer

Is law beyond the nation-state possible? Does compliance in horizontal settings work sufficiently well? What are the building blocks for a successful elicitation of compliance beyond the nation-state? What is special about the EU in this respect? These questions have guided our study. In this chapter we discuss the empirical findings of our study, some lessons in designing institutions to achieve high rates of compliance, and some special features of the EU as a polity. In the first section, we reject the principal hypothesis that reliable law and legal equality can be expected only within a national setting. The next section discusses in detail how different theoretical perspectives on compliance contribute towards understanding successful compliance beyond the nation-state. In addition, we argue that the interactive effects between variables from different theoretical perspectives are decisive in understanding compliance records. Finally, we discuss the practical and theoretical implications of our findings.

6.1   The winner is: The EU

The preceding chapters report the findings of three sets of comparisons. In each set, regulations are compared that are located at different political levels but are of very similar content and type. By keeping the policy type and the underlying interest structures more or less constant, we studied the effects of different political settings on rule compliance. Regulations on the control of subsidies have been formulated by the WTO and by the EU as well as within Germany. Redistribution among territorial units is institutionalized in both the EU and Germany. Trade in foodstuffs is regulated by the WTO and within the EU. In each set of cases we assessed the levels of compliance, by establishing both the overall rate of compliance and the capacity to handle compliance problems. The most striking result is that within each set of comparisons the level of compliance with EU regulations is better or at least as good as that with regulations at the other two levels. Moreover, the differences in rule-compliance between the WTO regulations and those German regulations that were examined

183

Table 6.1 *Relatively assessed compliance records*

Subsidies	EU > WTO ≥ Germany
Foodstuffs	EU > WTO
Redistributional mechanisms	EU ≥ Germany

in our study are negligible. In any case, the EU achieves the best rate of compliance and clearly prevails over the other two political settings (see table 6.1).

Such a positive result for the EU is quite astonishing. It completely contradicts the first principal hypothesis guiding our study. Regulations that have been developed and established within a national setting do not show a systematically better compliance record than similar regulations in other political settings. As to subsidy control, the national regulation has a lower level of compliance than the two regulations operating beyond the nation-state (with the EU faring better than the WTO). Moreover, while there is only a slight difference in the rate of compliance with redistributive mechanisms among territorial units, as implemented by the EU compared with Germany, it is possible, at a pinch, even here to support the argument that the EU achieves a better compliance record. Although we did not have a national case involving the trade in foodstuffs, in this area the EU secures a better rate of compliance than the WTO.

These counter-intuitive findings and our interpretation of them may be challenged on two counts. First, one may point to the low number of cases and argue that quantitative studies reveal a significant deficit regarding compliance in the EU. Secondly, one might argue that our findings do not contradict, but rather support the hypothesis that hierarchy is conducive to compliance, for the EU contains more elements of legal hierarchy than the relationship between the *Länder* in Germany. A detailed discussion of these two challenges will help us to specify our findings and to clarify our hypotheses.

6.1.1   *Patterns of non-compliance in the EU*

The European Commission and some commentators have argued more than once that the EU reveals significant deficiencies when it comes to the question of compliance (Krislov et al. 1986; Weiler 1988; and Snyder 1993).[1] For instance, Knill and Lenschow (1999: 613) describe

---

[1] See also: *Seventh Annual Report to the European Parliament on Commission Monitoring of the Application of Community Law*, COM(90) 288 final and *Sixteenth Annual Report to the European Parliament on Commission Monitoring of the Application of Community Law*, COM(99) 301 final.

compliance with EU regulations in the environmental field as a "prime example of ineffective implementation." In the same vein, Tallberg (2002) identifies three prominent forms of compliance problems in the EU. The first concerns non-compliance in terms of the *legal implementation of EU directives*, that is member states frequently fail to observe the time limits that are set down by the Council. In the 1990s, this resulted in the failure to comply with about 10 percent of all Community directives (Tallberg 1999). Secondly, the *application of EU rules* also seems to be commonly plagued by non-compliance. The Commission's initiation of infringement proceedings against member states under Article 226 (formerly Article 169) is usually taken as an indicator of this form of non-compliance. The frequency of these infringement procedures has grown over time and even exceeded 1,000 cases a year in the 1990s. Thirdly, as Tallberg (2002) also points out, a swift and diligent *implementation of ECJ decisions* has been anything but the rule. And indeed, the number of infringement judgments that have not been complied with at the end of each year has undergone a steady increase. At the end of 1998 the list of cases which had been decided by the European Court of Justice (ECJ), but not yet implemented by the member states involved, amounted to the substantial number of eighty-two. In three instances member state implementation has been overdue since 1990 (with appellate proceedings or a procedure as per Article 228 currently in progress). In one instance this has been the case since 1988 (see chapter 4, section 4.3).

These studies of compliance in the EU are helpful in many respects. They underline the fact that compliance in the EU is a problem and that its regulations and directives cannot be assumed to be self-enforcing. Political bargaining, the strategic misuse of legal procedures, and sometimes even open confrontation between the Commission and a member government are observable elements even within a highly juridified and legalized polity such as the EU. The BSE case provides a clear example of this (see chapter 4, section 4.4.1). The insights provided by such studies must, however, be put in perspective.

Compliance with most directives seems to be a matter of time, and data on the non-implementation of directives grossly overstates the degree of non-compliance. Given more time, the implementation record improves. For instance, at the time of writing the implementation of the internal market program, which was inadequate for some time, is almost complete. With the exception of Greece, all EU members now have a transposition rate of over 96 percent in implementing the internal market's legal framework. The average transposition deficit has been reduced from 6.3 percent in November 1997 to 2.5 percent in May 2001. This data underlines the fact that the enforcement of compliance must be understood as a process which is only properly understood when viewed over time.

Moreover, only a small proportion of infringement cases initiated actually reach a further stage in the process. Between 1978 and 1998, only about one-third of all cases reached the stage of reasoned opinions, and only about 10 percent were referred to the ECJ (see Jönsson and Tallberg 1998: 395). Similarly, measures of compliance in the EU must take into account the fact that both the body of legislation in force and the number of members have grown in recent decades. Taking these factors into account, the level of non-compliance is modest and has remained stable or even declined (Börzel 2001: 804).

Nevertheless, the number of infringements in the EU is significant. In general terms, however, data on the amount of work carried out by monitoring and adjudicating bodies seems to be a poor indicator of non-compliance, and must also be interpreted as an indicator of a well-functioning compliance enforcement system. Keohane et al. (2000: 474–475) point out, for instance, that the broader and less costly access to an international court or tribunal is, the more cases it will receive. According to data from Sands et al. (1999), the average number of cases processed annually at such institutions since their foundation is indeed highest in those that are most easily accessible: the ECJ leads with an average of over 100 cases a year, the WTO follows with 30.5 cases, which is clearly ahead of the old GATT dispute resolution system, which averaged 4.4 cases a year, with the ICJ processing just 1.7 cases a year. In short, some of the figures put forward as indicating a compliance problem in the EU may instead be seen as an indication of a well-working compliance system.

The most important reason for not overestimating the compliance problems of the EU is, however, one that puts the EU in perspective. *Ours is a relative argument. When similar policies are compared, the EU is more effective in eliciting compliance than other settings.* Although it is certainly true that all modern political systems face compliance problems, these difficulties may vary systematically according to different institutional contexts. Our research shows that the EU is a most successful case, and one to learn from.

6.1.2   *National settings and institutional hierarchy*

When lawyers and political scientists talk of hierarchy, they easily compound two aspects of the concept which do not necessarily belong together and therefore must be distinguished analytically. In this study we distinguish between institutional or legal hierarchy on the one hand and coercive or material hierarchy on the other. This distinction helps us to grasp better the polities that are the subject of this study.

The EU certainly displays a significant degree of legal hierarchy, now identified by many as a "constitutionalization of the treaty system." According to Stone Sweet and Caporaso (1998: 102), this phrase "refers to the process by which the EC treaties have evolved from a set of legal arrangements binding upon sovereign states, into a vertically integrated legal regime conferring judicially enforceable rights and obligations on all legal persons and entities, public and private, within EC territory. The phrase captures the transformation of an intergovernmental organization governed by international law into a multitiered system of governance founded on higher-law constitutionalism. Today, legal scholars and judges conceptualize the EC as a constitutional polity, and this is the orthodox position." In all issue areas covered by the so-called first pillar, the EU claims legal supremacy over the laws of the member states and exhibits undisputed elements of legal hierarchy.

To be sure, legal hierarchy reaches its limits in the EU when the most basic issues, such as the integrity of its democratic procedures and whether something is ultra vires, are involved. In particular, the German Federal Constitutional Court (*Bundesverfassungsgericht*) is not yet willing to accept the unrestricted supremacy of the ECJ over national constitutions. In an ideal/typical national setting, any such ultra vires conflicts and issues are resolved, or at least institutionalized, by means of a supreme institution that is empowered to make the ultimate decision. In the dynamic and still fast-developing multilevel governance system of the EU, a solution has yet to be found for resolving ultra vires issues. The conflict between the ECJ and the Federal Constitutional Court (*Bundesverfassungsgericht*) on the interpretation of the Maastricht Treaty[2] (as one of seven national claims to the superiority of their supreme court decisions) highlights this discrepancy, which some commentators argue is an indication that the EU remains bound to a horizontal political setting.[3] However, this caveat is of only limited importance when analyzing compliance with commitments that do not touch upon the most basic of democratic rights and procedures. When analyzing concrete cases of compliance enforcement, ultra vires conflicts rarely figure prominently. When adopting a constitutional approach to the analysis of the EU it may well be advisable to focus on ultra vires conflicts, but it is justifiable to regard the EU as a legally hierarchical polity when analyzing compliance with specific rules. The notion of legal hierarchy is captured in our concept of legalization.

Although the EU system shows strong elements of legal hierarchy, it does not have a *material hierarchy*, which means that it is not backed by

[2] *Bundesverfassungsgericht* (1993): BVerfGE 89, 155 (ruling of October 12, 1993).
[3] See the excellent and comprehensive treatment of this issue by Mayer (2000).

an independent agent with access to superior material resources. The presence of such a material hierarchy, according to constitutionalists and realists in international relations, distinguishes a federal state from a federation with other states. As Weiler (2000: 3–4) explains: "There is a hierarchy of norms: Community norms trump conflicting member state norms. But this hierarchy is not rooted in a hierarchy of normative authority or in a hierarchy of real power. Indeed, European federalism is constructed with a top-to-bottom hierarchy of norms, but with a bottom-to-top hierarchy of authority and real power." While the EU employs the principle of federalism, the center does not have the same capacity to coerce member units as it does in a federal state.

Moreover, the EU does not govern an integrated social community with a shared collective identity. According to communitarians, this type of community is closely linked to the nation-state in which people share memories and traditions (Miller 1995). Although the EU may possess some characteristics of a regional community, all available evidence supports the case that it is far closer to being a union of peoples than a national community (Offe 2001). The EU can therefore be characterized as a political system that has developed hierarchical legal relations which are independent of a material hierarchy and communal bonds and the means to resolve ultra vires conflicts. It is thus evident that a legal hierarchy, superior force in the form of a material hierarchy, and the existence of a civil community do not necessarily coincide.

The idea that legal and material hierarchy do not necessarily coincide is also supported by the case studies that focus on German regulations. Although it is true that from a constitutional perspective Germany's federal system is – in terms of both legal and material hierarchy – closer to the ideal/typical national setting than the EU, a policy-specific approach reveals striking differences. Constitutionalists would probably point out that in terms of legal hierarchy, the most important difference lies in the recognition of the Federal Constitutional Court (*Bundesverfassungsgericht*) as the supreme and ultimate arbiter in all legal matters. Furthermore, according to Article 37 of the German Basic Law the federal government has the legal competence to take the necessary federal coercive measures to urge a *Land* to fulfil its obligations, which includes the power to take over the legal competencies of a *Land* if that is deemed necessary for the execution of federal law. Although this power is limited by the principle of proportionality, and the need to gain the support of the majority of the *Länder*, it goes far beyond the legal competencies at the disposal of the EU. It is a federal *state* (Weiler 2000). However, when it comes to analyzing legal hierarchy in a policy-specific approach the picture becomes more complex. In at least one of the comparisons in this volume (subsidies), legal hierarchy is less developed in Germany than it is in the EU.

The major difference in terms of hierarchy between Germany and the EU on the constitutional level therefore is of a material rather than a legal substance. Apart from the control it exerts over military means, the federal government's most important resource through the *Länder* is its control over the federal budget. All *Länder* administer their budgets under tight financial constraints, and most of them depend on distributive payments from the federal government. Even if one argues that the federal government neither has a federal police force at its disposal, nor can it implement its policies by means of military coercion, its "power of the purse" means there is a strong case for attributing material hierarchy to the German constitutional setting.

The WTO, in comparison, has no elements of material hierarchy but a slowly developing and already significant legal hierarchy. Its law is at least formally accepted as binding on the contracting parties and the rulings of the Dispute Settlement Body (DSB) are – at least in most cases – followed even by major powers such as the US and the EU. Due to the recent development of legal hierarchy, the WTO is increasingly analyzed in constitutional terms (e.g. Petersmann 2000). In sum, we conclude that legal and material hierarchies are best conceptualized as two different variables which have no necessary linkage with each other. Our cases underline both the fact that legal hierarchy can exist without material hierarchy and that material hierarchy does not imply the existence of legal hierarchy.

We can therefore reject the assertion that a satisfactory level of compliance with inconvenient commitments can only be expected within a national setting with a material hierarchy at its disposal. The national setting is evidently not the decisive factor. In our set of cases there is no positive and even a slightly negative relationship between the national setting and the rate of compliance. Allowing for all due caution in the making of generalizations on the basis of a low number of cases, we can still quite confidently conclude that the national setting is by no means a *necessary* condition for a high rate of compliance with inconvenient regulations.

Clearly, this is not to say that hierarchy is unimportant for eliciting compliance. We certainly do not wish to advance the proposition that "co-operation under anarchy" (Oye 1986) is ideal for achieving a high rate of compliance. On the contrary, the next section shows that both legal hierarchy and material hierarchy, albeit in an indirect sense, are significant factors for explaining compliance. We also suggest that both legal and material hierarchies are capable of exploitation beyond the nation-state, thereby questioning the anarchy–hierarchy distinction, which is so prevalent in theories of international relations, as well as the distinction between "real law" and "international law" that is prevalent in traditional legal theory.[4] On the one hand, it is possible for legal hierarchy to develop in organizations beyond the nation-state. The EU's constitutionalized legal system, with its supremacy and direct effect, is a case in point. On the other hand, the material hierarchy that is especially characteristic in the relationship between the state and its citizens has been instrumentalized for the development of an institutional hierarchy outside the national setting. Thus, the monopoly of legitimate force that is well established within democratic nation-states remains important.

This monopoly of legitimate force was decisive in civilizing social relationships within state boundaries, and prepared the ground for the rule of law. Its pacifying effect can hardly be overestimated.[5] However, in the European multilevel system, as well as in the multilevel politics among the countries of the OECD, the sanctioning members – that is, the democratic nation-states – are qualitatively different agents from those who wielded the force in medieval society. They have already undergone the process of civilization, established constitutional constraints on state power and acknowledged both a legal and an ethical duty to respect the concerns of other nation-states. Relations between these civilized nation-states do not need to rely on an external agent with superior resources.[6] Both in the EU and among the most important contracting parties of the WTO, governments are well aware that co-operation and a generally high degree of compliance are necessary preconditions to provide the goods that are demanded on the domestic market, such as exotic but safe food, as well as to limit the race towards ever-increasing subsidies. Moreover, to some extent they improve compliance by giving the blessing of the national setting to institutions beyond the nation-state. The internalization of European and international law is a case in point.

In sum, the institutional setting of the EU is more successful in eliciting compliance than either Germany's federal setting or the WTO's international setting. This finding puts criticisms about deficits in the EU's record of compliance in perspective, and it shows that material hierarchy

[4] See Slaughter and Ratner (1999), who have edited a special issue of the *American Journal of International Law*, for a succinct overview of seven prevalent theories of international law.
[5] Among many others see Elias (1969).
[6] The promises of the liberal theory of international law are largely built on this assumption (see Slaughter 1995). See also the works that demonstrate that democracies do not wage war against one another (e.g. Russett and O'Neal 2001; Müller 2002).

Table 6.2 *Perspectives and variables*

Rational Institutionalism	• easy verification of rule-compliance • sanctioning does not involve high costs for the sanctioning party
Legalization	• autonomous third party supervision of rules (juridification) • supremacy and direct effect (legal internalization) • rules are individually and directly actionable (civil internalization)
Legitimacy	• participation of all executive addressees and all the associative targets of the regulation • involvement of the broader public in rule-formulation and application
Management	• sufficient capacities for implementation are available to all parties • flexibility through reflexivity

is not decisive in achieving a high rate of compliance. In the next section, we explain these findings in more detail.

6.2 Determinants and dynamics of compliance beyond the nation-state

While compliance with regulations in a horizontal setting is not necessarily worse than in a national setting, the degree of compliance between different horizontal settings varies significantly. In order to account for this variation, we draw on determinants of compliance identified by the four theoretical perspectives of compliance that are discussed in chapters 1 and 2. Table 6.2 reproduces this list from chapter 1. One of the aims of our discussion is to show that these different variables should not only be seen in isolation from one another, but their interaction and dynamics are important as well.

6.2.1 Rational institutionalism

Rational institutionalism in particular highlights two determinants of successful compliance: effective monitoring and the institutionalization of enforcement, such that the risks and costs for the complaining party are minimized. Subsidy control and the trade in foodstuffs demonstrate particularly well that these are indeed important aspects for ensuring compliance beyond the nation-state. For compliance with subsidy controls the EU fares better than the WTO, which itself does somewhat better than Germany. In ensuring compliance with the rules on the trade in foodstuffs, the EU seems to be more successful than the WTO, especially when it comes to handling compliance crises.[7] Rational institutionalism thus predicts that monitoring and the institutionalization of horizontal enforcement will be most effective within the EU setting and least effective in Germany, with the WTO lying somewhere in between. Our evidence supports this hypothesis.

6.2.1.1 *Monitoring*   The European Commission has many functions, but monitoring the compliance of member states with EU rules is certainly among its most prominent activities. On the one hand, the Commission itself commits a great deal of its resources to systematically collecting and assessing information on compliance with EU rules. The most important instruments are on-the-spot checks of national administrations and companies, as well as the procuring and processing of information on the application of EU law. On the other hand, the Commission also cooperates closely with firms, interest groups, consumer groups and national administrations to record and examine complaints about non-compliance. In this way, the Commission increases the resources that it devotes to monitoring. In particular, the capacity of the Commission to fight illegal subsidies benefits crucially from the integration of societal actors. Companies generally have a strong interest in making sure that their competitors do not receive illegitimate resources which disrupt the market mechanism and, probably more importantly to them, put them at a competitive disadvantage. Therefore, they may be seen as the Commission's most important allies in eliciting compliance with EU anti-subsidies law. Tallberg (2002) reports that there are almost four times as many external complaints as there are direct Commission inquiries, which act as a source for cases of suspected infringements. Equally important is the requirement placed on member states to notify the Commission of all relevant domestic legislation before it is enacted. This provision leaves the Commission with the option to outlaw any measure which might

---

[7] Regarding redistributional regulations, monitoring does not seem to be an institutional problem. The recipient of resources immediately notices when he no longer receives them. Moreover, the sanctioning of someone who is unwilling to help himself looks odd. In general, rational institutionalism can hardly account for the success of redistributive polices in settings without material hierarchy and in the absence of linkages. For these reasons we shall not discuss this set of comparisons in terms of rational institutionalism. However, if one were to, it appears vital that monitoring costs and the room for institutionalized sanctioning must not vary across the different levels, since they are largely determined by the properties of the policy itself. Moreover, in both cases the redistribution is managed by a centralized agency which would easily notice any non-compliance. Rational institutionalism would therefore predict that there would be no significant difference in terms of compliance across different political settings. This conclusion is clearly compatible with the findings of the study on redistributional regulations (see ch. 5, section 5.5).

endanger the integrity of the EU's legal system. All these activities take place before the Commission files an infringement procedure. The EU has thus developed an especially efficient combination of central and societal monitoring.

In contrast to the EU, the WTO mainly depends on decentralized, intergovernmental monitoring. The WTO procedures encourage governments which suspect other governments of infringing WTO rules to report their suspicion to the WTO. This type of monitoring, in combination with a centralized dispute settlement procedure, seems effective as long as it is border issues in trade relations that are concerned. Exporters can be expected to realize quickly when border tariffs and regulations increase. Now that the WTO deals also with behind-the-border issues (see Kahler 1995), it appears essential that it develops more independent, centralized monitoring mechanisms, which are open to complaints by companies. While the WTO has developed some monitoring capacities (e.g. the Trade Policy Review Body), no legal consequences are attached. They rely on the goodwill of the contracting parties and are somewhat deficient when compared to those measures implemented in the EU.

The WTO monitoring procedures look much more impressive, however, when they are compared with Germany's subsidy control procedures, where institutionalized monitoring between the German *Länder* is non-existent. Monitoring and the formulation of complaints against the activities of other *Länder* rely solely on the unilateral action of a single *Land*, with the consequence being that either they do not occur at all or, if they do, they do not reach the stage of a legal dispute settlement.

6.2.1.2 Sanctioning Both the EU and the WTO have set up sanctioning systems that impose fewer costs on the complaining party than would be the case in a purely anarchic setting. Until 1993, the EU had no sanctioning mechanisms at all. If states disregarded ECJ judgments, all the Commission could do was to start a renewed infringement procedure. Nor were states permitted to sanction each other. Only the Maastricht Treaty provided the Commission with the possibility of imposing a lump sum or penalty fine on member states who disregarded ECJ judgments. So far, the Commission has relied solely on daily penalty payments and has not used lump sum penalties. In any case, complainant member states do not carry the costs of sanctioning violators. The EU has developed a vertical coercion mechanism which more than offsets the gains of non-compliance.

With the WTO, the picture is rather mixed. While one could point to the dispute settlement mechanism, which contracting parties can count upon as a third party that is able to decide autonomously on matters of legality and sanctioning, it should be added that plaintiffs must be aware that complaints against other contracting parties might lead to legal retaliation and set off a chain reaction of counter-claims (cf. chapter 3). Busch and Reinhardt (2002) report that on average a complaint increases the probability that the target of that complaint will file a retaliatory suit within one year by fifty-five times. Furthermore, because any authorization to suspend trade concessions is limited to an amount which offsets the damage that has occurred to the plaintiff, contracting parties are factually free to choose between compliance and the limited consequences of non-compliance. In this sense, the WTO has institutionalized a tit for tat mechanism which may in most cases be considered beneficial for the complaining party,[8] but which has neither a deterrent nor a punishing effect – the sanctions are supposed only to offset the cost to the affected party – and are not without risk for the plaintiff, since they involve a horizontal mechanism.

Even such limited sanctioning mechanisms are unavailable to the German *Länder* in the case considered here. No sanctioning mechanisms whatsoever are available to punish illegal subsidies policies, and the only way for a *Land* to react to excessive subsidy payments by another *Land* is to do the same.

The compliance patterns observed in the case studies discussed match the expectations of rational institutionalism. Where the functions of monitoring and sanctioning are assumed by centralized institutions that make full use of transnational non-governmental actors, as in the case of the EU, compliance is the greatest. Where monitoring and sanctioning remains an intergovernmental function, as with the WTO, compliance works reasonably well. Where all the second-order costs of monitoring and sanctioning are borne by the complaining party, as in the case of subsidies policies in Germany, there is little compliance.

6.2.2   Legalization

To analyze legalization, we distinguish between the degree of legalization of a polity (such as the WTO, the EU or Germany) and the degree of legalization of specific policies (such as subsidy or foodstuffs policies). While the former refers to the overall legal design of a polity and addresses constitutional questions such as the question of *Kompetenz-Kompetenz* or the status of individuals as legal subjects in a given political order, the

---

[8] To be sure, economists would point to higher consumer prices and thus emphasize the costs that are involved in raising tariffs as a sanction. Decision-makers in the political sphere, however, rarely consider tariffs in a contested sector as costly.

latter refers to the manifestation of these overall designs with respect to actual policies. Furthermore, we distinguish between two aspects of legalization: juridification and internalization. Juridification refers to a process by which the settling of disputes surrounding the application of regulations is delegated to a third party. The greater the independence of the members of the adjudicatory body, measured, say, in terms of selection method and tenure (see Keohane et al. 2000: 461), and the more they apply legal reasoning (as opposed to bargaining), the higher the degree of juridification. Internalization refers to the degree to which the regulations of a larger system are legally and civilly internalized by the member's system. Legal internalization means that the legal norms of the higher political level are accepted by national or state courts without them having the option to veto them. In this way the law beyond the nation-state is enforced by domestic courts. Civilly internalized means that those affected by the regulations have actionable civil rights, or to put it differently, they have access to international or supranational courts.[9] A high degree of juridification *as well as* legal and civil internalization indicates legal hierarchy.

In terms of the *juridification of the polity*, the ranking of our cases is straightforward. The ECJ has a high level of independence. Its judges hold long tenures and it applies an advanced level of legal reasoning. Likewise, the German Federal Constitutional Court (*Bundesverfassungsgericht*) is undisputedly independent and it is a clear example of a highly juridified dispute settlement body. The new WTO dispute settlement mechanism follows closely behind on both these counts. As opposed to the GATT's old dispute settlement mechanism, its new DSB is comparatively independent and juridified.

When it comes to assessing *juridification in a policy perspective*, however, an important distinction must be made between the formal design of dispute settlement mechanisms and their factual competence and willingness to decide in specific cases. Although the Federal Constitutional Court, for example, was repeatedly asked by plaintiff *Länder* to give an opinion on the constitutionality of the level of redistribution, it always responded that any such question was of a political nature and was therefore beyond its competence. Likewise, the ECJ has no competence to decide on the level of redistribution between member states in the EU, but is – as with the Federal Constitutional Court – limited to assessing whether member states fulfill their legal obligations. Also in the federal

---

[9] See Zürn and Wolf (1999: 282–288) for a discussion of these concepts. They mainly build on Koh (1997). Keohane et al. (2000) conceptualize the degree of delegation to legalized dispute resolution beyond the nation-state in a way that is perfectly compatible with our thinking.

subsidies case the high degree of formal legalization did not translate into a policy-specific high degree of legalization, which was due to the hesitancy of the *Länder* to use that option for fear of instigating a process of centralization. It is only in the European subsidies case and the two foodstuffs cases, therefore, that a formal competence not only exists but was factually implemented and had an observable impact on the behavior of its addressees.

Legal internalization on the polity level is again furthest developed in the EU and the Federal Republic of Germany. The supremacy of European law over national law and the direct effect of ECJ case law through the preliminary-ruling procedure of Article 234 (formerly Article 177) ensure that European regulations (and some directives) in the subsidies and the foodstuffs cases have undeniable legal validity in all member states. Likewise, the Federal Constitutional Court enjoys unchallenged legal supremacy over all other national courts and all actions taken by governmental authorities. Compared to the ECJ and the Federal Constitutional Court, the DSB of the WTO lags behind in terms of legal internalization. Its rulings are accepted neither by the ECJ nor by domestic courts as creating legal obligations. Therefore, although it is highly juridified, it fares less well in terms of legal internalization.

In contrast to the widely held view that the EU's administration is isolated from its citizens, *civil internalization* on the *polity level* is rather well developed at the European level. Although it may take years for a suit filed by an individual to proceed all the way through the different national courts to the ECJ (cf. Joerges 2002b), it is at least possible for non-state actors to use European law to challenge the governmental action of a member state. In the subsidies and the foodstuffs cases, individuals not only have better access to dispute settlement bodies (via the Commission) than they do at the international level but also (in the subsidies case) as compared to the national level. The WTO, finally, shows no elements of civil internalization whatsoever. All legal proceedings must be initiated by the governments themselves, which are the only actors granted legal standing. The settling of disputes therefore remains an undertaking which is heavily influenced by political considerations and intergovernmental bargaining, and which is therefore of only limited effect for securing compliance.

These differences in general *civil internationalization* are partially reflected at the level of *specific policies*. In the subsidies and the foodstuffs cases, individuals have better access to the ECJ (via the Commission) than they do at the international level, as well as compared to the national level (in the subsidies case). Due to the purely intergovernmental character of the federal subsidies policy, the high degree of formal juridification and legal internalization in Germany has had no effect on the record of compliance of its *Länder*. Likewise, in the BSE case any affected citizen had the opportunity to file a legal suit against action taken by the German government, forcing it to comply with its obligations. Although it is true that civil internalization in redistributive policy is very low at the European level, the same applies to the German mechanism. Due to the traditional German legal requirement that individuals who wish to bring a legal claim must prove that significant damage has been inflicted on them (prohibition of collective action), no individual claim against a *Land* for non-compliance with the provisions of the redistributive mechanism would have any chance of proceeding.

In sum, the compliance records that are observed in the case studies support the conjectures that are derived from the theoretical perspective of legalization, which emphasize juridification and internalization on the level of specific policies, while the polity level does not play a role. In at least two of the three comparisons, it is the level with the higher degree of legalization in the given policy field which elicits the higher degree of compliance. The importance of legalization becomes especially clear in the comparison on subsidy controls. The most legalized level in this policy field is the EU, which achieves a better record of compliance than the less legalized WTO and a drastically better record than the non-legalized federal level in Germany. The effect of legalization can also be observed in foodstuffs policy. It is the EU's comparatively highly developed legal mechanisms which account for the better compliance rate with EU foodstuffs policy, whereas the WTO's less developed legalization shows serious functional deficiencies in its mechanisms for coping with alleged cases of non-compliance, leading to higher rates of non-compliance. Any unconditional optimism regarding the functional effectiveness of law as a steering mechanism for the pursuit of political order must, however, take into account that relying on courts to enforce compliance is highly time-consuming and carries no guarantee of success. The limitations of law as a steering mechanism are not only underlined by the failure of the WTO's DSB to make the EU comply with its decision on hormones, but are further emphasized by cases like Alcan (chapter 3), where it took seventeen years to recover illegal subsidies, or BSE (chapter 4), where it was only a political compromise that put an end to the dispute with Germany and years before the ECJ reached its judgment against France. Moreover, any assessment of the independent power of the law is well advised to take into account that its effectiveness presupposes its embeddedness in an institutional setting which follows the logic of rational institutionalism and acknowledges the importance of monitoring and sanctioning.

Strictly speaking, our findings on different levels of compliance are over-determined by the factors highlighted by rational institutionalism and legalization. We readily admit that the "too many variables, too few cases" objection applies to our study, especially when asked to discriminate between the independent effects of rationalist institution-building and of legalization.[10] Good records of compliance are, in our cases, generally accompanied simultaneously by both the principles of rational institution-building and legalization. Against the background of this close relationship between these independent variables, two comments are in order.

First, additional observations indicate that legalization has an *independent effect*. The first signs of improved compliance with the international trade regime over time provide a case in point. While the monitoring and sanctioning mechanisms did not change substantially in the course of the transformation from the GATT to the WTO regime, the level of juridification clearly did. Hence the insistence by John Jackson and a host of other scholars that the steady shift to more formal rules and processes in the GATT dispute resolution procedure, culminating in the WTO provision that panel decisions be automatically binding, has enhanced compliance.[11] Second, the explanation for the difference between the compliance record of the EU and that of the WTO must refer to legalization. The change in terms of rational institution-building does not suffice to explain this difference. Prior to 1993, the EU had an even weaker sanctioning system, yet its compliance record was at least as good as that of the GATT. Third, Börzel (2001) shows convincingly that regulations are much better complied with in the EU system than are directives. Since regulations automatically trigger legal internalization, this finding supports the notion of an independent effect from legalization.

Above all, however, it is the interplay between the features emphasized by rational institutionalism and legalization that makes the EU so effective in terms of securing compliance. Monitoring and sanctioning work better when backed up by legalization. As Hurd (1999: 400–401) points out, the effectiveness of sanctions increases when they are considered an outcome of a legal process. Legalization, in turn, only makes sense when monitoring works. Sophisticated legal proceedings would be considered shallow if only a small number of contested cases were dealt with in this way. In this sense, *the interactive effects of rational institution-building and legalization are most important*.

---

[10] Indeed, Abbott and Snidal (2000) consider legalization as part of rationalist institution-building.

[11] Jackson (1997, 1998); Petersmann (1997b). For a more critical view see Hudec (1993) and Goldstein and Martin (2000).

6.2.3   Legitimacy

Explaining compliance from the perspective of political legitimacy reveals further important insights. The exploration of the hypothesis that the probability of a satisfactory level of compliance is greater if all governmental *addressees* of a regulation are *involved* in the decision-making process behind it, and if the *affected* societal *parties* of a regulation, both the associative targets and all those affected by the rule, are *heard* both informally and formally, reveals the following. On the one hand, there is only weak empirical evidence to support the hypothesis that all the addressees of a regulation must have a fair chance of participation in the formulation of the rules, as this was the case to a large extent in almost all the cases we examined. One could even argue, as Dieter Wolf does in chapter 3, that the case in which the addressees and affected parties were least included and where a third party actor had the broadest discretionary powers, i.e. in the case of the European subsidies policy, shows an extraordinarily high degree of compliance, while it was precisely the strong position of the *Länder* in the application of the rules in the case of federal subsidies policy which prohibited their effectiveness. On the other hand, however, the foodstuffs cases, as discussed by Jürgen Neyer in chapter 4, provide evidence for exactly the opposite conclusion. In the two compliance crises that concerned the regulation of foodstuffs, it was essentially the disregard for the views of the EU member states (in the hormones case) and of France and Germany (in the BSE case) on the part of the Codex Alimentarius Commission (CAC) and the Commission, which provoked their protest and led to open non-compliance, temporarily or otherwise. Neither the EU in the hormones case nor France and Germany in the BSE case were prepared to accept the outcome of a narrow vote which refused to acknowledge the legitimacy of their concerns. Although the procedures according to which the decisions were taken could build on procedures that had been consented to, their outcome equated to a factual exclusion of concerns which were of the utmost importance to the defeated parties.

These two seemingly contradictory findings may be reconciled, however, if we qualify the legitimacy hypothesis by putting it into context with the democratic character of the rules' addressees: from this perspective, democratic governments have an inescapable obligation to promote those views which are viewed by a large domestic majority as highly sensitive. Any refusal to take such concerns seriously would amount to a disregard for domestic democratic procedures and would have little chance of withstanding public protest. Following this line of reasoning, a fundamental difference between the subsidies and the foodstuffs cases is that while the former can rely on a broad public acceptance of the need to limit governmental spending, and the lack of enforcement incites only the protest of a few interested parties (the affected company and its employees), the latter is an issue of concern to a much broader public and can rely on their unequivocal support for the most stringent possible regulations and a clear emphasis on the precautionary principle. It is therefore plausible to assume that, at least in cases of broad public concern, the satisfactory participation of all regulatory addressees in the decision-making process improves the rate of compliance, but that it is by no means a necessary or *sufficient requirement* for good compliance. Besides, participation alone is insufficient because the decision-making process must also be designed so that all legitimate concerns are taken into account and reflected in the policy-formulation.

Against this background, the relatively successful compliance rate of the EU, as compared to the WTO, may be explained by the systematic integration of the affected parties of a regulation into the decision-making processes of the EU. No other political institution beyond the nation-state has developed such far-reaching procedures for the involvement of non-state actors in will-formation and decision-making processes. By the mid-1990s, 693 formal EU-level interest groups had been established and 3,000 interest associations from every country and every conceivable sector had an office in Brussels (Aspinwall and Greenwood 1998: 3). In addition, the so-called comitology system has established a system of hearings that aims at integrating an unusually broad set of interests and perspectives in the decision-making process (Joerges and Falke 2000; Neyer 2000a). Such openness to interest groups, which frequently represent domestic affected parties, distinguishes the EU. No such developments can be observed in connection with the WTO, and even less so with respect to the GATT.

The more decisive argument in our view, however, relates to the social acceptance of a strong compliance and enforcement system by the broad, general public, which in the course of our studies emerged as the real weak point in securing compliance in horizontal settings. Legitimacy as such is neither necessary nor sufficient for improving compliance rates; monitoring, sanction and legalization are more decisive in this respect. Legitimacy, however, does back up the compliance mechanism and is thus necessary for developing strong secondary rules. The absence of legitimacy works as a disturbance variable in what would otherwise be very effective compliance systems. Even stable institutions, built under the guidance of rational institutionalism and, furthermore, legally and civilly internalized, reach the limit of their capacity to bring about compliance if national publics refuse to associate themselves with the

Table 6.3 *Inclusiveness of public spheres beyond the nation-state*

	Territorial dimension	
Functional dimension	Segmented	Integrated
Segmented	Fragmented sectoral publics	Fragmented national publics
Integrated	Sectoral transnational publics	Broad transnational publics

substantial demands of a regulation. *While institutions that build on the logic of rational institutionalism and legalization can elicit sufficiently high rates of overall compliance, legitimacy is decisive for effectively handling compliance problems.*

It is necessary to apply the distinction between broad publics, fragmented publics and sectoral publics to clarify the point. In all three cases it is important that the term "public" implies that an exchange of opinions takes place and that views and positions are not just issued, but that a discourse among competing claims can be observed. The term *broad public* refers to an ideal-typical democratic discourse among all the citizens of a given political system, which is mediated through newspapers and television, adopted by politicians, and characterized by an interactive exchange of views, opinions, and information. Such broad publics mostly arise within national contexts. A *fragmented public* is similar to a broad public in that it encompasses broad social groups which are mediated through newspapers or other forms of mass media. It differs from a broad public, however, in so far as the respective political system consists of a number of broad publics that are divided into separate and distinct territorial spheres which may from time to time take notice of each other but which generally do not exchange views or try to understand each other's concerns. In contrast to broad and fragmented publics, *sectoral publics* are formal or informal groups generated out of societal differentiation and stratification and which concern themselves with specific issues; their politically most important form is issue networks (Abromeit and Schmidt 1998; Peters 1994). Although these sectoral publics are often in a position to process far more complex matters and have a far more profound knowledge of the issue at hand than do broad publics, their social acceptance cannot be taken for granted (Eder, Hellmann and Trenz 1998: 324–328; Eder and Kantner 2000). Like broad publics, sectoral publics can be territorially integrated or fragmented (and see table 6.3).

The decisive point is that substantial compliance problems are likely to arise and are almost impossible to contain if the content of a regulation (i) moves from the agenda of sectoral publics onto the agenda of broad publics and (ii) becomes fragmented, i.e. is discussed separately by one or more national publics without reference to the debates of other national publics; and (iii) opposing opinions of the regulation are formed in different national publics. The power of such "public disturbances," which can be put down to the desire of governments to be re-elected, will even prevail if the regulation has previously been under deliberative negotiation among transnational sectoral publics. The dynamic that comes into play and jeopardizes compliance can only be avoided if a regulation is internalized at a societal level that exists beyond the nation-state, i.e. if the norms are given deliberative feedback by the broad public affected by the regulation. What is required, therefore, is a fair balance between the various interests that are based on the general political consent of the transnational community, as conveyed through argumentation.

At this point possibly the most crucial distinction between a post-national political system, such as the EU, and national political systems becomes clear: the level of integration or segmentation of the broad public. The debates over the appropriate reaction of the EU to the BSE crisis have undoubtedly become an issue of broad public interest but, at the same time, they reverted to the largely fragmented national publics, thereby upsetting the regulations that had been agreed on by the relevant sectoral public at EU level – which in this case was probably for the better. In the debate over Germany's interstate financial redistribution, by comparison, even the agitators on both sides were, in spite of their fundamental differences, forced to address both the interests of the *Land* which they represent as well as a common, integrated broad public at the national level. This not only facilitates negotiations over the establishment of a regulation, but substantially reduces compliance problems, so that there were no serious compliance crises in the German interstate financial redistribution regime. Nor did the EU redistributive mechanism fall into the trap of public disturbances because the fragmented national discourses did not lead to diametrically opposed positions. Finally, Europe's subsidy policy did not become an issue for the broad public and thus also caused no public disturbances when the member states were forced to change their policy. The difference between the Alcan and BSE cases is thus one between interest group and majoritarian policies (cf. Wilson and DiJulio 1995). Regarding EU foodstuffs policy, however, politicians are rewarded if they vigorously defend the opinion of their own national public, regardless of the legal or contractual circumstances and the facts of the case. While this was initially true for the British politicians in the BSE case, it was later equally valid for German and French politicians. In other words, the Achilles heel of international regulations is the existence of territorially fragmented publics, and this is felt most when policies generally attract a lot of attention but are at the same time perceived very differently by the respective national publics. Intergovernmental *arguing*, which is often viewed as a primary means of resolving problems beyond the state, is thus unlikely to bring about a desired result if it does not take into account the fact that the governments of democratic nation-states are not free to act as they please. Even if all the governments involved in a decision-making process embark on a perfectly deliberative discourse, by not integrating the affected parties and the broad public at home, they run the risk of provoking domestic protest, which will prevent them from implementing their decision, especially if it involves an issue of public concern. We believe that this is an important finding with increasing practical relevance. With the rise of globalization and more intrusive international institutions, the decoupling of effective compliance systems beyond the nation-state from national democratic legitimacy will become more frequent in the future. Hence, the growing necessity for public justification at the transnational level, so as to avoid the disturbance effect of absent legitimacy, which is becoming more important and potentially destructive for governance beyond the nation-state (cf. Zürn 2004).

One possible interpretation of this finding – that national publics are a "disturbance variable" – is to construe the EU's success as parasitic, feeding off the legitimacy of the member states. In this interpretation, the political system of the EU has only limited potential of its own to achieve independent legitimacy, but appropriates for its own use, so to speak, the legitimacy of the national constitutional state through legal internalization. However, the moment a concrete case lays bare the parasitic nature of the EU, compliance crises emerge. When it becomes clear that the rules are unpopular *and* are imposed from outside, the potential for resistance arises and polarized national publics can interfere with an otherwise smoothly running compliance system. Seen thus, a second interactive effect can be added to our explanatory variables. Legitimacy and compliance crises only become important when rationally designed institutions and legalization have established a strong compliance system. The power of the courts will then be countered from time to time by the power of the people.[12] This rather skeptical diagnosis of the EU as a polity with only limited legitimacy resources of its own, however, also paves the way for a more forward-looking understanding of the role of legitimacy

---

[12] Conversely, it can be assumed that there must be a substantial measure of legitimacy in the EU at the level of the political elite before legal internalization can proceed. In addition, in the light of the compliance conflicts described above, the development of the legitimacy of the EU also raises the interesting question whether instances of fragmented and polarized publics consume or create communities (cf. Eder, Hellmann and Trenz 1998).

in eliciting compliance. If it is true that broad public discourses are only likely to become a disturbance variable if they stand in opposition to specialized sectoral publics, one implication is that an important precaution against such disturbances is the integration of sectoral and broad publics. If sectoral and broad publics can be integrated by mediating between the competing claims of different publics, disturbances become less likely and the public may become a means of achieving constructive policy-making.

6.2.4   *Management*

The management approach starts with the expectation that states have a propensity to comply with their treaty obligations. When non-compliance occurs, it is, in this view, usually not because of a calculated weighing of the costs and benefits of norm adherence (which may be influenced by monitoring, sanctioning, and legalization) but instead because of insufficient capacity to implement the rules or the absence of regulatory flexibility in the light of changed circumstances. Sufficient capacities for implementation available to all parties and flexibility through reflexivity are therefore the two most important determinants of compliance in this perspective.

The lack of sufficient capacities to implement regulations which have been agreed upon does not help to explain the variance in our cases. On the basis of our data however, the resources hypothesis cannot be rejected altogether. The countries that we studied in our cases are usually considered exceptionally rich, in terms of financial, technological, and administrative means, and a lack of resources is rarely a cause for non-compliance.[13] Moreover, it seems that a shortage of resources is only relevant with respect to certain regulations. Only "positive" regulations require governments to undertake to do something, in contrast to "negative" regulations, which require them to refrain from doing something, and it is only when governments are expected to act that a lack of implementation resources becomes a problem. Refraining from doing something does not usually require vast material resources (see Zürn 1998: Chapter 6). However, although when states are required to refrain from doing something – as in the case of subsidy controls – resources do not constitute a significant problem, ambiguity and cheating do become more important causes of non-compliance. In such cases, juridification and even internalization are the best means of bolstering compliance. Therefore, when states with highly developed market economies and

---

[13] One partial exception was the EU demands on Great Britain in response to the BSE crisis in 1996 (see chapter 4).

well-functioning administrations agree to refrain from doing something, we do not expect compliance problems due to a lack of resources.[14] This may be quite different when we deal with "positive regulations" or countries with limited resources.

This point can be illustrated by data generated in other studies. Today, almost all of the measures required for the Single European Act (SEA) have been implemented in all the member states, and to a great extent without the administrative and financial support of the EU (see section 6.1). Moreover, the availability of resources is a much worse predictor of compliance in the case of negative regulations, which suggests that a lack of resources is not a major problem. The countries with the lowest rates of implementation of the single market program, Belgium and Italy, are clearly not those with the least administrative, technological and financial means (measured in GNP per capita). The countries with relatively few resources – such as Portugal and Greece – are among those member states in the lower-middle ranks in the implementation records of the SEA. By contrast, the real rates of reduction in sulfur dioxide emissions, as required by the Acid Rain Regime – a typical example of a positive regulation – fit almost perfectly with the level of GNP per capita. While only the rich countries, such as Sweden and Germany, had achieved reductions of over 50 percent between 1980 and 1989, poorer countries, such as Bulgaria or (the former) Czechoslovakia, were still at levels between plus 5 and minus 10 percent (Levy 1993: 114). In the EU, the correlation between a lower GNP per capita and implementation problems in the environmental field is not as clear and uniform as it is in the Acid Rain Regime, yet it is still remarkable (see Börzel 1999). A final remark in support of our point is that in dispute settlement processes over negative regulations, such as in the WTO, governments hardly ever try to justify their non-compliance by pointing to their own incapacity to implement the regulations in question. Rather, they generally refer to different interpretations of the contract or to infringements of the rules by the complainant.[15] It is a completely different situation with positive

---

[14] On the contrary, Tallberg (1999) argues that institutional incapacity is an important determinant of non-compliance. What he labels institutional incapacity seems to a large extent, at least implicitly, to be operationalized by the number of veto players at the national level. While this may indeed be a powerful means of accounting for varying compliance rates across countries, it seems a weak determinant for variance across policy fields. Moreover, it is debatable whether the number of veto players – usually used as a feature of the institutional structure of decision making – is a good indicator for administrative incapacity when complying with agreed rules.

[15] See e.g. Victor (2000) on WTO dispute settlement cases on: the European Community's ban on imports of bovine meat produced with growth hormones; Australia's ban on imports of fresh and frozen salmon; and Japan's ban on the import of numerous varieties of fruits and nuts.

regulations. The failure to implement positive regulations at the national level is often justified by insufficient resources and is accompanied by requests for international support.

The second aspect of the management approach – that is the degree to which the application of rules is flexible and is conducted by means of reflexive interaction – seems to be much more important for understanding the compliance records in at least two of our comparisons. Both in the foodstuffs and the redistributive cases, one of the most important reasons for the difficulties and the outright rejection of the regulation (without non-compliance or compliance crises necessarily taking place, however) was the addressees' perception that they had no fair chance to feed their concerns back into the adaptation of the rules so as to reflect their changing preferences and needs. The German net-payers' endeavor to alter the financial adjustment scheme to put a stronger emphasis on competition was blocked by the majority of *Länder* (which, nevertheless, accounted for only a minority of the population), which left little room for deliberative reflections on the adequacy of the mechanism. Likewise, in the two foodstuffs cases, decisions were dominated by strategic voting (in the CAC) or the bureaucratic rationality of the Commission and did not provide any opportunity to integrate the concerns of either important addressees or affected domestic parties. Certainly, the case of subsidy controls also underlines that flexibility may have a negative impact on the effectiveness of other rules already in force. That, however, must not be seen to contradict the general evidence of the importance of flexibility through reflexivity in promoting compliance: it might well be the case that the option to review older rules in the light of new demands is an important element in persuading addressees to comply. Against this background, flexibility through reflexivity can to some extent serve as a buffer, which balances out any lack of social acceptance, allowing a rule to be changed to suit social preferences, and thus pointing to a third interactive effect between our independent variables. Reflexivity comes at a price, however, namely the need to accept that compliance and effectiveness are two different variables which may sometimes prove to be difficult to realize at the same time.

The conclusions from these empirical results are relevant to at least three broader theoretical debates. First, they can be interpreted as supporting Mayntz's findings from the early 1980s that inquiries into the conditions for successful compliance and implementation require a multicausal research design because compliance can hardly ever be attributed to a single factor (cf. also Tsebelis 1995). The diversity of possible factors of influence at the national, transnational and international levels means that the reasons for a high degree of governmental compliance cannot be limited to any one of the three levels, but require instead a broad analysis with a variety of explanatory variables. Effective policies can be obstructed at any of the three levels. At the international level, a high degree of juridification is necessary to settle interpretational differences regarding the application of legal obligations, as well as to provide international institutions with the means to enforce legal obligations. At the transnational level, the integration of public interest groups is necessary in order that they can effectively voice their domestic concerns to the governance processes of postnational constellations. This participation is crucial for relieving the tension between domestic and intergovernmental rationalities and for generating social acceptance for international regulations. It can thus alleviate the Achilles heel of compliance in multilevel constellations, which is domestic resistance from lower units. What counts in the process of shaping postnational governance, therefore, is the search for a complex set of procedures which can bring about a continuous discursive process among international organizations, governmental addressees, and affected domestic parties on what are collectively acceptable regulations and the modalities of their application.

A second important finding is that although postnational politics has no international means of coercion whatsoever, the practice of intergovernmental co-operation reveals a far-reaching transformation of the modern understanding of sovereignty. Sovereignty can no longer be perceived as a combination of the internal monopoly on the legitimate exercise of force and the freedom from external legal constraints, but must be understood as the freedom to engage in collective problem-solving (cf. Chayes and Chayes 1995: 123). This "new sovereignty" is based on attaining the status of a trustworthy member of the international community. The fact that publicly justifiable arguments are presented for the vast majority of deviations from the requirements of international legal standards is not simply an expression of "cheap talk"; it is just as much a reflection of the basic commitment to the binding nature of international norms and the necessity felt to give a reason for their transgression which is acceptable to other governments. If a valid regulation were openly and intentionally violated without providing some form of justification, this would be tantamount to a unilateral rejection of the normative foundations underlying the international public order. Such a violation would inevitably be interpreted not only as an admission of untrustworthiness, but worse, as an admission of not *wanting* to be trustworthy. It would have to be interpreted as a declaration by the non-compliant government that it considers itself beyond the pale of the community of those who accept the law as an adequate means of promoting political integration. What the contracting party expresses through its compliance with the law is not merely the adaptation of its actions to a collective rationality, but its respect for the collective interest as a relevant guideline for its own actions (cf. Kratochwil 1989: 97).

The third theoretically relevant result is that the concerns about a widening gap between national democratic discourses and international policy-making can only to some extent be empirically substantiated by this study. True, governments can shield themselves from societal demands – as is particularly evident in European subsidizing policies – and in some cases, this strategy may even improve compliance with international obligations, but it is also true that a democratic government's actions remain linked to national public discourses and that it is hardly possible to implement international regulations in the face of explicit public protest. Just like national governance, international governance also requires a high degree of acceptance, not only on the part of its governmental addressees, but also on the part of those who are affected by the regulation. International regulations which cannot be sufficiently legitimized at the national level stand little chance of being implemented if they come up against widespread public opposition. Against this background, concerns about the emergence of a new *raison d'état* (Wolf 2000) seem exaggerated. What stands in fundamental contrast to the decoupling of international politics and national democracy is the growing need for the public justification of policies beyond the nation-state and the dependence of democratic politics on broad public consent.

6.3   Implications for the study of European integration

What is special about the EU? What are the key institutions of the European polity? What logic do they follow and how is legitimacy generated for this system? What is the driving force of European integration? What are the main features of the mechanisms by which decisions are made in this system? These are some of the key questions tackled by the study of European integration. Our study has implications for at least two of the most contested issues relating to European integration.

6.3.1   What kind of polity is the EU?

The EU is, above all, a political system that extensively utilizes law to create order and purpose. Law making and law enforcement take place within a structure that combines hierarchical and horizontal procedures. While there is clearly no central body with superior resources, the system has developed a well-established legal hierarchy and consented authority relations. The EU is an authoritative system that works without having to wield the threat of *brute* force. It does, however, utilize mechanisms of horizontal enforcement, the effectiveness of which depends on the shadow of nationally established monopolies of power. Although Walter Hallstein, President of the Commission from 1958–1967 and an ardent proponent of federalism, was certainly right to point out that the EU is a community of law, the EU is by no means entirely free from sanctions and force.

The Achilles heel of the system is therefore not the absence of superior force, but an insufficient degree of societal integration binding together the different political discourses in all the member states. Satisfactory compliance rates in the EU can be assured through rational institution building and legalization. However, the management of compliance crises, which take place especially when a regulation is heavily legalized, fails when societal integration does not back up the institutional system. Political integration through law is clearly more advanced than societal integration, as indicated by a strong feeling of common identity and an integrated broad public. Europe has undoubtedly become an increasingly political issue, but this is not the question at hand: the question is whether speakers in public discourses speak to national or European publics. So far, broad public discourses seem to be confined within the bounds of their respective national communities. If the outcomes of these fragmented national public discourses happen to be polarized, then the community of law comes under severe pressure and compliance crises become extremely hard to handle. In this sense, law in the EU is particularly deficient on one count. It does not satisfactorily fulfill its pivotal function of linking the normative framework of the social and political system with the real-world conditions of the regulation's addressees and other affected parties. To the extent that law cannot fulfill this function, due to the absence of societal prerequisites such as a common language and a common media system, it is vulnerable to a challenge to its legitimacy.

In the national setting, the law has had the capacity to serve its transformative function comparatively easily, because it has been able to build on a historically established common language, a common media system and a dense system of associations, which supported the exchange of positions, views and opinions. We would expect, therefore, that national policies, the design of which follows the logic of rational institutionalism and which are fully legalized, are most successful at eliciting compliance. In the EU, these social prerequisites are at least partially missing, and there is little evidence that this will change significantly in the near future. The challenge of the EU, therefore, is to embark on a historically novel endeavor to promote societal integration, mediate between fragmented broad publics, and encourage discursive interaction across borders without having the option of replicating the national experience. Its resources for achieving this task are far from overwhelming. However, there is little reason to be overly pessimistic, either. On the one hand, it should be pointed out that in the national setting, too, there were no broad public discourses prior to the setting up of authoritative institutions. These emerged subsequently with a growing civil awareness of the necessity for day-to-day societal coexistence. It has been argued as a consequence of this that the ethical–political self-consciousness of citizens is not a constant, but changes over time. Community-building in the national setting was not the product of a primordial "feeling of solidarity," but only emerged as the product of a legal institutionalization of civil communication (Habermas 1997: 191). It is thus not only possible, but even probable, that the establishment of European institutions will, in the long run, trigger a similar effect of consciousness-raising for cross-border affairs and eventually lead to the establishment of a true European public (see e.g. Schmalz-Bruns 1999).

These observations correspond to an understanding of the EU as a multilevel governance system (cf. Jachtenfuchs and Kohler-Koch 1996; Marks et al. 1996; Jachtenfuchs 2001). The multilevel governance concept sees the EU as a unique political system that is constituted by both nation-states and European institutions, each of which is defined in relation to the other. Moreover, the nation-states are so deeply enmeshed in the system of multilevel governance that they can no longer be thought of as discrete political systems. This feature makes the EU a political system. However, this emerging political system of multilevel governance also features the following characteristics that distinguish it clearly from other political systems:

- a territorial focus (*Staatsgebiet*) that is more loosely structured and more variable than territorial states, but is much more structured and much less variable than is the case with international governance;
- a constituency (*Staatsvolk*) that has developed only weak forms of identity and lacks the means to achieve an overarching public discourse;
- the absence of both an institutionalized supreme decision-making body (be it a parliament or a constitutional court) as well as a clear and uncontested hierarchy with a supreme authority holding a legitimate monopoly on force (*Staatsgewalt*).

Some of the more specific features of this system can already be identified (see Kohler-Koch 1999). Unlike many national political systems, the principal members of the EU multilevel governance structures are not individual citizens but corporate actors that work within highly organized and specialized subsystems. While individuals are to some extent legal subjects, the political sphere is exclusively populated by corporate actors. Seen from this perspective, the member states can be seen as

territorially defined interest organizations, which are functionally seg-
mented and operate side by side with functionally defined interest organizations. Furthermore, the participation of the members is primarily
motivated by an interest in problem-solving rather than their sense of a
common identity. Members share the notion of upgrading the common
interest rather than pursuing the common good. Moreover, the central
authority, so typical of the national setting, is substituted in the multilevel polity by a decision-mode which more closely resembles unanimity
than majority rule. Precedence is thus given to bargaining and deliberation, rather than majority voting, as a decision-making mechanism (Neyer
2003),[16] along with an enforcement mechanism that is horizontalized and
builds upon legal internalization as a substitute for a legitimate monopoly
on force. While these constitutional principles are admirably successful
in many respects (Neyer 2004), the still frequent exclusion of the people
at the European level means that there is a permanent danger of public protest at the national level. The lesson, therefore, is the same as in
many national settings: people excluded from the decision-making process are on average less willing to accept the outcomes of those processes.
A necessary condition for the future integration of Europe therefore is
not only a clever institutional design with the emphasis on monitoring,
legalization and independent sanctioning, but also a means of bridging
the still dominant divide that exists between the EU's political system and
its citizens.

6.3.2   What drives integration?

Our findings also have implications for theories seeking to explain the
causes and forces behind European integration. Since the start of the
integration process, there have been two main answers to the question
put by Lindberg and Scheingold (1970: v): "Once an enterprise like the
EC is launched, what accounts for its subsequent growth, stabilization
or decline?" One answer, neofunctionalism, emphasizes the unintended
spill-over effects of early decisions upon the development of the EU,
while intergovernmentalism, the other answer, lays stress on the powers
of member state governments.

The most recent neofunctionalist contributions point to the European Court and the role of law in the dynamics of integration. The key

---

[16] In a characterization of the EU as an example of "network governance," Eising and
Kohler-Koch (1999) and Kohler-Koch (1999) speak of consociation (see Lijphart 1977)
as the organizing principle (as opposed to majority rule). Indeed, the Council applied
majoritarian logic in only 14 percent of all decisions. All other decisions were taken
unanimously (Eriksen and Fossum 2000: fn. 7).

argument here is that the ECJ has managed to deepen integration and engineer greater compliance through its decisions than the member states had either expected or desired when they ratified the Treaty of Rome and subsidiary Community legislation (Burley and Mattli 1993; Mattli and Slaughter 1998). Alter (2001: 52) in particular has shown convincingly how national courts and domestic actors have – as a rule unintentionally – served as agents of European integration: "The central factor facilitating the expansion of EC law through judicial interpretation is the fact that the European court sits as an institution outside the domestic realm which can be used by domestic . . . and supranational actors to challenge national and European laws. The European legal system has become part of the policy-making process appealed to by those actors who lose during political negotiations over policy." Stone Sweet and Caporaso (1998: 100; see also Shapiro and Stone Sweet 2002) therefore speak of a theory of legal integration and identify three essentials for the construction of the European polity: "Viewed in dynamic relation to one another," they argue that "transnational exchange, transnational litigation and the production of Euro-rules can evolve interdependently, and in so doing constitute and reconstitute the supranational polity . . . Once constituted, the causal connections between social exchange, third party dispute resolution, and rule-making generate a dynamic, expansive logic to the construction of the legal system and therefore of the supranational polity."

Intergovernmentalists cast doubt on the existence of such a virtuous cycle. For them, it is the most powerful national governments, which themselves represent dominant national interest groups, that determine the course of European integration (Moravcsik 1998: 7). If integration goes too far, they are able to put a stop to it. A national backlash is always possible. Garrett (1992: 553; see also 1995) argues, along similar lines, that the ECJ's decisions are made to suit the dominant states' preferences and thus have no independent integrative force. "Decisions of the European Court are consistent with the preferences of France and Germany." If it were not so, the member states would have reconstructed the legal system (Garrett 1992: 556–559). "Member states could, if they choose, either ignore ECJ decisions or amend the legal order through multilateral action. The fact that governments have done neither to any important degree thus implies that the extant order serves their interests" (Garrett 1995: 172).

Our findings contribute to this debate. On the one hand, the role of legalization in eliciting compliance is central. Legalization does indeed lead member states to do things that they would not otherwise have wanted to do. By taking part in legalized interaction in the EU, or even the WTO, member states become participants in transnational legal discourses which involve not only governments but also parliaments, courts, and individuals (Slaughter, Stone Sweet and Weiler 1998; Neyer 2003). Member states gradually become socialized in an intensifying network of transnational legal reasoning, and even undergo a redefinition of their political identity. Today, it is no longer the sovereign nation-state which is the dominant paradigm of intergovernmental relations in the EU, but the legally bound member state (Walter 1999) which must observe its legal obligations and respect external restraints for the sake of its long-term interests. Legalization is therefore not only a means of satisfactorily ensuring the implementation of and compliance with the rules that have been agreed upon by member states, it is a process which impacts on the very identity of democratic states. In this sense, legal functionalism is right. Legalization contributes to the dynamics of European integration independently of the governments' preferences.[17] The dynamics of the compliance crises in the EU, discussed in chapters 3 and 4, clearly show that the nation-states and their governments cannot control the outcomes of the legal process.

On the other hand, however, the virtuous cycle can easily be broken. Compliance with European regulations is put seriously to the test if an issue comes on the *agenda* of a broader public discourse and the different national public discourses on the same issue are both *fragmented*, in the sense that they do not relate to one another, and *polarized*, in the sense that they lead to completely different outcomes. Under such circumstances, there is a strong incentive for national politicians to compromise their long-term interest in a legally constituted community in favor of short-term, domestic electoral concerns, thereby bringing the functional dynamics of European integration to a halt. Alter (2000: 490) puts it in a nutshell: "the very factors that have led to the success of the EU legal process in expanding and penetrating the national order have provoked national courts and European governments to create limits on the legal

---

[17] Our concept of legal internalization builds on and extends the *concept of socialization of states* (cf. Checkel 1998; Risse 2000; Hurd 1999: 388; Schimmelfennig 2000, 2001). The process of changing identities and preferences as a result of the internalization of norms and practices is indeed similar to the internalization of legal norms. At the same time, legal internalization builds on a construction of legitimacy, since no court in the world has the capacity to enforce its decisions. Thus, legal internalization refers to other mechanisms of internalization. Whereas constructivist socialization approaches lay emphasis on learning and persuasion, legal internalization makes use of pre-existing sources of legitimacy and builds on the plurality of domestic actors and on the division of powers. This is similar to the approach of Checkel (2001), who also suggests different ways in which institutions − conceptualized in social-constructivist terms − matter with respect to compliance.

process." While these findings to some extent support the intergovernmental point of view, they also diverge from it. It is neither the governments nor dominant economic interests that are principally responsible for orchestrating national backlashes against the virtuous cycle of legalization and integration, but rather national public opinion. Issues of legitimacy and the still fragmented character of the European public, rather than dominant economic interests, are the main dangers to the system. Therefore, the most important source of disruption for the virtuous cycle of legal integration and a disintegrative backlash may be fragmented national publics and is not necessarily national governments, which often feel constrained by popular demands when suggesting further integration, or national constitutional courts that have thus far been extremely careful to maintain their position as guardians of their national constitutions (Alter 2000: section 3).

The transformation process taking place in Europe, from an intergovernmental to a postnational multilevel governance system, can thus be divided into two different stages (Zürn 2001). The first stage is most plausibly regarded as a more or less *unintended, indirect outcome* of deliberate political responses to (perceived) functional demands and national interests. The continuous expansion of some regulations so that they increasingly deal with behind-the-border issues is a part of this first stage. This creates the need for credible commitments to the design of these more refined regulations and the development of supranational bodies to deal with monitoring and sanctioning, as well as intensified legalization.

The second stage of the transformation is much more *reflective*. When society and political actors begin to comprehend the change, they start to include in their considerations issues of legitimacy, trans-boundary identity and trans-boundary ethics. The pressures to improve the living conditions of people living thousands of miles away, as well as the debate on European identity and democracy, are the first signs of this reflective stage in the transformation process. Parallel to these developments, however, one can observe reactionary movements of a nationalist tendency and a growing awareness of the difficulties of designing democratic multilevel governance institutions. The outcome of this second stage of the transformation process has yet to be decided.

6.4   Political implications

The realization that a monopoly of force is not required to generate political union between territorial political units so as to create a durable, legalized political order is of special political significance, because it implies that constitutionalism is not exclusively restricted to the nation-state but can be extended to incorporate more than one state. However, these findings should not be used to corroborate a false, idealistic doctrine.

- First, they do not invalidate the modern understanding of a "monopoly of force." A monopoly on the use of legitimate force is and will remain a vital element in the relations between territorially defined political units and the addressees of regulations within these territories. *The national monopoly of force, therefore, is a necessary requirement for non-coercive and effective governance beyond the state.*

- Secondly, the absence of a monopoly of force beyond the nation-state does not imply that sanctions have no role to play in the relations between territorial units. On the contrary, political institutions for the regulation of relations between such units must be so constructed as to: (a) include mechanisms for the authoritative interpretation of rules (usually in the form of independent arbitration courts); (b) facilitate the disclosure of instances of transgression; and (c) establish procedures to deal with transgressors. In other words, *the institutionalization of enforcement mechanisms for the implementation of laws across more than one territorially defined political unit substitutes for the monopoly of force in the relations between these units.*

- Thirdly, governance beyond the nation-state must take advantage of the division of powers within the respective nation-states. As international and European regulations become legally and politically internalized, they not only improve in legal quality, but also improve their record of compliance. In other words, *the integration of European and international regulations into domestic legal systems significantly reduces the compliance problem that is inherent to regulations authorized by institutions beyond the nation-state.*

The theoretical and empirical evidence provided in this study on the effectiveness of the horizontal implementation of law thus dismisses the dichotomic reasoning of classical legal theories. The distinction – between the hierarchical, coercive implementation of norms and rules within a nation-state, and the horizontal *and* relatively non-coercive implementation of norms and rules beyond the nation-state – is too simplistic. A more adequate image for describing and understanding politics in postnational constellations is that of a multilevel governance system in which power is shared among different levels of decision making, which are (although empirically only imperfectly) brought together by the force of legal rules. While softer methods for achieving governance targets are gaining ground in the hierarchical political systems of nation-states, sanctioning mechanisms can be identified at different levels within the horizontally organized systems for the implementation of laws beyond the nation-state. In this respect, not only the formulation of laws, but also their implementation remains a legal issue. Under normal circumstances, the horizontal implementation of law is a highly stable means of eliciting compliance provided that it is integrated in a clever institutional design and shows a high degree of legal internalization. The EU achieves compliance rates comparable with those of the most successful nation-states (Jacobsen and Weiss 1998b). However, it does reveal one weakness. The European compliance mechanisms, developed within democratically constituted territorial units, soon proved to be inadequate when European and international regulations contradicted the perceived interests of a broad, and as yet nationally fragmented public.

This weak point gives some cause for talk of a crisis of multilateralism in general. The breakdown of the talks in Seattle, the battles in the streets of Genoa, the refusal of the American Congress to ratify the Test Ban Agreement in 2001, the missing US signature on the agreement for the establishment of an international criminal court, protests and the mediocre results of the EU intergovernmental conference in Nice, and last but not least the failure of the post-Nice Convention process – are these all signs of a chronic weakness? Can one even assert that such events point to the end of legally backed international institutions? We are convinced that in the age of globalization, effective international institutions are more of an imperative than ever. They must, however, take on a new shape in order to meet today's challenges. Without such a reform, there is a danger that those governance institutions so far established beyond the nation-state will be thwarted by the growing demands on societal justification. Executive multilateralism, which has guided relations between developed industrial countries ever since the end of World War II, must be substituted by a societally sanctioned – which ultimately means a democratically legitimized – form of multilateralism. Political proposals in favor of the further development of international institutions along the lines of a legalistic understanding of constitutionalization (Petersmann 2000) are well advised to respect the insight that valid law should not be decoupled from democratic procedures and public support. All three are intrinsically interconnected. The neglect of even one of them will not only give support to those who already point to the democratic deficit in postnational governance, but will also lead to increasing difficulties in eliciting compliance.

The realization of an institutional design going beyond executive multilateralism and legal constitutionalism is by no means unattainable. While such a design was, admittedly, not identified in any of the cases explored, if viewed over time both European and international institutions are clearly in a process of developing new mechanisms of transnational juridification and participation. This evidence can be interpreted as supporting our thesis that postnational governance need not choose between anarchy and full-blown hierarchy, but can (and does) realize new modes of governance which go beyond that dichotomy. A major reason for this process may well be the fact that most cases of open non-compliance are perceived by the EU, and also by the WTO, as institutional crises which trigger the search for new institutional solutions. Against this background, the increasing juridification of European and international politics, the extension of participation rights of the European Parliament, and the pursuit of new forms of participation for non-governmental actors in the EU and the WTO must also be understood as part of an institutional learning process with the attempt being to eliminate perceived deficits. Thus, while economic and political globalization may present a challenge to the institutional order of the national constellation, it is at the same time a chance to meet this challenge constructively, with a strategy of developing and improving the institutional characteristics necessary for effective and legitimate post-national constellations.

7   Compliance research in legal perspectives

Christian Joerges

7.1   *Da mihi facta, dabo tibi ius?* Introductory observations on an interdisciplinary agenda

"Compliance is not a legal problem." This is the traditional view of lawyers, which is by no means simply naive. Lawyers know of course about the problems of enforcement and the risks of litigation. But they are trained to find out whether some behavior is legal or illegal and they are paid to give good reasons that militate in favor of their client's viewpoints and interests. They can act on the assumption that no one will question that the enforcement of valid law in a *Rechtsstaat* is a matter of course, which is not susceptible to legal arguments and is hence beyond their professional responsibility. Compliance is something policemen, bailiffs and politicians should somehow ensure.

What is true for practicing lawyers is also true in legal academia. Research on compliance problems does not concern the validity of law and its normative contents. Such research could therefore be assigned to legal sociology – not a proper legal discipline. International law, however, has a different story to tell. In the account of Koh (1997), the issue of compliance constitutes the core problem of international law. The apparent contrast with the traditional perception of national legal systems is easy to understand. What lawyers can presume to exist within constitutional states, namely an authority that is entitled and committed to enforcing the law, is not available in the international system.

7.1.1   *Two assumptions and their implications*

These observations should suffice to explain why a project aiming at a comparison of compliance at different levels of governance should be prepared to respond to two skeptical objections. The first concerns the legal conceptualization of these three levels of governance in international, European, and national law. Implicit in the design of our project is the assumption that these differences are no longer as significant as

218

the inherited subdivision of legal disciplines suggests. A second, closely related assumption concerns the methodological status of compliance in legal reasoning. The thesis we submit may at first sight look more daring than the first, but it is in fact closely related. Not only European law, but national law as well, has to respond to the challenge of compliance. At all levels of governance, the legal system had to "internalize" compliance issues – compliance did become a *legal* problem.

The explanation and justification for these two assumptions will have to address two groups of contested and complex theoretical and methodological issues. We will stick to the analytical distinction between the legalization of national, European, and international governance on the one hand and the incorporation of compliance problems into the design of legal regulations and legal reasoning on the other.[1] To start with a very brief summary of inherited paradigms of legal disciplines seems best suited for an interdisciplinary discussion, simply because the parallels between legal and political science are so clearly visible. This is true not only for their formative eras, but also for their current efforts to reconceptualize what seems to be outdated or even discredited as factually and/or normatively inadequate. This reorientation forms the "trans-disciplinary" background problem for our project, which explains why interdisciplinary research has become increasingly important. While political scientists experience that law "matters" and legalization phenomena have to be integrated into their analyses of international and European governance, lawyers realize that the analytical models that integration research and international relations scholarship have developed can be used to inform the legal conceptualization of the international system and the European integration process.

The incorporation of compliance issues into law at all levels of governance is the second reference point and background problem. The problem is complex because the forms and strategies of incorporation remain specific to the level of governance at which they occur and are not readily apparent, either to political scientists or to lawyers. Section 7.3 will therefore proceed in three steps. Section 7.3.1 reviews the methodologies which already in the 1980s advocated a "post-interventionist" design of regulatory strategies, be it by redefining the tasks of the administration, regulatory bodies, and judiciary and/or a proceduralized understanding of the category of law. These innovations did not of course use the concept

---

[1] "Internalization" of compliance issues by the legal system would be a better charcterization had we not, in chapter 1, section 1.3.2, used the term "legal internalization" for the legal mechanisms (especially Article 234, formerly 177) ensuring that European law is treated as "law of the land" by national legal systems and the term "civil internalization" for the subjective rights of European citizens granted to them by European law.

of compliance. But it is important to realize that they did in fact advocate an "incorporation" of compliance issues. It is equally important to understand the similarities and differences of the incorporation problem at the European and international levels. Sections 7.3.2 and 7.3.3 will address these separately.

As will become apparent, the law differentiates not just between the national, European, and international levels of governance, but it must also find differentiating substantive answers to policies which seek to strengthen market mechanisms, correct market failures, or achieve redistributive effects. These distinctions have informed the selection of case studies presented in the previous chapters. Section 7.4 will review these studies from a legal perspective. That review will seek to substantiate what Henkin may have expected when he suggested that lawyers and political scientists should at least "hear each other" (Henkin 1979: 4): Legal discourses will remain normative and political scientists must not give up their explanatory ambitions even where they have identified converging and trans-disciplinary interests in the understanding of "compliance." We do not advocate a fusion of the disciplines. What we seek to demonstrate is that the law, in order to strengthen the social adequacy of its categories, has to understand in its own language the phenomena that political scientists explore. And vice versa: political scientists, if they want to do "justice" to what they explore and explain, will have to respect the facticity of normativity, i.e. the degree to which political processes are structured by normative arguments.[2] These problems will be taken up again more generally in the concluding section 7.5.

7.1.2   *A caveat and a third problem dimension*

It is unsurprising that the organizers of a project on the comparison of compliance at different levels of governance will defend the theses just outlined. It is important that they remain aware of the risks and difficulties their argument will have to face.

It is one thing to criticize the adequacy of inherited legal doctrines and methods, but quite another to replace them and pay the price of the changes. Despite their apparent inadequacy, the inherited theoretical and methodological paradigms of international law and national legal systems remain powerful, not just as ideologies but because of their inherent qualities, for which it is difficult to find substitutes. The defence of the inherited delineation between the legal and the extra-legal, between

---

[2] See chapter 1, especially section 1.4; see also Teubner (1987) and for a very lucid refinement Teubner (2004, at 1–5).

legal reasoning and inquiries into the real world and the enforcement of legal rules appeals to the very idea of the rule of law within constitutional democracies. Any request that the law should take seriously what happens in its shadow (or elsewhere in the real world) tends to assign legal validity to non-legal practices and risks compromising the claims and achievements of democracies, which seek to domesticate power within the nation by the rule of law. The "imperfections" of international law can be attributed to a perception of sovereignty as the ultimate authority. And nonetheless, the legal system is exposed to the erosion of its inherited reference framework. It is constantly forced to find practical responses to that challenge, and it is upon this that theorists have to reflect.

This is but a preliminary reminder of the third and most fundamental background problem of our project. The introductory section to chapter 1 designated this challenge very directly and ambitiously: the problem of compliance cannot be reduced to the questions of effectiveness and the problem-solving capacities of international regimes. The problem of "compliance" concerns the very notion of order. Issues of compliance are inextricably linked with issues of legitimacy. In a very straightforward normative turn, when discussing the reasons for compliance with rules, we will not be able to avoid discussions about the claims to validity of these rules. In Habermas's (2001: 113) strong formulation: we will be confronted with the questions of whether these rules "deserve" recognition. It is hardly possible to imagine a more difficult and more contested issue. It is nevertheless unavoidable. "The question that millions of lawyers around the world are regularly paid to answer is *not why* there is, or is not, compliance, *but what* does the law command?"[3] Their skills are needed to resolve what Michael Zürn has called the "intrinsic ambiguity" of law, and legal theorists call the inherent indeterminacy of law, or, if they are more constructively minded, the productivity of the "operation called *Verstehen*" (Abel 1948), the creative element of legal interpretation.[4] If our project documents how the inherent, internal, and endogenous normative logic and factual power of legal mechanisms can be taken into account in the design of compliance research, and if it also helps lawyers to realize and to overcome their naiveties and the simplicity of legal fictions, and encourages them to import non-normative reconstructions of the social world more reflexively into the legal system, we would have achieved a lot. The agenda we become entangled in through these explorations we label "constitutionalization."[5] "Constitutionalization,"

---

[3] Chapter 1, section 1.4.   [4] See sections 7.3.1.1 and 7.3.4.1.
[5] See chapter 1, section 1.4 and also chapter 6, sections 6.1.2 and 6.2.3.

in our understanding of the term, refers to the reflection of legitimizing secondary rules and principles when projecting primary rules.
This dimension is present in the legal systems of constitutional states.
Our insistence, however, that we have to redesign our analytical frameworks towards the emergence of new transnational governance structures
at the European and international levels, must not be misunderstood
as an equation of facts and norms. To rephrase: it is our core con-
tention that validity claims accompany the emergence of transnational
governance and suggestions for "improving" compliance ultimately have
the task of presenting notions of (normatively) legitimate transnational
governance.

7.2   The legacy of legal history: National, European, and international "governance"

Interdisciplinary studies cannot be more neutral and less biased than to
work within the concerned disciplines. The readiness of lawyers to engage
in research outside the law's doctrinal domains will be motivated by some
discontent with "normal" legal science. These underlying assumptions
cannot be discussed here comprehensively. But our premises and perspectives should at least become visible and transparent through the following
outline of the legal framework to which our analyses of compliance issues
refer.

These analyses touch upon no fewer than three distinct bodies of law
and legal disciplines: WTO-law and international law; European law;
and national (German) law. Each of these "levels of governance" is distinct. The varieties in the prevailing patterns of "juridification" and the
differences between the legal disciplines dealing with them cannot be discussed here in depth. They can, however, be illuminated using a reconstruction of "social models" underlying legal conceptualization, i.e. of
perceptions of the international system on which legal science has relied –
and it will immediately become apparent how strongly the paradigms that
law has inherited overlap with important traditions of international relations theory and integration research.[6] The models that are referred to
here do not represent the "real world" at some historical instance, or
mirror a consensus or quasi-hegemonic views of our academic ances-
tors. All they are meant to document are analogous perceptions of the

---

[6] Cf. chapter 1, section 1.1. For similar, yet much more elaborated analyses of these interde-
pendencies cf. Slaughter (2001) and recently Hathaway (2002: 1942–1962), both referring to the international system.

international system in legal and political sciences, assumptions that underlie both disciplines and reveal their complementarities.[7]

7.2.1   International law and the international system

This seems most obvious at the international level. "Compliance" can be understood, Koh (1997) has convincingly argued, as the core problem of international law; as a defect that could not be cured by invoking some higher law or enforcement power. And, indeed, if one conceives of the international system as constituted by relations between sovereign actors, the sovereign retains the highest legal authority; such an actor is by definition free to conclude agreements, but cannot be forced to comply with the principle of *pacta sunt servanda*. Political scientists understood "international relations" in a similar way. Whatever effects lawyers assigned to agreements and customary law, the "reality" of the international system remained "non-legal": a matter of power, diplomacy, interest, and strategic action.

The picture remains valid, even if one considers the differences between the pertinent legal subdisciplines. Since its formative period in the nineteenth century, private international law has underlined the equal standing (or normative equivalence) of the private law systems of nation-states. It has, however, also insisted on the freedom of states to spell out their own ideas of private "international" law, and the only conceivable means of achieving some practical uniformity was the international treaty. Similarly, and even more radically, sovereignty was defended in all legal areas concerned with regulatory policies; every state applies, or is supposed to apply, its own "public" law, to define autonomously its international ("extraterritorial") scope of application, and is not required to serve some other state's regulatory interests (Vogel 1965: 176–239). In such a world, "compliance" is a factual and political matter. The "lawyer" will interpret *de lege artis* treaties and customary law. Where he detects a breach of legal commitments, he will insist on the validity of his arguments and deplore the imperfections of international law.

---

[7] "Social models" ("*Sozialmodelle*"), i.e. representations of the social world *for the legal system*, provide links between the law and its social contexts. Their reconstruction helps to understand which basic concepts the law selects and how it adapts to social change. The concept was first introduced by the legal historian, Franz Wieacker (1953) (for a recent general analysis cf. Wielsch 2000: 166 ff.). The concept is of course controversial but certainly helpful for the understanding of a very general and fundamental issue. It designates bridges between the legal system and its contexts and it is a useful means of reconstructing the relation between legal and non-legal, e.g. economic or sociological perceptions of the social world. In the terminology of Luhmann as adapted by Teubner (2004: 17 ff.): legal systems have to accomplish some "structural coupling" between the law's own operations and the reflexion practices ("*Reflexionspraktiken*") of other social subsystems.

7.2.2   Nation-state law

National legal systems can be portrayed as an opposite to, a complement of, or a basis for, the international system: in a fully-fledged rule of law state, the compliance issue may be of great social and political importance. As a legal problem, it is non-existent. Law, by definition, requires "compliance" ("obedience"; cf. Koh 1997: note 5). Non-compliance with law triggers the machinery for the administration of coercive powers. To question compliance would be to question the rule of law itself. If some prevailing understanding of the law seems inconvenient, one has to question the *validity* of such interpretations, make use of the ambiguity or indeterminacy of law, plead for its reinterpretation, or rely on one's opportunity to promote legal change, or, in the last instance, turn to the legislature. To put all this slightly differently: "compliance" is a non-legal phenomenon, a problem the "lawyer as such" is not equipped to handle.

7.2.3   European law

The European (at the outset: "Economic") Community was a latecomer to the international arena which did not fit into the old dichotomy between national and international law. It was soon perceived as a *tertium* which required the development of new concepts. The success story of "integration through law" is, at the same time, a story of successful regime design and of intensifying regulatory politics that accordingly raises the standard for compliance. It is worth noting how cautiously the protagonists of integration used to define their agenda: when interpreting Article 169 (now 226) they contented themselves with purely formal signals (the duty to "implement" European legislation is "complied" with where something formally equivalent to the text prescribed by the Community is adopted at the national level), and they made cautious use of the authority of national courts and the interests of private actors. The implications of this for the compliance agenda are manifold and will concern us in the following sections: the quality and intensity of juridification has blurred the borderlines between "compliance" and "implementation," between political action and legal reasoning, and between governance through common rules versus commitments to transnational problem-solving. The core issues of international law looked less intriguing after their arrival in the European arena: this "organization" had no sovereign head of state but defined itself as a "Community." It had few coercive powers but managed to establish reasonably successful substitutes.

It was exactly this intermediate position of the EU, with its obvious reliance on law in the structuring of its internal relations, that generated our guiding research questions. The idea of a comparative evaluation of compliance at different levels implies that "legalization"[8] is a phenomenon of factual weight at all levels of governance, such that the differences between these levels might be gradual and the inherited dichotomies have become misleading. This is no longer a new insight. Compliance research on the EU tends to mirror its in-between position quite faithfully. As Tallberg (2002) has argued recently, compliance studies on the EU can adopt neither of the two main perspectives that compete with each other in the *international* arena: neither an "enforcement approach" emphasizing coercive strategies of monitoring and sanction, nor a management approach favoring a search for problem-solving, hold the key to compliance, but a prudent combination of both strategies. Our findings suggest a more radical departure from inherited perceptions in that they question the equation of "juridification" and enforceability, of law and coercion. To this second issue we will have to return.

7.3   Legal queries with compliance research

In the "old world," portrayed above, of two simplified ideal-types of international law and the law of the domestic state, "compliance" could be qualified as a primarily *sociological* and *political* problem that originated from the state of nature of the international system. Where compliance remains determined by non-legal factors, it can indeed most adequately be conceptualized as a causal, albeit complex, relationship. Political science seems best equipped to conduct pertinent inquiries, whereas efforts to impose legal discipline on the international system remain dependent upon some *cunning of reason*: on a convergence of interests, on political prudence or other mechanisms that ensure the conformity of legal and political rationality. Within a *Rechtsstaat*, a fully "juridified" polity, however, non-compliance will be perceived as an offense against the authority

---

[8] Our use of the term is explained in chapter 1, sections 1.1 and 1.3.2. The term "juri-didification" is defined there as the "process by which it is ensured that regulations fulfill certain criteria, such as clarity, pertinence, stringency, adaptability and a high degree of consistency both within themselves and in relation to other laws" (see also Abbott et al. 2000). The debates in legal theory to which this chapter refers have started with historical reflections. "Juridification" was introduced into the parlance of law and society studies as a translation of the notion of "*Verrechtlichung*" first used in the Weimar Republic by labour lawyer Fraenkel (1932), for example, in his critique of the use of law to domesticate class conflicts (cf. Teubner 1997: 9; Simitis 1997). It hence carries with it a perception of the ambivalent effects of the use of law, which were characterized first as depoliticization and later, e.g. (and most famously) as a destruction of social relations, a "colonialization of the life-world" by Habermas (1981; cf. for the pertinent chapter in English, Habermas 1985). "Legalization" analyses, as presented by Abbott et al. (2000), avoid such critical normative connotations.

of law and the competent bodies are expected to step in. Questions about the causes of deviations from legally required behavior might motivate some reconsideration of the contents of law. However, "good reasons" for disobedience should not cast doubt on the autonomy of the legal system to determine what is legal or illegal.

This rough sketch of traditional legal perceptions is of course meant to illustrate the need for their revision. That need is widely recognized in national and international law, and is particularly apparent in the EU context.[9] As already underlined, however, a "deconstruction" of inherited paradigms should not be undertaken lightly. The following analyses will focus on the methodological difficulties that lawyers have to overcome when embarking on such a venture. The risks we incur have, however, become unavoidable.

7.3.1   *The reflection of law on its effectiveness at national level*

Today's interdisciplinary research on compliance and its role in the new legislative processes that are being developed at the European and international levels has instructive precursors in the intense debates of the 1970s about the failures of strategies of welfare state legalization as well as their cures. These debates focused on three interrelated topics, which will be addressed separately.

The "indeterminacy problem". "Indeterminacy" is a term coined by the American Critical Studies Movement (Joerges 1989: 619 ff.) which reiterates much older insights (Curran 2003), albeit in a radicalized way. The insights concern discrepancies involved in producing and rationalizing legal decisions, the many dependencies of legal reasoning on implicit normative and factual assumptions, and the inability of law to "juridify" completely what happens in its application. "Legal method" in general and "statutory interpretation" in particular were the targets of these critiques.

The implementation problem. Discrepancies between legal programs, and especially between "purposive" legislation that is designed to achieve specific objectives and the actual impact of such laws on society, are a core concern of legal sociology, of effectiveness and of implementation research (famously summarized and analyzed by Teubner (1987)).

The "proceduralization of the category of law". It was the broadly experienced disappointment with "purposive" legal programs *and* a new sensitivity towards "intrusions into the life-world" through a legalization

---

[9] See section 7.3.2.

("*Verrechtlichung*"[10]) of social/welfarist policy goals that triggered the search for models of legal rationality that would fill the gaps left open by formalist legal techniques, and at the same time would cure the failures of the law's grip on social reality on the basis of some "grand theory," such as economic theories of law, systems theory or discourse theories (Teubner 1983; Wiethölter 1989).

All of these debates are of course open-ended, and it would be futile to try to review them here in any comprehensive way. What political scientists should be aware of, however, is the importance that these debates have for the perception and structuring of compliance issues.

7.3.1.1 Refining compliance definitions: Lessons from the debate on legal indeterminacy   However strongly one emphasizes the indeterminacy problem or downplays its practical importance, the difficulty of identifying unquestionable (or at least unquestioned) incidents of non-compliance becomes readily apparent as soon as one leaves the domain of the international system in its state of nature and moves into modern societies. These societies have been thoroughly "juridified." Every conflict in the private or public sphere and every move towards its solution can be, and very often is, observed and classified by the legal system's categories and its basic distinction between legal and illegal acts. The social importance of law is such that these perceptions matter: hardly any political or private actor takes them lightly. Such disregard would all too often be politically unwise and economically irrational. The most likely reaction to alleged non-compliance is not deferral. Instead of conceding that one's action was illegal, one first tries to produce evidence and a more or less sophisticated argument to the contrary; where acts of open "civil disobedience" do occur, they invoke some higher law and are undertaken with a view to achieving legal change.

Such observations could be categorized as sociological and would then not affect our research agendas – if there were "objective" observers available who would be in a position to distinguish between obedient and non-obedient behavior. That alternative, however, is not conceivable. The distinction between compliance and non-compliance occurs in an argumentative process, the outcome of which depends upon the moves of the parties to the conflict at stake and/or the choices and strategies of the courts or other bodies entrusted with its resolution.

These dark messages from the legal system were taken seriously in our debates and have inspired a refinement of compliance definitions. These refinements respect the normative dimensions of social actions; but they

---

[10] See note 8 above.

come at a price. Although the definitions used are all referring to observable behavior, the distinctions between "good compliance" (only minor divergence from the prescriptions of a norm, with discomfort not publicly voiced), "recalcitrant compliance" (negligible disregard but publicly voiced discomfort with a rule), "initial non-compliance" (significant difference and a change in behavior due to allegations and/or the decision of an authorized dispute settlement body), and a "compliance crisis" (significant difference, but no change in behavior even though the practice has been detected, alleged and/or outlawed) are, as the case studies document, difficult to "apply." Moreover, an evaluation of observed behavior has to take the institutional context within which it occurs into account. "Non-compliance" with a WTO dispute settlement ruling has a different legal meaning from non-compliance with a ruling of the ECJ – and the actors know this.[11]

Last but not least, it is theory which informs the observer of events about their meaning. This is the irrefutable consequence of the insight that, in the final instance, legal methodology does not provide a toolkit with which to arrive at *the* correct legal solution, but should rather be understood as aiding in the organizing and disciplining of legal reasoning. And even this insight is not the definitive answer to the indeterminacy problem. The ways in which legal science incorporates theoretical knowledge about social reality and the functions of law must not be equated fully with the theoretical constructions used by political science, neither in the more general conceptualization of whole disciplines[12] nor in the more specific reconstructions of the theoretical perspectives on compliance research, as presented in the introductory chapter.[13] Such theoretical assumptions must be adapted to the functions of the legal system, especially to its task in the resolution of conflicts. This mediating function was discussed intensively in the 1980s, when implementation studies brought to the fore the challenging discrepancies between the objectives of legal programs and their actual impact and functioning.

7.3.1.2 "Post-interventionist" legal programs: Lessons of the implementation[14] debate Compliance research originated in the international system. It is concerned with the respect shown by state

[11] See section 7.4.2.1 (discussion of BSE case analyzed in chapter 4); and also section 7.4.1.1 (discussion of *Länder* agreement on state aid analyzed in chapter 3).
[12] Cf. the remarks in section 7.1.2. above.   [13] Cf. chapter 1, section 1.3.
[14] The discovery of implementation problems by legal theorists preceded the discovery of legalization by international relations theorists by some decades. This is why the terminology in use among lawyers is somewhat different from that of international relations theorists (see also note 8 above). So are the examples used to illustrate these discoveries. However, these differences should not be overemphasized. As argued in the text,

actors (governments) towards their international commitments. Our project retains the focus of studies on state behavior at all of the three levels of governance that it explores. However, in its conceptualization of the normative quality of state commitments, it has also sought to overcome the distinctions between international, European, and national law, which have become the tradition of this discipline.[15] The lack of coercive power at the international level, the coercive nature of all legal rules at the national level, and the uneasy intermediate position of European law have informed the design of much compliance research and no longer offer reliable guidance. This is the background insight to the discovery of alternatives to coercion at the international level and is a widespread insight of compliance studies in the EU (Börzel 2002; Tallberg 2002). It is an insight arrived at through research on the impact of law, even though such studies could all assume that the law they dealt with was backed by coercive state power. The experience with the three types of studies on the impact of norms and/or law – compliance research, impact analyses, and implementation studies – sketched out by the introductory chapter,[16] corresponds to developments in the law in response to its experience of implementation gaps and regulatory failures and in its mission to establish European and international regulatory regimes.[17] The law's failures and innovations are related to the decline of sovereignty in the international arena, on the one hand, and to the growing dependence of the state and its administrative bodies on societal resources, on the other hand, which have led to the emergence of governance regimes in which governmental and non-governmental actors co-operate. This is a development which can be observed at all levels of governance, albeit at a different intensity and with specifics in which the differences of national, European, and international law remain clearly visible. It is a complementary move. Whereas at state level, coercive law sought to compensate for the failures of the purely legal approach to problem-solving, at international level the establishment of non-legal regimes and co-operative governance structures sought to compensate for the lack of coercive power.

The rise of these new governance regimes was at the national level understood as a response to the failures of law, which has been a famous

the borderlines between national, European, and international law are blurring. This is why the inspirations legal theory received from implementation research is of increasing importance at all "levels of governance."

[15] See chapter 1, section 1.1.

[16] In chapter 1, section 1.2.1. See the references to Victor, Raustiala and Skolnikoff (1998: 4); Young (1999b).

[17] Cf. chapter 3, sections 3.1.2, 3.2.2, and 3.3.1.

theme of the sociology of law and legal theory ever since Max Weber's diagnoses of the tensions between the values of legal formalism on the one hand, and the quests for a turn to substantive justice on the other (Weber 1967: 123–126, 329–343). Weber's analyses became a key reference point in analyzing the difficulties encountered by legal programs that were motivated by welfare (social) state reform when the legal system "implemented" them according to its own logic. In his reinterpretation of the Weberian distinction, Niklas Luhmann contrasted the welfarist goal-oriented "purposive" programs with the inherited "conditional" programming of legal decision making (Luhmann 1972, 227 ff.; 1973: 101 ff.; for a brilliant restatement see Luhmann 1993, 198 ff.). Such programs, Luhmann explained with the help of his sociological theory, were bound to fail since – due to their prospective nature that required answers to substantive issues – they were simply incompatible with the code of the legal system (a system operating with the legal/illegal distinction cannot know whether or not some ends are being properly pursued).

Luhmann observed the efforts of policy makers, law reformers and law and society studies closely. Does labor law protect or discipline employees and trade unions? Will co-determination ruin the German economy? Why are the effects of environmental legislation so limited? Why do poor consumers pay more and how can the law help them? What happens when the law regulates the parent-child relationship, teaching practices or school life? These were fascinating, multi-faceted and sometimes confusing debates. Gunther Teubner has most intriguingly spelled out the implications of Luhmann's abstract objections to the legal method. Implementation research and effectiveness studies,[18] he explained in a seminal contribution, were far too naive in assuming that law could be instrumentalized to achieve the social objectives of the political system, or that it would effectively transform the social world. Such efforts would end up in a regulatory dilemma (Teubner 1987: 19 ff.). Only through a redesign of legal programming to reflect these difficulties could the law become more faithful to the social objectives of welfare states. Instead of juridifying specific objectives directly, he suggested, "reflexive" law should focus on procedural rules and organizational prescriptions (Teubner 1983). Teubner's analyses were hardly representative of the *Zeitgeist* in their reliance on Luhmann's systems theory, but were so representative in their suggestions for the design of legal programs (Brüggemeier and Joerges 1983). It is these implications which compliance research must

[18] The terminological distinctions between compliance, implementation, and effectiveness studies explained in chapter 1 (see in particular section 1.2.1) were not in use when legal sociologists discovered the discrepancies between (national!) legal programs and their implementation.

be aware of. Once legislators, administrators, and courts (and policy makers!, cf. e.g. De Schutter et al. 2001) learn the lesson of "reflexive law" and "proceduralization," they will respond to the impasses of the legal and administrative system by the establishment of "governance regimes" which incorporate societal knowledge and the management capacities and skills of non-governmental actors, while reducing legal imperatives to principles and rules which only indirectly further the desired objectives (Hoffmann-Riem and Schmidt-Aßmann 1996; Zumbansen 2000: esp. at 67 ff.). This is not to say that such rules are necessarily more convenient and that compliance with them is so much easier to observe. But conflicts over the contested objectives are shifted into other arenas.

The legal theory and sociology of law debates on the failures of legal interventionism and the need for "post-interventionist" legal strategies owe much to the parallel discussions and differentiations in sociology and political science. Lowi's famous distinction between "constitutive" (market-making), "regulative" (market-correcting), and "(re)distributive" (market-breaking) policies (Lowi 1972), which we have taken up in our case studies,[19] corresponds to significant differences in legal programming. Market-constituting policies are widely equated with the "formally rational" legal programs that administrators and courts are best equipped to handle. Market-correcting policies that respond to some market failure ("economic" or "social" regulation) will typically resort to institutional provisions ensuring that non-legal, problem-resolving strategies are brought to bear upon decision-making processes. Redistributive policies are often judged to be so sensitive that they require legislative, rather than simply judicial or administrative, action.

Our case studies therefore cover fields in which a broad variety of legal techniques can be expected – and are in fact observed. Our additional aim, however, which is to take into account the transfer of ever more regulatory activities to transnational levels of governance, increases the complexity of our project still further, because the techniques of "post-interventionism" vary significantly at each level of governance. As has just been indicated, at the national level "purposive" legal programs have often increased their resort to "reflexive" or "procedural" strategies that include interactions between governmental and non-governmental actors. Insights into the dependence of the law's effectiveness on an adequate regulatory design as well as its dependence upon co-operation with non-governmental actors, apply equally forcefully to the transnational level, where states wish to ensure that the international commitments they have entered into generate their envisaged effects. International agreements will have

---

[19] Cf. chapter 1, section 1.2.2.

to go beyond the pure consent of the signatory states. Their effectiveness will often require the establishment of regime structures that include non-governmental actors. However, the conditions under which such co-operation is accomplished such that it functions constructively, differ significantly between the national, EU, and international levels. We address first the situation at the national level.

7.3.1.3 The concern for legitimacy   The ingenuity of governmental and non-governmental actors in making use of societal knowledge and management capacities has come at a (legal) price. This refinement to the regulatory strategies of regulatory agencies and/or the establishment of co-operative governance structures threatens the political authority of the constitutionally foreseen legislative and administrative bodies. Who bears the responsibility for the new forms of governance if they are no longer some form of visible government? Are the ideals of democratic governance under the rule of law in any way compatible with the exigencies of complex societies? Why should such queries as to the legally acceptable and normative legitimacy of post-interventionist governance structures concern political scientists and compliance research? If and because modern regulatory strategies are always incomplete in that they rely on problem-resolving processes, the "success" of such strategies cannot be exclusively measured by some predefined objective. Explanations rely not only on a causal relationship (however subtly defined that might be), but also on the communicative quality of such strategies. The normative exercises of lawyers are themselves a social "fact." If that is the case, one cannot obtain an adequate understanding of this reality, or hope to explain it, without taking its normative structuring seriously and one will have to take something like "the integrity of law as an explanatory variable for compliance."[20] To this intriguing issue we will have to return.

7.3.2   "Purposive" programs at the European level

Each of these three problems just discussed also presents itself at the European level – albeit in a somewhat different way. On the one hand, the legal system's need to reflect upon the conditions of the law's effectiveness is much more obvious in a Union, which lacks so many attributes of a "real" state. But, on the other hand, regulatory objectives must be accomplished without the help of comprehensive coercive powers or genuine administrative competencies. "Purposive" programs have, therefore, led to the establishment of even more ingenious governance structures, a

---

[20] See chapter 1, section 1.2.1.

development which has rendered the legitimacy of European governance particularly precarious.

7.3.2.1 Legal indeterminacy and the constitutional dimension of compliance disputes

What is true for legal texts "at home" must also be the same at the European level.[21] At first sight it is simply paradoxical that the EU continues to present European law successfully as a strictly legal product. Political scientists and legal theorists have quite thoroughly "unmasked" such perceptions (Burley and Mattli 1993); lawyers have offered disrespectful reconstructions of the operation of Europe's epistemic legal community (Schepel and Wesseling 1997). Even orthodox lawyers know that the acceptance of the orthodoxy of European law must rest upon extra-legal grounds.

One important factor which explains this paradox looks, at first sight, to be equally paradoxical. The resort to law and the willingness of so many actors to accept the self-description of the EU system can be understood as a quite deliberate response to, and compensation for, the weak political legitimacy of European governance (see, famously, Stein 1981; Weiler 1981), an explanation which has made a great impression on political scientists (see the review in Alter 2001 with many references). If, and because, this type of explanation for the stability of the European legal edifice is to be taken seriously, its stability should not be taken for granted. And indeed, both lawyers and political scientists have learned to understand the EU as a non-hierarchical or heterarchical system, in which competing and still partly autonomous "sovereigns" raise competing claims (on the legal background to the debate see, more extensively, Joerges 2002b).[22] This move in both disciplines suggests that "compliance" cannot occur as simple obedience, but will be embedded in a process of interaction about competing claims. If one starts from this understanding, it cannot come as a surprise if all the actors involved continue to present good legal reasons which support their positions, while at the same time developing short-term and long-term strategies by which they hope to promote their own agendas. On its own, the intensity of legalization is neither good nor bad for the discipline of the EU. The process

---

[21] Cf. sections 7.1.2 and 7.3.1.1 above.

[22] The Maastricht judgment of the German Constitutional Court (*Bundesverfassungsgericht* 1993: Judgment of 12.10.93 – 2 BvR 2134/92 and 2 BvR 2159/92, 3 Common Market Law Reports 225) is widely understood as an important signal of a new disobedience (see chapter 6, section 6.1.2). The text here understands – as does chapter 6 – the German decision to be symptomatic of much broader developments. The distinction between a legal hierarchy and a material hierarchy, used in chapter 6, section 6.1.2, expresses the same concern, although it might suggest that the move away from the orthodox legal understanding of the EU should be considered "illegal."

intensifies the interdependence between compliance and polity-building and enhances the need to explain why a European order "deserves" recognition. Two elements of this development deserve particular mention in the context of compliance studies.

The first element is the guardian function of the European commission. According to Article 226 (formerly Article 169), the Commission is supposed to monitor the compliance of the member states with their Treaty commitments, and is also entrusted with the right to call upon the ECJ to adjudicate in cases of their alleged non-compliance. To restrict this supervisory task to uninformative formalistic controls of the wording and timing of secondary legislation was (and often still is) one way of avoiding open political conflict and of simultaneously promoting integration through a legal agenda. With the deepening of market integration, the Commission has intensified its supervision and its strategies have become more sophisticated (Börzel 2002; Tallberg 2002). Does this amount to enforcement by "the carrot and the stick"? Or are softer management techniques more successful? (cf. Tallberg 2002: 34 ff.). Both strategies invoke the authority of the Commission as an interpreter of European law *and* make use of the discretion it enjoys when moving strategically as an institutional/political actor in the shadow of the law. In this sense, compliance can be understood as a "negotiated process" not only by political scientists (Börzel 2000: section 5.2.4), but also by lawyers – provided, however, such negotiations respect legal principles and co-operative duties.

The second element deserving particular mention is the resolution of European issues with the help of national courts. The doctrine of the direct applicability of European law as the "law of the (national) land"; the transformation of the freedoms laid down in the Treaty into subjective rights that private actors can invoke against their home countries and, since *Frankovich*,[23] the imposition of state liability for non-compliance are all legal moves that have enhanced the authority of European law by exploiting the authority enjoyed by national judiciaries at home.

Article 234 (formerly Article 177) proved to be an incredibly successful design that softened the supremacy claims of European law. The orthodox versions of these claims remain nevertheless extraordinary. Can it meaningfully be classified as an instance of "non-compliance" when national actors argue about the reach of Community law and insist on, as the German Constitutional Court did in its much criticized Maastricht judgment (*Bundesverfassungsgericht*; see fn. 22 above), a "co-operative" understanding of their relationship with the ECJ? (For a normative elaboration see Joerges 1996a; 2002b.)

---

[23] Cases 6, 9/90, *Frankovich and Bonifaci* v. *Italy* [1991] ECR I-5357.

Compliance research which focuses too narrowly on the behavior of the states in the EU would miss the "divide and rule" strategies that the Commission has at its disposal when co-operating directly with the sub-units of national administrations and, more importantly, when co-operating with private actors. Early studies on compliance with European law – which were, interestingly enough, undertaken by lawyers (Krislov et al. 1986; Weiler 1988; and Schwarze 1996) – mirror the normative background assumptions of their authors with their focus on the practice of states with regard to public and international law, and their reflection upon the intergovernmentalist paradigm that is common to both disciplines.[24] Later shifts towards the study of the Europeanization of the judicial branch (comprehensively analyzed by Slaughter et al. 1998; for illuminating insights in the field of labor law, see Sciarra 2001) renew and rewrite the "integration through law" paradigm by subtle observations about the role of courts in the promotion of legal developments and the settling of politically controversial issues. The legal basis of such a move from a hierarchical to a more interactive understanding of compliance is still underexplored and the potential of the European judiciary to face such challenges is far from clear. The observation, however, that compliance issues must be understood in the context of short-term controversies, as well as long-term strategies and political visions, should not come as any surprise to political scientists.[25] The ensuing nexus of compliance research with normative discourses will, nevertheless, be perceived as an unwelcome and certainly difficult challenge.[26]

7.3.2.2 The institutional specifics of regulatory politics at the Community level

The orthodox understanding of supremacy as a hierarchical relationship between the Community and its member states is particularly inadequate for explaining broad fields of regulatory politics. Two of our case studies analyze pertinent examples. Both of them differ considerably in substance as well as in institutional terms. The control of state aid forms part of the competition policy chapter of the EU Treaty (Articles 87–89). It is often characterized as an example of "good" economic regulation with provisions "institutionalizing" criteria of economic rationality to be used as a yardstick for assessing the validity of state policies Europe-wide. As the development of European antitrust policies in

---

[24] The famous analysis with which Weiler (1981) entered the stage of European studies used a similar dichotomy: intergovernmentalism dominating the political dimension of the EC and law bringing to bear its supranational quality.

[25] The controversy on the French refusal to lift the ban against imports of British beef (see the analysis in chapter 4) provides a telling example which we take up in section 7.4.2.1 below.

[26] See section 7.1.2 above and section 7.4 below.

general (see Wesseling 2000) and the many controversies accompanying the development of the Community's state aid regime in particular have revealed, the control of state aid has always been, and is bound to remain, a contested field in which member states continue to assert and defend their regulatory autonomy. Accordingly, the role of the Commission has never been restricted to applying a set of given principles or rules according to the standards of legal methodology, but has, in fact, acted as a true "regulator."

The adequacy of an interactive, rather than a hierarchical, understanding of Community-member state relations is even more apparent in the field of "social regulation," of which the case study in chapter 4 on the safety of beef examines a particularly prominent example. It is a field in which the need to accompany the "completion" of the internal market by "purposive" regulatory policies is uncontroversial. This need has led to the establishment of governance structures which have to master the threefold task of compensating for the lack of a genuine European administration, ensuring the integration of non-legal expertise into regulatory decision making, and managing the often sensitive political and economic controversies over foodstuffs.

EU committees, more or less formal semi-private and private networks, and, more recently, semi-autonomous agencies are the "institutions" upon which the management of the internal market relies. It is this complex web which generates policies, rules, and decisions which are then "complied with" by the very same actors who were engaged in their adoption. Agencies, committees, and less formal public/private networks are clearly all ad hoc creatures of necessity that respond in diverse ways to an unexpected and highly differentiated demand for European market regulation. As such, differences in their composition and mode of operation reflect a pragmatic impulse within the EU: a mix and match attitude, reminiscent of the early, experimental years of national administration-building, and responsive in turn to national, integrationist, public, private, and market interests.

Why should compliance research take note of this Kafkaesque world? The most obvious answer is that anyone trying to identify the actors of the compliance game simply cannot avoid getting entangled in the complex web that knits together Community, national, non-governmental, and governmental actors, as well as administrators, expert communities, and organized interests. Inextricably linked with this formal structure of the field is its mode of operation. Relying neither on purely "negative" integration strategies, nor on centralized welfarist-interventionist policies, European market integration has, in a discovery procedure of practice, given birth to an extensive and (crucially) a

socially/politically-detached sphere of private and self-determining economic interaction. While national markets were characterized by the
simple political pre-determination of social/ethical demands and their
subsequent administrative imposition upon market activities, the single
market is subject to an ongoing and openly political, administrative/
regulatory process, which is itself the forum in which competing public/
private, political/social, and national/supranational values and interests
are presented, identified, and accommodated.

The implications for the design of compliance research are manifold. To be sure, the "delegation" of regulatory tasks to a compound of
governmental and non-governmental actors is characteristic of modern
social regulation in general. The additional difficulty of the European
polity, however, is that, when establishing its regulatory machinery, it
had to resort to complex camouflage techniques. This, too, is a large
tribute to the European Community's orthodox legal heritage. A legal
doctrine that was developed by the ECJ in the late 1950s[27] is said to
exclude the entrustment of bodies which were unforeseen in the Treaties
with the exercise of discretionary regulatory powers. Respect for this principle has furthered the development of regulatory practices in which the
form of the legal framework differs markedly from its substantive regulatory functions. European "agencies" pool national competencies, but
have – formally speaking – no decision-making powers. In European regulatory committees one can easily identify national representatives and
Commission officials, but one will find it difficult to attribute decisions
to either the Community or the member states. Compliance research is
confronted with a difficult choice. It may orient itself along the formal
design of European regulatory policies. Its observations of compliance or
non-compliance will then fail to capture the full meaning of the events
it registers. The embeddedness of these events within complex webs of
interaction is much more difficult to describe. But it may well be that it
is upon this interactive process that the "quality" of European decision
making and, to a large degree, compliance actually depends.

7.3.2.3 Legitimacy problems of European governance   These
observations lead once again to the normative background of the assessment of compliance. In the field of European foodstuffs regulation, the
label "deliberative supranationalism" has been used to characterize a perspective for the disciplining of nation-states through supranational law,

[27] Case 9/56, *Meroni & Co Industrie Metallurgiche SpA* v. *High Authority of the ECSC* [1958]
ECR 133; Case 10/56, *Meroni & Co Industrie Metallurgiche SpA* v. *High Authority of the
ECSC* [1958] ECR 157.

the concomitant transformation of strategic intergovernmental interaction, and (last, but not least) the furthering of a deliberative quality in transnational patterns of interaction (Joerges and Neyer 1997a). Law is of central importance in all these respects. To substantiate this perspective with respect to the internal market: it is not the law's task to establish some transnational "administration," but rather to ensure the creation and maintenance of "good governance" that is responsive to the normative concerns and economic interests present in European societies. However severe the theoretical shortcomings of this idea may be (see, for a defense, Joerges 2002a), the need to substantiate a normative vision in which compliance conflicts can be understood and assessed seems irrefutable.

7.3.3   WTO "law" and "regulation"

Given that the legal character of the WTO regime has remained highly controversial and that WTO settlements cannot be enforced directly, it is unsurprising that the state aid and foodstuffs studies in chapters 3 and 4 follow the "classical" design of compliance research quite closely. "Compliance," where it occurs, needs to be explained, and a search for causal explanations seems to be the most promising research strategy. The WTO represents, however, a significant step towards a more intense legalization than is characteristic of international law. The debate on the "constitutional" dignity of the WTO (and previously of GATT) rules from which one derives a supremacy of WTO norms over European and national law, has gained such a momentum[28] that both states and the Community have to present their positions in much the same way as within European law. Similarly, WTO norms relate with a new intensity, at least in the fields under scrutiny in our case studies, to issues of economic and social regulation. For all these reasons, the questions that are addressed in the previous section on European law arise in a similar way at the WTO level. Is the WTO framework capable of achieving objectives of regulatory policy? How do the actors concerned respond to the supremacy claims of WTO-"law"? Can compliance studies avoid entering the debate on the legitimacy of transnational governance in the WTO framework?

      7.3.3.1 Regulation at the international level   "Purposive" legal programs, which promise to ensure the freedom and/or efficiency of markets, seek to correct market failures, or pursue distributive objectives,

---

[28] See the references in section 7.3.3.2 below.

require the establishment of some adequate regulatory machinery. Regulatory patterns and practices that were established within the EU differ significantly from the governance structures that have emerged at the international level. It does not follow, however, that barriers to international trade arising out of divergent regulations can only be overcome through the abolition of regulatory interventions ("negative integration") or their replacement by some supranational regime ("positive integration"). Europe has pursued both strategies. It has also found ways of avoiding a choice between these two alternatives. The rich jurisprudence of the ECJ on Article 28 (formerly Article 30) in particular has, again and again, documented how the dichotomy between "negative" and "positive" integration can be overcome through a "proceduralization" of the conflicts at issue: a search for criteria that render both polities compatible without forcing either of them to renounce legitimate regulatory concerns (see Joerges and Neyer 1997a: 284 ff.; Joerges 2002b).

It is small wonder that this jurisprudence has met with such wide acceptance. The ECJ's sensitivity towards "legitimate" national legislation when it searches for conflict resolutions that take into account both trade interests and regulatory concerns, seems to have contributed considerably to the positive compliance record of the European system – this at least is certainly the view among legal commentators, as confirmed by a systematic review of the comments on this jurisprudence. Many commentators on the opinions adopted by the WTO Panels and Appellate Bodies have underlined the quality of their reasoning (see Scott 2000; Gehring 2002 with many references).

Any more far-reaching equation of EU and WTO governance would, however, be premature. Both systems differ considerably in their "integration" standards and strategies. Governance within the EU is much more comprehensive and legalization is much more advanced than at international level. Important options for "positive" regulation which are available within the Community are not even conceivable at the international level. The EU can resort to its huge network of national bureaucracies, agencies, and epistemic communities. The WTO has no comparable machinery at its disposal. The international standards to which it can refer – food safety standards as adopted by the World Health Organization (WHO) and Food and Agriculture Organization (FAO) – do not enjoy a comparable political legitimacy (see Gehring 2002: 132 ff.; Joerges 2001: 17 ff.; Joerges and Neyer 2003). To this point, we will return in the discussion of the case studies.[29]

---

[29] See section 7.4.2 below.

7.3.3.2 Constitutionalizing the WTO? The controversy in the legal arena on the constitutional character of WTO-"law" is to be understood as a debate on the legitimacy of this regime. Political scientists are, by now, quite actively engaged in pertinent discussions. When assessing "compliance" with Appellate Body opinions, they tend to consider the controversy over the "legal nature" of the WTO system and the expectations that such qualifications raise.[30] Those who assign a "constitutional" quality to the WTO define the commitments of WTO members more strictly than the more cautious and prevailing view (e.g., Howse 1999; Howse and Nicolaïdis 2001; Hilf 2003; Schmid 2001; for a recent summary see Snyder 2003).

The WTO is a system in transition from an international organization to a more legalized, but quite unsettled, future. This description of its present state can point to a quite impressive record of the dispute settlement procedure – impressive both in terms of the quality of the reasoning, especially at the Appellate Body level, *and* in terms of the impact of these opinions. Could both features be explained by the "imperfect" legal status of the dispute settlement system? This is an interpretation Weiler suggests in an analysis which parallels his early work on the European Community: just as the Community was characterized by the simultaneous presence of law and politics (Weiler 1981), the WTO is now presented as incorporating both law *and* diplomacy (Weiler 2001). There is one important difference: in the case of the EC, Weiler found a factual equilibrium of supranational law and political intergovernmentalism, and he assigned normative validity to exactly this precarious balance. In the case of the WTO, GATT's heritage of diplomacy and the new intensity of the legalization of world trade relations have not achieved a new factual "equilibrium" that is paralleled by the constitutional quality of the interaction between diplomacy (ensuring internal legitimation) and legalized governance (de facto substituting this legitimacy). Weiler hesitates to call the WTO regime "law" even though he observes that lawyers are involved at all stages of dispute settlement and that the Appellate Body became "a court in all but name" (Weiler 2001).

Lawyers are trained in this kind of debate; political scientists less so. What political scientists can achieve is to translate the controversies they observe into the language of their discipline, which does not disregard the factual dimension of the legal controversies. The introductory and subsequent chapters of this book have done this through their reference to the four competing perspectives – and their readiness to inquire into the relationship between them. This is the adequate response to a system

---

[30] See chapter 6, sections 6.1.2, 6.2.1.1, 6.2.2, and 6.2.3.

in transition: "[T]hese different variables should not only be seen in isolation from one another, but their interaction and dynamics are important as well."[31]

In this type of analysis, the two disciplines do not merge, but remain compatible. And they arrive at questions that they can then retranslate into their own disciplinary languages. Did the changes that occurred in the transition from GATT to the WTO have a significant impact on the record of compliance? Could it be that the old diplomatic ethos of GATT did, in fact, cope quite successfully with the tensions between the objectives of GATT and their often controversial effects within national polities?

But, even assuming that intensified legalization went hand in hand with a better record of compliance, can this serve as a satisfactory explanation without further inquiries into the broader acceptance of WTO Panel reports and Appellate Body opinions at the governmental level and within national polities? Does it make a difference what normative grounds can be invoked to justify the impact? These questions point to the background agenda addressed in all the previous sections.

7.3.3.3 Legitimacy of WTO governance   It follows from the foregoing argument that validity claims for law require a theoretical perspective within which transnational governance is normatively legitimized, even at the international level. Again, it would be simply unproductive to plead for a merger of the disciplines. The adoption of a perspective on legitimacy, which emphasizes the democratic character of rules and seeks to redefine democratic ideals so that they become independent of their nation-state heritage,[32] is at least akin to the normative visions of "deliberative" supranationalism – as the concluding section will argue more extensively.

7.3.4   When lawyers and political scientists "at least hear each other," what is it that they understand? Some interim observations

Throughout the foregoing analyses we have sought to take Louis Henkin's advice seriously. Starting from the observation that there is a growing interest among political scientists in the study of compliance and the analysis of the legalization processes on the one hand, and in the internalization of compliance issues in legal methodology and the design of regulatory arrangements at all levels of governance, on the other hand, we have reconstructed legal perceptions of, and perspectives on, compliance

[31] Chapter 6, section 6.2.   [32] See chapter 6, section 6.3.1.

issues. Without repeating and summarizing these analyses, it should be possible now to take a further step, namely to designate three areas where the interests of both disciplines overlap and where each can learn from listening to the other.

7.3.4.1 Indeterminacy again   "How can you know it is compliance when you see it?" This rephrasing of a comment, originally concerning research on deliberative democracy (Lascher 1996), accompanied the whole project. The relation between rules and their application is of constitutive significance for the inherited self-perception of the legal profession. To confront political scientists with debates in legal theory on the so-called indeterminacy of law and then to insist that, paradoxically enough, the legal system handles the issue daily reasonably successfully, raises eyebrows. Such messages do indeed sound counter-intuitive. Our common sense tells us that we all know what Louis Henkin meant when he pointed out that "almost all nations observe almost all principles of international law and all of their obligations almost all of the time" (Henkin 1979: 47). Only gradually can one arrive at a common understanding of the issue of such an observation. Its methodological side has been compellingly defined: no legal rule can determine its own application (Wittgenstein 1971: I § 146; cf. Günther 1988: 120 ff.) This, however, is only part of the problem. Institutionally more intriguing is the steadily increasing dependence of the legal system upon non-legal expertise. This is again an "old" insight. Building upon Max Weber's theory of bureaucracy, Schluchter (1972: 145 ff.) and Feick (2000: 211 ff.) distinguish between "*Amtsautorität*" (the legal authority of the administration) and "*Sachautorität*" (the competence to find adequate answers to the problems legal provisions address). This dichotomy is present at all levels of governance. Similarly, the very fact that "market-making" and "market-correcting" policies pursue specific objectives, confronted us unavoidably with the debates on the effectiveness of goal-oriented ("purposive") legal norms and their compatibility with the ideals of the *Rechtsstaat*.

Political scientists who hear the same messages have to consider their implications in different contexts. Michael Zürn has taken the indeterminacy argument particularly seriously: compliance research, he argues, is to integrate the "intrinsic ambiguity" of law into its toolkit. The law is not simply out there in a way that would enable us to identify discrepancies between prescribed and actual behavior. Zürn's formula according to which "[c]ompliance and non-compliance are, at least at the margins, contested concepts"[33] does justice to the *fact* that the law is a

---

[33] See chapter 1, section 1.2.1; see also chapter 2, section 2.2.

moving target, with a huge machinery that is continually dedicated to the redefining of what is legal and illegal. But then he moves back into his not so normative disciplinary *Heimat*, first by developing a heuristic of "non-compliance" phenomena,[34] and from there, and inevitably so, to an exploration of "causes of and cures for non-compliance beyond the nation-state [in] four theoretical perspectives."[35]

This is not the step a lawyer can take. Lawyers have to translate the insights of political science back into the language of the legal system. The suggestion I adopt is to conceptualize "compliance" as "*Recht-Fertigung*" (*jus* and *justum facere*, law production) (cf. Wiethölter 1995; 2003).[36] That may sound somewhat esoteric. However, the term is well chosen and can even be re-exported. The inherent appeal of law to justice means, in Michael Zürn's translation, that political scientists are expected to "bring in the integrity of law as an explanatory variable for compliance."[37] "How can you see its integrity when you see it?" How can you avoid this *Gratwanderung* at the edges of facticity? It is a "fact" that in the contest over compliance actors appeal to notions of trans-personal ("objective") justice. It is also a "fact" that individual conflicts and controversies among statal actors are embedded into legal systems which seek social acceptability (legitimacy in an empirical sense) and promise to ensure justice (legitimacy in a normative sense).

7.3.4.2 Law beyond states and its "constitutionalization"   The preceding moves that travel back and forth between the two disciplines have implicitly and unavoidably touched upon two further contested issues. One is the category of law. Once we assign to law the regulatory tasks which it cannot resolve by distinguishing between legal and illegal acts, we can no longer content ourselves with invoking the authority of the state and its coercive power when explaining why a decision is "right" or "wrong." If it is not authority, must it then be reason? It is a long, but direct, way from this merger between law and justice to accepting that we should no longer reserve the category of law for legal norms backed by the coercive powers of the state.

The reasons for such a move are explored further in the following case studies, as will be the second implication of the interdependence between

---

[34] See Chapter 1, section 1.2.1.   [35] Such is the heading of chapter 1, section 1.3.
[36] A brief word of explanation: the term *Recht-Fertigungs-Recht* is a creation of Rudolf Wiethölter (2003). It refers to the normative tasks of law production. Translations are particularly delicate when they have to transmit the meaning of a freely constructed term into a not yet consolidated foreign semantic space. *Justum facere*, the Latin origin of justification, best transmits the meaning of *Recht-Fertigung*.
[37] See chapter 1, section 1.3.2.

facticity and normativity, namely the recognition that law "deserves." As explained above,[38] in our understanding, the notion of "constitutionalization" refers to the reflection of legitimizing secondary rules and principles when projecting primary rules. This dimension, we have argued, is present in the legal systems of constitutional states – and remains present at all levels of governance. This is a leitmotiv in all of the preceding sections. The connotations of "constitutionalization" are, however, problematic. The very use of the term to describe law beyond the state seems to imply that we envisage an analogy between domestic and transnational governance. An alternative to that term is Wiethölter's (2003) *Recht-Fertigungs-Recht* (a law ensuring the justice of law making). That alternative has its merits. Ease of translation is not among them (but see in a similar sense Frank I. Michelman's "law of law making" in Michelman 1999: 34).

7.4   Lessons from the case studies

The case studies selected for this project follow a pattern which is significant for both disciplines, albeit for different, discipline-specific reasons. The following sections will first complement the explanations given by my co-authors with their legal equivalents. The comments on each of the case studies will then specify what lawyers can learn from political science and where they must insist upon the autonomy of their discipline.

The comments will make use of the framework that is developed in the preceding sections. They take up the distinction between conditional and purposive legal programs. That dichotomy has inspired legal sociologists to differing explanations for the failures of law reforms; it has also inspired the turn in legal theory to "reflexive" law and "proceduralization,"[39] which implies the incorporation of compliance problems into the design of legal regulations and legal reasoning.[40] The second leitmotiv of the observations below is once again the problem of indeterminacy. As has been argued before, this problem is present everywhere in the legal system, but is becoming particularly troubling where the law seeks to "juridfy" purposive programs.[41] That insight leads to the third step of the argument: the less guidance the law provides for decision-makers, the more they will have to resort to other authorities, to "*Sachautorität*" rather than "*Amtsautorität*,"[42] to economic rationality or scientific expertise – or they will have to camouflage what they are really doing. To put it more constructively: they will have to deal with the legitimacy of their activities.

Our selection of cases was not motivated by the concerns of legal theory. Instead we sought to cover policy fields of exemplary importance. The control of state aid, the regulation of food safety, intergovernmental transfer payments in Germany's *Länderfinanzausgleich,* and the framework of the European Structural and Cohesion Funds can, according to Lowi's (1972) widely used terminology that is adopted by Michael Zürn in his introductory chapter,[43] be classified into examples of constitutive (market-making), regulative (market-correcting), and (re-) distributive (market-breaking) policies. These are not genuinely legal distinctions. Lawyers can nevertheless confirm the representativeness of these three types of policies. Even the aspects they emphasize are quite similar, despite the fact that legal discourses underline normative differences between these policies and their institutional implications. To repeat as well as develop aspects already discussed in the introductory sections: state aid law can be classified as a "market-making" policy where the control of state aid is committed to criteria of economic rationality as pursued by competition policy. Indeed, this *Ordnungspolitik* orientation is now widely accepted in the EU.[44] The regulation of food safety is in principle an uncontested "market-correcting" activity, even though the legitimacy and institutional design of the regulatory activities at the European and international levels are controversial issues.[45] Transfer payments at federal and European levels are interpreted by lawyers as commitments arising out of the solidarity present within the polity. This is why lawyers tend to assume that compliance with such commitments will be more likely in Germany than in the EU.[46]

As indicated, the translation of controversies over policies and resistance to their implementation into legal arguments can result in a very significant practical impact, which political scientists need to be aware of. The methodological debate, which the following comments again take up,[47] is somewhat more subtle. The legalization of market-making, market-correcting and market-breaking policies poses very different challenges within national law and at the different levels of governance.

7.4.1   *"Market-making": The case of state aid*

Dieter Wolf's findings on the success of state aid control seem counterintuitive. The European level performs best, although its administration is

---

[43] See chapter 1, section 1.2.2.   [44] Cf. section 7.4.1 below.
[45] Cf. section 7.4.2 below.   [46] But see section 7.4.3 below.
[47] See section 7.2.2 above.

notoriously small, its judicial system overburdened, and its enforcement powers very limited. Students of state aid law will be less surprised. The control of state aid granted by member states to national enterprises ranks very high on the agenda of Directorate General IV. The jurisprudence of the ECJ is extremely rich. Nowhere, neither at the national nor the international level is a comparably strong body of law available. If so much law on state aid control exists, this policy is obviously taken seriously by the actors involved. What can we find out about the reasons for it?

7.4.1.1 State aid defined   Comparative inquiries presuppose a workable definition of their object. Lawyers know where to look. According to Article 87(1) (formerly Article 92(1) EC Treaty) "any aid granted by a member state or through State resources in any form whatsoever . . . shall . . . be incompatible with the common market." This definition leads us into the normative world of law. The concept of state aid needs to be interpreted in the light of the objectives of the whole of chapter 1 of Title VI on competition policy (Articles 81–99, formerly Articles 85–94). It is inextricably linked with competence issues and the debates over Europe's "economic constitution." If the political scientist wishes to rely on the law, he would have to engage in a complex interpretative exercise. Resort to the jurisprudence of the ECJ does not offer an easy way out of this predicament (Schwendinger 2003; Ross 2000).

And even if they did offer an easy way out, can one compare compliance with Community law with the controls at the national and international levels? Dieter Wolf has sketched out the contents of the pertinent regimes separately.[48] The German *Länder* have sought to preserve the ambiguity of their commitments. Their agreement on a "codex" rather than hard law is indicative of their intention to take non-implementation lightly and to avoid litigation.[49] The sanctioning powers of the national government are on paper only. The GATT/WTO regime is not as rigid as that of the EU, but has nonetheless prompted much litigation. A comparative law study could identify some commonalities and many differences between the three levels of governance but would not provide a common legal yardstick for the assessment of compliance. Should one instead look for guidance in economic theory? The definitions used by economic theory are as closely embedded in disciplinary contexts as those of the lawyers.[50]

Dieter Wolf works with a broad definition, which comprises "any financial advantage (allocation of money, tax expenditure, transfer of valuable

[48] See chapter 3, sections 3.1.1, 3.1.2, and 3.1.3.
[49] See chapter 3, sections 3.1.1 and 3.2.
[50] See the references in Wolf's introductory section to chapter 3.

resources) given by a state authority (or in the name of a state authority) to an enterprise, which does not entitle the state authority to an adequate amount of marketable goods or rights (for example shares or ownership) in return for this financial support".[51] This definition captures the prevailing understanding of applicable statutory instruments. This is a pragmatic and workable response to queries into the problems of defining state aids and comparing different regimes. This pragmatism comes at an acceptable price. Having distanced himself from the self-understanding of the laws under scrutiny, Dieter Wolf cannot claim to analyze compliance with them. What he promises to find out is the compliance with the objectives that policy makers and regulators at all levels of governance promise to pursue.

7.4.1.2 *Normative implications*   Dieter Wolf's pragmatic definition of state aids has important normative implications. The first is a rejection of economic theories which would seek to justify state aids as a means, for example, of smoothening processes of change. Such theories enjoy little standing in today's expert communities. European policy makers cannot take them too seriously either after they have committed themselves to the establishment of an open European market. And yet, there are still serious legal objections to the steady expansion of state aid controls. These objections are based on the principle of enumerated powers, as enshrined in Article 5 (formerly Article 3(b)). State aid controls are based on those Community competences that are contained in the Treaty Chapter on competition policy. The traditional justification for state aids was based on economic policy considerations which the member states had not transferred to the Community. To subject their practices to the state aid regime is to impose upon them an "economic constitution" under which alternative economic strategies can no longer be pursued. As the many exceptions to the general prohibition in Article 87(1) EC show, the Community's own commitment to a "system of undistorted competition" (see Article 3(1)(g), formerly Article 3) is not as rigid as many of its exponents would like it to be. Equally importantly, under Article 87(2) EC, the Commission enjoys considerable discretion in the implementation of the provisions on state aid, and a unanimous Council may, in derogation from Article 87, "decide that aid . . . shall be considered to be compatible with the common market." Last, but not least, the jurisprudence of the ECJ is by no means easy to decipher. The ECJ is time and again confronted by new governance arrangements, which promise to pursue common interests (such as environmental

---

[51] *Ibid.*

protection) and use "state resources" only indirectly. All this is to say that state aid law remains a contested and increasingly complex field. Whether or not a member state is in "compliance" is very often difficult to tell.

The Community record of supervision and control remains as impressive as Wolf describes it. However, this record cannot be read as confirming the authority of a given body of European state aid law and its unquestioned acceptance by the member states. Both the jurisprudence of the ECJ and the patterns of secondary legislation are continuously engaged in processes of law production, a search for legal concepts which the national courts accept and apply. The Commission's role as an instigator of policy-making, an agenda-setter, and supervisor of member state policies is extremely important but is never unrestrained. What is impressive about European state aid policy is the disciplining of the whole policy process, not the obedience to substantive legal prerogatives.

7.4.1.3 Explanations and reasons   In Dieter Wolf's evaluation,[52] the good compliance record of the EU is best explained using the legalization approach. Rational institutionalism performs second best, whereas reflexivity and legitimacy cannot explain much.[53] The discrepancy with the expectations and suggestions in the preceding sections are not as substantial as they may at first glance appear. "Legalization" comprises judicialized ("triadic") dispute settlements, legal and civic internalization.[54] It is indeed highly plausible to attribute the strength of the European aid control schemes to these mechanisms. But it does not follow that they function regardless of the legitimacy of the policy and law producing processes established by the EU. It is characteristic of the *"Recht-Fertigung"*[55] under Articles 87–89 (formerly Articles 92–94 EC Treaty) that the Commission is bound to interact with member states, that concerned non-governmental actors have a voice in the process, and that the elaboration of policies respects agreed-upon principles and rules. The interests at stake are high and the process does have its weaknesses. But it is not unreasonable to assume that European state aid law "deserves" recognition and is hence on the whole legitimate, in the Habermasian sense of the term.[56] Dieter Wolf's skepticism stems primarily from the

---

[52] Chapter 3, sections 3.3.1–3.3.4 and 3.4.

[53] Cf. the descriptions of the approaches in chapter 1, section 1.3 and the summary in chapter 4, section 4.3.

[54] See chapter 3, section 3.3.2; chapter 1, section 1.3.2; and chapter 6, section 6.2.2.

[55] See on this term section 7.3.4.1 above.

[56] I am not aware of a study on state aid law which uses such an interpretative framework. For competition law in general, however, see Wesseling (2000).

observation that at national level the constant confirmation of competitive principles by all the concerned actors did not motivate the national
German government to make use of the powers at its disposal. It seems
quite obvious, however, that the notoriously weak shadow of the German
law cannot exert the same disciplining power that has been developed by
European law.

7.4.2   *"Market-correcting" regulation and polity building*

Foodstuffs regulation has been chosen as an exemplary field of social regulation, because the need to protect consumers from risks to their health
in Europeanizing and globalizing food markets is, in principle, uncontested and the regulatory machineries that have in fact been established
are impressive. There is a rich body of law with which the member states
of the EU and WTO members have to comply. Even those large parts
of foodstuffs regulation which function more or less smoothly and where
stable administrative routines have been established are a noteworthy
achievement. As Jürgen Neyer notes,[57] foodstuffs regulation has become
genuinely transnational. Europeanization has not harmonized national
law; it has initiated a process of re-regulation and modernization – and
this achievement is widely recognized (Joerges 1994). If one takes into
account that Europeanization was an innovative and demanding process,
the record of compliance with foodstuffs law seems equally impressive.
But the complex European regulatory machinery has no real equivalent
at the international level – neither quantitatively nor qualitatively.[58] The
focus of Jürgen Neyer's analysis on two causes célèbres, namely the BSE
crisis and the hormones in beef saga, has one advantage. In both cases,
the formal proceedings were overshadowed by very high politics. The
BSE crisis was, according to the Commissioner for Agriculture, Franz
Fischler, "the biggest crisis the European Union ever had." The hormones case concerned a long-lasting, transatlantic conflict; at stake were
important agricultural interests, public anxieties over health risks, as well
as feeding and eating habits and cultures. These dimensions of the conflicts were the context within which compliance issues arose. The real
challenge, however, was to the potential of the EU and the WTO to discipline the disagreements between the parties and to civilize the public
quarrelling.

7.4.2.1 BSE   In retrospect, the BSE crisis may one day turn
into a success story documenting the potential of the European system to

---

[57] Chapter 4, section 4.1.   [58] Chapter 4, section 4.5.3; see also Herwig 2004.

detect errors and trace institutional malfunctioning, to further the emergence of a European public space, to redefine the role of the European Parliament, and to reform its institutions thoroughly. So much has happened. The European Commission has reorganized its services; it has subsequently examined and established new institutional options; the European Parliament has gained new authority and constructively redefined its role in the supervision of the Commission. Equally remarkable is the fact that Europe, so often blamed for its democratic deficits, has brought the institutional malfunctions of its member states to the fore; regulatory capacities and performance at member state level have been improved rather than weakened; national regulators were exposed to critical observation both "vertically" and "horizontally" – and it seems obvious that this type of pluralism has the potential to grow into a productive type of "regulatory competition." Finally, a new institution, the European Food Authority, was established.[59] These interpretations might sound overly optimistic. Indeed, they should be read with a caveat: the new institutional setting is not yet in full operation (see Vos 2000; Chalmers 2003). And the performance of the legal system, upon which Jürgen Neyer's case study focuses, is not overly impressive.

These observations are not meant to downplay the queries with compliance that are described in chapter 4.[60] The compliance incident started when the Commission authorized the United Kingdom to export a range of beef products as from August 1, 1999.[61] That decision, however, was complied with by neither France nor Germany which explained that they would uphold their import bans. Their counter-alliance, however, did not prove to be stable. Both countries pursued different strategies. The French story is more dramatic. Its newly established *Agence Française de Sécurité Sanitaire des Aliments* (AFSSA), in an Advice of September 30, 1999, concluded that the risks associated with beef from the UK were still significant. Backed by this authority, the French government informed the European Commission on October 1, 1999, that it would not lift the import ban on British beef. The Commission did not give in. It sought, and received, confirmation of its position from its own new Scientific Steering Committee. On October 29, 1999, that Committee

---

[59] See COM(2001) 475 final announcing: "Today, the DG Health and Consumer Protection website publishes new pages on the European Food Authority providing an overview of the ongoing legislative process for establishing the Authority, an update on its future mission and the scope of its activities, tasks and organisational matters, as well as information on the ongoing work of the Interim Scientific Advisory Forum"; see http://europa.eu.int/comm/food/fs/efa/index_en.html. The new authority was soon (on January 21, 2002) formally established: see http://www.efsa.eu.int.

[60] See, especially, section 4.4.

[61] See Commission Decision 99/514, OJ 1999 No. L195/42.

unanimously concluded that the concern expressed by the AFSSA was unfounded.

But here the law ran into trouble. Could the Commission proclaim some kind of supremacy doctrine in the field of "science"? The Commission itself apparently had some doubts. It contented itself with threatening France with infringement proceedings, while searching for a "political" solution. However, after the AFSSA had once again confirmed its precautionary position, the French government officially declared on December 8, 1999 that it would not lift its embargo. On January 14, 2000, the Commission submitted a complaint to the European Court of Justice (ECJ). I wondered in a comment whether that step was to be taken seriously (Joerges 2001: 8). But Advocate General Mischo, in his opinion delivered on September 20, 2001,[62] concluded that, "by prohibiting the direct import from the United Kingdom of products eligible under the date-based export scheme, the French Republic has failed to fulfill its obligations," asserting *inter alia* that "a member state cannot take refuge behind the opinion issued by a national scientific body in order to oppose it [a decision backed by the authority of the Commission's Scientific Steering Committee (SSC)], at least where, as was the case here, the national body's objections subsequent to the SSC's opinion relied upon by the Commission when taking its decision have been submitted to the SSC for consideration and held to be unfounded by it" (para. 120). This is a puzzling intrusion of law into scientific expertise, which the Advocate General confirmed in the following paragraph: "While it can be accepted that an aspect of a tricky case may possibly have eluded the SSC initially, equally it cannot be accepted that, once the SSC has been informed of that matter, examined it and found it to lack pertinence, the Member State in question may challenge the scientific authority attached to the SSC's opinions, unless it proves a malfunction at the level of that body, a situation which, it is to be hoped, will never materialize, so dramatic would the effect be as regards the legitimacy of the action of the Community bodies."

The ECJ's reasoning was then indeed more cautious. Even though the ECJ confirmed that "by refusing to permit the marketing in its territory after 30 December 1999 of products subject to that scheme which are correctly marked or labeled, the French Republic has failed to fulfill its obligations," it did not endorse the Advocate General's reasoning fully. Instead, the ECJ examined and approved the fairness of the proceedings. The ECJ consequently appealed to the "juridification" of conflict resolution, examined the quality of the legal framework, and found that

[62] Case 1/00, *Commission v. France* [2001] ECR I-9989.

France could have defended its views adequately. This is not an assertion of blatant supremacy. And, ultimately, France could be expected to comply.

7.4.2.2 Hormones in beef In a comparative evaluation, the European level and the WTO level of governance contrast markedly in two respects (see Scott 2000: 144 ff., 159 ff.; see, also, Bernauer 2000a, 2000b; Victor 2000). On the one hand, governance in the European Union is certainly more comprehensive and legalization much more advanced than at the international level. On the other hand, the argumentative style of WTO opinions differs markedly from that of ECJ judgments: they employ extensive reasoning, rather than French formalism; deliberation and persuasion rather than dry juridical "top-down" deduction. The Appellate Body took much of the European reasoning really seriously (see Perez 1998; Joerges 2001). It adopted a broad understanding of the notion of "risk" and its "scientific justification," explaining that "it is not only risk ascertainable in a science laboratory . . . but also risk in human societies as they actually exist, in other words, the actual potential for adverse effects on human health in the real world where people live and work and die" that has to be evaluated.[63] This is why bad veterinary practices can constitute a risk. It was even accepted that the "intense concern" of European consumers rather than protectionist interests was the predominant motivation for introducing and upholding the hormones ban.[64] In the end, however, science won the contest for the metanorm, which all WTO members have to respect: the reports and studies, the Appellate Body found, did not sufficiently substantiate the carcinogenic or genotoxic potential of the contested hormones.[65]

This, however, by no means put an end to the hormones saga. The struggle over the proper interpretation and implementation of the Appellate Body's findings and recommendations went on (Joerges 2001). The Commission continued its fight for the recognition of the precautionary principle (Christoforou 2003; Majone 2002; see also Joerges and Neyer 2003).

The most recent effort of the EU to ensure the compatibility of its position with the DSB's opinion is its adoption of Directive 03/74/EC.[66] This Directive upholds the ban on the growth-promoting hormone oestradiol 17β plus five additional hormones, however allowing certain restricted

---

[63] See para. 187 in WT/DS26/AB/R, accessible at www.wto.org.
[64] *Ibid.*, para. 245.   [65] *Ibid.*, para. 200.
[66] Directive 03/74/EC concerning the prohibition on the use in stockfarming of certain substances having a hormonal or thyrostatic action and of beta-agonists, OJ 2003 No. L262/17.

use for therapeutic purposes or zootechnical treatment. The risk acceptance variables are explained in the preamble. The European Commission
underlined in a press release the EU commitment to WTO obligations.[67]
The impression of this move on the EU's critics will most probably be limited. When contrasting the compliance record of both systems, it seems at
any rate safe to conclude that the EU's record is better, even though it is
difficult to tell whether that victory should be attributed to the long calm-
ing down period before the ECJ handed down its judgment. The more
fundamental challenge of the BSE crisis and the hormones dispute, however, was the potential of the EU and the WTO to respond constructively
to a complex and politicized conflict. It is here where the EU has clearly
much more to offer. Michael Zürn and Jürgen Neyer suggest in their summarized conclusions on the conditions of compliance[68] that it is hardly
possible, let alone wise, for democratically elected and politically accountable actors to disregard serious public concerns in their constituency in
the name of legal supranationalism. That view is fully compatible with
a normative interpretation that looks at the responses to the BSE crisis
in the broader context of the formation of a European polity and the
constitutionalization of its multilevel system of governance. Rather than
complaining about some dedifferentiation of law and politics in the wake
of the crisis, one may read the desire of the public in France, and of French
and German institutions and politicians, not to be treated as "subjects"
of European decisions but as citizens and actors with a voice of their own
in European affairs. Similarly, one might interpret the EU's insistence
upon its reading of the principle of precaution, as against the outcomes
of WTO dispute settlements, as a defense of the legitimacy of European
political processes against a substitution of diplomacy by legalized decision making. We will return to this background to compliance problems
below.

7.4.3   "Market-breaking" redistribution: Germany's Länderfinanzausgleich and European funds

Jürgen Neyer's concluding observation in his analysis of European and
German redistribution schemes is surprising: the arrangements foreseen
at both levels "are very similar in terms of the range of actors they involve
and their redistributive intensity, as well as their similar degrees of monitoring, sanctioning, dispute settlement, legal and civil internalization,
and participation."[69] For political scientists, the surprise is for two main

---

[67] Commission press release of October 15, 2003, IP/03/1393.
[68] Chapter 6, section 6.2.3.   [69] Chapter 5, section 5.5.

reasons. Prominent analysts of the EU argue that redistributive politics are deeply political and depend for their acceptance upon majoritarian approval (Majone 2001). This conceptual argument is backed by what Jürgen Neyer characterizes as the "communitarian" presumption:[70] Germans may be ready to support fellow-Germans, but they cannot be expected to give their money to other Europeans.

Lawyers are less impressed. There is hardly a single conceivable norm which complies less with the criterion of "precision" given by Abbott et al. (2000: 412–415) as a constitutive feature of "legalization" than the constitutional provisions of Germany's Basic Law (Articles 72(3) and 106(3)) as well as Articles 158 ff. EU Treaty, which stipulate a legally binding commitment to solidarity among the *Länder* of Germany and the member states of the EU respectively. And yet, large sums of money are being distributed both within Germany and from the EU to economically weak regions, even though the solidarity that is allegedly required to bring about such commitments is a non-legal mystery.

Exactly because the basis of these redistributive commitments is indeterminate, compliance research has addressed the processes in which these vague provisions are concretized into clearer obligations. Thus, Neyer's contribution is not concerned with either the correctness or the irregularities in implementing pertinent secondary legislation and programs, but rather with explaining why these commitments are taken so seriously. His findings surprise and illuminate in many respects. His thesis that the European "interest-based form of integration" can easily compete with a "community-based form of integration" within nation-states is significant for the defenders of statehood and illuminates the state of the European polity. Equally plausible seems to be his suggestion that the resistance of the richer *Länder* in Germany to the continuation of the existing regime is indicative of an erosion of its legitimacy. The desire for more economic rationality and new incentive-based distributive schemes could bring about a Germany which is more like a Union and less like a federal republic.

7.4.4   Compliance with purposive programs

The control of state aid, the regulation of food safety, the intergovernmental transfer payments in Germany's *Länderfinanzausgleich* and the framework of the European Structural and Cohesion Funds are all purposive rather than legal programs. But complex legal regulations can never work with one side of that dichotomy alone. Our examples offer an

---

[70] Chapter 5, section 5.1.

interesting typology. The redistributive programs are the least legalized. They have only been weakly proceduralized. To a great extent their implementation is left instead to political negotiations. Foodstuffs regulation is a field in which scientific expertise and risk management have substituted conditional legal programs; but the law has responded by extensive proceduralization. European state aid law has only imperfectly institutionalized economic rationality. Member states again and again defend their autonomy and the law pays tribute to the unsettled controversies over Europe's "economic constitution." It therefore comes as no surprise that the case study on redistributive policies has become more of a report on the compliance with constitutional commitments than a study of compliance with legal rules. It is equally unsurprising that the study on the hormones controversy sheds light on the limits of governance through expertise, whereas the BSE controversy documents how Europe has learned to make prudent use of the proceduralization of foodstuffs regulation. Dieter Wolf could have found a lot of similar evidence in the field of state aid control. Since he decided not to focus on exemplary cases from a very broad field he was forced to work at a different level of abstraction, which made it possible for him to document the very remarkable progress of the European system in the establishment of its – imperfectly legalized – supervision and control of state aids. All of these observations confirm the significance of the "third dimension" of compliance, which is introduced in section 7.1.2 above and is continually touched upon throughout, namely the interdependence of compliance and legitimacy. To this topic we return in the following concluding comments.

7.5   A restatement and outlook

In a short essay published ten years ago, Habermas (1994b) described lawyers' and social scientists' treatment of law in general, and of the *Rechtsstaat* and democracy in particular, as opening up a kind of schism between the disciplines. Each discipline, he argued, tends to approach law according to its own logic, which cannot be communicated across the disciplinary borders. Lawyers restrict themselves to normative issues (and, specifically, to legal reasoning), whereas social scientists specialize in empirical dimensions (and their explanations). Habermas's observation related to the law of constitutional states, but it applies equally to European and international law.

Social scientists tend to perceive law – if they see it at all – from *external* perspectives. They do not engage in the business of a *lege artis* application of rules, but explore their impact on society, their effectiveness, or they analyze processes of implementation. They thus tend to avoid the prescriptive dimension of law; normative issues, as dealt with by lawyers, are an *aliud* to truly scientific operations. This situation corresponds precisely with the state of the non-relationship between the legal and social sciences – in the national as well as in the international context – that was sketched out in the introduction:[71] namely, the disregard of compliance issues by lawyers, and the preoccupation of political scientists with explanations for state behavior.

Our whole project was an effort to overcome these delineations. As we have asserted, the reconfigurations of our disciplines do not involve just an abstract normative agenda, but ongoing theoretical efforts. Reconfiguration occurs at all levels of governance. It has long been observed within nation-states, where legal policy has started to reflect the law's operation in complex societies. At the "highest" level of governance, the borderlines between law, soft law, and legal regimes have become blurred, and the definition of "law" has loosened the inherited links to states and their coercive powers.

These are by no means developments without risks. Throughout the whole project and in the preceding sections, we have pointed to their ambivalence and underlined the need to retain the law's commitment to democratic notions of legitimate governance and the need to regain a new equilibrium between "facticity" and "validity," the analytical reconstruction of governance structures and their normative qualities.

7.5.1   *The indeterminacy of law at all levels of governance*

What at first sight looks paradoxical is, upon closer inspection, easy to explain: it is the indeterminacy of law and the uncertainties involved in all interpretative efforts by academics and practitioners seeking to cope with that indeterminacy, which can motivate lawyers to listen to the explanatory effort of political scientists. And it is their understanding of the "intrinsic ambiguity" of law which can help them to develop sufficiently complex reconstructions of compliance phenomena and thereby allow them to take account of the productive dimension of legal practices.[72] This starting point is not in line with the expectations which political scientists tend to articulate when they turn to their neighboring discipline and try to uphold their methodological standards. The admonition of Abbott et al. (2000: 403) seems quite representative: "[D]efinitions should turn on a coherent set of identifiable attributes. These should be sufficiently few that situations can be readily characterized . . . and

---

[71] Sections 7.1 and 7.2.   [72] See sections 7.3.2.1 and 7.3.4.1 above.

sufficiently important that changes in their values will influence the process being studied."

We do not of course question the good disciplinary reasons for such quests. What we do insist upon is that these methodological virtues do not govern the life of the law. Legal systems have to accept the inevitability of the "operation called *Verstehen*," the insight that a rule cannot determine its own application and the gaps between "*Begründungs- und Anwendungs-diskursen*" (Günther 1988). All of these are efforts to understand and to cope with a very real phenomenon, which empirical research must not define away. This phenomenon is present at all levels of governance, although it differs with the intensity of legalization. It also varies with the methodological conventions of national, European, and international legal systems. Differences in legalization at the three levels of governance stem from differences in the coercive "quality" of norms (a legal asset, not a sociological one!) and make themselves felt in argumentative practices. And, more obviously, these differences are felt in the different perceptions of the "law's" context, especially in the different perceptions of the relationship between the legal and the political system. To recall only a single example: non-compliance with the law is rarely admitted openly in the juridified world of the constitutional nation-state. At the international level, the gap between what the law claims and the actual power it possesses is even wider; and the demand for, and the possibility of using, explanatory approaches is hence much higher.

7.5.2   *The turn to governance and its legal challenges*

One important implication of these insights into the productive dimension of legal practice in the context of our project is the possibility and relevance of comparisons: comparisons are possible because the differences between national, European, and international law have become gradual, but remain important because they are significant. All of this seems to us to be as irrefutable as it is uncomfortable. If compliance research sought to focus on uncontroversial interpretations, or on areas in which the resolution of controversies has been delegated to courts or court-like bodies, as Abbott et al. (2000: 401) seem to suggest it should, it would risk misstating the reality which it is expected to explore.

One important reason for the blurring of the differences between the once distinctive characteristics of national, European, and international law is "the turn to governance." This origin of that notion and the varieties of its meaning need not concern us here in any detail. We use it to designate actor configurations and problem-solving activities, which do not fit into the institutional frameworks that national, European, and international law foresaw, but which have instead emerged as responses to functional exigencies. These exigencies are twofold. In section 7.3.1.2 we underlined the needs of *national* legal systems to respond to the failures of regulatory law, to integrate expert knowledge, to resort to the management capacities of private enterprises, and to co-operate with non-governmental organizations. In the sections dealing with European and WTO law (7.3.2.2 and 7.3.3.1), Europeanization and globalization processes are identified as "external" promoters of governance arrangements which amount, in many important sectors, such as standardization, to the emergence of a type of legalization, which can be usefully characterized as "private transnationalism" (Schepel 2003: Chapter 2).

The career of the term is deeply rooted in the material question. "Governance" refers to the combination of activities that take place between the application of rules on the one hand, and the problem-solving that surrounds them on the other. The term disregards the public/private divide and hence faithfully mirrors modern regulatory practices. It comprises the governmental and non-governmental activities of bureaucracies, the judiciary, private firms, and associations. Last, but not least, we can apply the notion to the nation-state, within the EU, and beyond. The many actors and institutional levels that are often included in the concept may also mirror the many dimensions, complexities, and the transboundary character of the problems involved. Governance has been used to address our recognition that regulatory processes are not one-dimensional and administrative; on the contrary, regulation involves the interaction of very diverse contributors, including scientific expertise, law, economics, politics, consumer reactions, and the mass media, and it depends on preparatory research as much as on implementation (see Jachtenfuchs and Kohler-Koch 2003). It is important for lawyers to underline the point that "governance" comprises a broad variety of procedural standards, including both scientific quality and notions of justice (Sand 1998). Nonetheless, the concept seems to retain a positive, discriminating sense or message; namely, that we have an irrefutable need to "organize" our social and economic life, to build institutions, and to take political decisions (see Kohler-Koch 1999).

The problems that these practices pose for state-focused compliance research are not overly intriguing.[73] From a legal perspective, however,

[73] "[T]he focus on regulations which address themselves to territorially defined units does not imply an exclusion of societal actors from the study in general. On the contrary, we systematically differentiate between the immediate addressees of a regulation and those who are affected by it in other ways. While the former are those actors that are primarily required by the regulation to undertake or refrain from certain activities (and to whom the question of compliance or non-compliance applies), the number of those

the brave new world of governance gives rise to two interdependent queries. One concerns the erosion of the public/private distinction, a phenomenon which is gaining an ever more dramatic importance. The second concern may be less visible but seems even more intriguing. The legal system, as Luhmann (1993) has stressed so often, distinguishes between legal and illegal acts and operations. The operation of this binary code is now confronted everywhere with arrangements that seek to overcome the impasses of legal "solutions" to perceived problems. While governance arrangements seek the law's support, they also challenge the law's rule through a dejuridification of the polity. If, and because, governance "occurs" outside the formally envisaged institutions, normative yardsticks for their assessment are not easily available.

Within national legal systems, the turn to governance was accompanied (and even promoted) by new legal methodologies,[74] which inspired sophisticated concepts for the supervision of governance arrangements (see, e.g., Black 1996). Similar strategies were developed at the European level (e.g., Joerges, Schepel and Vos 1999; Schepel 2003: Chapter 6). This is not to say, however, that such suggestions, if they were noticed at all, have led to any consolidated opinion. The turn to governance leads lawyers into uncharted waters. Uncertainties are unavoidable exactly because governance "occurs" outside the formally envisaged institutions and the established normative yardsticks for their assessment are unavailable.

7.5.3   Constitutionalism, "Recht-Fertigung" and transnational governance

"Is law – understood as a normatively meaningful form of social regulation – conceivable or indeed possible beyond the nation-state?" Michael Zürn is well aware of the programmatic character of the question with which he opens this study.[75] He operates with a threefold assumption: (1) compliance issues are embedded in problems of social ordering; (2) the legitimacy of social ordering is inconceivable without law; (3) in postnational situations such law must lose its formerly constitutive links to the state.

---

who are ultimately affected by the regulation can be far greater than the number of its direct addressees . . . [W]e therefore include and distinguish between regulatory addressees, regulatory targets, and affected actors. However, only territorial political units – as regulatory addressees – appear as dependent variables. Regulatory targets and affected actors are included on the side of the independent variable" (chapter 1, section 1.2.2).

[74] Cf. section 7.3.2.2 above.   [75] Chapter 1, first sentence.

All of these assumptions point to highly topical theoretical debates in various legal disciplines, namely in legal theory and in European and international law.[76] "Constitutionalism" is the notion most widely used to reconstruct the interdependence of law and legitimacy. Deliberative theories of democracy are the most explicit in that respect. According to this tradition, "constitutionalism" is understood as a reflexive or circular operation. The specific quality or aspiration of constitutional law is that it legitimizes governance – gaining its own constitutive legitimacy from its embeddedness in democratic processes: "good" law is both the result of, and the precondition for, such deliberative political processes (Gerstenberg 1997: 9 ff.; programmatically for the EU see Eriksen and Fossum 2000; Eriksen, Fossum and Menéndez 2003).

This co-originality thesis emerged from reflections on constitutional states. This is why the "postnational constellation" is a fundamental challenge to theories of deliberative democracy: Is it conceivable that transnational governance can be legitimized through legal prescriptions, such that "good" transnational governance remains committed to rule-of-law ideals and the legitimacy of "law-mediated" transnational governance? Jürgen Neyer and I, with our concept of "deliberative supranationalism," have submitted a tentative answer, which was restricted to the conditions of European governance in a specific field (Joerges and Neyer 1997a; see also Joerges 2000 and 2003b). We conceptualized European law as a species of conflict of laws, a law which responds to "true conflicts" by principles and rules which are acceptable to all concerned polities – this is its supranational dimension. We have interpreted its resort to "deliberative" problem-solving as an alternative to hierarchical legal structures – and as a possible alternative path towards law-mediated legitimate governance in postnational situations. The notion of "constitutionalization," if understood as the search for law which would ensure the deliberative quality of decision-making processes, purified from its connotations with the state, captures the precarious legitimacy problematic of transnational governance, albeit somewhat unfortunately.[77] A study on compliance should not be expected to deliver comprehensive answers to these queries. Enough is achieved if it becomes apparent that our efforts to understand compliance have revealed common concerns. (1) The turn to governance forces lawyers to renew their understanding of constitutionalism. (2) Within national legal systems and even more so in postnational situations, this endeavor requires a radically procedural understanding of law, a continuous reflection on the context in which law emerges and

[76] See in particular sections 7.3.1.3, 7.3.2.3, and 7.3.3.3 above.
[77] See section 7.3.4.2 above.

on the conditions which favour its justice. (3) "Constitutionalization" means gradually to codify the insights that the process produces. Implicit in that term is the idea of law-mediated legitimacy. In that respect it is hopefully more precise and certainly more demanding than the quest for democracy protected by law in the constitutional state (cf. Joerges 2003, 2004).

All of these formulas relate to ongoing debates in legal science. They are not identical, but are compatible with the agenda spelled out in the previous chapters. As the introductory chapter underlines, deliberation has become "the normative leitmotiv that inspires the organization of transnational problem-solving and assessment. A supranational charter is, thereby, neither required to represent a territorial state nor does it presuppose the dissolution of national political systems. What it does require, however, is that the interests and concerns of non-nationals should be considered and legalized through juridification at levels beyond the nation-state and through the internalization of international regula-tions"[78] (see also Neyer 2003 with regard to the EU, and Zürn 2001 on the notion of complex governance beyond the nation-state; also Zürn and Wolf 1999). Similar ideas can be found elsewhere – among both lawyers and political scientists (see e.g. Picciotto 2000; Dryzek 1990, 1999). They may not yet have achieved the status of a theory. But they designate a promising three-dimensional agenda which is concerned with (1) the internalization of "compliance" issues by legal theories and the establishment of new governance arrangements; (2) the acceptance of gradualizing conceptions of law at all levels; and (3) the interplay of facticity and normativity in the generation of legitimacy.

---

[78] Chapter 1, section 1.4.4.

References

Abbott, Kenneth W. and Snidal, Duncan 2000, "Hard and Soft Law in International Governance," *International Organization* 54(3): 421–56.

Abbott, Kenneth W., Keohane, Robert O., Moravcsik, Andrew, Slaughter, Anne-Marie and Snidal, Duncan 2000, "The Concept of Legalization," *International Organization* 54(3): 401–19.

Abel, Theodore 1948, "The Operation Called Verstehen," *American Journal of Sociology* 54(3): 211–18.

Abromeit, Heidrun 1992, *Der verkappte Einheitstaat*, Opladen, Leske + Budrich.

Abromeit, Heidrun and Schmidt, Thomas 1998, "Grenzprobleme der Demokratie. Konzeptionelle Überlegungen," in Kohler-Koch, Beate (ed.), *Regieren in entgrenzten Räumen* (PVS Sonderheft 29), Opladen, West-deutscher Verlag, 293–320.

Adamantopoulos, Konstantinos A. 1988, *Das Subventionsrecht des GATT in der EWG*, Köln, Heymanns.

Alter, Karen J. 1998, "Who Are the 'Masters of the Treaty'? European Governments and the European Court of Justice," *International Organization* 52(1): 121–47.

Alter, Karen J. 2000, "The European Union's Legal System and Domestic Policy: Spillover or Backlash," *International Organization* 54(3): 489–518.

Alter, Karen J. 2001, *Establishing the Supremacy of European Law. The Making of an International Rule of Law in Europe*, Oxford University Press.

Alter, Karen J. and Meunier-Aitsahalia, Sophie 1994, "Judical Politics in the European Community. European Integration and the Path-Breaking Cassis de Dijon Decision," *Comparative Political Studies* 26(4): 535–61.

Anderson, Jeffrey J. 1995, "Structural Funds and the Social Dimension of EU Policy: Springboard or Stumbling Block?" in Leibfried, Stephan and Pierson, Paul (eds.), *European Social Policy. Between Fragmentation and Integration*, Washington, DC, Brookings Institution, 123–58.

Applebaum, Richard, Felstiner, William and Gessner, Volkmar (eds.) 2001, *Rules and Networks – The Legal Culture of Global Business Transactions*, Oxford, Hart.

Arbeiterkammer Bremen 1998. *Ländervergleich der Betriebsprüfung und Steuerfahndung. Ergebnisse der Untersuchung aus unveröffentlichten Steuerstatistiken*, *Arbeiterkammer Bremen*, unpublished paper (on file with the author).

Arend, Anthony Clark 1996, "Toward an Understanding of International Legal Rules," in Beck, Robert J., Arend, Anthony Clark and Vander Lugt, Robert

D. (eds.), *International Rules. Approaches from International Law and International Relations*, Oxford University Press, 289–310.

Arendt, Hannah 1961, *Between Past and Future*, New York, Viking Press.

Armstrong, Kenneth A. 1998, "Legal Integration: Theorizing the Legal Dimension of European Integration," *Journal of Common Market Studies* 36(2): 155–74.

Aspinwall, Mark and Greenwood, Justin 1998, "Conceptualizing Collective Action in the European Union. An Introduction," in Aspinwall, Mark and Greenwood, Justin (eds.), *Collective Action in the European Union. Interests and the New Politics of Associability*, London, Routledge, 1–30.

Avery, Natalie, Drake, Martine and Lang, Tim 1993, "Internationale Harmonisierung lebensmittelrechtlicher Normen. Eine Studie über die Codex Alimentarius Kommission," *EPD Entwicklungspolitik, Materialien* II/93.

Axelrod, Robert 1984, *The Evolution of Cooperation*, New York, Basic Books.

Axelrod, Robert and Keohane, Robert O. 1986, "Achieving Cooperation under Anarchy: Strategies and Institutions," in Oye, Kenneth A. (ed.), *Cooperation under Anarchy*, Princeton, NJ, Princeton University Press, 226–54.

Backes, Peter 1995, "Die neuen Streitbeilegungsregeln der Welthandelsorganisation (WTO). Zu den Auswirkungen im nationalen Recht der USA," *Recht der Internationalen Wirtschaft* 41(11): 917–19.

Baker, Betsy 1992, "Eliciting Non-Party Compliance with Multilateral Environmental Treaties: U.S. Legislation and the Jurisdictional Bases for Compliance Incentives in the Montreal Ozone Protocol," *German Yearbook of International Law* 35, 333–65.

Becker, Peter 1977, "Politikverflechtung in der Gemeinschaftsaufgabe 'Verbesserung der regionalen Wirtschaftsstruktur'," in Scharpf, Fritz W., Reissert, Bernd and Schnabel, Fritz (eds.), *Politikverflechtung II. Kritik und Berichte aus der Praxis*, Kronberg/Ts, Hain, 29–38.

Benz, Arthur and Eberlein, Burkard 1999, "The Europeanization of Regional Policies: Patterns of Multi-Level Governance," *Journal of European Public Policy* 6(2): 329–48.

Bernauer, Thomas 2000a, "Solving Conflicts of Interest among Governments, Consumers, and Producers I," *Swiss Political Science Review* 6(2): 79–99.

Bernauer, Thomas 2000b, "Solving Conflicts of Interest among Governments, Consumers, and Producers II," *Swiss Political Science Review* 6(3): 85–127.

Bilal, Sanoussi and Polmans, Roel 1999, "Is State Aid in Decline? Trends of State Aid to Industry in the Member States of the European Union," in Bilal, Sanoussi and Nicolaides, Phedon (eds.), *Understanding State Aid Policy in the European Community. Perspectives on Rules and Practice*, Maastricht, European Institute of Public Administration, 47–80.

Black, Julia 1996, "Constitutionalising Self-Regulation," *Modern Law Review* 59(1): 24–55.

Bleckmann, Albert 1977, "Die Beihilfenkompetenz der Europäischen Gemeinschaften. Ein Beitrag zum Prinzip der begrenzten Ermächtigung," *Die Öffentliche Verwaltung* 30(17): 615–19.

Bleckmann, Albert 1984, "Ordnungsrahmen für das Recht der Subventionen. Gutachten D für den 55. Deutschen Juristentag," *Verhandlungen des Deutschen Juristentags* 55(1): D1–D115.

Bliss, Julia Christine 1987, "GATT Dispute Settlement Reform in the Uruguay Round: Problems and Prospects," *Stanford Journal of International Law* 23(1): 31–55.

Böckenförde, Ernst 1969, "Entstehung und Wandel des Rechtsstaatsbegriffs," in Ehmke, Horst (ed.), *Festschrift für Adolf Arndt*, Frankfurt/M, Europäische Verlagsanstalt, 53–76.

Bogdandy, Armin von 1999, *Supranationaler Föderalismus als Wirklichkeit und Idee einer neuen Herrschaftsform. Zur Gestalt der Europäischen Union nach Amsterdam*, Baden-Baden, Nomos.

Böhret, Carl, Jann, Werner and Kronenwett, Eva 1980, "Handlungsspielräume und Steuerungspotential der regionalen Wirtschaftsförderung," in Bruder, Wolfgang and Ellwein, Thomas (eds.), *Raumordnung und staatliche Steuerungsfähigkeit* (PVS-Sonderheft 10/1979), Opladen, Westdeutscher Verlag, 76–110.

Börzel, Tanja A. 1999, *Why There Is No Southern Problem: On Environmental Leaders and Laggards in the European Union*, EUI Working Paper, RSC 99/16, Florence, European University Institute.

Börzel, Tanja 2000, *Private Actors on the Rise? The Role of Non-State Actors in Compliance with International Institutions*, Bonn, Max-Planck-Projektgruppe on Common Goods.

Börzel, Tanja 2001, "Non-Compliance in the European Union," *Journal of European Public Policy* 8(5): 803–24.

Börzel, Tanja 2002, "Non-State Actors and the Provision of Common Goods. Compliance with International Institutions," in Hértier, Adrienne (ed.), *Common Goods: Reinventing European and International Governance*, Lanham, MD, Rowman & Littlefield, 155–78.

Boss, Alfred and Rosenschon, Astrid 1998, *Subventionen in Deutschland*, Kieler Diskussionsbeiträge 320, Kiel, Institut für Weltwirtschaft.

Boss, Alfred and Rosenschon, Astrid 2000, *Subventionen in Deutschland: eine Aktualisierung*, Kieler Diskussionsbeiträge 356, Kiel, Institut für Weltwirtschaft.

Boss, Alfred and Rosenschon, Astrid 2002, *Subventionen in Deutschland: Quantifizierung und finanzpolitische Bewertung*, Kieler Diskussionsbeiträge 392/393, Kiel, Institut für Weltwirtschaft.

Bothe, Michael 1996, "The Evaluation of Enforcement Mechanisms in International Environmental Law," in Wolfrum, Rüdiger (ed.), *Enforcing Environmental Standards: Economic Mechanisms as Viable Means?*, Berlin, Springer, 13–38.

Boyle, Alan E. 1991, "Saving the World? Implementation and Enforcement of International Law Through International Institutions," *Journal of Environmental Law* 3(2): 229–45.

Break, George 1985, "The Tax Expenditure Budget. The Need for a Fuller Accounting," *National Tax Journal* 38(3): 261–65.

Breuel, Birgit 1988, "Was geschieht zur Subventionsprävention? Niedersächsische Gesetzesinitiativen im Bundesrat," *MIT-Jahrbuch* 1988, 43–6.

Brösse, Ulrich 1999, *Industriepolitik*, München, Oldenbourg.

Brüggemeier, Gert and Joerges, Christian (eds.) 1984, *Workshop zu Konzepten des post-interventionistischen Rechts*, Zentrum für Europäische Rechtspolitik, Materialien 4, Bremen, Zentrum für Europäische Rechtspolitik.

Bull, Hans Peter 1999, "Finanzausgleich im 'Wettbewerbsstaat' – Bemerkungen zur neuen Föderalismustheorie und zu ihrer Bedeutung für den Länderfinanzausgleich," *Die Öffentliche Verwaltung* 52(7): 269–81.

Bull, Hedley 1977, *The Anarchical Society. A Study of Order in World Politics*, Basingstoke, Macmillan.

Burley, Anne-Marie and Mattli, Walter 1993, "Europe before the Court: A Political Theory of Legal Integration," *International Organization* 47(1): 41–76.

Busch, Marc L. and Reinhardt, Eric 2002, "Testing International Trade Law: Empirical Studies of GATT/WTO Dispute Settlement," in Kennedy, Daniel L. M. and Southwick, James D. (eds.), *The Political Economy of International Trade Law: Essays in Honor of Robert E. Hudec*, New York, Cambridge University Press, 457–81.

Caldeira, Gregory A. and Gibson, James L. 1995, "The Legitimacy of the Court of Justice in the European Union: Models of Institutional Support," *American Political Science Review* 89(2): 356–76.

Cameron, James 1996, "Compliance, Citizens, and NGOs," in Cameron, James, Werksman, Jacob and Roderick, Peter (eds.), *Improving Compliance with International Environmental Law*, London, Earthscan Publications, 29–42.

Cameron, James and Campbell, Karen (eds.) 1998, *Dispute Resolution in the World Trade Organisation*, London, Cameron May.

Cameron, James, Werksman, Jacob and Roderick, Peter (eds.) 1996, *Improving Compliance with International Environmental Law*, London, Earthscan Publications.

Caporaso, James A. 1996, "The European Union and Forms of State: Westphalian, Regulatory or Post-Modern," *Journal of Common Market Studies* 34(1): 29–52.

Caporaso, James 1997, "Does the European Union Represent an N of 1?," *ECSA Review* 10(3): 1–5.

Caporaso, James A. 2000, "Changes in the Westphalian Order: Territory, Public Authority, and Sovereignty," *International Studies Review* 2(2): 1–28.

Chalmers, Damien 2003, " 'Food for Thought': Reconciling European Risks and National Habits," *Modern Law Review* 66(4): 532–62.

Charney, Jonathan I. 1997, "Third Party Dispute Settlement and International Law," *Columbia Journal of Transnational Law* 36(1): 65–89.

Chayes, Abram and Chayes, Antonia Handler 1990, "From Law Enforcement to Dispute Settlement," *International Security* 14(2): 147–64.

Chayes, Abram and Chayes, Antonia Handler 1993, "On Compliance," *International Organization* 47(2): 175–205.

Chayes, Abram and Chayes, Antonia Handler 1995, *The New Sovereignty. Compliance with International Regulatory Agreements*, Cambridge, MA, Harvard University Press.

Checkel, Jeffrey T. 1998, "The Constructivist Turn in International Relations Theory. A Review Essay," *World Politics* 50(1): 328–48.

Checkel, Jeffrey T. 2001, "Why Comply? Social Learning and European Identity Change," *International Organization* 55(3): 553–88.

Christoforou, Theofanis 2003, "The Precautionary Principle and Democratizing Expertise: A European Legal Perspective," *Science and Public Policy* 30(3): 205–11.

Classen, Claus Dieter 1997, "Anmerkung zu EuGH, Rs. C24/95, Urteil vom 20.3.1997," *Juristenzeitung* 52(14): 724–6.

Cowles, Maria Green, Caporaso, James A. and Risse, Thomas (eds.) 2001, *Transforming Europe. Europeanization and Domestic Change*, Ithaca, NY, Cornell University Press.

Cummins, Jason G., Harris, Trevor S. and Hassett, Kevin A. 1995, "Accounting Standards, Information Flow, and Firm Investment Behavior," in Feldstein, Martin, Hines, James R. and Hubbard, R. Glenn (eds.), *The Effects of Taxation on Multinational Corporations*, Chicago, University of Chicago Press, 181–224.

Curran, Vivian G. 2003, "Formalism and Anti-Formalism Traditions in French and German Judicial Methodology," in Joerges, Christian and Ghaleigh, Navraj S. (eds.), *Darker Legacies of Law in Europe: The Shadow of National Socialism and Fascism over Europe and its Legal Traditions*, Oxford, Hart, 205–28.

Curtis, Craig, Thurman, Quint C. and Nice, David C. 1991, "Improving Legal Compliance by Noncoercive Means: Coproducing Order in Washington State," *Social Science Quarterly* 72(4): 645–60.

Datta, Lois-Ellin and Grasso, Patrick G. (eds.) 1998, *Evaluating Tax Expenditures: Tools and Techniques for Assessing Outcomes*, San Francisco, Jossey-Bass.

De Schutter, Olivier, Lebessis, Notis and Paterson, John (eds.) 2001, *Governance in the European Union*, Luxembourg, Office for Official Publications.

Deutsche Bundesbank 2000, "Die Entwicklung der Subventionen in Deutschland seit Beginn der neunziger Jahre," *Monatsbericht <Deutsche Bundesbank>* 52(12): 15–29.

Deutscher Bundestag (ed.) 1982, *Fragen der Subventionspolitik*, "Zur Sache"—Themen parlamentarischer Beratung 3/82, Bonn, Deutscher Bundestag.

Di Fabio, Udo 1996, "Gefahr, Vorsorge, Risiko: Die Gefahrenabwehr unter dem Einfluß des Vorsorgeprinzips," *Jura* 18(11): 566–74.

Doering, Thomas 2003, "German Public Banks Under the Pressure of the EU Subsidy Proceedings," *Intereconomics* 38(2): 94–101.

Downs, George W., Rocke, David M. and Barsoom, Peter N. 1996, "Is the Good News About Compliance Good News About Cooperation?," *International Organization* 50(3): 379–406.

Dryzek, John S. 1990, *Discursive Democracy*, Cambridge University Press.

Dryzek, John S. 1999, "Transnational Democracy," *Journal of Political Philosophy* 7(1): 30–51.

Dworkin, Ronald 1986, *Law's Empire*, Cambridge, MA, Belknap.

Dworkin, Ronald 1991, *Taking Law Seriously: New Impressions with a Reply to Critics*, London, Duckworth.

Easson, Alex 1994, "Integration Through Law: The Court of Justice and the Achievement of the Single Market and the European Union," in Michelmann, Hans J. and Soldatos, Panayotis (eds.), *European Integration: Theories and Approaches*, Lanham, MD, University Press of America, 77–97.

Ebert, Werner and Meyer, Steffen 1999, "Die Anreizwirkungen des Finanzausgleichs," *Wirtschaftsdienst* 79(2): 106–14.

Eckert, Dieter 1995, "Die neue Welthandelsordnung und ihre Bedeutung für den internationalen Lebensmittelhandel," *Zeitschrift für das gesamte Lebensmittelrecht* 3, 365–93.

Eder, Klaus and Kantner, Cathleen 2000, "Transnationale Resonanzstrukturen in Europa. Eine Kritik der Rede vom Öffentlichkeitsdefizit in Europa," in Bach, Maurizio (ed.), *Die Europäisierung nationaler Gesellschaften* (Kölner Zeitschrift für Soziologie und Sozialpsychologie – Sonderheft 40), Opladen, Westdeutscher Verlag, 306–31.

Eder, Klaus, Hellmann, Kai-Uwe and Trenz, Hans-Jörg 1998, "Regieren in Europa jenseits öffentlicher Legitimation? Eine Untersuchung zur Rolle von politischer Öffentlichkeit in Europa," in Kohler-Koch, Beate (ed.), *Regieren in entgrenzten Räumen* (PVS-Sonderheft 29), Opladen, Westdeutscher Verlag, 321–44.

Eggers, Barbara 1998, "Die Entscheidung des WTO Appellate Body im Hormonfall. Doch ein Recht auf Vorsorge?," *Europäische Zeitschrift für Wirtschaftsrecht* 9(5–6): 147–51.

Eick, Christian 1981, "Wirtschaftssubventionen. Anmerkungen zu einer aktuellen Debatte," *Bremer Zeitschrift für Wirtschaftspolitik* 4(4): 5–43.

Eising, Rainer and Kohler-Koch, Beate 1994, "Inflation und Zerfaserung: Trends der Interessenvermittlung in der Europäischen Gemeinschaft," in Streeck, Wolfgang (ed.), *Staat und Verbände* (PVS-Sonderheft 25/1994), Opladen, Westdeutscher Verlag, 175–206.

Eising, Rainer and Kohler-Koch, Beate 1999, "Governance in the European Union. A Comparative Assessment," in Kohler-Koch, Beate and Eising, Rainer (eds.), *The Transformation of Governance in the European Union*, London, Routledge, 266–84.

Elias, Norbert 1969, *Über den Prozeß der Zivilisation. Soziogenetische und psychogenetische Untersuchungen*, Bern, Francke.

Elster, Jon 1992, "Arguing and Bargaining in the Federal Convention and the Assemblée Constituante," in Malnes, Raino and Underdal, Arild (eds.), *Rationality and Institutions. Essays in Honour of Knut Midgaard*, Oslo, Universitetsforlaget, 13–50.

Elster, Jon 1998a, "Introduction," in Elster, Jon (ed.), *Deliberative Democracy*, Cambridge University Press, 1–18.

Elster, Jon 1998b, "Deliberation and Constitution Making," in Elster, Jon (ed.), *Deliberative Democracy*, Cambridge University Press, 97–122.

Engels, Rainer 1996, *Die Codex Alimentarius Kommission und der Einsatz von Hormonen in der Tierernährung. Vorsorgeprinzip oder blindes Vertrauen in die Wissenschaft*. Form Umwelt & Entwicklung, Bonn, BUND.

Eriksen, Erik Oddvar and Fossum, John Erik (eds.) 2000, *Democracy in the European Union: Integration Through Deliberation?*, London, Routledge.

Eriksen, Erik O., Fossum, John E. and Menéndez, Agustín José (eds.) 2003, *Developing a Constitution for Europe*, London, Routledge.

European Parliament 1997, *Report by the Temporary Committee of Inquiry Into BSE on Alleged Contraventions or Maladministration in the Implementation of Community Law in Relation to BSE, Without Prejudice to the Jurisdiction of the Community and National Courts*, PE 220.544/fin., Luxembourg, Office of Official Publications.

European Parliament and European Commission 1999, *The European Union and Food Security: Lessons from the BSE Crisis*, Luxembourg, Office of Official Publications.

Evers, Tilmann 1994, "Supranationale Staatlichkeit am Beispiel der Europäischen Union: Civitas Civitatum oder Monstrum?," *Leviathan* 22(1): 115–34.

Falke, Josef 1996, "Comitology and other Committees: A Preliminary Empirical Assessment," in Pedler, Robert H. and Schaefer, Guenther F. (eds), *Shaping European Law and Policy. The Role of Committees and Comitology in the Political Process*, Maastricht, European Institute of Public Administration, 117–66.

Falkenkötter, Thomas 1996, "Der Streit um die sächsischen VW-Beihilfen – Anlaß für grundsätzliche Klärung?," *Neue Juristische Wochenschrift* 49(41): 2689–94.

Färber, Gisela 1989, "Subventionen in der Sozialen Marktwirtschaft. Subventionsbegriff und Subventionspolitik in der Bundesrepublik Deutschland im Lichte gewandelter finanzpolitischer Konzeptionen," in Fischer, Wolfram (ed.), *Währungsreform und Soziale Marktwirtschaft. Erfahrungen und Perspektiven nach 40 Jahren* (Schriften des Vereins für Socialpolitik N.F. 190), Berlin, Duncker & Humblot, 319–43.

Färber, Gisela 1995, *Binnenmarktgerechte Subventionspolitik in der Europäischen Gemeinschaft. Strukturen, Normen und Defizite*, Frankfurt/M, Campus.

Färber, Gisela 1996, "Regionen in der Finanzverfassung der Europäischen Union – Probleme und Reformvorschläge," *Steuer und Wirtschaft* 73(4): 379–94.

Feick, Jürgen 2000, "Wissen, Expertise und regulative Politik: Das Beispiel der Arzneimittelkontrolle," in Werle, Raymund and Schimank, Uwe (eds.), *Gesellschaftliche Komplexität und kollektive Handlungsfähigkeit*, Frankfurt/M, Campus, 208–33.

Finnemore, Martha 1996, *National Interests in International Society*, Ithaca, NY, Cornell University Press.

Finnemore, Martha and Toope, Stephen J. 2001, "Comment on Legalization and World Politics," *International Organization* 55(3): 743–58.

Fraenkel, Ernst 1932, "Die politische Bedeutung des Arbeitsrechts," in Ramm, Thilo (ed.), *Arbeitsrecht und Politik*, Neuwied, Luchterhand, 247–60.

Franck, Thomas M. 1990, *The Power of Legitimacy Among Nations*, Oxford University Press.

Franck, Thomas M. 1995, *Fairness in International Law and Institutions*, Oxford, Clarendon Press.

Franz, Wolfgang 1992, "Keynesianische Beschäftigungstheorie und Beschäftigungspolitik," *Aus Politik und Zeitgeschichte* B 12/92, 25–31.

Franzmeyer, Fritz 1993, "Die Europäische Wirtschafts- und Währungsunion: Ausbau der gemeinschaftlichen Kohäsionspolitik," *Integration* 16(2): 95–102.

Garrett, Geoffrey 1992, "International Cooperation and Institutional Choice. The European Community's Internal Market," *International Organization* 46(2): 533–60.

Garrett, Geoffrey 1995, "The Politics of Legal Integration in the European Union," *International Organization* 49(1): 171–81.

Garrett, Geoffrey, Kelemen, R. Daniel and Schulz, Heiner 1998, "The European Court of Justice, National Governments, and Legal Integration in the European Union," *International Organization* 52(1): 149–76.

Gaubatz, Kurt Taylor 1996, "Democratic States and Commitment in International Relations," *International Organization* 50(1): 109–39.

Gawron, Thomas and Rogowski, Ralf 1996, "Effektivität, Implementation und Evaluation. Wirkungsanalyse am Beispiel von Entscheidungen des Bundesverfassungsgerichts," *Zeitschrift für Rechtssoziologie* 17(2): 177–220.

Gehring, Thomas 1996, "Arguing und Bargaining in internationalen Verhandlungen. Überlegungen am Beispiel des Ozonschutzregimes," in Prittwitz, Volker von (ed.), *Verhandeln und Argumentieren. Dialog, Interessen und Macht in der Umweltpolitik*, Opladen, Leske+Budrich, 207–38.

Gehring, Thomas 2002, "Schutzstandards in der WTO? Die schleichende Verknüpfung der Welthandelsordnung mit standardsetzenden internationalen Institutionen," in Jachtenfuchs, Markus and Knodt, Michèle (eds.), *Regieren in internationalen Institutionen*, Opladen, Leske + Budrich, 111–39.

Gerstenberg, Oliver 1997, *Bürgerrechte und Demokratie*, Frankfurt/M, Suhrkamp.

Gerstenberg, Oliver 2000, "Justification (and Justifiability) of Private Law in a Polycontextual World," *Social and Legal Studies* 9(3): 419–29.

Gerstenberg, Oliver and Sabel, Charles F. 2002, "Directly-Deliberative Polyarchy, An Institutional Ideal for Europe?," in Joerges, Christian and Dehousse, Renaud (eds.), *Good Governance in Europe's Integrated Market*, Collected Courses of the Academy of European Law, vol. XI/2, Oxford University Press, 289–341.

Gessner, Volkmar and Budak, Ali Cen 1998, *Emerging Legal Certainty: Empirical Studies on the Globalization of Law*, Aldershot, Ashgate.

Gibson, James L. 1989, "Understandings of Justice: Institutional Legitimacy, Procedural Justice, and Political Tolerance," *Law and Society Review* 23(3): 469–96.

Gibson, James L. and Caldeira, Gregory A. 1993, "The European Court of Justice: A Question of Legitimacy," *Zeitschrift für Rechtssoziologie* 14(2): 204–22.

Gibson, James L. and Caldeira, Gregory A. 1998, "Changes in the Legitimacy of the European Court of Justice: A Post-Maastricht Analysis," *British Journal of Political Science* 28(1): 63–91.

Giddens, Anthony 1994, *Beyond Left and Right. The Future of Radical Politics*, Cambridge, Polity Press.

Godt, Christine 1998, "Der Bericht des Appellate Body der WTO zum EG-Einfuhrverbot von Hormonfleisch. Risikoregulierung im Weltmarkt," *Europäisches Wirtschafts- und Steuerrecht* 9(6): 202–9.

Goldstein, Judith 1996, "International Law and Domestic Institutions. Reconciling North American 'Unfair' Trade Laws," *International Organization* 50(4): 541–64.

Goldstein, Judith, Kahler, Miles, Keohane, Robert O. and Slaughter, Anne-Marie 2000, "Introduction: Legalization and World Politics," *International Organization* 54(3): 385–99.

Goldstein, Judith and Martin, Lisa L. 2000, "Legalization, Trade Liberalization, and Domestic Politics: A Cautionary Note," *International Organization* 54(3): 603–32.

Goodin, Robert 1988, "What Is So Special About Our Fellow Countrymen?," *Ethics* 98(4): 663–86.

Götz, Volkmar 1984, "Rückforderung von Subventionen," *Neue Zeitschrift für Verwaltungsrecht* 3(8): 480–5.

Grande, Edgar and Jachtenfuchs, Markus (eds.) 2000, *Problemlösungsfähigkeit der Europäischen Union*, Baden-Baden, Nomos.

Greven, Michael Th. 2000, "Can the European Union Finally Become a Democracy?," in Greven, Michael Th. and Pauly, Louis W. (eds.), *Democracy Beyond the State?*, Lanham, Rowman & Littlefield, 35–62.

Grieco, Joseph M. 1990, *Cooperation Among Nations. Europe, America, and Non-Tariff Barriers to Trade*, Ithaca, NY, Cornell University Press.

Griller, Stefan 2000, "Judicial Enforceability of WTO Law in the European Union: Annotation to Case C-149/96, Portugal v. Council," *Journal of International Economic Law* 3(3): 441–72.

Günther, Klaus 1988, *Der Sinn für Angemessenheit. Anwendungsdiskurse in Moral und Recht*, Frankfurt/M, Suhrkamp.

Haas, Peter M. 1998, "Compliance with EU Directives: Insights from International Relations and Comparative Politics," *Journal of European Public Policy* 5(1): 17–37.

Haas, Peter M., Keohane, Robert O. and Levy, Marc A. (eds.) 1993, *Institutions for the Earth: Sources of Effective International Environmental Protection*, Cambridge, MA, MIT Press.

Habermas, Jürgen 1981, *Theorie des kommunikativen Handelns.* Vol. 2, Frankfurt/M, Suhrkamp.

Habermas, Jürgen 1985, "Law as Medium and Law as Institution," in Teubner, Gunther (ed.), *Dilemmas of Law in the Welfare State*, Berlin, de Gruyter, 203–20.

Habermas, Jürgen 1994a, *Faktizität und Geltung. Beiträge zur Diskurstheorie des Rechts und des demokratischen Rechtsstaats*, Frankfurt am Main, Suhrkamp.

Habermas, Jürgen 1994b, "Über den inneren Zusammenhang von Rechtsstaat und Demokratie," in Preuß, Ulrich K. (ed.), *Zum Begriff der Verfassung*, Frankfurt/M, Fischer, 83–94. [= Jürgen Habermas 2001, "Constitutional Democracy: A Paradoxical Union of Contradictory Principles?," *Political Theory* 29(6): 766–81].

Habermas, Jürgen 1997, *Die Einbeziehung des Anderen: Studien zur politischen Theorie*, Frankfurt/M, Suhrkamp.

Habermas, Jürgen 2001, "Remarks on Legitimation through Human Rights," in Habermas, Jürgen (ed.), *The Postnational Constellation: Political Essays*, Cambridge, Polity, 113–29.

Hall, Peter A. 1989, "Introduction," in Hall, Peter A. (ed.), *The Political Power of Economic Ideas. Keynesianism across Nations*, Princeton University Press, 3–26.

Hancher, Leigh 1994, "State Aids and Judicial Control in the European Community," *European Competition Law Review* 15(3): 134–50.

Harlow, Carol 1996, "Francovich and the Problem of the Disobedient State," *European Law Journal* 2(3): 199–225.

Hart, Herbert Lionel Adolphus 1972, *The Concept of Law*, Oxford, Clarendon.

Harzem, Kerstin 1988, *Subventionen aus der Sicht der Neuen Politischen Ökonomie*, Köln, Deutscher Institut Verlag.

Hasenclever, Andreas, Mayer, Peter and Rittberger, Volker 1997, *Theories of International Regimes*, Cambridge University Press.

Hathaway, Oona A. 2002, "Do Human Rights Treaties Make a Difference?," *Yale Law Journal* 111(8): 1935–2038.

Heinemann, Friedrich 1998, *EU-Finanzreform. Eine Synopse der politischen und wissenschaftlichen Diskussion und eine neue Reformkonzeption*, Gütersloh, Bertelsmann Stiftung.

Heise, Arne, Mülhaupt, Bernd, Seifert, Hartmut, Schäfer, Claus, Störmann, Wiebke and Ziegler, Astrid 1998, "Begutachtung des Wirtschaftsstandorts Deutschland aus einer anderen Sicht," *WSI Mitteilungen* 51(6): 393–417.

Held, David 1995, *Democracy and the Global Order. From the Modern State to Cosmopolitan Democracy*, Cambridge, Polity Press.

Henkin, Louis 1979, *How Nations Behave. Law and Foreign Policy*, New York, Columbia University Press.

Héritier, Adrienne 1996, "The Accommodation of Diversity in European Policy Making and its Outcomes: Regulatory Policy as a Patchwork," *Journal of European Public Policy* 3(2): 149–67.

Héritier, Adrienne, Knill, Christoph and Mingers, Susanne 1996, *Ringing the Changes of Europe: Regulatory Competition and the Transformation of the State – Britain, France, Germany*, Berlin, de Gruyter.

Herwig, Alexia 2004, "Transnational Governance Regimes for Foods Derived From Bio-Technology and Their Legitimacy," in Joerges, Christian, Sand, Inger-Johanne and Teubner, Gunther (eds.), *Transnational Governance and Constitutionalism*, Oxford, Hart, 199–222.

Hilf, Meinhard 1991, "Settlement of Disputes in International Economic Organizations: Comparative Analysis and Proposals for Strengthening the GATT Dispute Settlement Procedures," in Petersmann, Ernst-Ulrich and Hilf,

Meinhard (eds.), *The New GATT Round of Multilateral Trade Negotiations: Legal and Economic Problems*, Deventer, Kluwer, 285–322.

Hilf, Meinhard 2001, "Power, Rules and Principles: Which Orientation for WTO/GATT Law?," *Journal of International Economic Law* 4(1): 111–30.

Hilf, Meinhard 2003, "Die Konstitutionalisierung der Welthandelsordnung. Struktur, Institutionen und Verfahren," *Berichte der Deutschen Gesellschaft für Völkerrecht* 2003, 257–82.

Hilf, Meinhard and Eggers, Barbara 1997, "Der WTO-Panelbericht im EG/USA-Hormonstreit. Anstoß zum grenzenlosen Weltbinnenmarkt oder Eigentor der WTO?," *Europäische Zeitschrift für Wirtschaftsrecht* 18, 559–66.

Hilf, Meinhard and Reuß, Matthias 1997, "Verfassungsfragen lebensmittelrechtlicher Normierung im europäischen und internationalen Recht," *Zeitschrift für das gesamte Lebensmittelrecht* 24(3): 289–302.

Hoekman, Bernard M. and Mavroidis, Petros C. 1996, "Policy Externalities and High-Tech Rivalry: Competition and Multilateral Cooperation Beyond the WTO," *Leiden Journal of International Law* 9(2): 273–318.

Hoekman, Bernard M. and Mavroidis, Petros C. 2000, "WTO Dispute Settlement, Transparency and Surveillance," *World Economy* 23(4): 527–42.

Hoffmann-Riem, Wolfgang and Schmidt-Aßmann, Eberhard (eds.) 1996, *Öffentliches Recht und Privatrecht als wechselseitige Auffangordnungen*, Baden-Baden, Nomos.

Holmes, Oliver W. 1897, "The Path of Law," *Harvard Law Review* 10, 458–78.

Hooghe, Lisbeth (ed.) 1996, *Cohesion Policy and European Integration. Building Multi-level Governance*, Oxford University Press.

Horn, Norbert 1996, *Einführung in die Rechtswissenschaft und Rechtsphilosophie*, Heidelberg, C. F. Müller.

Howard, Christopher 1995, "Testing the Tools Approach: Tax Expenditures Versus Direct Expenditures," *Public Administration Review* 55(5): 439–47.

Howard, Christopher 1997, *The Hidden Welfare State. Tax Expenditures and Social Policy in the United States*, Princeton, NJ, Princeton University Press.

Howse, Robert 1999, "Adjudicative Legitimacy and Treaty Interpretation in International Trade Law: The Early Years of WTO Jurisprudence," in Weiler, Joseph H. H. (ed.), *The EU, the WTO and the NAFTA: Towards a Common Law of International Trade*, Oxford University Press, 35–70.

Howse, Robert and Nicolaïdis, Kalypso 2001, "Legitimacy and Global Governance: Why Constitutionalizing the WTO Is a Step Too Far," in Porter, Roger B., Sauve, Pierre, Subramanaian, Arvind and Zampetti, Beviglia (eds.), *Efficiency, Equity, and Legitimacy: The Multilateral Trading System at the Millennium*, Washington, DC, Brookings Institution Press, 227–52.

Hrbek, Rudolf 1996, "Eine politische Bewertung der VW-Beihilfen-Kontroverse," *Wirtschaftsdienst* 76(10): 506–9.

Hübl, Lothar and Legler, Harald 1983, *Der Subventionskodex der Länderwirtschaftsminister angewendet auf ausgewählte Finanzhilfen an die gewerbliche Wirtschaft. Gutachten im Auftrag des Niedersächsischen Ministers für Wirtschaft und Verkehr*, Hannover, Niedersächsisches Institut für Wirtschaftsforschung.

Hudec, Robert E. 1993, *Enforcing International Trade Law. The Evolution of the Modern GATT Legal System*, Salem, NH, Butterworth.

Hudec, Robert E. 1999, "The New WTO Dispute Settlement Procedure: An Overview of the First Three Years," *Minnesota Journal of Global Trade* 8(1): 1–53.

Hurd, Ian 1999, "Legitimacy and Authority in International Politics," *International Organization* 53(2): 379–408.

Hurrell, Andrew 1993, "International Society and the Study of Regimes. A Reflective Approach," in Rittberger, Volker (ed.), *Regime Theory and International Relations*, Oxford, Clarendon Press, 49–72.

Ikenberry, G. John 1993, "Creating Yesterday's New World Order: Keynesian 'New Thinking' and the Anglo-American Postwar Settlement," in Goldstein, Judith and Keohane, Robert O. (eds.), *Ideas and Foreign Policy. Beliefs, Institutions, and Political Change*, Ithaca, NY, Cornell University Press, 57–86.

Ipsen, Hans Peter 1972, *Europäisches Gemeinschaftsrecht*, Tübingen, Mohr.

Jachtenfuchs, Markus 2001, "The Governance Approach to European Integration," *Journal of Common Market Studies* 39(2): 245–64.

Jachtenfuchs, Markus and Kohler-Koch, Beate 1996, "Regieren im dynamischen Mehrebenensystem," in Jachtenfuchs, Markus and Kohler-Koch, Beate (eds.), *Europäische Integration*, Opladen, Leske + Budrich, 15–44.

Jachtenfuchs, Markus and Kohler-Koch, Beate 2003, "Regieren und Institutionenbildung," in Jachtenfuchs, Markus and Kohler-Koch, Beate (eds.), *Europäische Integration*, Opladen, Leske + Budrich, 11–48.

Jackson, John H. 1978, "The Jurisprudence of International Trade: The DISC Case in GATT," *American Journal of International Law* 72(4): 747–81.

Jackson, John H. 1997, *The World Trading System: Law and Policy of International Economic Relations*, Cambridge, MA, MIT Press.

Jackson, John H. 1998, "Designing and Implementing Effective Dispute Settlement Procedures: WTO Dispute Settlement, Appraisal and Prospects," in Krueger, Anne O. (ed.), *The WTO as an International Organization*, Chicago, University of Chicago Press, 161–80.

Jackson, John H. 1999, *The World Trade Organization. Constitution and Jurisprudence*, London, Royal Institute of International Affairs.

Jackson, John H. 2000, *The Jurisprudence of GATT and the WTO. Insights on Treaty Law and Economic Relations*, Cambridge University Press.

Jacobson, Harold K. and Weiss, Edith Brown 1998a, "A Framework for Analysis," in Weiss, Edith Brown and Jacobson, Harold K. (eds.), *Engaging Countries. Strengthening Compliance with International Environmental Accords*, Cambridge, MA, MIT Press, 1–18.

Jacobson, Harold K. and Weiss, Edith Brown 1998b, "Assessing the Record and Designing Strategies to Engage Countries," in Weiss, Edith Brown and Jacobson, Harold K. (eds.), *Engaging Countries. Strengthening Compliance with International Environmental Accords*, Cambridge, MA, MIT Press, 511–54.

Joerges, Christian 1989, "Politische Rechtstheorie and Critical Legal Studies: Points of Contacts and Divergencies," in Joerges, Christian and Trubek,

David M. (eds.), *Critical Legal Thought: An American-German Debate*, Baden-Baden, Nomos, 597–643.

Joerges, Christian 1994, "Rationalisierungsprozesse im Recht der Produktsicherheit: Öffentliches Recht und Haftungsrecht unter dem Einfluß der Europäischen Integration," *Jahrbuch für Umwelt- und Technikrecht* 27, 141–78.

Joerges, Christian 1996a, "Taking the Law Seriously: On Political Science and the Role of Law in the Process of European Integration," *European Law Journal* 2(2): 105–35.

Joerges, Christian 1996b, *The Emergence of Denationalized Governance Structures and the European Court of Justice*, Arena Working Paper 16/1996, Oslo, Arena.

Joerges, Christian 1997, "Scientific Expertise in Social Regulation and the European Court of Justice: Legal Frameworks for Denationalized Governance Structures," in Joerges, Christian, Ladeur, Karl-Heinz and Vos, Ellen (eds.), *Integrating Scientific Expertise into Regulatory Decision-Making. National Traditions and European Innovations*, Baden-Baden, Nomos, 295–324.

Joerges, Christian 2000, "Interactive Adjudication in the Europeanisation Process? A Demanding Perspective and a Modest Example," *European Review of Private Law* 8(1): 1–16.

Joerges, Christian 2001, "Law, Science and the Management of Risks to Health at the National, European and International Level. Stories on Baby Dummies, Mad Cows and Hormones in Beef," *Columbia Journal of European Law* 7(1): 1–19.

Joerges, Christian 2002a, " 'Deliberative Supranationalism' – Two Defences," *European Law Journal* 8(1): 133–51.

Joerges, Christian 2002b, "The Law in the Process of Constitutionalizing Europe," in Eriksen, Erik O., Fossum, John E. and Menéndez, Agustín J. (eds.), *Constitution Making and Democratic Legitimacy*, Arena Report 5/2002, Oslo, Arena, 13–48.

Joerges, Christian 2003, "Comitology and the European Model? Towards a Recht-Fertigungs-Recht in the Europeanisation Process," in Neyer, Jürgen et al. (eds.), *The Forging of Deliberative Supranationalism in the EU*, Arena Report 02/2003, Oslo, Arena, 501–40.

Joerges, Christian 2004, "Constitutionalism and Transnational Governance: Exploring a Magic Triangle," in Joerges, Christian, Sand, Inger-Johanne and Teubner, Gunther (eds.), *Transnational Governance and Constitutionalism*, Oxford, Hart, 339–75.

Joerges, Christian and Falke, Josef (eds.) 2000, *Das Ausschußwesen der Europäischen Union. Praxis der Risikoregulierung im Binnenmarkt und ihre rechtliche Verfassung*, Baden-Baden, Nomos.

Joerges, Christian and Neyer, Jürgen 1997a, "From Intergovernmental Bargaining to Deliberative Political Processes: The Constitutionalisation of Comitology," *European Law Journal* 3(3): 273–99.

Joerges, Christian and Neyer, Jürgen 1997b, "Transforming Strategic Interaction into Deliberative Problem-Solving. European Comitology in the Foodstuffs Sector," *Journal of European Public Policy* 4(4): 609–25.

Joerges, Christian and Neyer, Jürgen 2003, "Politics, Risk Management, WTO Governance and the Limits of Legalisation," *Science and Public Policy* 30(3): 219–25.

Joerges, Christian, Schepel, Harm and Vos, Ellen 1999, *The Law's Problems with the Involvement of Non-governmental Actors in Europe's Legislative Process: The Case of Standardisation Under the "New Approach"*, EUI Working Paper Law 9/99, Florence, European University Institute.

Joerges, Christian and Vos, Ellen (eds.) 1999, *European Committees: Social Regulation, Law and Politics*, Oxford, Hart.

Jönsson, Christer and Tallberg, Jonas 1998, "Compliance and Post-Agreement Bargaining," *European Journal of International Relations* 4(4): 371–408.

Kahler, Miles 1995, *International Institutions and the Political Economy of Integration*, Washington, DC, Brookings Institution.

Kelemen, R. Daniel 2001, "The Limits of Judicial Power: Trade-Environment Disputes in GATT/WTO and the EU," *Comparative Political Studies* 34(6): 622–50.

Kelsen, Hans 1966, *Principles of International Law*, New York, Holt, Rinehart, Winston.

Kent, Ann 1995, "China and the International Human Rights Regime. A Case Study of Multilateral Monitoring, 1989–1994," *Human Rights Quarterly* 17(1): 1–47.

Keohane, Robert O. 1984, *After Hegemony: Collaboration and Discord in the World Political Economy*, Princeton University Press.

Keohane, Robert O. 1986, "Reciprocity in International Relations," *International Organization* 40(1): 1–27.

Keohane, Robert O. 1997, "International Relations and International Law: Two Optics," *Harvard International Law Journal* 38(2): 487–502.

Keohane, Robert O., Moravcsik, Andrew and Slaughter, Anne-Marie 2000, "Legalized Dispute Resolution: Interstate and Transnational," *International Organization* 54(3): 457–88.

Kesper, Irene 1998, *Bundesstaatliche Finanzordnung, Grundlagen, Bestand, Reform*, Baden-Baden, Nomos.

Kielmansegg, Peter Graf 1994, "Läßt sich die Europäische Gemeinschaft demokratisch verfassen?," *Europäische Rundschau* 22(2): 23–33.

Kielmansegg, Peter Graf 2003, "Integration und Demokratie (mit Nachwort zur 2. Auflage)," in Jachtenfuchs, Markus and Kohler-Koch, Beate (eds.), *Europäische Integration*, Opladen, Leske + Budrich, 49–83.

Kiemmer, Paul 1986, "Die Kontroverse um die Daimler-Benz-Beihilfe," *Wirtschaftsdienst* 66(11): 550–4.

King, Gary, Keohane, Robert O. and Verba, Sidney 1994, *Designing Social Inquiry. Scientific Inference in Qualitative Research*, Princeton University Press.

Kiss, Alexandre-Charles 1996, "Compliance with International and European Environmental Obligations," *Hague Yearbook of International Law* 9, 45–54.

Klein, Eckart 1998, "The Reporting System under the International Covenant on Civil and Political Rights," in Klein, Eckart (ed.), *The Monitoring System of Human Rights Treaty Obligations*, Berlin, Berlin-Verlag, 17–30.

Knill, Christoph and Lenschow, Andrea 1999, "Neue Konzepte – alte Probleme? Die institutionellen Grenzen effektiver Implementation," *Politische Vierteljahresschrift* 40(4): 591–617.

Koh, Harold Hongju 1997, "Why Do Nations Obey International Law?," *Yale Law Journal* 106(8): 2599–659.

Kohler-Koch, Beate 1992, "Interessen und Integration. Die Rolle organisierter Interessen im westeuropäischen Integrationsprozeß," in Kreile, Michael (ed.), *Die Integration Europas* (PVS-Sonderheft 23/1992), Opladen, Westdeutscher Verlag, 81–119.

Kohler-Koch, Beate 1994, "Changing Patterns of Interest Intermediation in the European Union," *Government & Opposition* 29(2): 166–80.

Kohler-Koch, Beate 1999, "The Evolution and Transformation of European Governance," in Kohler-Koch, Beate and Eising, Rainer (eds.), *The Transformation of Governance in the European Union*, London, Routledge, 14–35.

Komuro, Norio 1995, "The WTO Dispute Settlement Mechanism – Coverage and Procedures of the WTO Understanding," *Journal of World Trade* 29(4): 5–96.

Koskenniemi, Martti 2002, *The Gentle Civilizer of Nations. The Rise and Fall of International Law 1870–1960*, Cambridge University Press.

Krasner, Stephen D. (ed.) 1983, *International Regimes*, Ithaca, NY, Cornell University Press.

Krasner, Stephen D. 1999, *Sovereignty. Organized Hypocrisy*, Princeton University Press.

Kratochwil, Friederich 1989, *Rules, Norms, and Decisions. On the Conditions of Practical and Legal Reasoning in International Relations and Domestic Affairs*, Cambridge University Press.

Krieger-Boden, Christiane and Lammers, Konrad 1996, *Subventionsabbau in räumlicher Perspektive: Wirkungszusammenhänge und Schlussfolgerungen*, Kieler Diskussionsbeiträge 280, Kiel, Institut für Weltwirtschaft.

Krislov, Saul, Ehlermann, Claus-Dieter and Weiler, J. H. H. 1986, "The Political Organs and the Decision-Making Process in the United States and the European Community," in Cappelletti, Mauro, Seccombe, Monica and Weiler, Joseph H. H. (eds.), *Integration through Law. Methods, Tools and Institutions: Political Organs, Integration Techniques and Judicial Process*, Berlin, de Gruyter, 3–112.

Krüger, Malte 1998, "Kann Industriepolitik die Wettbewerbsfähigkeit verbessern?," in Donges, Juergen B. and Freytag, Andreas (eds.), *Die Rolle des Staates in einer globalisierten Wirtschaft*, Stuttgart, Lucius & Lucius, 217–35.

Lahnstein, Manfred 1978, "Probleme des kooperativen Föderalismus aus finanzpolitischer Sicht des Bundes," *WSI Mitteilungen* 31(8): 434–42.

Laird, Sam 1999, "The WTO's Trade Policy Review Mechanism – From Through the Looking Glass," *World Economy* 22(2): 741–64.

Lang, Jochen, Naschold, Frieder and Reissert, Bernd 1998, *Management der EU-Strukturpolitik*, Berlin, Edition Sigma.

Lang, Winfried (ed.) 1995, *Sustainable Development and International Law*, London, Graham & Trotman.

Lascher, Edward L. 1996, "Assessing Legislative Deliberation: A Preface to Empirical Analysis," *Legislative Studies Quarterly* 21(4): 501–19.

Lasok, K. P. E. 1990, "The Commission's Powers Over Illegal State Aids," *European Competition Law Review* 11(3): 125–7.

Laursen, Finn and Vanhoonacker, Sophie (eds.) 1992, *The Intergovernmental Conference on Political Union*, Maastricht, European Institute of Public Administration.

Lavdas, Kostas A. and Mendrinou, Maria M. 1999, *Politics, Subsidies and Competition. The New Politics of State Intervention in the European Union*, Aldershot, Elgar.

Lee, Philip and Kennedy, Brian 1996, "The Potential Direct Effect of GATT 1994 in European Community Law," *Journal of World Trade* 30(1): 67–89.

Leibfried, Stephan and Pierson, Paul (eds.) 1995, *European Social Policy. Between Fragmentation and Integration*, Washington, DC, Brookings Institution.

Levy, Marc A. 1993, "European Acid Rain. The Power of Tote-Board Diplomacy," in Haas, Peter M., Keohane, Robert O. and Levy, Marc A. (eds.), *Institutions for the Earth. Sources of Effective International Environmental Protection*, Cambridge, MA, MIT Press, 75–132.

Levy, Marc A., Young, Oran R. and Zürn, Michael 1995, "The Study of International Regimes," *European Journal of International Relations* 1(3): 267–330.

Lewis, Jeffrey 1998, *The Institutional Problem-Solving Capacities of the Council. The Committee of Permanent Representatives and the Methods of Community*, MPIFG Discussion Paper 98/1, Köln, Max-Planck-Institut für Gesellschaftsforschung.

Liemt, Gijsbert van (ed.) 1992, *Industry on the Move: Causes and Consequences of International Relocation in the Manufacturing Industry*, Geneva, International Labour Organization.

Liese, Andrea 2001, *Staaten am Pranger. Zur Wirkung internationaler Regime auf die innerstaatliche Menschenrechtspolitik*, PhD thesis, Universität Bremen.

Lijphart, Arend 1977, *Democracy in Plural Societies. A Comparative Exploration*, New Haven, Yale University Press.

Lind, E. Allan 1995, "Verfahrensgerechtigkeit und Akzeptanz rechtlicher Autorität," in Bierbrauer, Günter, Gottwald, Walther and Birnbreier-Stahlberger, Beatrix (eds.), *Verfahrensgerechtigkeit. Rechtspsychologische Forschungsbeiträge für die Justizpraxis*, Köln, Otto Schmidt, 3–19.

Lindberg, Leon N. and Scheingold, Stuart A. 1970, *Europe's Would-Be Polity. Patterns of Change in the European Community*, Englewood Cliffs, NJ, Prentice Hall.

Link, Werner 1998, *Die Neuordnung der Weltpolitik. Grundprobleme globaler Politik an der Schwelle zum 21. Jahrhundert*, München, Beck.

Lowi, Theodore 1972, "Four Systems of Policy, Politics and Choice," *Public Administration Review* 32(4): 298–310.

Luhmann, Niklas 1972, *Rechtssoziologie 2*, Reinbek, Rowohlt.

Luhmann, Niklas 1973, *Zweckbegriff und Systemrationalität*, Frankfurt/M, Suhrkamp.

Luhmann, Niklas 1993, *Das Recht der Gesellschaft*, Frankfurt/M, Suhrkamp.

278   References

Lukas, Martin 1995, "The Role of Private Parties in the Enforcement of the Uruguay Round Agreements," *Journal of World Trade* 29(5): 181–206.

Macrory, Richard 1992, "The Enforcement of Community Environmental Laws: Some Critical Issues," *Common Market Law Review* 29(2): 347–69.

Maduro, M. Poiares 1998, *We, the Court. The European Court of Justice and the European Economic Constitution*, Oxford, Hart.

Majone, Giandomenico 1994, "The Rise of the Regulatory State in Europe," *West European Politics* 17(3): 77–101.

Majone, Giandomenico 1998, "Europe's 'Democratic Deficit': The Question of Standards," *European Law Journal* 4(1): 5–28.

Majone, Giandomenico 2001, "Nonmajoritarian Institutions and the Limits of Democratic Governance: A Political Transaction-Cost Approach," *Journal of Institutional and Theoretical Economics* 157(1): 57–78.

Majone, Giandomenico 2002, "What Price Safety? The Precautionary Principle and its Policy Implications," *Journal of Common Market Studies* 40(1): 89–109.

Mancini, G. Federico 1991, "The Making of a Constitution for Europe," in Keohane, Robert O. and Hoffmann, Stanley (eds.), *The New European Community. Decisionmaking and Institutional Change*, Boulder, CO, Westview, 177–94.

Marks, Gary 1992, "Structural Policy in the European Community," in Sbragia, Alberta M. (ed.), *Euro-Politics. Institutions and Policymaking in the "New" European Community*, Washington, DC, Brookings Institution, 191–224.

Marks, Gary 1997, "Does the European Union Represent an N of 1?," *ECSA Review* 10(3): 2–3.

Marks, Gary, Scharpf, Fritz W., Schmitter, Philippe C. and Streeck, Wolfgang (eds.) 1996, *Governance in the European Union*, London, Sage.

Martin, Lisa L. 1993, "The Rational State Choice of Multilateralism," in Ruggie, John Gerard (ed.), *Multilateralism Matters. The Theory and Practice of an International Form*, New York, Columbia University Press, 91–121.

Mattli, Walter and Slaughter, Anne-Marie 1998, "Revisiting the European Court of Justice," *International Organization* 52(1): 177–209.

Mayer, Franz C. 2000, *Kompetenzüberschreitung und Letztentscheidung. Das Maastricht-Urteil des Bundesverfassungsgrichts und die Letztentscheidung über ultra-vires Konflikte in Mehrebenensystemen. Eine rechtsvergleichende Betrachtung von Konflikten zwischen Gerichten am Beispiel der EU und der USA*, München, Beck.

Mayntz, Renate (ed.) 1980, *Implementation politischer Programme. Empirische Forschungsberichte*, Königstein/Ts, Athenäum.

McDougal, Myres S., Lasswell, Harold D. and Reisman, W. Michael 1968, "Theories about International Law: Prologue to a Configurative Jurisprudence," *Virginia Journal of International Law* 8, 188–299.

McGowan, Francis 2000, "Competition Policy: The Limits of the European Regulatory State," in Wallace, Helen and Wallace, William (eds.), *Policy-Making in the European Union*, Oxford University Press, 115–47.

McLarty, Taunya 1994, "GATT 1994 Dispute Settlement: Sacrificing Diplomacy for Efficiency in the Multilateral Trading System?," *Florida Journal of International Law* 9(2): 241–75.

Mearsheimer, John 1994, "The False Promise of International Institutions," *International Security* 19(3): 5–49.

Mearsheimer, John 2002, *The Tragedy of Great Power Politics*, New York, W.W. Norton.

Mendrinou, Maria 1996, "Non-Compliance and the European Commission's Role in Integration," *Journal of European Public Policy* 3(1): 1–22.

Meng, Werner P. 1990, "The Hormone Conflict Between the EEC and the United States Within the Context of GATT," *Michigan Journal of International Law* 11(4): 819–39.

Mestmäcker, Ernst-Joachim 1994, "On the Legitimacy of European Law," *Rabels Zeitschrift für ausländisches und internationales Privatrecht* 58(4): 615–35.

Michelman, Frank I. 1999, *Brennan and Democracy*, Princeton University Press.

Miles, Edward, Underdal, Arild, Andresen, Steinar, Wettestad, Jørgen, Skjærseth, Jon Birger and Carlin, Elaine M. 2002, *Explaining Regime Effectiveness: Confronting Theory with Evidence*, Cambridge, MA, MIT Press.

Miller, David 1988, "The Ethical Significance of Nationality," *Ethics* 98(4): 647–62.

Miller, David 1995, *On Nationality*, Oxford, Clarendon Press.

Mills, Geoffrey and Rockoff, Hugh 1987, "Compliance with Price Controls in the United States and the United Kingdom During World War II," *Journal of Economic History* 47(1): 197–213.

Mitchell, Ronald B. 1994, "Regime Design Matters. International Oil Pollution and Treaty Compliance," *International Organization* 48(3): 425–58.

Mitchell, Ronald B. and Keilbach, Patricia M. 2001, "Situation Structure and Institutional Design: Reciprocity, Coercion, and Exchange," *International Organization* 55(4): 891–917.

Moravcsik, Andrew 1997a, "Does the European Union Represent an N of 1?," *ECSA Review* 10(3): 3–4.

Moravcsik, Andrew 1997b, "Warum die Europäische Union die Exekutive stärkt: Innenpolitik und internationale Kooperation," in Wolf, Klaus Dieter (ed.), *Projekt Europa im Übergang? Probleme, Modelle und Strategien des Regierens in der Europäischen Union*, Baden-Baden, Nomos, 211–69.

Moravcsik, Andrew 1998, *The Choice for Europe. Social Purpose and State Power from Messina to Maastricht*, Ithaca, NY, Cornell University Press.

Morgan, T. Clifton and Schwebach, Valerie L. 1997, "Fools Suffer Gladly: The Use of Economic Sanctions in International Crises," *International Studies Quarterly* 41(1): 27–50.

Morgenthau, Hans J. 1949, *Politics Among Nations. The Struggle for Power and Peace*, New York, Knopf.

Morrow, James D. 1994, *Game Theory for Political Scientists*, Princeton University Press.

Müller, Harald 2002, "Antinomien des demokratischen Friedens," *Politische Vierteljahresschrift* 43(1): 46–81.

Müller, Harald and Risse-Kappen, Thomas 1990, "Internationale Umwelt, gesellschaftliches Umfeld und außenpolitischer Prozeß in liberaldemokratischen Industrienationen," in Rittberger, Volker (ed.), *Theorien der internationalen Beziehungen. Bestandsaufnahme und Forschungsperspektiven*, PVS-Sonderheft 21, Opladen, Westdeutscher Verlag, 375–400.

280   References

Müller, Ulrich 1984, "Ordnungspolitische Vorkehrungen zur Durchsetzung der GATT-Regeln," *Zeitschrift für Wirtschaftspolitik* 33(2–3): 261–76.

Nägele, Frank 1996, *Regionale Wirtschaftspolitik im kooperativen Bundesstaat. Ein Politikfeld im Prozeß der deutschen Vereinigung*, Opladen, Leske+Budrich.

Nägele, Frank 1997, "Die 'graue Eminenz' der regionalen Wirtschaftspolitik. Zur regionalpolitischen Bedeutung der EG-Beihilfenkontrolle in der Bundesrepublik Deutschland," *Staatswissenschaften und Staatspraxis* 8(1): 109–30.

Neuhaus, Karl Herbert 1987, *Möglichkeiten und Grenzen einer zentralen Erfassung von Subventionen der Länder*, Schwerpunkt Finanzwissenschaft/ Betriebswirtschaftliche Steuerlehre – Arbeitspapier 11, Trier, Universität Trier.

Neyer, Jürgen 1999, "Legitimes Recht oberhalb des demokratischen Rechtsstaates? Supranationalität als Herausforderung für die Politikwissenschaft," *Politische Vierteljahresschrift* 40(3): 390–414.

Neyer, Jürgen 2000a, "Risikoregulierung im Binnenmarkt: Zur Problemlösungsfähigkeit der europäischen politischen Verwaltung," in Falke, Josef and Joerges, Christian (eds.), *Das Ausschußwesen der EU. Praxis der Risikoregulierung im Binnenmarkt und ihre rechtliche Verfassung*, Baden-Baden, Nomos, 257–328.

Neyer, Jürgen 2000b, "Risk Regulation and the Power of the People: Lessons from the BSE-Crisis," *European Integration online Papers (EIoP)* 4(6) (http://eiop.or.at/eiop/texte/2000-006a.htm).

Neyer, Jürgen 2003, "Discourse and Order in the EU. A Deliberative Approach to Multi-Level Governance," *Journal of Common Market Studies* 41(4): 687–706.

Neyer, Jürgen 2004, "Explaining the Unexpected: Effectiveness and Efficiency in European Policy-Making," *Journal of European Public Policy* 11(1): 19–38.

Nicolaides, Phedon 2002, "The New Frontier in State Aid Control: An Economic Assessment of Measures that Compensate Enterprises," *Intereconomics* 37(4): 190–97.

Nicolaysen, Gert 1996, "Der Streit um die VW-Beihilfen aus juristischer Sicht," *Wirtschaftsdienst* 76(10): 503–6.

Nieder-Eichholz, Markus 1995, *Die Subventionsordnung. Ein Beitrag zur finanzwirtschaftlichen Ordnungspolitik*, Berlin, Duncker & Humblot.

O'Brien, Robert 1997, *Subsidy Regulation and State Transformation in North America, the GATT and the EU*, Basingstoke, Macmillan.

O'Connell, Mary Ellen 1992, "Enforcing the New International Law of the Environment," *German Yearbook of International Law* 35, 293–332.

O'Connell, Mary Ellen 1995, "Enforcement and the Success of International Environmental Law," *Indiana Journal of Global Legal Studies* 3(1): 47–64.

Offe, Claus 2001, "Gibt es eine europäische Gesellschaft? Kann es sie geben?," *Blätter für deutsche und internationale Politik* 46(4): 423–35

Ostrom, Elinor 1990, *Governing the Commons. The Evolution of Institutions for Collective Action*, Cambridge University Press.

Oye, Kenneth A. 1986, "Explaining Cooperation under Anarchy: Hypothesis and Strategies," in Kenneth A. Oye (ed.), *Cooperation under Anarchy*, Princeton, NJ, Princeton University Press, 1–24.

Peffekoven, Rolf 1994, "Reform des Finanzausgleichs – eine vertane Chance," *Finanzarchiv* N.F. 51(3): 281–311.

Perez, Oren 1998, "Reconstructing Science: The Hormones Conflict Between the EU and United States," *European Foreign Affairs Review* 3(4): 563–82.

Peters, Bernhard 1991, *Rationalität, Recht und Gesellschaft*, Frankfurt/M, Suhrkamp.

Peters, Bernhard 1994, "Der Sinn von Öffentlichkeit," in Neidhardt, Friedhelm (ed.), *Öffentlichkeit, öffentliche Meinung, soziale Bewegung* (Kölner Zeitschrift für Soziologie und Sozialpsychologie, Sonderheft 34), Opladen, Westdeutscher Verlag, 42–76.

Petersmann, Ernst-Ulrich 1991, "Strengthening the GATT Dispute Settlement System: On the Use of Arbitration in GATT," in Petersmann, Ernst-Ulrich and Hilf, Meinhard (eds.), *The New GATT Round of Multilateral Trade Negotiations: Legal and Economic Problems*, Deventer, Kluwer Law, 323–43.

Petersmann, Ernst-Ulrich 1997a, "Darf die EG das Völkerrecht ignorieren?," *Europäische Zeitschrift für Wirtschaftsrecht* 8(11): 325–31.

Petersmann, Ernst-Ulrich 1997b, "International Trade Law and the GATT/WTO Dispute Settlement System 1948–1996. An Introduction," in Petersmann, Ernst-Ulrich (ed.), *International Trade Law and the GATT / WTO Dispute Settlement System*, London, Kluwer Law International, 3–122.

Petersmann, Ernst-Ulrich 1997c, *The GATT/WTO Dispute Settlement System. International Law, International Organizations and Dispute Settlement*, London, Kluwer Law International.

Petersmann, Ernst-Ulrich 1998, "How to Reform the United Nations? Lessons from the 'International Economic Law Revolution'," *Aussenwirtschaft* 53(2): 193–231.

Petersmann, Ernst-Ulrich 2000, "From 'Negative' to 'Positive' Integration in the WTO. Time for 'Mainstreaming Human Rights' into WTO Law?," *Common Market Law Review* 37(6): 1363–82.

Petersmann, Ernst-Ulrich 2002, "Constitutionalism and WTO Law: From a State-Centred Approach Towards Human Rights in International Economic Law," in Kennedy, Daniel L. M. and Southwick, James D. (eds.), *The Political Economy of International Trade Law. Essays in Honor of Robert E. Hudec*, Cambridge University Press, 32–67.

Petersmann, Ernst-Ulrich and Jaenicke, Günther (eds.) 1992, *Adjudication of International Trade Disputes in International and National Economic Law*, Fribourg, Switzerland, Fribourg University Press.

Picciotto, Sol 2000, *Democratizing the New Global Public Sphere* (http://www.lancs.ac.uk/staff/lwasp/demglobpub.pdf).

Plank, Rosine 1987, "An Unofficial Description of How a GATT Panel Works and Does Not," *Journal of International Arbitration* 4(4): 53–102.

Pollack, Mark A. 1995, "Regional Actors in an Intergovernmental Play. The Making and Implementation of EC Structural Policy," in Rhodes, Carolyn and Mazey, Sonia (eds.), *The State of European Union. Vol. 3: Building a European Polity*, Boulder, CO, Lynne Rienner, 361–90.

Pollack, Mark A. 1997, "Representing Diffuse Interests in EC Policymaking," *Journal of European Public Policy* 4(4): 572–90.

Polley, Romina 1996, "Die Konkurrentenklage im Europäischen Beihilfenrecht. Klagebefugnis und Rückforderung bei rechtswidrig gewährten Beihilfen," *Europäische Zeitschrift für Wirtschaftsrecht* 7(10): 300–5.

Ponce-Nava, Diana 1995, "Capacity-Building in Environmental Law and Sustainable Development," in Lang, Winfried (ed.), *Sustainable Development and International Law*, London, Graham & Trotman, 131–6.

Pressman, Jeffrey L. and Wildavsky, Aaron 1984, *Implementation*, Berkeley, University of California Press.

Raustiala, Kal 1995, *The Domestication of International Commitments*, Working Paper WP-95-115, Laxenburg, IIASA.

Raustiala, Kal 1997, "Domestic Institutions and International Regulatory Cooperation. Comparative Responses to the Convention on Biological Diversity," *World Politics* 49(4): 482–509.

Raustiala, Kal and Slaughter, Anne-Marie 2002, "International Law, International Relations and Compliance," in Carlsnaes, Walter, Risse, Thomas and Simmons, Beth A. (eds.), *Handbook of International Relations*, London, Sage, 538–58.

Raustiala, Kal and Victor, David G. 1998, "Conclusions," in Victor, David G., Raustiala, Kal and Skolnikoff, Eugene B. (eds.), *The Implementation and Effectiveness of International Environmental Commitments: Theory and Practice*, Cambridge, MA, MIT Press, 659–707.

Reinicke, Wolfgang 1998, *Global Public Policy. Governing without Government?*, Washington, DC, Brookings Institution Press.

Renzsch, Wolfgang 1991, *Finanzverfassung und Finanzausgleich. Die Auseinandersetzungen um ihre politische Gestaltung in der Bundesrepublik Deutschland zwischen Währungsreform und deutscher Vereinigung (1948–1990)*, Bonn, Dietz.

Renzsch, Wolfgang 1994, "Föderative Problembewältigung. Zur Einbeziehung der neuen Länder in einen gesamtdeutschen Finanzausgleich ab 1995," *Zeitschrift für Parlamentsfragen* 25(1): 116–38.

Rieger, Elmar 1995, "Politik supranationaler Integration. Die Europäische Gemeinschaft in institutionentheoretischer Perspektive," in Nedelmann, Brigitta (ed.), *Politische Institutionen im Wandel* (Kölner Zeitschrift für Soziologie und Sozialpsychologie Sonderheft 35), Opladen, Westdeutscher Verlag, 349–67.

Risse, Thomas 2000, " 'Let's Argue!': Communicative Action in World Politics," *International Organization* 54(1): 1–40.

Risse-Kappen, Thomas 1996, "Exploring the Nature of the Beast: International Relations Theory and Comparative Policy Analysis Meet the European Union," *Journal of Common Market Studies* 34(1): 53–80.

Rittberger, Volker and Zürn, Michael 1991, "Regime Theory: Findings from the Study of 'East-West Regimes'," *Cooperation and Conflict* 26(2): 165–183.

Ritter, Markus 1997, "Das WTO-Übereinkommen und seine Auswirkungen auf das Deutsche und Europäische Lebensmittelrecht. Hormonrückstände in Lebensmitteln als künftiger Standard?," *Europäische Zeitschrift für Wirtschaftsrecht* 8(5): 133–8.

Romano, Cesare P. R. 1999, "The Proliferation of International Judicial Bodies: The Pieces of the Puzzle," *New York University Journal of International Law and Politics* 31(4): 709–52.

Rosenschon, Astrid 1991, "Subventionen in den alten Bundesländern," *Weltwirtschaft* (1): 76–90.

Rosenstock, Manfred 1995, *Kontrolle und Harmonisierung nationaler Beihilfen durch die Kommission der Europäischen Gemeinschaften*, Frankfurt/M, Lang.

Ross, Malcolm 2000, "State Aids and National Courts: Definitions and Other Problems. A Case of Premature Emancipation?," *Common Market Law Review* 37(2): 401–23.

Russett, Bruce and O'Neal, John R. 2001, *Triangulating Peace. Democracy, Interdependence, and International Organization*, New York, W.W. Norton.

Sachverständigenrat zur Begutachtung der gesamtwirtschaftlichen Entwicklung 1992, *Für Wachstumsorientierung – gegen lähmenden Verteilungsstreit, Jahresgutachten 1992/1993*, Stuttgart, Metzler-Poeschel.

Sack, Jörn 1997, "Von der Geschlossenheit und den Spannungsfeldern in einer Weltordnung des Rechts," *Europäische Zeitschrift für Wirtschaftsrecht* 8(21): 650–1.

Sand, Inger-Johanne 1998, "Understanding the New Forms of Governance: Mutually Interdependent, Reflexive, Destabilised and Competing Institutions," *European Law Journal* 4(2): 271–93.

Sands, Philippe, Mackenzie, Ruth and Shany, Yuval (eds.) 1999, *Manual on International Courts and Tribunals*, London, Butterworths.

Scharpf, Fritz W. 1994, *Optionen des Föderalismus in Deutschland und Europa*, Frankfurt/M, Campus.

Scharpf, Fritz W. 1997, *Games Real Actors Play. Actor-Centered Institutionalism in Policy Research*, Boulder, CO, Westview.

Scharpf, Fritz W. 1999, *Governing in Europe: Effective and Democratic?*, Oxford University Press.

Scharpf, Fritz W., Reissert, Bernd and Schnabel, Fritz 1976, *Politikverflechtung: Theorie und Empirie des kooperativen Föderalismus in der Bundesrepublik*, Kronberg/Ts, Hain.

Scheffler, Dietrich 1993, "Juristische Aspekte der Subventionsproblematik im GATT," *Recht der Internationalen Wirtschaft* 39(5): 401–9.

Schepel, Harm 2003, *The Constitution of Private Governance. Product Standards in the Regulation of Integrating Markets*. PhD thesis, Florence: European University Institute (forthcoming with Hart Publishing, Oxford).

Schepel, Harm and Wesseling, Rein 1997, "The Legal Community: Judges, Lawyers, Officials and Clerks in the Writing of Europe," *European Law Journal* 3(2): 105–30.

Schimmelfennig, Frank 2000, "International Socialization in the New Europe. Rational Action in an Institutional Environment," *European Journal of International Relations* 6(1): 109–39.

Schimmelfennig, Frank 2001, "The Community Trap: Liberal Norms, Rhetorical Action, and the Eastern Enlargement of the European Union," *International Organization* 55(1): 47–80.

Schluchter, Wolfgang 1972, "Aspekte bürokratischer Herrschaft," in Schluchter, Wolfgang (ed.), *Studien zur Interpretation der fortschreitenden Industriegesellschaft* (re-edited Frankfurt/M, Suhrkamp 1985), 145–76.

Schmalz-Bruns, Rainer 1999, "Deliberativer Supranationalismus. Demokratisches Regieren jenseits des Nationalstaates," *Zeitschrift für Internationale Beziehungen* 6(2): 185–244.

Schmid, Christoph 2001, *A Theoretical Reconstruction of WTO Constitutionalism and its Implications for the Relationship with the EU*, EUI Working Paper Law, 5/2001, Florence, European University Institute.

Schmid, Heiko Thorsten 1989, *Regionale Wirtschaftsförderung – Schranke des "Modells Baden-Württemberg"? Eine Untersuchung über Gründe und Effekte des Festhaltens an einem umstrittenen Politikbereich*, Konstanz, Hartung-Gorre.

Schmidt, Helmut 1977, "Verantwortung und Solidarität in Staat und Gesellschaft. Interview des Bundeskanzlers," *Bulletin des Presse- und Informationsamtes der Bundesregierung*, 69, 647–51.

Schneider, Heinrich 1969, "Zur politischen Theorie der Gemeinschaft," *Integration* 2(1): 23–44.

Schneider, Jens-Peter 1996, "Konkurrentenklagen als Instrumente der europäischen Beihilfeaufsicht," *Deutsches Verwaltungsblatt* 111(22): 1301–9.

Scholz, Rupert 1998, "Zum Verhältnis von europäischem Gemeinschaftsrecht und nationalem Verwaltungsverfahrensrecht. Zur Rechtsprechung des EuGH im Fall 'Alcan'," *Die Öffentliche Verwaltung* 51(7): 261–8.

Schoppa, Leonard J. 1999, "The Social Context in Coercive International Bargaining," *International Organization* 53(2): 307–42.

Schuppert, Gunnar Folkert 1995, "Der bundesstaatliche Finanzausgleich – Status-quo-Denken oder Reformprojekt," *Staatswissenschaften und Staatspraxis* 6(4): 675–93.

Schütterle, Peter 1994, "Das Interesse der Konkurrenten in der EG-Beihilfenkontrolle nach Art. 92ff. EGV," *Europäische Zeitschrift für Wirtschaftsrecht* 5(9): 265–9.

Schütterle, Peter 1995, "Die Beihilfenkontrollpraxis der Europäischen Kommission im Spannungsfeld zwischen Recht und Politik," *Europäische Zeitschrift für Wirtschaftsrecht* 6(13): 391–6.

Schwarze, Jürgen 1996, "Länderbericht Deutschland," in Schwarze, Jürgen (ed.), *Das Verwaltungsrecht unter europäischem Einfluß. Zur Konvergenz der mitgliedstaatlichen Verwaltungsrechtsordnungen in der Europäischen Union*, Baden-Baden, Nomos, 123–228.

Schwendinger, Gerd 2003, *Deutsche Rundfunkgebühren – "staatlich oder aus staatlichen Mitteln gewährt"? Zugleich eine kritische Bestandsaufnahme der Rechtsprechung des EuGH zur staatlichen Zurechenbarkeit von Beihilfen gemäß Art. 87 Abs. 1 EGV*, EUI Working Paper Law 05/03, Florence, European University Institute.

Sciarra, Silvana 2001, "Integration Through Courts: Article 177 as a Pre-federal Device," in Sciarra, Silvana (ed), *Labour Law in the Courts. National Judges and the European Court of Justice*, Oxford, Hart Publishing, 1–30.

Scott, Joanne 2000, "Trade and Environment in the EU and WTO," in Weiler, Joseph H. H. (ed.), *The EU, the WTO and the NAFTA: Towards a Common Law of International Trade*, Oxford University Press, 125–68.

Seeleib-Kaiser, Martin 2001, *Globalisierung und Sozialpolitik: Ein Vergleich der Diskurse und Wohlfahrtssysteme in Deutschland, Japan und den USA*, Frankfurt/M, Campus.

Seidel, Martin 1984, "Grundfragen des Beihilfenaufsichtsrechts der Europäischen Gemeinschaften," in Börner, Bodo and Neundörfer, Konrad (eds.), *Recht und Praxis der Beihilfen im Gemeinsamen Markt*, Köln, Heymanns, 55–82.

Seidel, Martin 1985, "Aktuelle Rechtsprobleme der Subventionsgewährung und der Beihilfenaufsicht in der Europäischen Wirtschaftsgemeinschaft," in Schwarze, Jürgen (ed.), *Integrationsrecht. Beiträge zu Recht und Politik der Europäischen Gemeinschaft*, Baden-Baden, Nomos, 61–84.

Seidel, Martin 1992, "Das Subventionsrecht der Europäischen Gemeinschaften," *Orientierungen zur Wirtschafts- und Gesellschaftspolitik* 51: 25–30.

Selznick, Philip 1985, "Focusing Organizational Research on Regulation," in Noll, Roger G. (ed.), *Regulatory Policy and the Social Sciences*, Berkeley, CA, University of California Press, 363–7.

Selznick, Philip 1992, *The Moral Commonwealth. Social Theory and the Promise of Community*, Berkeley, CA, University of California Press.

Senti, Richard 1986, *GATT: Allgemeines Zoll- und Handelsabkommen als System der Welthandelsordnung*, Zürich, Schulthess.

Senti, Richard 2000, *WTO – System und Funktionsweise der Welthandelsordnung*, Zürich, Schulthess.

Sevilla, Christina R. 1997, *A Political Economy Model of GATT/WTO Trade Complaints*, Harvard Jean Monnet Working Paper 5/97, Cambridge, MA, Harvard University.

Shackleton, Michael 1993, "Keynote Article: The Delors II Budget Package," *Journal of Common Market Studies* 31, Annual Review, 11–25.

Shapiro, Martin and Stone Sweet, Alec 2002, *On Law, Politics and Judicialization*, Oxford University Press.

Siebert, Horst (ed.) 1990, *Reforming Capital Income Taxation*, Tübingen, Mohr.

Siebert, Horst (ed.) 1995, *Locational Competition in the World Economy*, Tübingen, Mohr.

Siebert, Horst 2000, *Zum Paradigma des Standortwettbewerbs*, Tübingen, Mohr Siebeck.

Siedentopf, Heinrich and Ziller, Jacques (eds.) 1988, *Making European Policies Work: Implementation of Community Legislation in the Member States*, London, Sage.

Simitis, Spiros 1987, "Juridification of Labour Relations," in Teubner, Gunther (ed.), *Juridification of Social Spheres*, Berlin, de Gruyter, 113–62.

Simmons, Beth A. 2000a, "The Legalization of International Monetary Affairs," *International Organization* 54(3): 573–602.

Simmons, Beth A. 2000b, *Compliance in International Relations*, paper prepared for delivery at the 2000 Annual Meeting of the APSA, August 31–September 3, 2000, Washington, DC.

Simonis, Heide 1979, "Thesen zu einer Neugestaltung der Subventionspolitik," *Wirtschaftsdienst* 59(5): 215–18.

Sinnaeve, Adinda 1999, "State Aid Control: Objectives and Procedures," in Bilal, Sanoussi and Nicolaides, Phedon (eds.), *Understanding State Aid Policy in the*

European Community. Perspectives on Rules and Practice, Maastricht, European Institute of Public Administration, 13–27.

Sinnaeve, Adinda 2001, "Die ersten Gruppenfreistellungen: Dezentralisierung der Beihilfenkontrolle?," *Europäische Zeitschrift für Wirtschaftsrecht* 12(3): 69–77.

Slaughter, Anne-Marie 1993, "International Law and International Relations Theory: A Dual Agenda," *American Journal of International Law* 87(2): 205–39.

Slaughter, Anne-Marie 1995, "International Law in a World of Liberal States," *European Journal of International Law* 6(4): 503–38.

Slaughter, Anne-Marie 2001, *International Law and International Relations*, Hague Academy of International Law: Receuil des Cours 285 (2000), The Hague, Martinus Nijhoff.

Slaughter, Anne-Marie and Ratner, Steven R. 1999, "The Method is the Message," *American Journal of International Law* 93(2): 410–23.

Slaughter, Anne-Marie, Stone Sweet, Alec and Weiler, J. H. H. 1998, *The European Court and National Courts – Doctrine and Jurisprudence: Legal Change in its Social Context*, Oxford, Hart.

Slot, Piet Jan 1990, "Procedural Aspects of State Aids: The Guardian of Competition Versus the Subsidy Villains?", *Common Market Law Review* 27(4): 741–60.

Slot, Piet Jan 1999, "EC Policy on State Aid: Are the Procedures 'User-Friendly'? The Rights of Third Parties," in Bilal, Sanoussi and Nicolaides, Phedon (eds.), *Understanding State Aid Policy in the European Community. Perspectives on Rules and Practice*, Maastricht, European Institute of Public Administration, 81–97.

Slotboom, Marco M. 2002, "Subsidies in WTO Law and in EC Law: Broad and Narrow Definitions," *Journal of World Trade* 36(3): 517–42.

Smith, Jackie, Chatfield, Charles and Pagnucco, Ron (eds.) 1997, *Transnational Social Movements and Global Politics: Solidarity Beyond the State*, Syracuse University Press.

Smith, Mitchell P. 1996, "Integration in Small Steps: The European Commission and Member-State Aid to Industry," *West European Politics* 19(3): 563–82.

Smith, Mitchell P. 1998, "Autonomy by the Rules: The European Commission and the Development of State Aid Policy," *Journal of Common Market Studies* 36(1): 55–78.

Snyder, Francis 1993, "The Effectiveness of European Community Law: Institutions, Processes, Tools and Techniques," *Modern Law Review* 56(1): 19–54.

Snyder, Francis 2003, "The Gatekeepers: The European Courts and WTO Law," *Common Market Law Review* 40(3): 313–67.

Somogyi, Arpad 1999, *Assuring Science Based Decisions – Determining the Appropriate Level of Protection: Threshold of Regulations/Implementation*. Conference on International Food Trade Beyond 2000: Science-Based Decisions, Harmonization, Equivalence and Mutual Recognition – Melbourne, Australia, October 11–15, 1999 (http://europa.eu.int/comm/dgs/health_consumer/library/speeches/speech24_en.html.).

Staudt, Erich 1987, "Technologie- und Regionalpolitik der Länder: Vom Leistungs- zum Subventionswettbewerb," *List Forum* 14(2): 93–110.

Stehn, Jürgen 1996, *Subsidies, Countervailing Duties, and the WTO: Towards an Open Subsidy Club*, Kieler Diskussionsbeiträge 276, Kiel, Institut für Weltwirtschaft.

Stein, Arthur A. 1983, "Coordination and Collaboration: Regimes in an Anarchic World," in Krasner, Stephen D. (ed.), *International Regimes*, Ithaca, Cornell University Press, 115–40.

Stein, Eric 1981, "Lawyers, Judges, and the Making of a Transnational Constitution," *American Journal of International Law* 75(1): 1–27.

Steinberg, Richard H. 2002, "In the Shadow of Law or Power? Consensus-Based Bargaining and Outcomes in the GATT/WTO," *International Organization* 56(2): 339–74.

Stevens, Christopher 1996, "EU Policy for the Banana Market: The External Impact of Internal Policies," in Wallace, Helen and Wallace, William (eds.), *Policy-Making in the European Union*, Oxford University Press, 325–51.

Stone, Alec 1994, "What is a Supranational Constitution? An Essay in International Relations Theory," *Review of Politics* 56(3): 441–74.

Stone Sweet, Alec 1997, "The New GATT. Dispute Resolution and the Judicialization of the Trade Regime," in Volcansek, Mary L. (ed.), *Law Above Nations. Supranational Courts and the Legalization of Politics*, Gainesville, University of Florida Press, 118–41.

Stone Sweet, Alec and Brunell, Thomas 1998, "Constructing a Supranational Constitution. Dispute Resolution and Governance in the European Community," *American Political Science Review* 92(1): 63–80.

Stone Sweet, Alec and Caporaso, James 1998, "From Free Trade to Supranational Polity. The European Court and Integration," in Sandholtz, Wayne and Stone Sweet, Alec (eds.), *European Integration and Supranational Governance*, Oxford University Press, 92–133.

Streeck, Wolfgang 1995, "From Market Making to State Building? Reflections on the Political Economy of European Social Policy," in Leibfried, Stephan and Pierson, Paul (eds.), *European Social Policy. Between Fragmentation and Integration*, Washington, DC, Brookings Institution, 389–431.

Subak, Susan 1997, "Verifying Compliance with an Unmonitorable Climate Convention," *International Environmental Affairs* 9(2): 148–68.

Széll, Patrick 1995, "The Development of Multilateral Mechanisms for Monitoring Compliance," in Lang, Winfried (ed.), *Sustainable Development and International Law*, London, Graham & Trotman, 97–109.

Tallberg, Jonas 1999, *Making States Comply. The European Commission, the European Court of Justice and the Enforcement of the Internal Market*, Lund, Studentlitteratur.

Tallberg, Jonas 2002, "Paths to Compliance: Enforcement, Management, and the European Union," *International Organization* 56(3): 609–44.

Teubner, Gunther 1983, "Substantive and Reflexive Elements in Modern Law," *Law and Society Review* 17(2): 239–85.

Teubner, Gunther 1987, "Juridification – Concepts, Aspects, Limits, Solutions," in Teubner, Gunther (ed.), *Juridification of Social Spheres*, Berlin, de Gruyter, 3–48.

References

Teubner, Gunther 1997, "'Global Bukowina': Legal Pluralism in the World Society," in Teubner, Gunther (ed.), *Global Law Without a State*, Aldershot, Dartmouth, 3–28.

Teubner, Gunther 2000, "Privatregimes: Neo-Spontanes Recht und duale Sozialverfassungen in der Weltgesellschaft?," in Simon, Dieter and Weiss, Manfred (eds.), *Zur Autonomie des Individuums. Liber Amicorum Spiros Simitis*, Baden-Baden, Nomos, 437–53.

Teubner, Gunther 2004, *Netzwerk als Vertragsverbund. Virtuelle Unternehmen, Franchising, Just-in-time in sozialwissenschaftlicher und juristischer Sicht*, Baden-Baden, Nomos.

Thagesen, Rikke and Matthews, Alan 1997, "The EU's Common Banana Regime: An Initial Evaluation," *Journal of Common Market Studies* 35(4): 615–27.

Thomas, Ingo P. 1994, "Finanzausgleich und Kohäsion in der Europäischen Union," *Die Weltwirtschaft* 4: 472–91.

Thomas, Kenneth P. 2000, *Competing for Capital: Europe and North America in a Global Era*, Washington, DC, Georgetown University Press.

Trachtman, Joel P. 1999, "The Domain of WTO Dispute Resolution," *Harvard International Law Journal* 40(2): 333–77.

Trachtman, Joel P. and Moremen, Philip M. 2003, "Costs and Benefits of Private Participation in WTO Dispute Settlement: Whose Right Is It Anyway?," *Harvard International Law Journal* 44(1): 221–50.

Tsebelis, George 1995, "Decision Making in Political Systems," *British Journal of Political Science* 25(3): 289–325.

Tyler, Tom R. 1990, *Why People Obey the Law*, New Haven, Yale University Press.

Tyler, Tom R. 1997, "Procedural Fairness and Compliance with the Law," *Schweizerische Zeitschrift für Volkswirtschaft und Statistik* 133(2/2), 219–40.

Underdal, Arild 1998, "Explaining Compliance and Defection: Three Models," *European Journal of International Relations* 4(1): 5–30.

Underdal, Arild 2002, "One Question, Two Answers," in Miles, Edward, Underdal, Arild, Andresen, Steinar, Wettestad, Jørgen, Skjærseth, Jon Birger and Carlin, Elaine M. 2002, *Explaining Regime Effectiveness: Confronting Theory with Evidence*, Cambridge, MA, MIT Press, 3–46.

Van Miert, Karel 2000, *Markt, Macht, Wettbewerb. Meine Erfahrungen als Kommissar in Brüssel*, Stuttgart, Deutsche Verlagsanstalt.

Väyrynen, Raimo 1997, "International Stability and Risky States: The Enforcement of Norms," in Schneider, Gerald and Weitsman, Patricia A. (eds.), *Enforcing Cooperation. Risky States and International Management of Conflict*, Basingstoke, Macmillan, 37–59.

Vermulst, Edwin and Driessen, Bart 1995, "An Overview of the WTO Dispute Settlement System and its Relationship with the Uruguay Round Agreement – Nice on Paper but Too Much Stress for the System?," *Journal of World Trade* 29(2): 131–62.

Vervaele, John A. (ed.) 1999, *Compliance and Enforcement of European Community Law*, The Hague, Kluwer Law International.

Victor, David G. 2000, "The Sanitary and Phytosanitary Agreement of the World Trade Organization: An Assessment After Five Years," *New York University Journal of International Law and Politics* 32(4): 865–937.

Victor, David G., Raustiala, Kal and Skolnikoff, Eugene B. 1998, "Introduction and Overview," in Victor, David G., Raustiala, Kal and Skolnikoff, Eugene B. (eds.), *The Implementation and Effectiveness of International Environmental Commitments: Theory and Practice*, Cambridge, MA, MIT Press, 1–46.

Vogel, David 1997, *Trading Up. Consumer and Environmental Regulation in a Global Economy*, Cambridge, MA, Harvard University Press.

Vogel, David and Kessler, Timothy 1998, "How Compliance Happens and Doesn't Happen Domestically," in Weiss, Edith Brown and Jacobson, Harold K. (eds.), *Engaging Countries. Strengthening Compliance with International Environmental Accords*, Cambridge, MA, MIT Press, 19–37.

Vogel, Klaus 1965, *Der räumliche Anwendungsbereich der Verwaltungsrechtsnorm*, Frankfurt/M, Metzner.

Voigt, Rüdiger 1999, *Globalisierung des Rechts*, Baden-Baden, Nomos.

Volcansek, Mary L. (ed.) 1997, *Law Above Nations: Supranational Courts and the Legalization of Politics*, Gainsville, University Press of Florida.

Vos, Ellen 2000, "EU Food Safety Regulation in the Aftermath of the BSE Crisis," *Journal of Consumer Policy* 23(3): 227–55.

Wallace, Helen 1983, "Distributional Politics. Dividing up the Community Cake," in Wallace, Helen, Wallace, William and Webb, Carole (eds.), *Policy-Making in the European Community*, Chichester, John Wiley, 81–113.

Walter, Christian 1999, "Die Europäische Menschenrechtskonvention als Konstitutionalisierungsprozeß," *Zeitschrift für ausländisches und öffentliches Recht* 53(4): 961–81.

Walthes, Frank 1996, *Europäischer Finanzausgleich*, Berlin, Duncker & Humblot.

Waltz, Kenneth 1979, *Theory of International Politics*, Reading, MA, Addison-Wesley.

Weaver, R. Kent 1986, "The Politics of Blame Avoidance," *Journal of Public Policy* 6(4): 371–98.

Weber, Max 1967, *Rechtssoziologie*, Neuwied, Luchterhand.

Weber, Max 1980, *Wirtschaft und Gesellschaft*, Tübingen, Mohr.

Weiler, Joseph H. H. 1981, "The Community System: The Dual Character of Supranationalism," *Yearbook of European Law* 1: 257–306.

Weiler, Joseph H. H. 1988, "The White Paper and the Application of Community Law," in Bieber, Roland, Dehousse, Renaud, Pinder, John and Weiler, Joseph H. H. (eds.), *1992: One European Market?*, Baden-Baden, Nomos, 337–58.

Weiler, Joseph H. H. 1991, "The Transformation of Europe," *Yale Law Journal* 100(8): 2403–83.

Weiler, Joseph H. H. 1993, "Journey to an Unkonown Destination: A Retrospective and Prospective of the European Court of Justice in the Arena of Political Integration," *Journal of Common Market Studies* 31(4): 417–46.

Weiler, Joseph H. H. 1994, "A Quiet Revolution: The European Court of Justice and its Interlocutors," *Comparative Political Studies* 26(4): 510–34.

Weiler, Joseph H. H. 1998, "Europe: The Case Against the Case for Statehood," *European Law Journal* 4(1): 43–62.

Weiler, Joseph H. H. 2000, *Federalism and Constitutionalism: Europe's Sonderweg*, Harvard Jean Monnet Working Paper 10/00, New York University School of Law.

Weiler, J. H. H. 2001, "The Rule of Lawyers and the Ethos of Diplomats: Reflections on the Internal and External Legitimacy of WTO Dispute Settlement," *Journal of World Trade* 35(2): 191–207.

Weiler, Joseph H. H., Haltern, Ulrich R. and Mayer, Franz C. 1995, "European Democracy and its Critique," *West European Politics* 18(3): 4–39.

Weiss, Edith Brown and Jacobson, Harold K. (eds.) 1998, *Engaging Countries. Strengthening Compliance with International Environmental Accords*, Cambridge, MA, MIT Press.

Weitsman, Patricia A. and Schneider, Gerald 1997, "Risky States: Implications for Theory and Policy Making," in Schneider, Gerald and Weitsman, Patricia A. (eds.), *Enforcing Cooperation. Risky States and International Management of Conflict*, New York, St. Martin's Press, 283–94.

Werksmann, Jacob (ed.) 1996, *Greening International Institutions*, London, Earthscan.

Werner, Georg 1995, *Subventionsabbau – gesetzliche Zwänge schaffen. Vorschläge zur Ergänzung des Haushaltsgrundsätzegesetzes zwecks besserer Kontrolle und Kürzung von Subventionen*, Wiesbaden, Karl-Bräuer-Institut des Bundes der Steuerzahler.

Wesseling, Rein 2000, *The Modernisation of EC Antitrust Law*, Oxford, Hart.

Westlake, Martin 1997, " 'Mad Cows and Englishmen' – The Institutional Consequences of the BSE Crisis," *Journal of Common Market Studies* 35(Annual review): 11–36.

Wettestad, Jorgen 1999, *Designing Effective Environmental Regimes. The Key Conditions*, Cheltenham, Edward Elgar.

Wieacker, Franz 1953, *Das Sozialmodell der klassischen Privatrechtsgesetzgeber und die Entwicklung der modernen Gesellschaft*, Karlsruhe, C. F. Müller.

Wielsch, Dan 2000, *Freiheit und Funktion. Zur Struktur- und Theoriegeschichte des Rechts der Wirtschaftsgesellschaft*, Baden-Baden, Nomos.

Wiethölter, Rudolf 1989, "Proceduralisation of the Category of Law," in Joerges, Christian and Trubek, David M. (eds.), *Critical Legal Thought: An American-German Debate*, Baden-Baden, Nomos, 501–10.

Wiethölter, Rudolf 1995, "Zur Argumentation im Recht: Entscheidungsfolgen als Rechtsgründe," in Teubner, Gunther (ed.), *Entscheidungsfolgen als Rechtsgründe*, Baden-Baden, Nomos, 89–120.

Wiethölter, Rudolf 2003, "Recht-Fertigungen eines Gesellschafts-Rechts," in Joerges, Christian and Teubner, Gunther (eds.), *Rechtsverfassungsrecht: Recht-Fertigungen zwischen Sozialtheorie und Privatrechtsdogmatik*, Baden-Baden, Nomos, 1–18.

Wilson, James Q. and DiJulio, John J. 1995, *American Government*, Lexington, MA, Heath.

Winkler, Roland 1999, "Das 'Alcan'-Urteil des EuGH – eine Katastrophe für den Rechtsstaat?," *Die Öffentliche Verwaltung* 52(4): 148–52.

Winter, J. A. 1993, "Supervision of State Aid: Article 93 in the Court of Justice," *Common Market Law Review* 30(2): 311–29.

Winter, Jan A. 1999, "The Rights of Complainants in State Aid Cases: Judicial Review of Commission Decisions Adopted Under Article 88 (ex 93) EC," *Common Market Law Review* 36(3): 521–68.

Wittgenstein, Ludwig 1971, *Philosophische Untersuchungen*, Frankfurt/M, Suhrkamp.

Wolf, Klaus Dieter 2000, *Die Neue Staatsräson – Zwischenstaatliche Kooperation als Demokratieproblem in der Weltgesellschaft*, Baden-Baden, Nomos.

Wolters, Christian 1998, *Die BSE Krise. Agrarpolitik im Spannungsfeld zwischen Handelsfreiheit und Konsumentenschutz*, Frankfurt/M, Europäischer Verlag der Wissenschaften.

Wozniak, Jennifer 1999, *The Commission and the Member States. The Evolution of Regional Policy*, paper presented at the Sixth Biennial Conference of the ECSA, Pittsburgh, June 2–5, 1999.

Young, Oran R. 1979, *Compliance and Public Authority: A Theory with International Application*, Baltimore, MD, Johns Hopkins University Press.

Young, Oran R. 1999a, *Governance in World Affairs*, Ithaca, NY, Cornell University Press.

Young, Oran (ed.) 1999b, *The Effectiveness of International Environmental Regimes. Causal Connections and Behavioral Mechanisms*, Cambridge, MA, MIT Press.

Young, Oran R. and Levy, Marc A. 1999, "The Effectiveness of International Environmental Regimes," in Young, Oran (ed.), *The Effectiveness of International Environmental Regimes. Causal Connections and Behavioral Mechanisms*, Cambridge, MA, MIT Press, 1–32.

Zangl, Bernhard 1999, *Interessen auf zwei Ebenen. Internationale Regime in der Agrarhandels-, Währungs- und Walfangpolitik*, Baden-Baden, Nomos.

Zangl, Bernhard 2001, "Bringing Courts Back In: Normdurchsetzung im GATT, in der WTO und der EG," *Swiss Political Science Review* 7(2): 49–80.

Zimmermann, Horst 1979, "Vergleichbarkeit in der Subventionsberichterstattung des Bundes," *Finanzarchiv* N.F. 37(3): 459–75.

Zimmermann, Horst 1990, "Gewichtsverlagerung im föderalen Staatsaufbau unter EG-Einfluß?," *Wirtschaftsdienst* 70(9): 451–6.

Zippel, Wulfdiether 1993, "Die ordnungspolitischen Probleme von Subventionen und die Beihilferegeln von EGKSV und EWGV," in Zippel, Wulfdiether (ed.), *Ökonomische Grundlagen der europäischen Integration. Eine Einführung in ausgewählte Teilbereiche der Gemeinschaftspolitiken*, München, Vahlen, 61–81.

Zonnekeyn, Geert A. 2000, "The Status of WTO Law in the EC Legal Order: The Final Curtain?," *Journal of World Trade* 34(3): 111–25.

Zuleeg, Manfred 1974, *Subventionskontrolle durch Konkurrentenklage*, Frankfurt/M, Metzner.

Zuleeg, Manfred 1978, "Nationales Subventionsrecht als Wirkungsfeld und Wirkungsfaktor des europäischen Subventionsrechts. Landesbericht Bundesrepublik Deutschland," in Börner, Bodo and Bullinger, Martin (eds.), *Subventionen im Gemeinsamen Markt*, Köln, Heymanns, 7–55.

Zumbansen, Peer 2000, *Ordnungsmuster im modernen Wohlfahrtsstaat. Lernerfahrungen zwischen Staat, Gesellschaft und Vertrag*, Baden-Baden, Nomos.

Zürn, Michael 1992, *Interessen und Institutionen in der internationalen Politik. Grundlegung und Anwendungen des situationsstrukturellen Ansatzes*, Opladen, Leske+Budrich.

Zürn, Michael 1998, *Regieren jenseits des Nationalstaates. Denationalisierung und Globalisierung als Chance*, Frankfurt/M, Suhrkamp.

Zürn, Michael 2000, "Democratic Governance Beyond the Nation-State: The EU and Other International Institutions," *European Journal of International Relations* 6(2): 183–221.

Zürn, Michael 2001, "Political Systems in the Postnational Constellation: Societal Denationalization and Multilevel Governance," in Volker Rittberger (ed.), *Global Governance and the United Nations System*, Tokyo, United Nations University Press, 48–87.

Zürn, Michael 2004, "Global Governance under Legitimacy Pressure," *Government & Opposition* (forthcoming).

Zürn, Michael and Wolf, Dieter 1999, "European Law and International Regimes: The Features of Law Beyond the Nation State," *European Law Journal* 5(3): 272–92.

Index

For EU product safety concerns, contact us at Calle de José Abascal, 56–1°,
28003 Madrid, Spain or eugpsr@cambridge.org.

www.ingramcontent.com/pod-product-compliance
Ingram Content Group UK Ltd.
Pitfield, Milton Keynes, MK11 3LW, UK
UKHW042153130625
459647UK00011B/1314